Communication Works

Eleventh Edition

Teri Kwal Gamble
College of New Rochelle

Michael Gamble
New York Institute of Technology

SPC 1608
Special Edition for Valencia College

 Learning Solutions

Boston   Burr Ridge, IL   Dubuque, IA   New York   San Francisco
St. Louis   Bangkok   Bogotá   Caracas   Lisbon   London   Madrid
Mexico City   Milan   New Delhi   Seoul   Singapore   Sydney   Taipei   Toronto

The McGraw·Hill Companies

COMMUNICATION WORKS, Eleventh Edition
SPC 1608
Special Edition for Valencia College

2 3 4 5 6 7 8 9 0 QDB QDB 14 13 12

ISBN-13: 978-0-07-766160-1
ISBN-10: 0-07-766160-5

Learning Solutions Consultant: Kimberly Wollschlager
Learning Solutions Specialist: Jeff Schmitt
Production Editor: Nina Meyer
Printer/Binder: Quad/Graphics

BRIEF CONTENTS

C O N T E N T S

PART 1   THE ESSENTIALS OF COMMUNICATION

CHAPTER 6
Listening, Feedback, and Critical Thinking *139*

PART 4 COMMUNICATING TO THE PUBLIC

CHAPTER 11
The Speaker and the Audience: The Occasion and the Subject *291*

CHAPTER 12
Researching, Supporting, and Outlining Your Speech *323*

TERI KWAL GAMBLE AND MICHAEL W. GAMBLE both earned PhDs in communication from New York University. They are full professors of communication and award-winning teachers, with Teri at the College of New Rochelle and Michael at the New York Institute of Technology in Manhattan. As co-founders of Interact Training Systems, a communication consulting firm, they have conducted seminars, workshops, and short courses for numerous business and professional organizations across the United States.

The Gambles are co-authors of several textbooks and training systems, including *Public Speaking in the Age of Diversity; Interpersonal Communication in Theory, Practice and Context;* and *Literature Alive!* Their trade books include *Sales Scripts That Sell, Phone Power,* and *The Answer Book.*

Teri and Michael live in New Jersey and spend much of their time exploring how and why communication works. Their personal favorite communicators are their children—their son, Matthew Jon, who has his doctorate in biochemistry and is now a scientist, and their daughter, Lindsay Michele, who received her MBA in marketing, ran the New York City Marathon, teaches this course, and works in real estate.

Teri and Michael Gamble with son Matthew and daughter Lindsay.

What if:

- You could help your students think critically about communication and its relevance to their lives?

- You could get them interested in learning why and how communication works in the 21st century?

- You could facilitate their developing communication skills for college and beyond?

- You had access to a print and digital program built around your course objectives?

How do we accomplish these goals?

The new edition of *Communication Works* applies a new **critical thinking framework** to its core content, now in a more user-friendly 15-chapter organization. We have retained and revised the text's practical approach to communication, with a focus on the ways in which diversity, technology, social media, and ethical concerns enrich and complicate our world. Students will learn what role communication plays in their lives today, in the classroom, and tomorrow, in the working world. And with **Connect Communication,** instructors and students have a print *and* digital solution to meet the needs of their course.

The Critical Thinking Framework

The critical thinking framework of this text is based on Bloom's taxonomy, which guides students from lower-order thinking skills (remembering, understanding) to higher-order skills (analyzing, evaluating, and creating), thereby enhancing their understanding. This framework is introduced at the beginning of the chapter and reinforced throughout:

- **Learning objectives** at the beginning of the chapter provide goals for the student requiring various levels of understanding.

  After completing this chapter, you should be able to demonstrate mastery of the following learning outcomes:

  LO1 **Define** communication.

  LO2 **Explain** the essential elements of communication and their interaction using representative communication models.

  LO3 **Describe** the core principles of communication.

  LO4 **Analyze** how digital media are transforming communication in ways good and bad.

  LO5 **Evaluate** the benefits of communicating effectively.

  LO6 **Apply** guidelines for improving your communication effectiveness.

- **Repetition of learning objectives** in the margin show students where each concept is covered and reminds them what the learning outcome should be.

  ## Why We Communicate

  LO5
  Evaluate the benefits of communicating effectively

  As we see, every communication experience serves one or more functions. For example, communication can help us discover who we are, help us establish meaningful relationships, or prompt us to examine and try to change either our own attitudes and behaviors or the attitudes and behaviors of others.

  TO GAIN SELF-UNDERSTANDING AND INSIGHT INTO OTHERS
  One key function of communication is self-other understanding: insight into ourselves and others. When you get to know another person, you also get to know yourself. others. if you learn b

- The **Review, Reflect, and Apply** feature appears at key points in the chapter, allowing students to test whether they have mastered the learning objective at different levels of Bloom's taxonomy.

  ## Review, Reflect, & **Apply**

  ### Recall
  Describe what is meant by the statement, "Communication is dynamic."

  ### Understand
  Give an example in which the irreversibility of communication caused difficulties for you.

- **An end-of-chapter summary,** based on the learning objectives presented at the beginning of the chapter, allows students to review their understanding of the material covered.

  ## The Wrap-Up

  SUMMARY

  LO1 **Define** *communication.*
  Communication is the deliberate or accidental transfer of meaning. Human communication takes place interpersonally (one to one), in small groups (one to a few), in public forums (one to many), via the media, or online.

  LO2 **Explain** the essential elements of communication and their interaction using representative communication models.
  The essential elements of communication are people, messages, channels, noise, context, feedback, and effect. Models of communication illustrate the communication process in action.

Communication Works
for Instructors

Powered by Connect Communication

Communication Works is available to instructors and students in traditional print format, as well as online within an integrated assignment and assessment platform. These online tools, collectively called Connect Communication, make managing assignments easier for instructors—and make learning and studying more motivating and efficient for students.

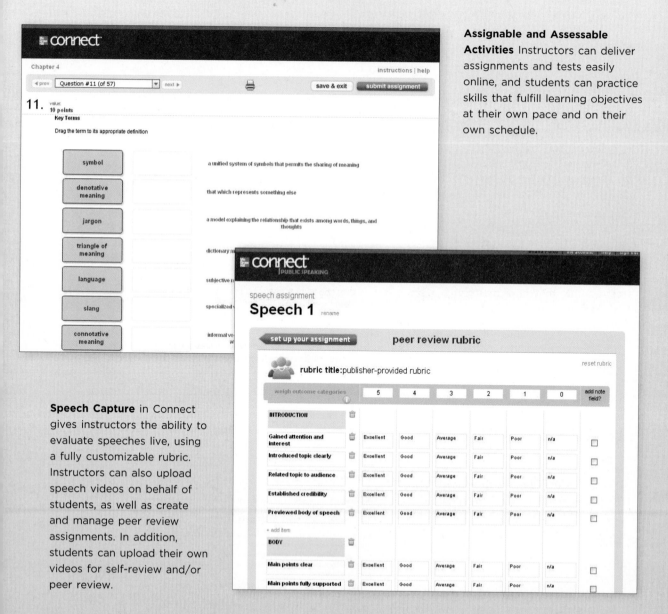

Assignable and Assessable Activities Instructors can deliver assignments and tests easily online, and students can practice skills that fulfill learning objectives at their own pace and on their own schedule.

Speech Capture in Connect gives instructors the ability to evaluate speeches live, using a fully customizable rubric. Instructors can also upload speech videos on behalf of students, as well as create and manage peer review assignments. In addition, students can upload their own videos for self-review and/or peer review.

Communication Works
for Students

LearnSmart This adaptive diagnostic tool helps students "know what they don't know"—while guiding them to experience and learn what they *don't* know through interactivities, exercises, and readings.

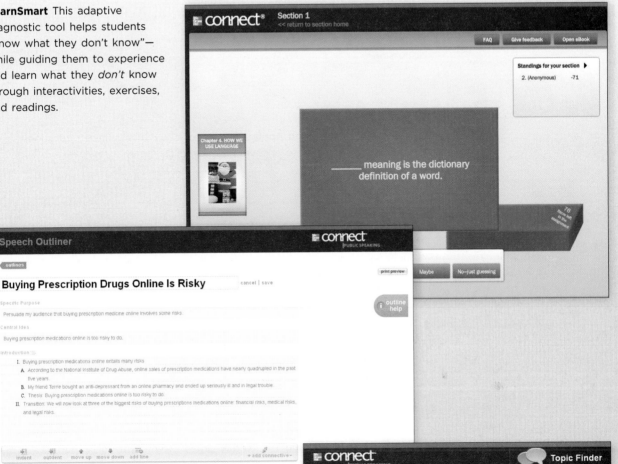

Outline Tool, with enhanced user interface, guides students systematically through the process of organizing and outlining their speeches. Instructors can customize part of the outliner, and also turn it off if they don't want students to use it.

Topic Finder, as well as access to EasyBib and Survey Monkey online tools. The Topic Finder helps students select a topic for speech assignments. EasyBib is a Web-based tool that simplifies and automates the formatting of citations and bibliographies. Survey Monkey, also a Web-based tool, helps students create and manage audience-analysis questionnaires.

Key Features and Learning Aids

Communication Works includes several types of feature boxes that reinforce our emphasis on critical thinking, multiculturalism, ethics, and technology in a practical format. Questions for each feature encourage reflection or can be used for class discussion.

Review, Reflect, & Apply

New **Review, Reflect, and Apply** feature provides critical thinking questions at the end of each section to encourage students to evaluate, analyze, and apply the material.

Skill Builder

Skill Builders These individualized activities encourage students to observe and consider communication, to assess its effects, and to experience the insights and practice they need to become effective communicators.

Exploring Diversity

Exploring Diversity These sections provide a glimpse into the way culture influences communication and reflects the needs of an increasingly diverse student audience.

Ethics & Communication

Ethics and Communication This feature draws attention to the importance of ethical communication in all facets of life.

MediaWise

Media Wise These segments underscore the expanding role of technology and media in today's world, helping students to examine the impact on their lives.

Communication Checklist

Communication Skills These checklists at the end of each chapter give students simple and practical tips for improving their communication skills.

Chapter-by-Chapter Changes

Chapter 1: Revised discussion of communication models including the transactional model. New sections on communication confidence and the top qualities employers seek in new hires.

Chapter 2: Expanded discussion of the complexity of cultural identity and the diversity in our own back yards. New coverage of the role technologies play in creating community and flattening out our world.

Chapter 3: New section on popularity and bullying and the influence of Facebook on identity. Enhanced discussion of how to improve perceptual skills.

Chapter 4: Expanded explanation of the Triangle of Meaning and the influence of technology. New discussions on polarizing language, linguistic relativity, and the influence of neuroscience on our understanding of language.

Chapter 5: New coverage on the impact of appearance.

Chapter 6: Enhanced coverage of the role of critical thinking in developing communication competence. New exploration of the effects of digital media on listening.

Chapter 7: New sections on technology's effects on relationships, Schutz's FIRO theory, and Duck's serial construction of meaning model. Enhanced discussion of lying and defriending.

Chapter 8: More coverage on the changing nature of friendships and professional relationships. Enhanced discussion of conflict management strategies, including DESC scripts. Revised organization of factors in attraction and emotions in relationships. New topics include media rants and confessionals, friends-with-benefits, and frenemies.

Chapter 9: Enhanced coverage of working in teams. Revised discussions of brainstorming, problem solving, and decision making. New coverage of motivation bias, decision ambivalence, and the impact of social media and crowdsourcing on decision making.

Chapter 10: Expanded coverage of leadership, groupthink, and the impact of culture. New section on the popularity of online groups and their impact on conflict.

Chapter 11: Revised organization of the chapter. Refined staircase model of speech process.

Chapter 12: We help students understand the integrated nature of speech development and organization. We did a better job of explaining the parts of an outline.

Chapter 13: Relocated section on presentation aids. New discussion of Photoshop. Enhanced coverage of PowerPoint.

Chapter 14 and Chapter 15: Updated speech examples. Enhanced coverage of ethics and faulty reasoning.

Appendix: *Interviewing and Developing Professional Relationships.* New discussion of the nature of professional relationships. Revised coverage of impression management, the role of social networking, and the use of video chat software.

Online Unit: *Mass Communication and Media Literacy.* Expanded coverage of media literacy. New discussion on how technology affects the brain.

Teaching and Learning with *Communication Works*

CREATE

Design your ideal course materials with McGraw-Hill's *Create*—www.mcgrawhill create.com! Rearrange or omit chapters, combine material from other sources, and/or upload your syllabus or any other content you have written to make the perfect resources for your students. Search thousands of leading McGraw-Hill text-books to find the best content for your students, then arrange it to fit your teaching style. You can even personalize your book's appearance by selecting the cover and adding your name, school, and course information. When you order a *Create* book, you receive a complimentary review copy. Get a printed copy in 3 to 5 business days or an electronic copy (eComp) via e-mail in about an hour.

Register today at www.mcgrawhillcreate.com, and craft your course resources to match the way you teach.

Tegrity Campus

Tegrity Campus is a service that makes class time available all the time by auto-matically capturing every lecture in a searchable format for students to review when they study and complete assignments.

With a simple one-click process, you capture all computer screens and correspond-ing audio. Students replay any part of any class with easy-to-use browser-based viewing on a PC or Mac.

With Tegrity Campus, students quickly recall key moments by using the unique search feature. Students can efficiently find what they need, when they need it, across an entire semester of class recordings.

Help turn all your students' study time into learning moments immediately sup-ported by your lecture. To learn more about Tegrity, watch a 2-minute Flash demo at http://tegritycampus.mhhe.com.

Online Learning Center

- The **Instructor's Manual** incorporates tools for both new and experienced instructors, including learning objectives, chapter outlines, topics for discussion, skill-building activities, worksheets, and additional resources.
- **PowerPoint Slides** include illustrations from the text.
- **Test Bank** This resource offers multiple-choice, true or false, and essay questions for each chapter. McGraw-Hill's computerized EZ Test allows the instructor to create customized exams using the publisher's supplied test items or the instructor's own questions. A version of the test bank is also provided in Microsoft Word files for instructors who prefer that format.

CourseSmart

CourseSmart offers thousands of the most commonly adopted textbooks across hundreds of courses from a wide variety of higher education publishers. It is the only place for faculty to review and compare the full text of a textbook online, providing immediate access without the environmental impact of requesting a printed exam copy. At CourseSmart, students can save up to 50 percent off the cost of a printed book, reduce their impact on the environment, and gain access to powerful Web tools for learning, including full text search, notes and highlighting, and e-mail tools for sharing notes among classmates. Learn more at **www.coursesmart.com**.

McGraw-Hill Campus

McGraw-Hill Campus is the first of its kind institutional service providing faculty with true single sign-on access to all of McGraw-Hill's course content, digital tools, and other high-quality learning resources from any learning management system (LMS). This innovative offering allows for secure and deep integration and seamless access to any of our course solutions such as McGraw-Hill Connect®, McGraw-Hill Create™, McGraw-Hill LearnSmart™, or Tegrity®. McGraw-Hill Campus includes access to our entire content library, including eBooks, assessment tools, presentation slides, and multimedia content, among other resources, providing faculty open and unlimited access to prepare for class, create tests/quizzes, develop lecture material, integrate interactive content, and much more.

ACKNOWLEDGMENTS

The contributions and collective wisdom of many people, including past and present students, the instructors who have been so loyal and helpful to us over the years, and the consummate professionals at McGraw-Hill, demonstrate that it takes a dedicated team to produce a text. We are ever grateful to all those people for the attention, nurturing, and care they have given *Communication Works* through the years.

We offer our heartfelt gratitude to the extremely talented editorial team at McGraw-Hill. We are especially thankful to executive editor Susan Gouijnstook for her vision and commitment to this book; our development editor, Briana Porco, for her creativity, endless energy, professionalism, skillful editing, and fresh insights; and Rhona Robbin for being there and believing in us. We value the relationship we have built with each of you and will always consider you our friends. We also want to thank Sheryl Rose for her careful reading and good decisions; Manish Sharma for his attention to detail; and Ruth Sakata Corley, the text's production editor. In addition, we offer kudos to Emily Tietz, the photo editor, and Jeanne Schreiber for the book's fresh design.

We also want to thank Leslie Oberhuber and the marketing team for their attention to this book, enthusiasm, and exceptionally creative approaches.

We especially thank our reviewers for their insightful advice that has resulted in this edition's improvements:

MANUSCRIPT REVIEWERS

Donna Acerra, *Northampton Community College*

Luann Adams, *Mid-State Technical College*

Tanya Biami, *Cochise College*

Diana Bifano, *Palm Beach State College-Lake Worth*

Marilyn Brimo, *Mt. Hood Community College*

Shannon M. Brogan, *Kentucky State University*

Judy Cannady, *Ozarka College*

Michael Caudill, *Western Carolina University*

Grace L. Coggio, *University of Wisconsin-River Falls*

Sue Cox, *Wallace State Community College*

Philip Dalton, *Hofstra University*

Jennifer Del Quadro, *Northampton Community College*

Morris Ellis, *Harding University*

Jay Frasier, *Lane Community College*

Jodi Gaete, *Suffolk County Community College*

Jean Hennessey, *Merrimack College*

Douglas Hoehn, *Bergen Community College*

Michael James, *Harding University*

Aaron Kaio, *Mt. Hood Community College*

Linda Kalfayan, *Westchester Community College*

Charles J. Korn, *Northern Virginia Community College-Manassas*

Erica Lamm, *Northern Virginia Community College-Annandale*

Kurt Lindemann, *San Diego State University*

Marian Lyles, *Seattle Central Community College*
Arlene MacGregor, *Massachusetts Maritime Academy*
John Marlow, *Hawaii Community College*
Jan Oehlschlaeger, *South Seattle Community College*
Marcie Pachter, *Palm Beach State College-Lake Worth*
Miri Pardo, *St. John Fisher College*
Tami Phillips, *University of Central Arkansas*

Danna Prather, *Suffolk County Community College*
Jennifer Rainey, *Northern Virginia Community College-Annandale*
Robert Ritchie, *Harding University*
Anthony Roberto, *Arizona State University*
Jack R. Shock, *Harding University*
Blair Thompson, *Western Kentucky University*

CONNECT CONTRIBUTORS

Donna Acerra, *Northampton Community College*
Marilyn Brimo, *Mt. Hood Community College*
Josie DeGroot Brown, *Southern Illinois University-Edwardsville*

Jan Oehlschlaeger, *South Seattle Community College*
Miri Pardo, *St. John Fisher College*
Charlene Widener, *Hutchinson Community College*

Finally, we thank Matthew and Lindsay, our children, for their insights and support. When all is said and done, they are our reasons for loving life.

Teri Kwal Gamble

Michael W. Gamble

Communication Works

ELEVENTH EDITION

Communication: Begin Right Here!

1

After completing this chapter, you should be able to demonstrate mastery of the following learning outcomes:

LO1 **Define** communication.

LO2 **Explain** the essential elements of communication and their interaction using representative communication models.

LO3 **Describe** the core principles of communication.

LO4 **Analyze** how digital media are transforming communication in ways good and bad.

LO5 **Evaluate** the benefits of communicating effectively.

LO6 **Apply** guidelines for improving your communication effectiveness.

Welcome to *Communication Works!* Since you're reading this textbook, most likely you're a college student eager to acquire new skills to use in your personal life and professional career. If you're like many twenty-first-century individuals, you communicate with others both face-to-face and in cyberspace. Your cell phone lets you reach anyone at any time. You use it to text and to tweet. You may also log on to Facebook, LinkedIn, or FourSquare to connect with others. You live your life and maybe a "second life," a fantasy or alternative life you create and live online. Like most of us, your goal is to live as fulfilling a life as possible. And to do so, you will need to make communication work.

What is your favorite means of communication? If given the choice, would you prefer to text, tweet, post an update on Facebook, talk via cell, or meet face-to-face? For some, connecting with another person, actually talking to that person can cause discomfort. Technology makes it possible for someone to contact you without having to be in your physical presence. It frees that person to say what they want without fear of being interrupted or even listening to your response. Others still prefer connecting with the important people in their lives in person. Social media and technology can also broaden the network of people with whom we can communicate. Some enjoy that far-reaching communication, while others choose not to use Twitter, Facebook, or Skype to engage vast networks of individuals. So the choice is yours—connect remotely or in person, be anonymous or yourself. However you connect, whether in a social network or a social circle, your goal is to make communication work for you. That, too, is the goal of this book!

Today, job-specific talent, technical expertise, and graduation from a prestigious school do not guarantee upward mobility or attainment of goals. Many of us get our jobs because of our **social capital,** that is, our social connections or social networks—the people we know—rather than our human capital—what we know.[1] Our workplaces are prime environments for connecting with others. The Internet has made finding out what we don't know a lot easier. Anyone with a computer is able to gather nearly as much intelligence as the CIA, access as much data as exists in the Library of Congress, and engage in conversations with people around the world at any hour.[2]

social capital
social connections or networks

One factor shared by people who ascend both the professional and the personal ladders of success is superior communication skills. When you are a skilled communicator, you can sell ideas to people who otherwise might not have been open to them.[3] While not guaranteed, people with good communication skills are more likely to be promoted rapidly, happy in relationships, and believe their lives are rich and fulfilling. That is why this book can be of value to you. Whatever your age, sex, marital status, or employment history, it is never too late to learn skills that will enrich and improve the quality of your life. You are not born knowing how to make communication work. You learn and develop communication skills, a process that will continue throughout your life. That is why we designed this book to provide a program for lifelong learning. If you desire to improve your ability to relate to people in your social life, job, or academic life, now is the time to start making communication work!

What Is Communication?

We are all communicators. We engage in intrapersonal (with ourselves), dyadic (one to one), small-group (one to a few), public (one to many), and mass communication (communication that is shared across great distances with potentially large audiences through a technological device or mass medium). We also engage in computer-assisted or online communication. Every time we knowingly or unknowingly send a verbal or nonverbal message to anyone, communication takes place.[4] We define **communication** as the deliberate or accidental transfer of meaning. It is the process that occurs whenever someone observes or experiences behavior and attributes meaning to that behavior. As

communication
the deliberate or accidental transfer of meaning

long as what someone does or says (his or her symbolic behavior) is interpreted as a message—as long as the behavior of one person affects or influences the behavior of another—communication is occurring. Since we spend more time communicating than doing anything else, our communication skill level helps shape our personal, social, work, and professional relationships. Communication is our link to the rest of humanity and serves a number of purposes, as these examples reveal:

> Talk and change the world.
>
> —Slogan espoused by a group of U.S. senators who happened to be female

> Communication is the vehicle which allows humans to recall the past, think in the present, and plan for the future.
>
> —Roy Berko

> I once had a boyfriend who was Mr. Text-o-Rama. He never wanted to talk but he always wanted to text. To him the only way to communicate was via thumb. . . . New media professor Barb Iverson says, "Digital natives instinctively emote through their thumbs and don't consider a relationship 'official' until their Facebook or MySpace profile says it is."
>
> —As reported by Natalie Y. Moore on *Chicago Public Radio*

Which of these observations do you agree with? Which do you find most applicable to your own communication experiences?

Because our focus is communication, it makes sense to define and distinguish among the types of communication also used.

- During **intrapersonal communication,** you think about, talk with, learn about, reason with, and evaluate yourself.

- When you engage in **interpersonal communication,** you interact with another, learn about him or her, and act in ways that help sustain or terminate your relationship.

- When you participate in **group communication,** you interact with a limited number of others, work to share information, develop ideas, make decisions, solve problems, offer support, or have fun.

- Through **public communication,** you inform and persuade the members of an audience to hold certain attitudes, values, or beliefs so that they will think, believe, or act in a particular way. You can also function as a member of an audience, in which case another person will do the same for you.

- During **mass communication,** the media entertain, inform, and persuade you. You, in turn, have the ability to use your viewing and buying habits to influence the media.

- During **online, or machine-assisted, communication,** you navigate cyberspace as you converse, research, and exchange ideas, and you build relationships with others using computers and the Internet.

Whatever the nature or type of communication, however, the communicative act itself is characterized by the interplay of certain elements.

intrapersonal communication
communication with the self

interpersonal communication
the relationship level of communication

group communication
interaction with a limited number of persons

public communication
communication designed to inform, persuade, or entertain audience members

mass communication
the transmission of messages that may be processed by gatekeepers prior to being sent to large audiences via a channel of broad diffusion

online, or machine-assisted, communication
the building of relationships using computers and the Internet

Review, Reflect, & Apply

Recall
List the different types of communication one may encounter.

Understand
Give examples of how you engage in each type of communication.

Create
Taking your cue from the definition and quotations included here, form your own working definition of communication.

Identify five people with whom you had a sustained interaction this week. For each person you name, indicate the nature of your relationship (for example, instructor, parent, boss, friend, significant other), the context in which the interaction occurred (classroom, office, home, online), the channel(s) used to communicate the messages that were sent and received, and the outcome(s) of the exchange (what happened as a result of your communicating). Finally—and this is most important—evaluate your communication effectiveness in each interaction by rating it on a scale of 1 to 5, where 1 represents extremely ineffective and 5 represents extremely effective, giving your reason(s) for each rating.

Rate Yourself as a Communicator

Person	Context	Channel(s)	Outcome(s)	Rating W/Reason(s)
_____	_____	_____	_____	_____
_____	_____	_____	_____	_____
_____	_____	_____	_____	_____
_____	_____	_____	_____	_____
_____	_____	_____	_____	_____

1. After reviewing your self-evaluations, would you replay any of the interactions if given the opportunity? How?

2. If it were up to you, would you prefer to increase or decrease the number of exchanges you have that are virtual as opposed to face-to-face? Why?

Elements of Communication: Picturing the Communication Model

LO2

Explain the essential elements of communication and their interaction using representative communication models.

essentials of communication
those components present during every communication event

senders
persons who formulate, encode, and transmit a message

receivers
persons who receive, decode, and interpret a message

All communication interactions have certain common elements that together help define the communication process. The better you understand these elements, the easier it will be for you to develop your own communicative abilities. Let's begin by examining the **essentials of communication,** those components present during every communication event.

PEOPLE

Obviously, human communication involves people. Interpersonal, small-group, and public communication encounters take place between and among all types of **senders/receivers** (persons who encode and send out and decode and take in messages). Although it is easy to picture a communication experience beginning with a sender and ending with a receiver, it is important to understand that during communication the role of sender does not belong exclusively to one person and the role of receiver to another. Instead, the processes of sending and receiving occur simultaneously. Reflecting this fact, in *That's Not What I Meant!* linguist Deborah Tannen writes, "Communication is a continuous stream in which everything is simultaneously a reaction and an instigation, an instigation and a reaction."[5] Thus, when we communicate with one or more people, we simultaneously send and receive.

MESSAGES

During every communication encounter, we all send and receive both verbal and nonverbal messages. What you talk about, the words you use to express your thoughts and feelings, the sounds you make, the way you sit and gesture, your facial expressions, and perhaps even your touch or your smell all communicate information. In effect, a **message** is the content of a communicative act. Some messages we send are private (a kiss accompanied by "I love you"); others are public and may be directed at hundreds or thousands of people. We send some

message
the content of a communicative act

messages purposefully ("I want you to realize . . . ") and others accidentally ("I had no idea you were watching . . . or 'lurking'"). Everything a sender or receiver does or says is a potential message as long as someone is there to interpret it.

CHANNELS

Channels are the media we use to carry messages. We can classify channels according to (1) which of our senses carries or receives the message, (2) whether the message is being delivered verbally, nonverbally, or both, and (3) the primary means of communication we use to deliver the message, that is, whether we use face-to-face interaction, computer-mediated communication, text messaging, or a mass medium such as television. Thus, we are multichannel communicators. Let's see how this works.

channels
media through which messages are sent

We receive sound messages (we hear noises from the street), sight messages (we see how someone looks), taste messages (we enjoy the flavor of a particular food), smell messages (we smell the cologne a friend is wearing), and touch messages (we feel the roughness of a fabric). Which channel are you most attuned to? Why? To what extent do you rely on one or more channels while excluding or ignoring others? Effective communicators are adept at switching channels. They recognize that communication is a multichannel experience.

The following dialogue between a husband and a wife illustrates the multichannel nature of communication:

> **Wife:** What's the matter with you? You're late again. We'll never get to the Adamses' on time.
>
> **Husband:** I tried my best.
>
> **Wife:** (Sarcastically) Sure, you tried your best. You always try your best, don't you? (Shaking her finger) I'm not going to put up with this much longer.
>
> **Husband:** (Raising his voice) You don't say! I happen to have been tied up at the office.
>
> **Wife:** My job is every bit as demanding as yours, you know.
>
> **Husband:** (Lowering his voice) OK. OK. I know you work hard too. I don't question that. Listen, I really did get stuck in a conference. (Puts his hand on her shoulder) Let's not blow this up. Come on. I'll tell you about it on the way to Bill and Ellen's.

What message is the wife (the initial source-encoder) sending to her husband (the receiver-decoder)? She is letting him know with her words, her voice, and her physical actions that she is upset and angry. Her husband responds in kind, using words, vocal cues, and gestures in an effort to explain his behavior. Both are affected by the nature of the situation (they are late for an appointment), by their attitudes (how they feel about what is occurring), and by their past experiences.

NOISE

In the context of communication, **noise** is anything that interferes with or distorts our ability to send or receive messages. Although we are accustomed to thinking of noise as a particular sound or group of sounds, noise can have both internal and external causes. Internal noise is attributed to a communicator's psychological makeup, intellectual ability, or physical condition. External noise is attributed to

noise
anything that interferes with or distorts the ability to send and receive messages

the environment. Thus, noise includes distractions such as a loud siren, a disturbing odor, and a hot room; personal factors such as prejudices, daydreaming, and feelings of inadequacy; and semantic factors such as uncertainty about what another person's words are supposed to mean.

CONTEXT

Communication always takes place in a **context,** or setting. Sometimes a context is so natural that we hardly notice it. At other times, however, the context exerts considerable control over our behavior. Consider how your present environment affects the way you act toward others or determines the nature of the communication encounters you share with them. Consider as well the extent to which certain environments might cause you to alter your posture, manner of speaking, attire, or means of interacting.

FEEDBACK

Whenever we communicate with one or more persons, we receive information in return. The verbal and nonverbal cues that we perceive in reaction to our communication

context
the setting

feedback
information returned to a message source

positive feedback
a behavior-enhancing response

function as **feedback.** Feedback tells us how we are coming across. A smile, a frown, a chuckle, a sarcastic remark, a muttered thought, or simply silence in response to something we did or said can cause us to change, continue, or end a transaction. Feedback that encourages us to continue behaving as we are is **positive feedback;** it enhances whatever behavior is in progress. In contrast, **negative feedback** extinguishes a behavior; it serves a corrective rather than a reinforcing function. Thus, negative feedback can help eliminate unwanted, ineffective behaviors. Note that the terms *positive* and *negative* should not be interpreted as "good" and "bad"; these terms simply reflect the way the responses affect behavior.

Both positive and negative feedback can emanate from internal or external sources. **Internal feedback** is feedback you give yourself as you monitor your own behavior or performance during a transaction. **External feedback** is feedback from others who are involved in the communication event. To be an effective communicator, you must be sensitive to both types of feedback.

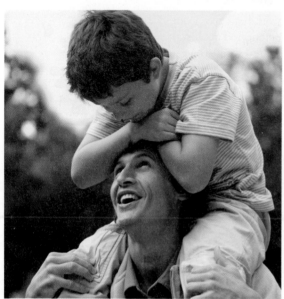

Communication can cause us to feel happy and loved.

EFFECT

As people communicate, they are changed in some way by the interaction. Communication has an **effect** and can be viewed as an exchange of influences.

An effect can be emotional, physical, cognitive, or any combination of the three. Communication can elicit feelings of joy, anger, or sadness (emotional); it can cause you to fight, argue, become apathetic, or evade an issue (physical); or it can lead to new insights, increased knowledge, the formulation or reconsideration of opinions, silence, or confusion (cognitive). Since effects are not always visible or immediately observable, there is obviously more to communication than meets the eye, or the ear.

Models of Communication

Now that we have examined the basic elements of communication, we are ready to see how our understanding can be reflected in a picture, or model, of the communication process.

Through communication, we share meaning with others by sending and receiving messages—sometimes intentionally and sometimes unintentionally. Communication thus includes every element that could affect two or more people as they knowingly or unknowingly relate to one another.

At this point, we need to reiterate that communication occurs whenever one person assigns significance or meaning to the behavior of another. But, you might ask, will knowing this enable you to understand or establish better and more satisfying relationships with your friends, spouse, employer, parents? The answer is yes. If you understand the processes that permit people to contact and influence each other, if you understand the forces that can impede or foster the development of every kind of effective communication, then you stand a better chance of communicating effectively yourself. Models of communication, like the ones in Figures 1.1 and 1.2, explain and help you visualize the process we employ to initiate and maintain communicative relationships with others. You will find these models useful tools in discovering how communication operates and in examining your own communication encounters.

The model in Figure 1.1 is a transactional model of communication. It depicts communication as a continuous circle with both communicators simultaneously performing sender and receiver responsibilities. Each individual pictured is sending and

negative feedback
a response that extinguishes behavior in progress

internal feedback
a response you give yourself

external feedback
a response from another

effect
the commmunication outcome

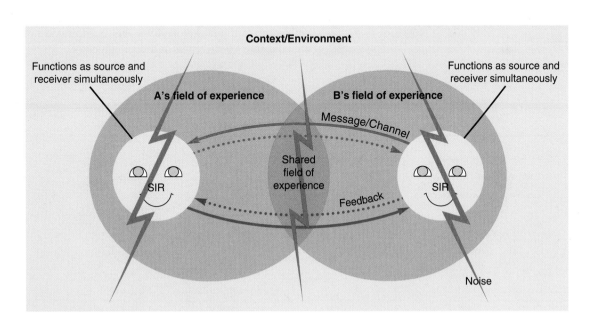

FIGURE 1.1

Gamble and Gamble's Model of Communication.

Communication is a continuous and simultaneous transaction.

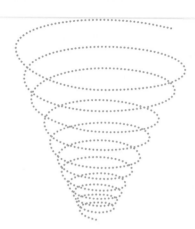

FIGURE 1.2

Dance's Communication Helix.

SOURCE: From *Human Communication Theory: Original Essays* by Frank E. X. Dance. Holt, Rinehart & Winston. Copyright © 1967 by Frank E. X. Dance. Used by permission of the author.

receiving messages (including feedback) through one or more channels at the same time as the other, suggesting that their messages will build upon and affect one another. Each person's field of experience—their culture, past experiences, education, biases, and heredity—will influence the interaction, as well as the extent to which their fields of experience overlap. In theory, the more individuals communicate with each other, the more overlap they create. In addition, we see that noise can enter the interaction at any point—for example, it can pop up in the message, be present in the channel, come from one's field of experience, or derive from the context. Such noise can affect the sending and/or the receiving abilities and effectiveness of the communicators.

Another model of communication, devised by communication theorist Frank Dance[6] (see Figure 1.2), depicts the communication process in a more abstract way. It is interesting because it plays with the concept of communication as an artist might. Dance's spiral, or helix, represents the way communication evolves or progresses in a person from birth to the present moment. This model emphasizes the fact that each person's present behavior is affected by his or her past experience and, likewise, that present behavior will have an impact on future actions. Thus, Dance's helix indicates that communication has no clearly observable beginning and no clearly observable end.

By playing with Dance's model, we can picture two communication spirals as meeting in a number of different ways, one of which is shown in Figure 1.3. The point where the spirals touch is the point of contact; each time a contact occurs, messages are sent and received by the interactants. Some helical spirals touch each other only once during a lifetime, whereas others crisscross or intertwine in a pattern that indicates an enduring relationship. Furthermore, the spirals (interactants) may sometimes develop in similar ways (grow together) and sometimes develop in different ways (grow apart; see Figure 1.4).

The understanding you now have should provide you with some of the background you will need as you work to increase your effectiveness as a communicator.

Review, Reflect, & **Apply**

Recall

Name the essential elements of communication.

Understand

Explain what makes communication transactional.

FIGURE 1.3

Meeting of Helixes.

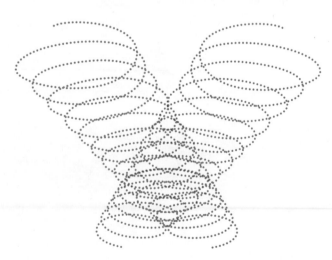

FIGURE 1.4

Model of Communication in Relationships.

How Good a Communicator Are You? Understanding Core Communication Principles

Simply communicating frequently does not mean that you are as effective a communicator as you could be. Too often, we neglect problems with our communicative relationships. When we lack sensitivity and fail to consider the feelings of others, for example, our relationships suffer. There is no such thing as being too effective at establishing, maintaining, and controlling personal and public contacts with others. Being mindful of the principles discussed in this section can help you to improve your communication skills.

LO3

Describe the core principles of communication.

COMMUNICATION IS DYNAMIC

When we call communication a dynamic process, we mean that all its elements constantly interact with and affect each other.[7] Since all people are interconnected, whatever happens to one person determines in part what happens to others.

Like the humans who compose them, relationships constantly evolve. Nothing about communication is static. Everything is accumulative. We communicate as long as we are alive. Thus, every interaction we engage in is part of connected happenings. As we learned from Dance's model, our present communication experiences may be thought of as points of arrival from past encounters and as points of departure for future ones. Do your experiences support this?

COMMUNICATION IS UNREPEATABLE AND IRREVERSIBLE

Every human contact you experience is unique. It has never happened before, and never again will it happen in just the same way. Our interpretation of the adage "You can never step into the same river twice" is that the experience changes both you and the river forever. Similarly, a communication encounter affects and changes people so that the encounter can never happen in exactly the same way again. Thus, communication is both unrepeatable and irreversible. We can neither take back something we have said nor erase the effects of something we have done. And although we may be greatly influenced by our past, we can never reclaim it. In the words of a Chinese proverb, "Even the emperor cannot buy back one single day." Do you think this proverb is accurate?

COMMUNICATION HAS NO OPPOSITE

People often assume that communication is purposeful and that we communicate only because we want to communicate. While this is sometimes true, it is also true that sometimes we communicate without any awareness of doing so—and just as often even without wanting to.

Whenever we are involved in an interaction, we respond in some way. Even if we choose not to respond verbally, even if we maintain absolute silence and attempt not to move a muscle, our lack of response is itself a response, constitutes a message, influences others, and communicates. We can never voluntarily stop behaving—because behavior has no opposite. No matter how

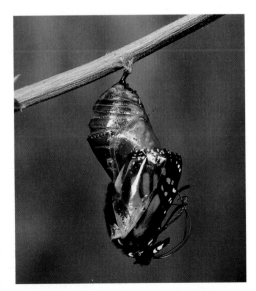

Experience changes us forever.

hard we try, we cannot *not* communicate, because all behavior is communication and therefore is a message.

COMMUNICATION IS AFFECTED BY CULTURE

As we will learn in Chapter 2, how we formulate and interpret messages depends on our culture. Cultural diversity, including race, ethnicity, gender, and age, influences the meanings we attribute to communication. Cultural differences exist not only between persons who speak different languages but between persons who speak the same language as well. Every cultural group has its own rules or preferences for interaction. When these are ignored or unknown, we are likely to misinterpret the meaning of messages received and miscalculate the impact of messages sent.

COMMUNICATION IS INFLUENCED BY ETHICS

Every time we communicate, we decide implicitly or explicitly whether we will do so ethically. Ethics are the moral principles, values, and beliefs that the members of society use to guide behavior. Since communication has consequences, it involves judgments of right and wrong. When the agreed-upon standards of behavior are violated, the behavior is judged unethical. For example, most of us expect those with whom we interact to be honest, play fair, respect our rights, and accept responsibility for their actions.

Review, Reflect, & Apply

Recall

Describe what is meant by the statement, "Communication is dynamic."

Understand

Give an example in which the irreversibility of communication caused difficulties for you.

Evaluate

Outline what distinguishes an effective communicator from a poor one using the core principles of communication.

Apply

Show how improving a specific communication skill can resolve a problem in your personal, academic, or professional life.

COMMUNICATION IS COMPETENCE-BASED

According to communication scholar Osmo Wiio, if communication can fail, it will.[8] The problem we face is determining how we can prevent communication from failing. One solution is to make wise choices. In certain situations, some messages are appropriate and okay to say to particular receivers while others are not.

While we all have different communication strengths and weaknesses, we can all benefit from getting better at communicating. When we add to our knowledge and make a commitment to develop the skills to apply that knowledge across an array of communication situations or contexts, we gain communication competence. For example, included among the skills necessary for effective communication is the ability to think critically. When we can think critically, we have the ability to examine ideas reflectively and to decide what we should and should not believe, think, or do, given a specific set of circumstances.[9]

MEDIA AND TECHNOLOGY ARE TRANSFORMING COMMUNICATION

LO4

Analyze how digital media are transforming communication in ways good and bad.

As media critic Marshall McLuhan cautioned, "The medium is the message."[10] In McLuhan's view, different channels of communication affect the way a sender encodes a message and the way a receiver responds to a message. The same words delivered face-to-face, on paper, via text or via radio or television do not constitute the same message. The channel of communication changes things. For example, terminating a relationship by texting our partner is very different from delivering such news in person. What channel would you use, for example, to say "good-bye"? Which channel would you use to tell someone "I'm sorry"? What about "I love you"?

New forms of communication also alter our communication experiences. According to media scholar Neil Postman, a new technology does not merely add or subtract something; it changes everything. Postman contends that our culture is now a **technopoly**—a culture in which technology monopolizes the thought-world.[11] Technology continues to speed up communication as it brings the world into our living rooms and bedrooms, offices and cars. Instead of valuing sequential understanding and careful logic, we now value immediate gratification and emotional involvement. Technology has also given us the ability to interact in more ways, more quickly, and with more people than ever before. For example, we experienced the Middle East uprisings and the earthquake, tsunami, and nuclear energy plant crises in Japan as these events occurred. E-mail, Skype, and YouTube make it possible for us to see, interact with, and visit with people across the country and around the world.

We are evolving new ways of discovering ideas and information; new ways of relating with friends and strangers; and new ways of learning about our world, our identities, and our futures. As we expand our real and virtual communication repertoires, as we live not only our real life but an online life, we need to ask and try to answer a number of questions: What changes are digital media creating in us? How are they influencing our social and emotional lives and cultural sensibilities? How are they altering our desire to relate to others—that is, our desire to communicate? What does it mean to be a communicator in a digital age?

For one thing, whether you are e-mailing, texting, or blogging, online messages tend to be more permanent. Ethically challenged individuals can access your files, private messages may be made public, or messages you send may be used against you or forwarded to someone you had no intention of communicating with. On the other hand, when online it is easier to find people who share your interests.

technopoly
a culture in which technology monopolizes the thought-world

Smart phones and laptops keep us connected. In your opinion, are they facilitating or impeding human interaction?

In addition, you can choose to remain anonymous. You decide what aspects of yourself to reveal to others or whether you wish to remain disguised. Also, unless you post your picture, you are more likely to be evaluated on the basis of what you write, rather than how you look.

Like television in the 1950s, digital media are society-altering devices affecting personal interaction. Parents used to cry, "Please turn off the television." Now they plead, "Please turn off the computer and come watch television with us." Or quite possibly, parents today are just as plugged in as their kids, with Facebook accounts of their own. Undeniably, many are spending more and more time on the Internet. Some contend the Internet is addictive; others say it's destroying inner lives. Both are claims once made about television. Television was once everything, in the same way the Internet has now taken over. In either case, the machines we have are shaping our consciousness.[12]

What do your Internet experiences reveal? In what ways does the time you spend online contribute to social or antisocial activity? Do you find that Internet use is isolating, adding to the time you spend alone? Do you find it promotes active engagement with others, facilitating more social time? Does online time complement or displace the time you spend face-to-face? Compare your answers with these research findings: For every minute that individuals spend on the Internet, the time they spend alone increases by 35 to 40 seconds.[13] It is harder to be engaged with others while Internet engaged (see Figure 1.5).[14] Some 33 percent of college students spend over 10 hours each week online, and almost 20 percent spend over 20 hours a week on the Internet. That's more time than college students spend using television and radio (see Figure 1.6).[15] Internet

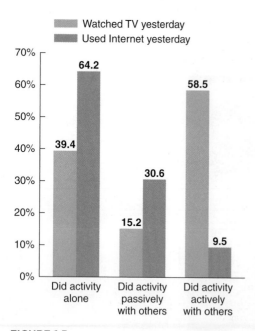

FIGURE 1.5

Sociability of the Internet versus Television.

NOTE: For those who spent time watching Television, N = 3,304. For those who spent time online, N = 757. Percentages can sum to greater than 100% because categories are not mutually exclusive.
SOURCE: Reprinted by permission of BurstMedia.

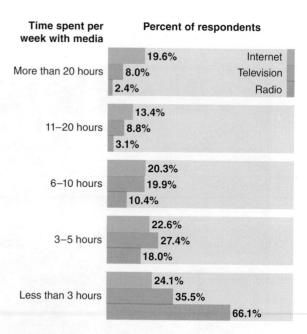

FIGURE 1.6

College Students Are Online, Even When Watching Television.

NOTE: Respondents were 18- to 24-year-old college students.
SOURCE: Reprinted by permission of BurstMedia.

TABLE 1.1 Percentage of College Students Who Actively Participate in Online Activity

	Female College Students	Male College Students
Instant messaging	57.2%	62.3%
Downloading music/MP3 files/online concerts	51.2%	55.0%
Pursuing school/work activities	60.2%	44.9%
Playing online games	49.3%	46.4%
Reading entertainment news/gossip	47.8%	44.9%
Listen to Internet radio	45.8%	43.5%
Reading local/national/international news	46.3%	42.5%
Viewing streaming video	34.3%	49.3%
Shopping	41.8%	35.3%
Researching health/medical information	32.8%	21.7%
Reading sports scores and news	10.4%	34.8%
Searching local restaurant/club listings	16.9%	23.6%
Reading news on fashion/trends	23.9%	17.4%
Reading horoscope	22.9%	9.1%
Looking up weather info	5.5%	6.8%

NOTE: Participants were college students aged 18-24 years old.
SOURCE: Reprinted by permission of BurstMedia.

users also spend less time talking on the phone with friends and family. In addition, for every extra hour of Web-time, Internet users report spending less time with traditional media.

The most common Internet communication endeavors are e-mail and instant messaging, with some 90 percent of Internet users reporting themselves to be e-mailers. A little over 30 percent of users engage in entertainment online, participating in computer games and the like. Over 25 percent of users enter chat rooms—frequently interacting with anonymous, rather than known, others. Internet users also multitask. Approximately 50 percent of college students use the Internet while watching television, and a little less than half are online while listening to the radio. (See Table 1.1 for an overview of online activities in which college students participate.)[16] Where do you fit into these findings?

To be sure, participation in online communication activity has risen dramatically since the beginning of the millennium. In 2000, there were some 12,000 blogs; in 2010, the number increased to 141 million. One hundred million Google

NON SEQUITUR © 2004 Wiley Miller. Dist. By UNIVERSAL UCLICK. Reprinted with permission. All Rights Reserved.

Understand

Explain how technology alters our communication experiences.

Evaluate

Identify the pros and cons of online versus face-to-face communication, giving examples of situations suited to each.

searches were conducted in 2000; two billion searches were done in 2010. We sent a scant 400,000 text messages in 2000; that figure rose to 4.5 billion in 2010. The average person spent 2.7 hours a week online in 2000; in 2010, she spent more than 18 hours a week online.[17] In fact, it is no longer uncommon to be awakened by a text message.[18]

A question to consider is this: Does what happens online stay online, or do our online experiences affect our offline realities?[19] The cell phone, for example, is no longer just a means of social interaction, it is also a source of news and public information, as well as a medium through which we express our social identity.[20] In addition, texting has changed the way we communicate. We may be reluctant to make a telephone call to deliver certain kinds of messages, but we are willing to send those messages via text. Are there messages that you prefer to send by texting rather than by talking face-to-face with another person? The more socially anxious you are, the more you may prefer "to play it safe," and the greater the likelihood that you will use text messaging as a preferred means of forming and managing close personal relationships.[21] New media give us new communication options.

Why We Communicate

LO5

Evaluate the benefits of communicating effectively

As we see, every communication experience serves one or more functions. For example, communication can help us discover who we are, help us establish meaningful relationships, or prompt us to examine and try to change either our own attitudes and behaviors or the attitudes and behaviors of others.

TO GAIN SELF-UNDERSTANDING AND INSIGHT INTO OTHERS

One key function of communication is self-other understanding: insight into ourselves and others. When you get to know another person, you also get to know yourself; and when you get to know yourself, you learn how others affect you. We depend on communication to develop self-awareness.

We need feedback from others all the time, and others are constantly in need of feedback from us. Interpersonal, small-group, public, and media communications offer us numerous opportunities for self-other discovery. Through communication encounters we are able to learn why we are trusting or untrusting, whether we can make our thoughts and feelings clear, under what conditions we have the power to influence others, and whether we can effectively make decisions and resolve conflicts and problems.

Today, it is a given that we will need to interact with persons who are culturally different from us. To attempt to insulate ourselves from such intercultural contacts is virtually impossible, nor is it desirable. It is through communication that we can reveal to others what is important to us and what we stand for, as well as learn what is important to them and what they stand for.

TO FORM MEANINGFUL RELATIONSHIPS

In building relationships, we cannot be overly concerned with ourselves but must consider the needs and wants of others. It is through effective communication that our basic physical and social needs are met.

Does Reality TV Reflect Reality?

In reality-type television programs, such as *Survivor, American Idol, The Bachelor,* and *America's Next Top Model,* people are thrown together, filmed continuously, and frequently isolated from or permitted to have only limited contact with the outside world as they compete against each other in an effort to win money, fame, and/or love. A pop-culture trend, these shows have ratings that prove huge numbers of people view them. Critics ask whether shows like these, which emphasize wealth, beauty, and popularity, are "in reality" promoting the worst in human behavior. What is more, they ask, do programs that place people in unusual situations—situations that exist in a setup environment and deviate from most of the everyday experiences that the vast majority of us have—reflect reality at all?[22]

What do you think? Does reality television reflect reality? What values do your most and least favorite reality television shows promote? What do your most and least favorite shows suggest about human nature? What do they reveal about our competitiveness and the role competition plays in our lives? In your opinion, are shows like these symptomatic of **hyper-competitive culture,** the belief that one needs to defeat another in order to achieve one's goals? And what do they reveal about our communication ethics? Will people do anything to win? Do these shows encourage us to live in the here and now? Do they fuel our materialistic greed and our desires for what is superficial by making us eager to sacrifice privacy, relationships, common sense, and morality in the drive to acquire great wealth, fame, and beauty? And what do they suggest about us as viewers? Have we become, as author Clay Calvert suggests, a "voyeur nation"?

Psychologists tell us that we need other people just as we need water, food, and shelter. When we are cut off from human contact, we become disoriented and maladjusted, and our life itself may be placed in jeopardy. People who are isolated from others—people who lack satisfying social relationships—are more likely to experience health problems and to die early than people who have an abundance of satisfying relationships.

Communication offers each of us the chance to satisfy what psychologist William Schutz calls our "needs for inclusion, control, and affection."[23] The **need for inclusion** is our need to be with others, our need for social contact. We like to feel that others accept and value us, and we want to feel like a full partner in a relationship. The **need for control** is our need to feel that we are capable and responsible, that we are able to deal with and manage our environment. We also like to feel that we can influence others. The **need for affection** is our need to express and receive love. Since communication allows each of these needs to be met, we are less likely to feel unwanted, unloved, or incapable if we are able to communicate meaningfully with others.

Communication also gives us the chance to share our personal reality with people from our own culture, as well as people from different cultures. Whether we live in an East Coast urban area, a southern city, a desert community, a home in sunny California, a village in Asia, a plain in Africa, or a town in the Middle East, we all engage in similar activities when we communicate. We may use different symbols, rely on different strategies, and desire different outcomes, but the processes we use and the motivations we have are strikingly alike. Equally significant is the fact that insensitivity to another's needs and preferred ways of interacting can hamper our ability to relate effectively.

TO INFLUENCE OTHERS

During interpersonal, small-group, public, mediated, and online communication, people have ample opportunities to influence each other subtly or overtly. We spend much time trying to persuade one another to think as we think, do

hyper-competitive culture
the contention that one needs to defeat another to achieve one's goals

need for inclusion
the need for social contact

need for control
the need to feel we are capable and responsible

need for affection
the need to express and receive love

Exploring **Diversity**

Over 24 years ago, researcher Gordon Allport wrote the following in his now-classic *The Nature of Prejudice:*

> See that man over there?
>
> Yes.
>
> Well, I hate him.
>
> But you don't know him.
>
> That's why I hate him.

Why does lack of knowledge or familiarity breed hate? Why might we experience hate when encountering people from a new or unfamiliar culture or group? Although Allport was writing over two decades ago, his comments remain true today. Why? To what extent do you believe that enhanced self–other understanding can help resolve this predicament? Explain.

what we do, like what we like. Sometimes our efforts meet with success, and sometimes they do not. In any case, our experiences with persuasion afford each of us the chance to influence others so that we may try to realize our own goals.

FOR CAREER DEVELOPMENT

Employers are concerned about the lack of communication skills in new hires. Among their perennial complaints are poor written communication and pre-sentation skills of applicants. Employers report that recent college grads tend to ramble when asked to explain something, have difficulty making a point, and are prone to sending e-mails that are far too casual and read more like text messages.[24]

There is a positive relationship between the ability to communicate and career success. Employers seek to hire people who know how to make communication work. If you develop the abilities to speak so that others listen, listen when others speak, critically evaluate what you read and hear, adapt to differences in cultural perspectives, handle conflicts and solve problems, and make sound decisions, then you will exhibit skills valued by employers.[25]

In fact, most careers require interaction with others, making strong communica-tion skills a requisite for being hired. Among the most important skills employers seek in hires are communication skills (listening, oral, and written), interpersonal skills, teamwork and problem-solving skills, planning and organizing skills, analytical/research skills, multicultural sensitivity, and adaptability—the very skills we focus on in this text.[26]

LO6

Apply guidelines for improving your communication effectiveness

Communication Skills

PRACTICE EFFECTIVE COMMUNICATION

The major purpose of this book is to help you gain an understanding of communication and to assist you in developing your skills at interpersonal, small-group, public, mass, and online communication. Engaging with the following tasks will give you a great start:

Become Actively Involved in the Study of Communication

Once you commit to putting the principles we have discussed into practice, you will be on your way to becoming a better communicator. Use the learning objectives to clarify your personal communication objectives as you make your way through the book. Use the Skill Builder, Thinking Critically, Exploring Diversity, Ethics & Communication, and Media Wise boxes to further explore what you must know and do to become a more effective communicator.

Set and Track Personal Goals

Focus on mastering and maintaining these skills and work to eliminate ineffective behaviors.

- The ability to understand and communicate with yourself
- An appreciation of the extent to which gender, culture, media, and new technologies affect communication
- The capacity to listen to and process information
- Sensitivity to silent messages that you and others send
- Knowledge of how words affect you and those with whom you relate
- An understanding of how relationships develop
- An understanding of how feelings and emotions affect relationships
- Learning how to disagree without being disagreeable
- An understanding of how beliefs, values, and attitudes affect the formulation and reception of messages and the development of speaker-audience relationships

Believe in Yourself

Above all else, you need to believe that you are worth the time and effort required to develop your communication skills. You also need to believe that developing these skills will immeasurably improve the quality of your life.

The Wrap-Up

SUMMARY

LO1   **Define** *communication.*

Communication is the deliberate or accidental transfer of meaning. Human communication takes place interpersonally (one to one), in small groups (one to a few), in public forums (one to many), via the media, or online.

LO2   **Explain** the essential elements of communication and their interaction using representative communication models.

The essential elements of communication are people, messages, channels, noise, context, feedback, and effect. Models of communication illustrate the communication process in action.

LO3   **Describe** the core principles of communication.

Communication reflects a number of general principles. First, since communication is a dynamic process, each interaction is part of a series of interconnected communication events. Second, every communication experience is unique, unrepeatable, and irreversible. Third, communication has no opposition. Fourth, culture influences communication. Fifth, it is influenced by ethics. Sixth, it is competence-based.

LO4   **Analyze** how digital media are transforming communication.

New forms of communication are altering the nature of our communication experiences. We use more ways of relating to others than ever before. As we expand our virtual communication repertoires, including the use of e-mail and instant messaging, we increase some forms of communication and limit others.

LO5   **Evaluate** the benefits of effective communication.

Effective communication promotes self-other understanding, helps us establish meaningful relationships, enables us to examine and attempt to change the attitudes and behavior of others, and enhances career development. Developing communication skills is a life-long process. This book explains the strategies you can use to assess your own communication abilities, improve the effectiveness of your communication relationships, and enhance the quality of your life.

LO6   **Apply** guidelines for improving your communication effectiveness.

Once you become actively involved in the study of communication, commit to setting and tracking personal goals, and believe in yourself, you are on the road to mastering communication skills to last a lifetime.

KEY CHAPTER TERMINOLOGY

channels 7

communication 4

context 8

effect 8

essentials of communication 6

external feedback 8

feedback 8

group communication 5

hyper-competitive culture 17

internal feedback 8

interpersonal communication 5

intrapersonal communication 5

mass communication 5

message 6

need for affection 17

need for control 17

need for inclusion 17

negative feedback 8

noise 7

online, or machine-assisted, communication 5

positive feedback 8

public communication 5

receivers 6

senders 6

social capital 4

technopoly 13

Nonverbal Communication:
Silent Language Speaks

After completing this chapter, you should be able to demonstrate mastery of the following learning outcomes:

LO1 **Define** *nonverbal communication*, and explain its characteristics and functions.

LO2 **Discuss** the following types of nonverbal messages: *Body Language, Voice, Space and Distance, Appearance, Color, Clothing and Artifacts, Time, Touch,* and *Smell.*

LO3 **Describe** how nonverbal cues can help distinguish truth telling from lying.

LO4 **Identify** the ways in which differences in gender and cultural background influence nonverbal behavior.

LO5 **Discuss** the influence of technology on nonverbal communication.

LO6 **Practice** using and observing nonverbal cues.

We believe that learning to interpret and send nonverbal messages effectively will benefit you. Frequently more powerful than words, nonverbal communication often provides reasons for how others respond to us.

> *What you are speaks so loudly that*
> *I cannot hear what you say.*
>
> —Ralph Waldo Emerson

Recently, customs inspectors at John F. Kennedy Airport carefully watched hundreds of passengers get off a flight from South America. As people moved past them, they looked for telltale body language indicative of exceptional nervousness. One man caught their attention. His lips were so chapped and dry they appeared white and "his carotid artery was jumping out of his neck." They took the man aside and discovered that he had paid cash for a business-class ticket, even though he was a low-paid service worker. X-rays revealed that the man had swallowed several bags of heroin pellets.

Since 9/11, the science of spotting nervous or threatening behavior has gained respect. According to one security consultant, "well-trained body language profilers might have spotted and questioned some of the September 11th hijackers" using basic behavior pattern recognition work. In fact, security personnel positioned at airports and in office buildings are now trained to watch for darting eyes and hand tremors in addition to identifying other cues of suspicious behavior. For example, they are being taught that our lips get thinner when we become angry, and our blink rate increases when we become nervous. They now know that our nostrils flare when we are aroused, and our blood flow increases, reddening our skin when we prepare for a physical or mental fight.[1]

Communicating Without Words

LO1

Define nonverbal communication, and explain its characteristics and functions.

Do you know people who have had trouble establishing and maintaining good relationships at work and in their personal lives, but can't figure out why? The answer may be that they lack the nonverbal communication skills essential for social success.[2] Some of us have trouble picking up on social cues that others of us use regularly and take for granted. The nonverbally skill-less are, for all practical purposes, communication clueless. The founder of psychoanalysis, Sigmund Freud, once wrote: "He that has eyes to see and ears to hear may convince himself that no mortal can keep a secret. If his lips are silent, he chatters with his fingertips; betrayal oozes out of him at every pore."

We all communicate nonverbally. In a normal two-person conversation, the verbal channel carries less than 35 percent of a message's meaning; this means that more than 65 percent of the meaning is communicated nonverbally (see Figure 5.1).[3] For instance, consider this example describing the impact of nonverbal behavior by former president Bill Clinton:

I've seen him do it a million times, but I can't tell you how he does it. . . . The right-handed part. I can tell you what he does with his left hand. He's a genius with it. He might put that hand on your elbow . . . or your bicep, like he's doing now. Basic move. He's interested in you. He's honored to meet you. But if he gets any higher, if he gets on your shoulder . . . it's not as intimate. He'll share a laugh with you, a light secret. And if he doesn't know you, but wants to share emotion . . . he'll lock you in a two-hander. You'll see when he shakes hands with you. . . .[4]

By analyzing nonverbal cues, we can enhance our understanding of what is really being said when people talk. The nonverbal level can also help us define the nature of each relationship we share. With practice, we can learn to use the nonverbal mode to provide us with "ways of knowing" that would not otherwise be available to us.[5]

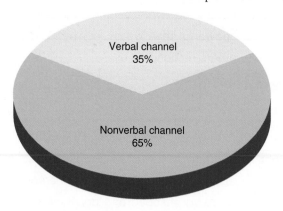

Verbal channel
35%

Nonverbal channel
65%

FIGURE 5.1
Communication of Social Meaning.

Facecrime

In the classic novel *1984,* author George Orwell describes the potential power and possible dangers of nonverbal communication:

> It was terribly dangerous to let your thoughts wander when you were in any public place or within range of a telescreen. The smallest thing could give you away. A nervous tic, an unconscious look of anxiety, a habit of muttering to yourself—anything that carried with it the suggestion of abnormality, of having something to hide. In any case, to wear an improper expression on your face (to look incredulous when a victory was announced, for example), was itself a punishable offense. There was even a word for it in Newspeak: *facecrime,* it was called.

Do you recognize the importance nonverbal cues play in impression formation?

1. Can you read people's faces?　○ Yes　○ No
2. Recall an instance when someone accused you of committing a *facecrime.* What about your demeanor might have led to that accusation?
3. Are you able to detect a person's mood based on his or her voice?　○ Yes　○ No
4. Cite an instance when someone didn't need to tell you the emotion he or she was feeling because you could tell it from the person's voice and vica versa. What cues did you use?
5. Can you tell how interested people are in you by where they stand in relation to you?　○ Yes　○ No
6. If a consultant worked with you to improve your use of nonverbal cues, what changes do you imagine he or she would suggest you make?

Characteristics of Nonverbal Communication: Cues and Contexts

What is nonverbal communication? The term **nonverbal communication** designates all the kinds of human messages and responses not expressed in words.

nonverbal communication the kinds of human messages and responses not expressed in words

The twinkle in his eye, the edge in her voice, the knowing look of his smile, the rigidity of her posture, the confidence in his walk, her dress, his hairstyle, where she sits, how closely he stands in relation to another, her eagerness to arrive early—each of these cues contains clues regarding the attitudes, feelings, and personality of the displayer. Often, however, we are virtually unaware of what we do with our body, our voice, or the space around us when we interact with others.

Sometimes we consciously use nonverbal cues to send specific messages. Our use of nonverbal cues is then purposeful. For example, we may smile when meeting someone for the first time, shake hands firmly when greeting the person who will interview us for a job, or wear a flag lapel pin as a sign of our patriotism.

If, at this very moment, someone were to photograph you, what could others surmise by examining the photograph? How are you sitting? Where are you sitting? How are you dressed? What would your facial expression reveal about your reaction to this chapter?

Like verbal communication, nonverbal communication is ambiguous. (Think about the example we just gave—the photograph of you reading this chapter. Would different people interpret the photograph the same way?) Like words, nonverbal messages may not mean what we think they do. Thus, we have to be careful not to misinterpret them. Don't be surprised if you find that the real

Toni Smith, the basketball player with her back to the flag, used her nonverbal behavior to express her attitude toward U.S. foreign policy.

reason a person left a meeting early is quite different from what you assumed. All nonverbal communication must be evaluated or interpreted within the context in which it occurs.

Furthermore, verbal and nonverbal messages can be—and often are—contradictory. When we say one thing but do another, we send an incongruent, or **mixed message** that can impede communication. Whenever you detect an incongruity between nonverbal and verbal (word-level) messages, you will probably benefit by paying greater attention to the nonverbal messages. Researchers in communication believe that nonverbal cues are more difficult to fake than verbal cues—hence the importance of examining the nonverbal dimension.

mixed message
message that occurs when words and actions contradict each other

Review, Reflect, & **Apply**

Recall

List different kinds of nonverbal cues.

Understand

Describe the message(s) that each of those cues might communicate.

Apply

Using your own experience with nonverbal communication, devise a scenario that provides a meaningful context for one of these cues.

Functions of Nonverbal Communication

Nonverbal communication serves an array of communicative functions that can work both independently of and in conjunction with verbal messages to clarify meaning. Knapp and Hall identify a number of these functions.[6]

MESSAGE REINFORCEMENT OR COMPLEMENTATION

Nonverbal cues reinforce the verbal message by adding redundancy. A woman says, "I love you," to her fiancé and covers her partner's face with kisses. An instructor asks,

What does this cartoon suggest regarding the importance of nonverbal communication? How have you used another person's body language to enhance communication?

"Did you complete the assignment?" and you reply, "Sure did!" and make an OK sign with your fingers. Message reinforcement occurs when the nonverbal and verbal messages complement each other.

MESSAGE NEGATION

Nonverbal cues can also contradict or negate a verbal message—such as a man who says to his lover, "I need us to spend more time apart," as he moves closer with each word spoken. Such a message is contradicted or canceled by the communicator's nonverbal cues. The interaction represents a double message—the nonverbal cues and the words spoken are at odds with each other. Remember, the nonverbal message is usually the more accurate reflection of meaning.

MESSAGE SUBSTITUTION

Nonverbal cues can replace or substitute for verbal cues. A hand gesture lets everyone know you're OK. A shrug of the shoulders lets others know when someone doesn't care about something. Placing your finger over your lips can indicate that you'd like everyone in the room to stop talking. In each case, instead of words being spoken, an action is performed.

MESSAGE ACCENTUATION OR INTENSIFICATION

Nonverbal cues also can be used to underscore or intensify parts of a verbal message. Slowing down speech to emphasize the meaning and importance of key words, smiling when you say, "It's nice to meet you," and clutching your hair when you say, "I'm so angry I could pull my hair out!" are nonverbal cues that accent or emphasize the verbal messages sent.

MESSAGE REGULATION

Finally, nonverbal cues help regulate the back-and-forth flow of person-to-person interaction. We direct conversational turn taking with nonverbal cues. With eye contact, posture, gestures, and voice, we signal that we have finished speaking or indicate who should talk next. Nonverbal cues help us manage and control communication. They provide the traffic signals for verbal exchanges.

Types of Nonverbal Messages

LO2

Discuss the following types of nonverbal communication: Body Language, Voice, Space and Distance, Appearance, Color, Clothing and Artifacts, Time, Touch, and Smell.

For us to use nonverbal cues effectively, we must understand them. In the coming section, we examine the following types of nonverbal messages: body language, voice, space and distance, appearance, colors, clothing and artifacts, time, touch, and smell. As we will see, the nonverbal cues that fall within these categories do not occur in isolation; they interact, sometimes supporting and sometimes contradicting one another.

BODY LANGUAGE: KINESICS

kinesics
the study of the relationship between human body motion, or body language, and communication

Kinesics is the study of the relationship between body motion, or body language, and communication. Body language includes facial expression (particularly eyebrows, forehead, eyes, and mouth), posture, and gestures. Thus, hand movements, a surprised stare, drooping shoulders, a knowing smile, and a tilt of the head are all part of kinesics. The role of signing and gestures in learning garnered attention when it was reported that infants and toddlers who learn to use and read gestures may learn to read faster and do better on future IQ tests than children who do not.[7] Consciously using multiple channels facilitates communication.

Facial Expressions

How well do you read faces? Research has shown that many people are able to decipher facial cues with great accuracy, but others lack this ability. Unpopularity, poor grades, and a variety of other problems that plague schoolchildren may be attributed to an inability to read the nonverbal messages of teachers and peers. According to psychologist Stephen Norwicki, "Because they are unaware of the messages they are sending, or misinterpret how other children are feeling, unpopular children may not even realize that they are initiating many of the negative reactions they receive from their peers."[8] Your ability to read someone's face increases when you know the person, understand the context of the interaction, and are able to compare and contrast the person's facial expressions with others you have seen him or her make.

Of all the nonverbal channels, the face is the single most important broadcaster of emotions. Since we cannot put the face away, we take great pains to control the expressions we reveal to others.

How do we do this? We use the following **facial management techniques:** intensifying, deintensifying, neutralizing, and masking. When we intensify an emotion, we exaggerate our facial responses. Have you ever pretended you loved a gift when in reality you couldn't stand it? When we deintensify an emotion, we deemphasize our facial expressions so that others will judge our reactions to be more appropriate. Were you ever very angry with a professor but were compelled to restrain yourself because you feared the professor's response if you let your anger show? When we neutralize an emotion, we avoid displaying it at all. Sometimes neutralization is an attempt to display strength, as when we are saddened by the death of a relative but want to appear brave. In U.S. culture, men neutralize fear and sadness more frequently than women do. Finally, when we mask an emotion, we replace it with another to which we believe others will respond more favorably. Thus, we sometimes conceal feelings of jealousy, disappointment, or rage.

Your facial appearance also influences judgments of your attractiveness.[9] In addition, it affects others' assessment of you as being dominant or submissive.[10] Thus, we speak of a baby face, a face as cold as ice, a face as strong as a bulldog's, and so on. What words would you use to describe your own face?

By now you are probably beginning to realize the importance of observing facial expressions. But what should you watch for? For purposes of analysis, a person's face can be divided into three general areas: (1) the eyebrows and forehead, (2) the eyes, and (3) the mouth. Let us focus on each area separately.

Eyebrows and Forehead If you raise your eyebrows, what emotion are you showing? Surprise is probably most common, but fear may also be expressed by raised eyebrows; when you are experiencing fear, the duration of the movement will probably be longer.

The brows help express other emotions as well. Right now, move your brows into as many configurations as you can. With each movement, analyze your emotional response. What do the brows communicate?

The forehead also helps communicate your physical and emotional state. A furrowed brow suggests tension, worry, or deep thought. A sweating forehead suggests nervousness or great effort.

Eyes The second of the three areas is the eyes. Ralph Waldo Emerson noted, perceptively, "The eyes of men converse at least as much as their tongues." What do your eyes reveal to others?

Many expressions refer to the eyes—"shifty eyes," "the look of love," "the evil eye," "look me in the eye." Various eye movements are associated with emotional expressions: A downward glance suggests modesty; staring suggests coldness; wide eyes suggest wonder, naivete, honesty, or fright; and excessive blinking suggests nervousness and insecurity. Researchers have also shown that as we begin to take an interest in something, our blinking rate decreases and our pupils dilate.

The direction of eye gaze also provides interesting insights. For example, have you considered in what direction people look when they are not looking directly at you—and what that might signify? Richard Bandler and John Grinder, two of the founders of neurolinguistic programming, have developed a number of interesting theories. They suggest that people look in one direction when they try to remember something seen or heard and in another direction when they try to invent something.

facial management techniques
the means we use to control the expressions we reveal to others

To test their hypothesis, ask yourself the following series of questions; pay attention to any patterns in the direction you look while thinking of a response.

Questions That Evoke Visually Remembered Images

What color are your mother's eyes?

What color is your instructor's hair?

Questions That Evoke Visually Invented Images

How would you look in purple and green hair?

What would your home look like after it had been ravaged by fire?

Questions That Evoke Auditorily Remembered Images

Can you hear your favorite music?

Can you hear music you dislike?

Questions That Evoke Auditorily Invented Images

How would your dog sound singing "Mary Had a Little Lamb"?

What would King Kong sound like tiptoeing through the tulips?

Bandler and Grinder suggest that a right-handed person will look in the directions shown in Figure 5.2. Do your experiences confirm their findings? Could a lawyer or negotiator ask questions and then use these findings to determine whether the person answering had invented the reply? Could a CIA agent use the technique to determine if an informant was telling the truth? If the findings are valid, presumably the answer is yes. The agent, for example, could inquire about where hostages were being held: "What does the house look like? Did you see terrorist members there?" If the informant looked up and to the right, he or she might be creating images rather than actually remembering; in other words, the informant might be lying.

FIGURE 5.2

How Direction of Gaze Varies According to the Nature of the Item under Consideration.

Whatever your conclusions about the direction of eye gaze, it is important to maintain eye contact with others to recognize not only when others are not looking at you but where they are looking. Because these cues are not consciously controlled, they will seldom mislead us.

How long we look or gaze at a person or thing also communicates a message. In our culture, it is deemed acceptable to stare at animals and inanimate objects, such as paintings or sculptures, but rude to stare at people. Instead of staring at others, we are supposed to practice **civil inattention,** avoiding sustained eye contact and letting our eyes rest only momentarily on people (in other words, keeping our eyes to ourselves). Although it is permissible to look at someone we do not know for one or two seconds, after that we are expected to move our eyes along.

Despite civil inattention, in any gathering, the first thing most people do is eye one another. Eye contact indicates whether the communication channel is open. It is much easier to avoid talking or listening to people if we have not made eye contact with them. Eye contact between people also offers clues to the kind of relationship they share. For one thing, it can signal a need for inclusion or affiliation. People who have a high need for affiliation will frequently return the glances of others. There is a high degree of eye contact between people who like each other. We also increase eye contact when

civil inattention

the polite ignoring of others so as not to infringe on their privacy communicating with others if the physical distance between us is increased.

Of course, we must keep in mind that culture influences eye contact. Some cultures use eye contact more than we do; some use it less. Arabs engage in more direct eye contact and the Japanese in less eye contact than is typical of Americans. The Japanese, in fact, believe that prolonged eye contact is a sign of disrespect. Japanese children learn at an early age to avoid direct eye contact and to direct their gaze to the area of the Adam's apple instead.[11]

The fact is, the eyes have much to tell us.

Mouth People who do not smile are perceived to be unfriendly, uninterested in others, or bored. People respond more favorably to those who smile.[12]

Like the eyes, the lower facial area has much to communicate. For example, some people smile with just the mouth and lips. For others, the smile appears to consume the entire face. As a child, were you ever told to "wipe that smile off your face"? Why? Besides happiness, what can a smile communicate?

The presence or absence of eye contact indicates whether a communication channel is open or closed. What does the eye contact of these people suggest about their relationship?

How does your face look when you are not smiling—when it is at rest? Some faces have a neutral expression; others have a frown, snarl, or habitual smile—that is, the corners of the mouth seem to turn up naturally.

When you choose to smile, how do people react to your smile? People often find that others will return a smile to those who smile at them but will look away from, or avoid stopping to speak to, a person whose lips are pursed in a frown. To what extent do your experiences confirm this?

Both men and women tend to smile when seeking approval, but in general, women smile more frequently than men do. Women tend to smile even when given negative messages.[13] Why do you think this is so?

Recently, marketers for products such as Yahoo and cappuccino machines began using the images of women sticking out their tongues in ads. According to nonverbal communication researcher Maureen O'Sullivan, "the mouth is a sexual orifice," and the gesture of "sticking out one's tongue can have multiple meanings. It can be an act of rudeness, disgust, playfulness, or outright sexual provocation." She believes we are seeing more tongues in ads because marketers are running out of body parts to expose.[14] What do you think?

Posture

How many times have you heard the following admonitions?

"Stand up straight!"

"Why are you hunched over that desk?"

What kinds of nonverbal messages does your posture send to others? The way we hold ourselves when sitting or standing is a nonverbal broadcast, giving others information that they use to assess our thoughts and feelings.

Research provides enough information for us to draw some general conclusions about how others are likely to interpret our posture. Nancy Henley, in her book

Body Politics, suggests that "the bearing with which one presents oneself proclaims one's position in life."[15] Television and film support this premise by frequently contrasting the upright bearing of a wealthy person with the submissive shuffle of a servant or the slumped demeanor of a nobody. In line with this, researcher Albert Mehrabian notes that when people assume inferior roles, they reflect this by lowering their heads. In contrast, when they assume superior roles, people often raise their heads.

Each of us has certain expectations regarding the postures we expect others to display. For instance, we might expect a high-ranking military officer to adopt an extremely straight and somewhat official posture. Henley suggests that standing tall, in and of itself, helps a person achieve dominance.

Another aspect of posture to consider is how we lean, or orient ourselves, when we communicate. If you were speaking to someone who suddenly turned or leaned away from you, would you consider that a positive sign? Probably not. We usually associate liking and other positive attitudes with leaning forward, not withdrawing. When you are communicating with others, a slight forward tilt of your upper body may indicate that you are interested in what they have to say. Mehrabian found that we lean either left or right when communicating with a person of lower status than ourselves. This right or left leaning is a part of our more relaxed demeanor.[16] Thus, when we say, "I'm looking forward," can you predict the direction we tend to lean?[17]

Gestures

We learn to gesture before we learn to speak. If you've ever watched a young child perform the arms-raised "pick me up now" request, you know this. According to researchers, learning the meaning of gestures is important for children to understand the meaning of words, and understanding the meaning of their children's gestures is vital for parents.[18] The movements of our arms, legs, hands, and feet carry important nonverbal data. For instance, the way you position your arms sends information about your attitudes. Cross your arms in front of you. Do you feel closed off from the world? Stand up and put your hands on your hips. How does this stance make you feel? Next, clasp your arms behind your back in a self-assured manner. Then, hold your arms stiffly at your sides, as if you were a nervous speaker. Finally, dangle your arms at your sides. Become aware of the arm positions that you habitually use. What message does each of these positions communicate?

Nonverbal Cues and Status

Do you think if you were taller, spoke louder, and were perceived by others as more dominant, it would help you advance in your career? One female chief executive officer persists in wearing stiletto heels even though she is five feet, nine inches tall. She believes they make her appear more intimidating.[19] Another male CEO, six feet, three inches tall, in the midst of heated negotiations, puts his hand on the shoulder of those shorter than him, crowding into their personal space, attempting to demonstrate decisiveness and dominance. Another CEO says that he would rather be bald than short.[20] In fact, in *Blink*, author Malcolm Gladwell notes that 30 percent of Fortune 500 CEOs are at least six feet, two inches tall, versus just 4 percent of all men.[21] According to Stanford University professor Lara Tiedens, business people acquire status by looking directly at others, using an open stance and vigorous gestures, speaking loudly in a deep voice, interrupting at will, and leaning in close to reduce the space of others while expanding their own. Thus, she recommends that, to advance, you try to be seen as taller and louder, even borderline rude.[22] Others counter that chest beating and shouting matches are passé, akin to bullying, and a waste of time. Where do you stand?

Our legs also convey information about us. Try standing as a model would stand. Next, sit down and put your feet up on a desk or table. Then stand with your feet wide apart. Does this last stance make you feel more powerful? Why? The distribution of body weight and the placement of legs and feet can broadcast stability, femininity, masculinity, anger, happiness, or any number of other qualities. When communicating, choose the stance that most accurately reflects your goals. Keep in mind that crossing one's legs does not necessarily play well from country to country. In fact, it is perceived as highly offensive in Turkey and Ghana.

Gestures do not have universal meanings. Consider, for example, our "OK" gesture made by forming a circle with the thumb and forefinger. In Japan, the thumb and forefinger making a circle is used as a symbol for money. To most Americans, this joining of thumb and forefinger signifies that all is positive; the French and Belgians, in contrast, would interpret the gesture as meaning "you're worth zero."[23]

A lack of universality in gesturing can create problems for global advertisers. For years, in its advertisements for insurance, Allstate implied that it offers consumers security and protection by using the image of a person holding out his or her hands while a voice-over intones, "You're in good hands with Allstate." The ad failed in Germany, however, because in that country hands held out symbolize begging rather than security and protection.[24]

VOICE: PARALANGUAGE

Your friend asks you a question, and you matter-of-factly reply, "Mmhmm." Another person shares a revealing piece of gossip with you, and you shout, "Huh!" Reading about the ethical lapses of some politicians, you click your tongue: "Tsk, tsk, tsk." These elements of speech that are not standard words are a part of **paralanguage.** How good you are at using paralanguage determines whether or not you will be able to do your part to convey the meaning of a message to others.[25]

In many ways, you either play your voice—like a musical instrument—or are a victim of your voice. Would you ever advise someone to get a new voice? What

paralanguage
vocal cues that accompany spoken language

© Peter Steiner/The New Yorker Collection/www.cartoonbank.com.

"You're right. It does send a powerful message."

about yourself? Are you happy with the sound of yours? Have you ever heard how you sound on a tape of a meeting or on your answering machine? Does your tone go up and down, or do you speak in a monotone? Can you tell a good story, or do your words fall flat? If a new hairstyle and a new outfit are part of the job search, why aren't we similarly concerned with the sound of our voice? According to voice expert Thomas Murry, depth of knowledge and impact of voice are equally important in who gets hired and who succeeds in business.[26] Albert Mehrabian estimates that 38 percent of the meaning of a message delivered during face-to-face conversation is transmitted by voice or vocal cues.[27] Frequently, *how* something is said is *what* is said.

Among the elements of paralanguage are pitch, volume, rate, and pauses. Let us examine these elements of paralanguage more closely.

Pitch is the highness or lowness of the voice; it is the counterpart of pitch on a musical scale. We tend to associate higher pitches with female voices and lower pitches with male voices. We also develop vocal stereotypes. We associate low-pitched voices with strength, sexiness, and maturity and high-pitched voices with helplessness, tenseness, and nervousness. Although we all have what is termed a characteristic, or **habitual, pitch,** we have also learned to vary our pitch to reflect our mood and generate listeners' interest.

pitch
the highness or lowness of the voice

habitual pitch
the characteristic pitch one uses

Some people tend to overuse one tone to the exclusion of others. These people have monotonous voices characterized by too little variety of pitch. Other people speak at or near the upper end of their pitch scale, producing very fragile, unsupported tones. One way to discover a pitch that is not overly high is simply to yawn. Try it now. Permit yourself to experience a good stretch; extend your arms to shoulder level and let out a vocalized yawn. Do it again. Now count to 10 out loud. To what extent does the pitch of your voice appear to have changed? Is it more resonant? It should be. If you indulge yourself and yawn once or twice before stressful meetings or occasions, you will be able to pitch your voice at a more pleasing level.

Volume, or degree of loudness, is a second paralinguistic factor that affects perceived meaning. Some people cannot seem to muster enough energy to be heard by others. Others blast through encounters. Have you ever sat in a restaurant and heard more of the conversation at a table several feet away than you could hear at your own table? Volume frequently reflects emotional intensity. Loud people are often perceived as aggressive or overbearing. Soft-spoken people are often perceived as timid or polite.

The **rate,** or speed at which we speak, is also important. Do you, for example, expect high-pressure salespeople to talk rapidly or slowly? Most often, they speak very quickly. Similarly, those who are selling gadgets in department stores or on television also speak at a quick clip to retain the audience's interest and involvement. With regard to persons from other cultures, increased rate enhances judgments of credibility.[28]

Of course, more stately or formal occasions require slower speaking rates broken by planned pauses or silences. (Politicians at rallies typically punctuate their speeches with pauses that function almost as applause signs.) Frieda Goldman-Eisler, a communications researcher, has concluded that two-thirds of spoken language comes to us in chunks of fewer than six words.[29] Therefore, knowing when to pause is an essential skill. Pauses slow the rate of speech and give both sender and receiver a chance to gather their thoughts. Unfortunately, many people feel that all pauses must be filled and consciously or unconsciously seek ways to fill them. Frequently, we fill a pause with meaningless sounds or phrases: "Er—huh—uh—"; "You know? You know?" "Right! Right!" "OK! OK!" Such **nonfluencies** disrupt the natural flow of speech. Since pauses are a natural part of communication, we should stop trying to eliminate them. Instead, we should give pauses a chance to function.

Silence, the absence of both paralinguistic and verbal cues, also serves important communicative functions.[30] Silence, for example, can allow you time to organize your thoughts. It can also be used to alert receivers that the words you are about to share are important. In addition, choosing not to speak to someone at all can be a forceful demonstration of the indifference one person feels toward another and can be a very powerful message of disconfirmation. Silence can also be used as a form of punishment after an argument or as a conflict to indicate that one person is still angry with the other. Silence, as we see, can communicate a number of meanings. It can indicate that two people are so comfortable

Yawning can help you discover your optimum pitch.

volume
the degree of loudness of the voice

rate
speaking speed

nonfluencies
meaningless sounds or phrases that disrupt the flow of speech

silence
the absence of both paralinguistic and verbal cues

"I think I've finally found my own voice."

with each other that they do not feel a need to talk, or in a different context, it can reveal a person's shyness, by suggesting discomfort or the inability to keep a conversation moving. On the other hand, silence may simply indicate that you, at the moment, agree with what is being said or simply have nothing to say.

Besides communicating emotional content, the voice also communicates personal characteristics. Listening to a voice can sometimes help you identify the speaker's individual characteristics. For instance, on the telephone we are frequently able to determine a speaker's sex, age, vocation, and place of origin even though we have never met him or her. We also tend to associate particular voice types with particular body or personality types. For example, what type of appearance would you expect in a person who has a breathy, high-pitched voice? How do you think a person who has a throaty, raspy voice would look? As a communicator, you should be aware that your voice suggests certain things about you.

Research also reveals that we not only distrust but also lose confidence in a person when a foreign accent makes it difficult for us to understand him or her. Thus, distrust could be attributed to incomprehension as well as prejudice.[31] Whatever its source, unfortunately, the presence of a foreign accent can cause some people to judge non-native speakers as less credible than they actually are.

SPACE AND DISTANCE: PROXEMIC AND ENVIRONMENTAL FACTORS

Office space is shrinking, thus affecting workers' "me space" and their sense of privacy.[32] How much of the space on our planet do you call your own? How much space do you carry around with you? Are there times when people encroach on your

Silence can indicate how comfortable two people are in each other's presence.

space? In his book *The Hidden Dimension*, Edward Hall uses the term **proxemics** for human beings' "use of space."[33] *Proxemics* is the study of the space that exists between us as we talk and relate to each other, as well as the way we organize the space around us in our homes, offices, and communities. Architects and interior designers, for example, are using proxemics to humanize hospitals. In hospitals with soft lighting, single rooms, relaxing gardens, and artwork, patients heal more quickly, nurses remain more loyal to employers, and doctors perform better. By adding therapeutic touches to a typically sterile environment, such as providing patients with views of trees from their windows and more accessibility for family and friends to visit, patients have speedier and fuller recoveries.[34] Seating patterns, for example, influence our communicative behavior. How might another environment, such as a school, use an understanding of proxemics to encourage learning?

proxemics
the study of the use of space

Distances—Intimate, Personal, Social, Public

Hall identified four distances that we keep between ourselves and other people, depending on the type of encounter and the nature of the relationship:

intimate distance: 0 to 18 inches

personal distance: 18 inches to 4 feet

social distance: 4 to 12 feet

public distance: 12 feet to limit of sight

Intimate distance ranges from the point of touch to 18 inches from the other person. At this distance, physical contact is natural. We can wrestle, and we can make love. Our senses are in full operation. They are easily stimulated but also easily offended if we find ourselves in an uncomfortable situation. Have you ever had someone come too close to you and wanted that person to back off? Did you

intimate distance
a distance ranging from the point of touch to 18 inches from a person

The amount of distance between us depends on the nature of our encounter and our relationship to each other. What do the distances between each of these interactants communicate to you about the relationships?

personal distance
a distance ranging from 18 inches to 4 feet from a person

social distance
a distance ranging from 4 feet to 12 feet from a person

yourself back away? Sometimes we are forced to endure intimate distance between ourselves and strangers in crowded buses, trains, and elevators. How do you feel and respond in such situations?

Hall's **personal distance** ranges from 18 inches to 4 feet. When communicating at this distance, you can still hold hands or shake hands with another person. This is the most common distance between people talking informally in class, at work, or at parties, and we are apt to conduct most of our conversations within this range. If you reduce personal distance to intimate distance, you are likely to make the other person feel uncomfortable. If you increase it, the other person is likely to begin to feel rejected.

Hall's **social distance** ranges from 4 feet to 12 feet. At the social distance—in contrast to the personal distance—we are not likely to share personal concerns. By using social distance, we can keep people at more than arm's length. Thus, this is a safer distance, one at which we would communicate information and feelings that are not particularly private or revealing. Many of our conversations at meals and at business conferences or meetings occur within this space. In business, the primary protector of social space is the desk. Of course, the greater the distance between people, the more formal their encounters. (At a social gathering, you can normally tell how well people know one another by examining how close they stand to each other.)

Public distance (12 feet and farther) is commonly reserved for strangers with whom we do not wish to have an interaction. Distances at the farther end of the range are well beyond the area of personal involvement and make interpersonal communication very unlikely. People waiting in an uncrowded lobby for an elevator frequently use public distance. It can be assumed that if a person opts for public distance when he or she could have chosen otherwise, that person does not care to converse.

What happens when we violate distance norms? Researchers tell us that the outcomes of such violations can be positive. For example, if the approaching person is perceived to be attractive or is viewed as a high-reward source, our evaluation of the approacher may become more favorable, especially if the distance violation is accompanied by other behaviors, such as compliments.[35]

Spaces—Informal, Semi-Fixed-Feature, and Fixed-Feature

The nature of our environment affects the amount of distance we are able to maintain between ourselves and others. Researchers in nonverbal communication divide environmental spaces into three classifications: informal, semi-fixed-feature, and fixed-feature. These categories are based on the perceived permanence of any physical space.

Informal space is a highly mobile, quickly changing space that ranges from intimate to public (from no space between us and others to 25 feet or more). Informal space functions as a personal bubble that we can enlarge to keep people at a distance or decrease to permit them to get closer.

In contrast to the high mobility of informal space, **semi-fixed-feature space** uses objects to create distance. Semi-fixed features include chairs, benches, sofas, plants, and other movable items. (Some office walls and partitions can be classified as semi-fixed features, since they are designed to be relocated as spatial requirements change.) Researchers find that barriers such as desks reduce interaction. One study of doctor-patient relationships found that patients were more at ease speaking with a physician seated in a chair across from them than they were when the physician was sitting behind a desk.[36] Why do you think this was so? In many public places, if interaction is desired, the space will usually contain chairs facing each other. Such arrangements are found in bars, restaurants, and lounges. In contrast, the chairs in waiting rooms at airports and bus terminals are often bolted together in long parallel rows.

Fixed-feature space contains relatively permanent objects that define the environment around us. Fixed features include immovable walls, doors, trees, sidewalks, roads, and highways. Such features help guide and control our actions. For example, most classrooms are rectangular, with windows along one side, usually to the students' left. The window location also determines the front of the room. Shopping malls and department stores rely on fixed features to help route pedestrian traffic in certain directions that will increase sales. The next time you shop in a carefully designed store, examine its fixed features. Can you walk, unimpeded, to any department, or are you carefully "directed" through the perfumes, lingerie, and knickknacks? Why?

Territoriality and Personal Space

Another aspect of proxemics is our need for a defined territory. Some animals mark their territory by urinating around its perimeter and will defend their area

public distance
a distance of 12 feet and farther from a person

informal space
space that is highly mobile and can be quickly changed

semi-fixed-feature space
space in which objects are used to create distance

fixed-feature space
space that contains relatively permanent objects

Guarded Territory and the New Need for Security

A majority of persons living in the United States would like to live in a gated community.[37] Gated communities require that someone allows you to enter or that you have a permit that affords you the right of entry. They are typically protected by armed guards, gates, walls, or fences. As in Robert Frost's poetic line "Good fences make good neighbors," security devices and details in gated communities keep their members feeling safe by keeping out those whom the community does not want let in. Sometimes tire-piercing or other antiterrorist devices are used to guard against false entry into the community.

The prime motivator for living in a gated community is the desire for personal safety. On the other hand, because gated communities signal that outsiders should stay out, critics contend that social fragmentation is the cost society pays to allow those living inside them to feel secure. Thus, the fear is that gated communities precipitate in-groups and out-groups who compete for rights to use the same space.

Where do you stand? Are gated communities a good idea? Are there other kinds of living arrangements that could produce security without closing off a community to the outside world?

---

territoriality
the need to demonstrate a possessive or ownership relationship to space

against invaders. Human beings also stake out space, or territory, and territoriality is an important variable in interpersonal communication. What examples of **territoriality**—the need to demonstrate a possessive or ownership relationship to space—can you remember encountering? Are you familiar with "Dad's chair"? "Mom's bureau"? How do you feel when someone invades your room—your territory? What happens when someone stands too close to you? How are you treated when you enter another person's territory?

To establish territory, we use **markers,** items that reserve our space, set boundaries that help distinguish space, or identify a space as ours. At the library, for instance, you may spread your things out, over, and across the table, so that others will not find it easy to enter your territory. In large corporations, a person's status is often reflected by the size of his or her space. Thus, the president may be accorded a large top-floor territory, while a clerk is given a desk in a second-floor room amid a number of other desks and office machines. Regardless of the size of our location, however, we identify with it and frequently act as if we own it.

APPEARANCE

Do we live in a looks-based culture? Are people discriminated against because of how they look? If so, in an image-consumed culture, short men and unattractive women are at a disadvantage. For example, statistics reveal that persons perceived as unattractive receive lower salaries and even longer prison sentences than their more attractive counterparts. U.S. society seems to sanction this appearance bias by allowing attractive people to receive more advantages, or what some call "a beauty premium."[38]

Body Talk, Clothes Talk

1. The treatment of black characters on television may influence racial attitudes. It appears that the body language and facial expressions actors express tend to be less favorable when they are responding to someone who is black, unconsciously affecting viewers' attitudes about race. When, however, black characters were treated better than white characters, viewers showed improved conscious attitudes toward blacks.[39] How do you suggest these findings be used in the media?

2. Advertisers, aided by celebrity use and endorsements, have turned the clothing we wear into billboards and/or picket signs, soliciting our participation in promoting both high-status name brands and support for controversial issues. For example, some of us wear clothing or carry artifacts featuring the name or logo of designers such as Gucci or Louis Vuitton. We pay extra to wear name brands and then advertise them for free. Others of us wear shirts emblazoned with the name of our favorite sports team or player. And still others of us wear T-shirts that reveal our attitude on religion or spirituality, or various social and political issues. For example, we have T-shirts that picture Jesus and the message "Put Down the Drugs and Come Get a Hug," "War is Not the Answer," or "It's Easier to Get a Gun Than a Haircut." Again, celebrities also help to popularize these kinds of messages.

In your opinion, does the First Amendment protect the wearing of such clothing in schools and public spaces? What about the wearing of clothing that bears the names or colors of gangs or announces a wearer's discriminatory attitudes toward a specific co-culture or minority group? What messages, if any, would you consider to be unwearable?

When it comes to height, for example, tall people tend to "come out on top" whether in elections or job interviews.[40] When it comes to weight, a cold shoulder and brusque treatment are routinely given to people who are perceived as obese.[41] In fact, men make $789 more a year for every extra inch of height, while obese women tend to get substantially lower wages than women of average weight.[42] For some reason, it is still acceptable to stigmatize fat people by turning them into scapegoats for all kinds of societal problems and making weight an obstacle to their career success. For example, one job interviewee reported:

> As soon as I shook the interviewer's hand, I knew she would not hire me. She gave me a look of utter disdain, and made a big deal about whether we should take the stairs or ride the elevator to the room where we were going to talk. During the actual interview, she would not even look at me.[43]

Even physicians are influenced by the appearance of obese patients; the higher a patient's body mass, the less respect doctors express for the patient.[44] Does the stigmatization of obese people affect you? Does society's treatment give you permission to think there is something wrong with larger people? People judged to be attractive date more, earn higher grades, and are rated as more persuasive and likable than others.[45] Obsessing on being attractive may cause men to engage in bodybuilding, women to diet, and both men and women to turn to plastic surgery as a solution to feeling unattractive.[46] Thanks to the proliferation of Western models of beauty and success, even in South Korea, parents spend large sums of money for treatments that are supposed to make their children taller because short kids are ostracized.[47]

Judgments of race are also based on clues the face and body provide. For marketers, ethnic ambiguity—the multiracial face of youth—is becoming the new American beauty. Advertisers judge a face whose heritage is hard to determine

markers
items that reserve one's space

Does Rihanna's outfit support her image?

artifactual communication
the use of personal adornments

as most desirable. Ethnic mixing is changing the face of attractiveness—and influencing casting choices in advertisements and films.[48]

CLOTHING AND ARTIFACTS

Since people make inferences about our age, social and economic status, educational level, group membership, athletic ability, personality, and relationships to others by the way we dress, our use of **artifactual communication** (the use of personal adornments, such as clothing, jewelry, makeup, hairstyles, and beards) provides important nonverbal cues.

We use artifacts to create an image or a first impression. For example, some of us wear glasses even though our eyes are perfectly normal or we could wear contact lenses instead, believing, rightly or wrongly, that glasses make us appear more intelligent, interesting, or mysterious.[49]

How we dress influences how we behave. Consider singer Rihanna. Does Rihanna's dress support her behavior? Given the kind of music she sings, could she just as easily wear more prim and proper attire? Why or why not? While Rihanna purposefully wears such clothing to her job, could you wear the same or similar clothing to yours? Unless you are a singer or dancer, you probably answered this question with "Are you kidding?" or "No way." The clothing we wear to work should support the job roles and functions we perform.

It is clear that we react to people on the basis of their clothing. In the early stages of a relationship, clothing and appearance affect first impressions and exert influences that lead to acceptance or rejection. In addition, judgments regarding our success, character, dominance, and competence are made on the basis of the type of clothing and jewelry we wear.[50]

Typically, we respond more positively to those we perceive to be well dressed than we do to those whose attire we find questionable or unacceptable. We are also more likely to respond to requests from or follow the lead of well-dressed individuals, including persons in uniform, than we are to listen to or emulate those whose dress suggests lower status or lack of authority.[51]

COLORS: MEANINGS AND ASSOCIATIONS

Do you currently have a favorite color? A few years ago, one color authority, the Pantone Color Institute, named blue iris as its color of the year, noting: "Blue Iris brings together the dependable aspects of blue, underscored by a strong, soul-searching purple cast. Emotionally, it is anchoring and meditative with a touch of magic."[52] Acknowledging this, the advertising and marketing company JWT noted that "blue is the new green," particularly as it denotes ecological concerns.[53] One year earlier, the favored color had been chili pepper red. The leader of the Color Association, Margaret Welch, said bamboo, a yellow-green, was her personal color of the year, adding that it "just has a power. You know, these are very insecure times."[54]

FIGURE 5.3

Favored Colors

SOURCE: "The New Hue for 2011," The Wall Street Journal, Dec. 9, 2010, p. D8.

Color affects us emotionally and physiologically. Look at the color palette representing favored colors for the past decade in Figure 5.3.

Colors seem to have more than a passing effect on us. It has been found that color affects us emotionally and physiologically. Today, red is about authority and self-confidence.[55] Recent studies also reveal that while the color red makes people's work more accurate, the color blue makes them more creative. Thus red may increase memory, while blue may make a group brainstorming session more effective.[56] (See Figure 5.4.) Red excites the nervous system, while blue has a calming effect, lowering blood pressure, heart rates and respiration rates.

In the past decade, an increasing number of U.S. companies have chosen to be associated with the color blue: "Big Blue" (IBM), JetBlue (an airline), BlueKite (a wireless technology company), Blue Martini (a software company), and Blue Nile, to name just a few. According to the executive director of the Pantone Color Institute, "Blue is invariably connected with sky and water. The

Seeing Red, Seeing Blue

A study of 600 people who performed tasks on computer screens with red, blue or neutral backgrounds found that the red group did better on tests of attention to detail, while the blue group did better at creative tasks.

RECALLING WORDS

Some participants were asked to complete a detail-orientated task: studying and later recalling a list of 36 words. People in the red group recalled more words correctly than those in the blue group, with fewer false recollections.

Source: *Science*

THINKING CREATIVELY

Other participants tried a creative task, thinking of as many creative uses as possible for a brick. Each group produced the same number of suggestions, but a panel of judges rated those of the blue group to be the most creative.

FIGURE 5.4

Seeing Red, Seeing Blue

SOURCE: The New York Times, February 6, 2009 issue. Copyright © 2009. Used by permission of The New York Times Co.

sky has never fallen and water has never gone away. It has dependability and constancy."[57]

TIME: COMMUNICATIVE VALUE OF CHRONEMICS

chronemics
the study of the use of time

Chronemics is the study of how we use time to communicate. The meaning of time differs not only around the United States but also around the world.[58] While some people are preoccupied with time, others regularly waste it. While some are typically early, others are chronically late. While some travel through life with a sense of urgency, others amble through it at a more leisurely pace. Some people function best in the morning (the early birds), while others perform best at night (the night owls). Chronemics expert Robert Levine notes that clock addiction is difficult to break. Because the West is becoming more devoted to the clock by the minute, altering the pace of your life poses numerous challenges.

Do you have enough time for most of your activities? Are you usually prepared for exams or assignments? Do you arrive for appointments on time, early, or late? Recent surveys reveal that tardiness is a chronic problem among chief executive officers of corporations, who arrive late for 6 in 10 meetings.[59] Edward Hall says that "time talks."[60] What does your use or misuse of time say about you? To what extent do others communicate with you by their use of time?

Would you make real estate tycoon Donald Trump wait for a meeting with you, or would you arrive on time or even early? When negotiating a real estate transaction, a group of Chinese millionaires once made Trump wait for them—close to an hour. Do you feel that they were sending a message?

How long we wait for something or someone is related, first, to the value we place on whatever it is we are waiting for and, second, to our own status. We are taught to value what we wait for. In fact, if something is too readily available, we may decide we do not want it after all. Status determines who waits. If we are "important," others usually have access to us only by appointment; thus, it is easier for us to make others wait—and difficult or impossible for others to make us wait.

How well do you structure your time? In his book *The Time Trap*, Alex MacKenzie lists several barriers to the effective use of time:

attempting too much (taking on too many projects at once)

estimating time unrealistically (not realizing how long a project will take)

procrastinating (putting it off, and off, and off . . .)

allowing too many interruptions (letting yourself be distracted by telephone calls, friends, and so on)[61]

Do any of these apply to you? How might you go about improving your use of time?

Our sense of time is even reflected in how we use technology. For example, in text messages and e-mails, commas now appear rarely. Some observers believe that the disappearing comma is a metaphor for the frenetic pace of life today.[62] The comma, after all, signals a pause—the need to slow down before moving on, and slowing down is not what we seem to be doing. Instead, we multitask.

Wherever we go, we find people feverishly using iPads, PDAs, and cell phones even when dining at a restaurant or in meetings with others.

TOUCH: HAPTICS

Another category of nonverbal communication is touch, also referred to as **haptics.** According to researchers, touch is "one of the most provocative, yet least well understood" of nonverbal behaviors.[63] Yet all humans need to touch and be touched.[64] Research reveals that a hug and 10 minutes of hand-holding with a romantic partner greatly reduce the harmful physical effects of stress. It appears that, because touch lowers stress hormones, such loving contact protects us throughout the day.[65] Especially for women, hugs, by buffering them from stress, do their hearts good.[66] Thus, touch expresses specific emotions—even if the touch lasts only five seconds—sometimes more quickly than words, and even in the absence of words.[67] Touch is a significant means of emotional expression. For example, students who receive a supportive touch on the back or arm from a teacher volunteer in class nearly twice as often as those students who were untouched. A doctor's sympathetic touch causes the patient to believe the doctor spent more time with him or her than patients whom the doctor did not touch. A warm, reinforcing touch has the power to strengthen relationships.[68]

How accessible are you to touch?

The amount of touching we do or find acceptable is, at least in part, culturally conditioned. Where do you touch your father? Your mother? Your brother? Your sister? A friend of the same sex? A friend of the opposite sex? In general, women are more accessible to touch than are men. Touch also correlates positively with openness, comfort with relationships, and the ability to express feelings.[69] Both men and women will often kiss women in greeting; men who meet usually shake hands. Usually, men touch women more than women touch men.[70] Physical contact between males is often limited to contact sports, such as football and soccer.

The kind of touch believed appropriate depends upon the kind of relationships individuals share and the situation they find themselves in. One system of analysis identifies the following touch categories: functional-professional (touch that is impersonal or businesslike, such as the kind of touch that occurs when a doctor examines a patient); social-polite (touch used to acknowledge another person, such as a handshake); friendship-warmth (touch that expresses appreciation or warm feelings for another person, such as a pat on the back); love-intimacy (touch occurring in romantic relationships, such as a hug or kiss); and sexual arousal (the most intimate kind of personal contact used to express physical attraction).[71] *Mirasmus*, a Greek word meaning "wasting away," was the term used in the nineteenth and early twentieth centuries to describe how some babies placed in orphanages or hospitals failed to thrive. These infants were dying due to a lack of physical contact. Today, in part because of the threat of sexual harassment, teachers refrain from touching students, and employers avoid touching employees. Is it possible that a lack of touch contributes to perceptions that schools and workplaces are cold and uncaring places?

Touch can also reflect status. High-status people touch others and invade their space more than do people with lower

haptics
the study of the use of touch

You cannot shake hands with a clenched fist.

—Golda Meir

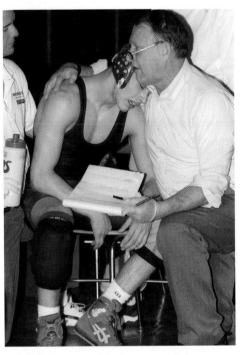

Touch facilitates the expression of feelings.

status.[72] The person who initiates touch is usually the one with the higher status. Nancy Henley points out that we are unlikely to go up to our boss and pat him or her on the shoulder.[73] Would you put your arm around the president of your college or university? Why? Would your behavior change if you met the president at a party? Probably not. The president, however, might well put an arm around you or another student. The person who initiates touching usually also controls the interaction.

Touch, of course, functions importantly in sexual communication. If people hold hands, we assume they have a romantic interest in one another. Are we right? Most American women use a variety of lotions to keep their hands soft to the touch.

How we use touch sends many messages about us. It reveals our perceptions of status, our attitudes, and even our needs. In his book *The Broken Heart*, psychologist James L. Lynch establishes a correlation between many diseases—particularly heart disease—and loneliness.[74] Lynch tells the story of one man, hooked up to heart-monitoring devices, who was in a coma and near death. When a nurse would walk into his room and hold his hand for a few moments, his heartbeat would change from fast and erratic to slow and smooth.

SMELL: OLFACTICS

olfactics
the study of the sense of smell

What do happiness and contentment smell like? **Olfactics,** the study of the sense of smell, could help us find the answer. Industries are based around our preoccupation with smells and odors. We put on perfumes or colognes and deodorants, clean ourselves with scented soaps, freshen our breath with mouthwash, spray our homes with scented sprays, and burn scented candles in an effort to increase perceptions of attractiveness by enhancing our smell as well as the smell of our home or surroundings.

What kinds of messages does smell send? While some cultures consider the natural smells of both people and the environment to be normal, large numbers of Americans are obsessed with masking natural odors and substituting what they perceive to be more pleasant ones.

Smells are associated with attraction, often triggering our emotions or romantic feelings. What smell triggers what emotion depends on our associations, memories, and to some degree, culture. For example, in the United Kingdom, the smell of root beer is reviled whereas people in the United States think it smells good. In England, sarsaparilla and wintergreen, ingredients in root beer, are also used in medicine.[75] Researchers have also studied how smell, specifically pheromones, chemicals emitted by one individual to evoke behavior in another individual, contributes to sexual arousal. Women, research reveals, prefer men whose smell resembles their own.[76] Recently, researchers have also shown that homosexual and heterosexual men respond differently to two odors that may play a part in sexual arousal, with gay men responding similar to women.[77]

Interestingly, smell aids memory recall—both good and bad. In fact, our sense of smell sharpens when something

Review, Reflect, & Apply

Recall

Describe the various ways in which nonverbal messages are communicated.

Understand

Discuss how nonverbal messages have both helped and inhibited your ability to communicate with others.

Evaluate

Argue for or against the use of nonverbal cues as a means of judging another individual's social status.

bad happens, alerting us to the odor, and helping us steer clear of impending danger.[78] Give examples of how smell has triggered good and bad memories for you.

Truth, Deception, and Nonverbal Communication

Actors and actresses use nonverbal cues to encourage us to suspend our disbelief and accept them as persons whom they are not. They carefully rehearse the parts they play, down to the smallest gestures and artifacts. As a result, they are able to control the nonverbal cues they exhibit, so that they present the characters being performed in exactly the way they desire.

What about the rest of us? We, too, may use nonverbal cues to create false impressions in others. While the aim of some deceptive communication is to help receivers save face (we try to appear calm when we are nervous) or to protect oneself from the embarrassment that bluntness can cause ("Yes, I love your new hairstyle," we say when we hate it), the goal of too many deceivers is to take advantage of those with whom they are interacting. Most of us, however, do not rehearse for every one of our person-to-person encounters. Our lives are not that plotted or planned. We do not map out the nonverbal cues we will use during our continuing interactions with others. But what if we could, and what if we did? Would others be able to discern our intentions? Would they be able to tell that we were not really feeling what we were expressing?

In general, people tend to pay closer attention to the nonverbal cues of persons whom they do not trust or whom they suspect may be lying than they do to the rest of the people with whom they interact.[79] Those who plan and rehearse the deceptive messages they are sending tend to be self-confident and experience no guilt about their deception. They are least likely to be suspected by others and, therefore, least likely to be uncovered as liars. This, to be certain, is not necessarily a good thing for those of us trying to detect deceptiveness in others.

Some of us are better at nonverbal deception than others. For example, persons whose occupations require that they sometimes act differently than they feel are most successful at deception. Included in this group are lawyers, diplomats, and salespersons.[80] Researchers also tell us that, as we age, most of us become better liars.[81] Those among us who are high self-monitors are also usually better dissemblers than those of us who possess less self-awareness.

Those of us who are better at nonverbal detection than others are more watchful. Unsuccessful liars are vulnerable to leakage, deception clues that careful observers pick up. Sometimes, it is a change in expression on the face, a movement of the body, a vocal inflection, a deep or shallow breath, a long pause, a slip of the tongue, a microfacial expression, or an ill-timed or inappropriate gesture.[82] The following cues are used to spot lies: split-second flashes of emotion on a person's face, asymmetrical expressions (one-sided smiles, frowns, or shrugs),

LO3

Describe how nonverbal cues can help distinguish truth-telling from lying.

Review, Reflect, & **Apply**

Recall

Identify the types of behaviors that can be used to determine when a person is lying.

Understand

Describe the various aims for creating false impressions.

Analyze

Attempt to determine how frequently people attempt to deceive one another by keeping track of the number of times in one day you detect a leakage cue. For each instance you observe, ask yourself whether your intuition about the person is supported or contradicted by your behavioral observation.

a higher than normal blink rate, unusually dilated pupils, nonverbal indicators occurring in rapid succession rather than simultaneously, and expressions that are fixed (look pasted on). How do you protect yourself from being lied to? While there are no specific nonverbal clues that indicate someone is lying, one book went so far as to provide readers with 46 clues to deception.[83] Although the context of the behavior must always be considered, among the nonverbal behaviors typically exhibited by deceivers are increased eye blinking, hand fidgeting, posture shifts, the making of speech errors, rising pitch, and hesitations.[84]

Who do you believe is better at nonverbal deception, a child or an adult? Why?

Gender and Nonverbal Behavior: Masculine and Feminine Styles

LO4

Identify the ways in which differences in gender and cultural background influence nonverbal communication.

visual dominance
a measure calculated by comparing the percentage of looking while speaking with the percentage of looking while listening

The ways men and women use nonverbal communication often reflect societal practices. While men, for example, are expected to exhibit assertive behaviors that demonstrate their power and authority, women are expected to exhibit more reactive and responsive behaviors. Thus, men often talk more than women and interrupt women more frequently than they are interrupted by women.[85]

During interactions, while both men and women gaze primarily at each other's face, men tend to be more visually dominant than women. We measure **visual dominance** by comparing the percentage of looking while speaking with the percentage of looking while listening. When compared with women, men display higher levels of looking while speaking and lower levels when listening. Thus, the visual dominance ratio of men is usually higher than that of women and, again, reflects the use of nonverbal cues to reinforce perceptions of social power.[86]

Men may use space and touch to assert their dominance over women. Men are much more likely to touch women than women are to touch them. Again, women are usually the recipients of touching actions, rather than the initiators. Men also tend to claim more personal space than women, and they more frequently walk in front of women than behind them. Thus, in general, males are the touchers, not the touchees, the leaders rather than the followers.

What kinds of nonverbal cues do women display more than men? According to body language experts, whereas power posture was in vogue in the 1990s, women now slouch more, using it to express rebelliousness, boredom, and wealth. In fact, what has come to be known as "the sultry slouch" remains a virtual fashion accessory for women.[87] In contrast to their posture of noninvolvement, women tend to smile and show emotion more often than men do. In general, they are more expressive than men are and exhibit higher levels of involvement during person-to-person interaction. Women stand closer to one another than men do. Women also use nonverbal signals to draw others into conversations more than men do. While women demonstrate an interest in affiliation, men generally are more interested in establishing the strength of their own ideas and agendas.[88] In

How might a crowded train affect persons from contact and noncontact cultures?

addition, when tests are given to assess nonverbal decoding ability, including the ability to read another person's feelings by relying on vocal or facial cues, females usually outperform males.[89]

Culture and Nonverbal Behavior

People throughout the world use nonverbal cues to help them express themselves. Members of **contact cultures**—that is, cultures that promote interaction and encourage displays of warmth, closeness, and availability—tend to stand close to each other when conversing, seek maximum sensory experiences, and touch each other frequently. This is not the case, however, among members of **low-contact cultures,** where such behaviors are discouraged. Saudi Arabia, France, and Italy are countries with contact cultures; their members relish the intimacy of contact when conversing. In contrast, Scandinavia, Germany, England, and Japan are low- or lower-contact cultures, whose members value privacy and maintain more distance from each other when interacting.[90]

In similar fashion, people from different cultures may not display emotion or express intimacy in the same ways. Among the members of Mediterranean cultures, for example, it is normal for emotive reactions to be uninhibited. Thus, it is common for the cultures' members to express a feeling like grief or happiness together with open facial displays, magnified gestures, and vocal cues that support the feeling. On the other hand, neither the Chinese nor the Japanese readily reveal their inner feelings in public, preferring to display less emotion, maintain more self-control, and keep their feelings to themselves; for these reasons, they often appear to remain expressionless.[91] In contrast, persons in the United States are likely to be emotionally expressive and to smile freely.

The cultural background of the individuals communicating also affects their use of personal space and touch. Americans stand farther apart when conversing

contact cultures
cultures that promote interaction and encourage displays of warmth, closeness, and availability

low-contact cultures
cultures that maintain more distance when interacting

What kind of statement does a tattoo or a tongue or belly button ring make? Do you believe such artifacts signal defiance, independence, or something else? What inferences are persons who do not use such personal adornments likely to make about those who do?

than do persons from Middle Eastern cultures. Whereas Americans expect persons who live next door to them to be friendly and to interact with them, the Japanese do not share this expectation. Consequently, whereas the Japanese may view Americans as overly friendly, Americans may conclude that the Japanese are unfriendly, cold, and distant. Middle Easterners are apt to do a significant amount of touching; they walk with their arms around each other and are apt to touch each other during conversations a lot more than are persons from noncontact cultures.

Even when the nonverbal cues displayed in different cultures are the same, they do not necessarily convey the same meaning. In the United States, for example, a head nod symbolizes agreement or consent, while in Japan it means only that a message was received. Hand signals can be confusing to those not tuned in to the culture. For example, people in the United States use their hand pointing at their chest when they talk about themselves. The Japanese use their forefinger pointed at their nose. Similarly, diverse cultures feel differently about silence. Whereas in the United States we are apt to perceive another person's silence as a negative and to infer that he or she is too self-absorbed, is not listening, is not interested, or has nothing of value to add to a conversation, other cultures interpret silence in a more favorable light. In Asian countries, for example, silence is frequently preferred to speech.

Culture also affects use of space. In an effort to enhance the relationships between the external environment and the inner self, the Chinese, and now others, use feng shui (pronounced "fung-SHWAY"), the ancient Chinese art of

Review, Reflect, & Apply

Recall

List some of the differences between the nonverbal communication styles of men and women.

Understand

Give examples that illustrate the relationship between culture and nonverbal behaviors.

Evaluate

Take note of the nonverbal behaviors you observe in a given day, and discuss the extent to which they reflect gender- and culture-specific practices.

Etiquette

If interactions speak louder than words, then it is important to be aware of how the local customs of different countries can guide communication. A lack of knowledge can cause perceptions in natives of an assault on traditional values. In contrast, exhibiting cultural intelligence, the ability to engage in cross-cultural code switching, can facilitate the establishment of effective relationships with people from diverse countries and cultures. Consider the lessons inherent in the following two situations:

1. Refusing a drink when in Russia on business can cause a problem because drinking is a social tradition that Russian business people use to gauge whom they are dealing with, and to see if they can trust you.[92]

2. When the Middle Eastern version of the reality program *Big Brother* aired in the Arab world, one segment had a handsome Saudi kiss a Tunisian beauty. The kiss led to protests and accusations of moral depravity among viewers who already objected to unrelated men and women sharing a house. The show was taken off the air.[93]

Nonverbal behavior and interaction etiquette do not necessarily transfer from one culture to another. Imagine that you are preparing to do business with the people of another country of your choosing. What nonverbal understandings would you need to facilitate success?

---

placement, to add harmony and balance to living spaces. Feng shui introduces the five elements in nature into design: earth, fire, water, wood, and metal. For example, it uses green plants to bring the outdoors inside, and red candles and fabrics to increase energy.[94] The goal is to arrange space, furniture, walls, colors, and objects to promote blessings and to harness the life force (chi).

For us to experience more effective interaction with people from different cultures, we must make the effort to identify and understand the many ways each culture shapes nonverbal communication. Acknowledging that our communication style is not intrinsically better than others will contribute to more successful multicultural exchanges.

Technology and Nonverbal Communication

Nonverbal communication is alive and well in cyberspace. Just as those who communicate in cyberspace rely on established netiquette guidelines for the standards of behavior acceptable during their online interactions, so they have also evolved a system of written symbols to help reinforce those standards. These symbols, called **emoticons,** replace physical gestures and facial expressions, substitute for nonverbal cues, and help those engaged in online dialogues convey action, emotion, and emphasis.[95]

Emoticons, or relational icons, help add personalization and more expressive emotional exchanges to computer-mediated communication as a way to approximate the warmth and intimacy of face-to-face interactions. Thus, emoticons, are used also at times to indicate subtle mood changes.[96] For example, a symbol called the smiley face looks like :-) and indicates the humorous intent of the sender. It may wink mischievously, ;-), or frown, :-(, depending on whether the online comment is to be interpreted humorously or sarcastically. Similarly, capitalizations and asterisks, such as GREAT and ***, convey a user's emphasis and enthusiasm.

LO5

Discuss the influence of technology on nonverbal communication.

emoticons
symbols that replace nonverbal cues during machine-assisted communication

A Carnegie Mellon University professor, Scott E. Fahlman, believes he was the first to use three keystrokes—a colon followed by a hyphen and a parenthesis—as a horizontal "smiley face" in a computer message, paving the way for emoticons to express sentiments that might otherwise be misinterpreted online.

The following list contains other emoticons that can be used to describe a communicator's physical or emotional condition or to depict feelings and actions that straight text alone could not depict. These symbols are commonly understood by online users.

:-P	someone sticking out the tongue
= :-O	someone screaming in fright, their hair standing on end
:-&	someone whose lips are sealed
!#!^*&:-	a schizophrenic[97]

Of course, persons unfamiliar with online culture would more than likely be confused by the use of emoticons. Lacking more conventional social context cues, they would not be able to use the symbols to achieve understanding.

Since online communicators probably are not able to hear each other, they have also created a shorthand to describe their reactions. For instance, they may describe themselves as "rolling on the floor laughing" with the abbreviation ROFL.

Technological changes are affecting our nonverbal communication in other ways as well. According to Nelson Thall, the president and chief executive officer of the Marshall McLuhan Center on Global Communication, the current variety in fashion is an outgrowth of the electronic technological revolution. According to Thall, "Our clothing is an extension of our skin, just like a hammer is a technological extension of our hand."[98] Thall contends that since computers and the Internet allow people to be nationless, sexless, and ageless, fashion now reflects that option. We now dress similarly across borders and wear clothing that is technologically friendly, with room for cell phones, beepers, PDAs, and so on. We even have a wearable computer, also known as a personal optical mobile appliance or personal multimedia appliance. An increasing percentage of the U.S. population ages 15 to 50 now also carry or wear a wireless computing and communications device. Within this decade, future-casters believe that the cell phone will similarly become a wearable device, woven into the fabric of our clothes to ensure it will always be accessible.

In addition, in our security-conscious age, technology is also being called into play to aid in person identification and behavior analysis by helping with the reading of nonverbal cues. The CIA, for example, has commissioned two research centers, the Salk Institute and Carnegie Mellon University's Robotics Institute, to try to teach computers to watch for detailed facial-language clues. Hidden computers are also used to pick up stress in the speech patterns of travelers when they check in at airports.[99]

When all is said and done, we may be able to signal a hug using an emoticon, but we still have not created a way to actually hug someone via a computer screen.[100] So, e-mail may save us time, but being there for those who matter to us says more.

Has technology become an accessory? Is it now a regular part of your wardrobe? Does wearing it help enhance your credibility?

Review, Reflect, & Apply

Understand

Explain how established guidelines for netiquette can help set the standard for online interactions.

Apply

Compose a message to a friend, keeping in mind the guidelines of netiquette, and using emoticons where appropriate.

Analyze

Analyze your own use of emoticons on a day-to-day basis, citing instances in which they have clarified or distorted your meaning.

Communication Skills

PRACTICE USING AND OBSERVING NONVERBAL CUES

The following guidelines should prove helpful as you continue to develop your ability to make valid judgments and decisions on the basis of nonverbal communication.

Observe the Communicators

Ask yourself if the sex, age, or status of the communicators will exert an influence on their relationship. Assess to what extent, if any, attractiveness, clothing, or physical appearance should affect the interaction. Determine if, in your own mind, the communicators' dress is appropriate to the environment. Decide if the communicators appear to like each other and to have similar goals.

Observe Body Language

What does each communicator's facial expression reveal? Assess the extent to which you believe the facial expressions are genuine.

Analyze significant bodily cues.

Assess the extent to which the interactants mirror each other's posture. Ask yourself how posture supports or contradicts their status relationship. Analyze when and why the communicators alter their postures.

Watch the eye behavior of the participants. Determine if one looks away more than the other. Determine if one stares at the other.

Listen for Vocal Cues

Assess whether the communicators are using appropriate vocal volumes and rates of speaking, given their situation. Determine if and how the way something that is said verbally supports or contradicts what is being said nonverbally. Analyze how and when silence is used. Be responsive to signals of nervousness and changes in pitch.

Examine Appearance, Clothing, Artifacts, and Color

Determine how the appearance, clothing and artifacts of a person can affect your first impression of him or her. Ask if the person's dress, role, and behavior are congruent. In what ways, if any, do the colors worn by someone or adorning a room influence perception and behavior?

Observe the Effects of Time, Touching, and Smell

Observe how you and others treat time. Analyze the meanings of touch or touch-avoidance behavior. Watch to see if participants touch each other at all. Determine, if you can, why they touched and how it affected them. Was it appropriate or inappropriate to the situation? Also determine the ways that smell attracts or repels interaction.

Examine the Environment

For any nonverbal interaction, ask yourself if any environmental stimuli are likely to affect it. Determine if other people present could influence the communicators. Attempt to determine whether colors and decor will have an impact on the nature and tone of the communication. Analyze the amount of space available to the interactants. Determine whether architectural factors might alter the outcome. Where are chairs, tables, passageways, and desks situated? Why did the interactants situate themselves as they did? What type of behavior would we expect to see in this environment?

The Wrap-Up

SUMMARY

LO1

Define *nonverbal communication* and explain its characteristics and functions.

Nonverbal communication includes all the human responses that are not expressed in words. Over 65 percent of the meaning of a message is communicated nonverbally. Perceiving and analyzing nonverbal cues can help us understand what is really happening during a conversation.

LO2

Discuss the following types of nonverbal messages: *body language, voice, space and distance, appearance, colors, clothing and artifacts, time, touch, and smell.*

Nonverbal messages fall into the preceding main categories. All constitute significant sources of information. Body language or kinesics includes facial expressions, posture, eye gaze and eye contact, and gestures. Voice or paralanguage includes the analysis of pitch, volume, rate, and pauses—factors affecting the expressiveness of the human voice. Space and distance or proxemic factors include considering both the space that exists between us when converse, as well as the way we organize space in our homes, offices, and communities. Appearance includes aspects of attractiveness, height, and weight. Color includes a consideration of both psychological and physiological effects. Clothing and artifacts finds us analyzing the effects of dress, hair, and body adornments. People are apt to make inferences about us based on our appearance or dress. Time or chronemics finds us focusing on how time is organized, used and responded to. Touch or haptics includes an analysis of messages sent through the presence or absence of touch. And smell or olfactics includes the consideration of how smell influences perceptions of people and our behavior.

LO3

Describe how nonverbal cues can help distinguish truth telling from lying.

Deception detection is important for societal, professional, and personal reasons. Accuracy in determining truthfulness depends on the ability to decipher leakage clues.

LO4   **Identify** the ways in which differences in gender and cultural background influence nonverbal behavior.

The use of nonverbal cues is affected by variables such as gender and culture. The ways men and women use nonverbal cues reflect societal practices. To a large degree, people modify their use of nonverbal cues depending on the culture they belong to or identify with.

LO5   **Discuss** the influence of technology on nonverbal communication.

Nonverbal communication is also affected by whether communication is occurring online or offline. Those who communicate online rely on the guidelines of netiquette, which can include expressive and relational icons called emoticons.

LO6   **Practice** using and observing nonverbal cues.

You can improve your effectiveness as a nonverbal communicator by focusing on, analyzing, and interpreting all aspects of nonverbal behavior.

KEY CHAPTER TERMINOLOGY

artifactual communication 124

chronemics 126

civil inattention 112

contact cultures 131

emoticons 133

facial management techniques 111

fixed-feature space 121

habitual pitch 116

haptics 127

informal space 121

intimate distance 119

kinesics 110

low-contact cultures 131

markers 122

mixed message 108

nonfluencies 117

nonverbal communication 107

olfactics 128

paralanguage 115

personal distance 120

pitch 116

proxemics 119

public distance 121

rate 117

semi-fixed-feature space 121

silence 117

social distance 120

territoriality 122

visual dominance 130

volume 117

Listening, Feedback, and Critical Thinking

After completing this chapter, you should be able to demonstrate mastery of the following learning outcomes:

LO1 **Define** listening and explain its role in communication.

LO2 **Distinguish** among four types of listening: appreciative, comprehensive, critical, and empathic.

LO3 **Use** the HURIER model to explain the six stages of listening.

LO4 **Describe** the factors that contribute to ineffective listening.

LO5 **Summarize** the kinds of feedback listeners can provide.

LO6 **Discuss** critical thinking and its impact on listening.

LO7 **Explain** how gender, culture, and media and technology influence listening.

LO8 **Demonstrate** effective listening.

Do you know someone who never seems to pay attention when you speak to him or her? How do you feel when your words fall on deaf ears? How frustrated do you become when the person you are talking to either ignores you or tells you that she or he is listening but is actively engaged in something else? Can someone really listen to you while looking at another person or pursuing another activity like texting? By contrast, do you know someone whose attention never wavers when talking with you, whose eyes lock on yours, whose facial expressions announce interest in you, and whose questions and ability to paraphrase demonstrate an understanding of you? If you do, then you know a person who knows what it means to be an effective listener.[1]

To get what you want in your career, stop talking and start listening.

—Anonymous

Listening is not just hearing what someone tells you word for word. You have to listen with a heart.

—Anna Deavere Smith

The Chinese character for "listening" (see Figure 6.1) combines a number of symbols representing the ears, the eyes, and the heart, suggesting that when we listen, we need to give our undivided attention and should not rely on our ears alone but should use our eyes and our hearts as well. In your opinion, do most of the people you know accomplish this goal? Do you?

Listening and Communication

LO1

Define listening and explain its role in communication.

Famed American author Ernest Hemingway is said to have spoken the following words: "I like to listen. I have learned a great deal from listening. Most people never listen." On the basis of your personal experiences, do you think Hemingway's conclusion is right? Do most people never listen?

One college student, Brett Banfe, convinced that he had failed miserably in listening to others, vowed to correct his failing by remaining silent for a year: "I noticed I wasn't really listening to people. I was just waiting for people to stop talking so I could chime in," Banfe said.[2] "I'd wait for them to stop talking, then I'd start talking. Because . . . my opinion was the right one anyway. It was like, 'Thanks a lot for your input, but here's how it really happened.'"[3] While you may think that the action taken by Brett Banfe seems extreme, far too often listening is something we take for granted. However, listening is a difficult, intricate skill, and like other skills, it requires training and practice.

Listening affects all kinds of communication. From the time the alarm clock rings until the late news winds up, we are inundated with things to listen to. As we proceed through our day and as we move from person to person, from class to lunch, from formal discussions to casual conversations, we are constantly called on to listen. We are expected to listen to others whenever we interact face-to-face with friends and acquaintances, use the telephone, attend meetings, participate in interviews, take part in arguments, give or receive instructions, make decisions based on information received orally, and generate and receive feedback.

Ear

Eyes

Undivided
Attention

Heart

FIGURE 6.1

We Do Not Listen with Our Ears Alone, as the Chinese Character for Listening Reveals.

Are You Listening?

Answer the following series of questions about how you listen.

1. When involved in a conversation with another person, how often do you find yourself thinking that what the other person is saying is unimportant?

   a. always   b. sometimes   c. never   _____

2. How frequently do you find yourself silently criticizing the mannerisms or the appearance of an individual with whom you are conversing?

   a. always   b. sometimes   c. never   _____

3. How often do you find yourself becoming overstimulated by something another person says?

   a. always   b. sometimes   c. never   _____

4. How often do you find yourself jumping ahead of the person speaking—perhaps even completing his or her thoughts?

   a. always   b. sometimes   c. never   _____

5. How frequently do you interrupt a person speaking with you?

   a. always   b. sometimes   c. never   _____

6. How often do you fake paying attention to someone?

   a. always   b. sometimes   c. never   _____

7. How frequently do you find yourself distracted by something when listening?

   a. always   b. sometimes   c. never   _____

8. How often do you try to avoid listening to difficult content?

   a. always   b. sometimes   c. never   _____

9. How often do you find yourself personally antagonized by another person using emotion-laden words?

   a. always   b. sometimes   c. never   _____

10. How often do you give your complete attention to someone expressing a point of view that conflicts with yours?

    a. always   b. sometimes   c. never   _____

    _____ Total

Score your answers as follows: If your answer to a question is always, award yourself 1 point. If your answer is sometimes, award yourself 5 points. If your answer is never, award yourself 10 points. Total your score. Based on your answers and resulting score, describe and, if necessary, critique your listening behavior.

LISTENING IS MORE THAN HEARING

Listening and hearing are not the same thing. Most people are born with the ability to hear. **Hearing** is a process that occurs automatically and requires no conscious effort on your part. If the physiological elements within your ears are functioning properly, your brain will process the electrochemical impulses received, and you will hear. However, what you do with the impulses after receiving them belongs to the realm of listening.

What is listening? **Listening** is a deliberate process through which we seek to understand and retain aural (heard) stimuli. Unlike hearing, listening depends on a complex set of skills that must be acquired. Thus, whereas hearing simply happens to us and cannot be manipulated, listening requires us to make an active, conscious effort to comprehend and remember what we hear. Thus, while hearing requires no understanding, listening requires analysis and the desire for full understanding. Furthermore, who we are affects what we listen to. In your environment, from minute to minute, far too many sounds bombard you for you to be able to pay attention to each one. Thus, in listening, you process the external sounds of your environment to select those that are relevant to you, your activities, and your interests. This is not to say that listening is just an external process. It is also an internal process. We listen to the sounds we hear, and we listen to what others say, but we also listen to what we say aloud and what we say to ourselves in response. Self-talk—listening to what you say to

hearing
the involuntary, physiological process by which we perceive sound

listening
the deliberate, psychological process by which we receive, understand, and retain aural stimuli

Have you ever felt like Lucy does in this cartoon—angry because the person you were talking to was focused on something other than your words? What did you do?

yourself—can help you make sense of the way you listen to and react to the people in your life. (Do you ever talk to yourself? Are you your own best listener? Most of us are.)

LISTENING TAKES EFFORT

While all of us continually engage in activities that require us to listen, some of us fail to pay enough attention to the role listening plays in these activities and in our relationships.

How Responsive a Listener Are You?

Although we expect others to listen to us, we sometimes ignore our ethical responsibility to listen to them. We fake listening or do not listen as carefully as we could. Consequently, problems due to ineffective listening occur.

At one time, a poll of American teenagers indicated that as many as half of them believed that communication between themselves and their parents was poor—and that a primary cause was poor listening. Parents, too, often feel that communication is failing. One woman was convinced that her daughter must have a severe hearing problem and took her to an audiologist. The audiologist tested

"I'm sorry, dear, I wasn't listening. Could you repeat what you've said since we've been married?"

both ears and reported back to the distraught parent: "There's nothing wrong with her hearing. She's just tuning you out."

A leading cause of the high divorce rate (approximately half of all marriages in the United States end in divorce) is the failure of husbands and wives to interact effectively. They don't listen to each other or respond to each other's messages. Presidents of major companies also identify listening as one of their major communication problems.[4] One nationwide survey revealed that 14 percent of each workweek is wasted as a result of poor listening. That amounts to about seven weeks of work per year.[5] A survey of personnel managers also identified listening as the skill most needed at work if work teams are to succeed.[6]

When we make the ethical commitment to listen to others, we focus and attend fully to them without allowing competing thoughts or stimuli to divert our attention. In effect, we practice **mindfulness**—by emptying our minds of personal concerns and interfering emotions, and choosing to focus on the person and what is happening in the here and now—a skill many of us find difficult to master.[7]

When we are mindful, we fully engage ourselves in the moment, paying careful attention to the here and now. We focus completely on what another person says and does. We do not judge the other, but demonstrate our interest in understanding his or her ideas. If we fail at listening, does it mean we are mindless?

Effective listeners—people who not only know how to listen but also want to listen—make better employers and employees, doctors and patients, friends and significant others.[8] Many people enroll in professional courses focused on how to improve listening skills,[9] but you have that opportunity now.

mindfulness
emptying one's mind of personal concerns and interfering emotions, and choosing to focus on the person and the here and now

Do You Prepare to Listen?

Think back over the years you have spent as a student. Did you receive training in writing? Reading? Speaking? The answer to each of these questions is probably

Do you make an active, conscious effort to comprehend and remember what you hear?

yes. In fact, many children now learn to read and write before they start school, and reading and writing skills are taught and emphasized throughout our educational careers. But what about listening? Of the four communication skills—reading, writing, speaking, and listening—listening has received the least attention from educators, yet listening is the fundamental process through which we initiate and maintain relationships, and it is the primary process through which we take in information.

Do You Use Listening Time Wisely?

A recent study revealed that college students like you spend as much time listening to media as engaged in interpersonal communication. Some 55.4 percent of a college student's day is now spent listening, while only 17.1 percent of it is spent reading, 16.1 percent speaking, and 11.4 percent writing.[10] We spend more time listening than engaging in other forms of communication. These results hold true on the job, where listening is an integral element in creating relationships with others at work.[11] In fact, employees of Fortune 500 companies spend the majority of their day—approximately 60 percent of it—listening.[12]

The use of digital media complicates this picture by distracting you. What happens when you're digitally distracted? Does being used to receiving quick bursts of information or tweets of information make it difficult for you to listen to and make sense of more detailed and complex information?[13] Imagine a typical digital day for you. (See Table 6.1.) According to a study by the Kaiser Family Foundation, young people use media seven hours, 38 minutes a day. But that number is actually more like 10 hours and 45 minutes when the time spent multitasking is included—more time than a typical day at a full-time job or in school.[14]

Take a moment to review your personal listening situation. Think of interactions you have had that were complicated because you or someone else failed to listen effectively. For example, when was the last time you jumped to a wrong conclusion? Missed an important word? Failed to realize you were not being understood? Reacted emotionally or let yourself become distracted? Far too often, instead of listening, we daydream our way through our daily contacts—we take side trips or otherwise tune out what is said to us. In other words, we adopt destructive "unlistening" behaviors.

Most people estimate that they listen with 70 to 80 percent accuracy. This means they believe that they can listen to others and accurately retain 70 to 80 percent of what is said. However, researchers like Ralph Nichols tell us that most of us actually listen at only 25 percent efficiency—that is, instead of retaining 75 percent of what we hear, we lose 75 percent.[15]

TABLE 6.1 A Digital Day

Average Daily Media Use, Including Multi-Talking Among 8–18-Year-Olds	
Television content	4 hours, 29 minutes
Music/audio	2 hours, 31 minutes
Computer	1 hour, 29 minutes
Video games	1 hour, 38 minutes
Movies	25 minutes

SOURCE: "Generation M²: Media in the Lives of 8–18-Year-Olds," The Kaiser Family Foundation, January 2010.

FIGURE 6.2

Serial Communication.

SOURCE: William Haney. *Communication and Organizational Behavior.* Homewood, IL: Irwin, 1973.

Message → Information is subtracted from original message → Information is added to original message → Original message is distorted

Do You Listen Accurately?

Although most of us have supposedly had many years of practice in listening, errors are extremely common. According to communication theorist William Haney, we frequently run into problems when we use **serial communication,** or chain-of-command transmissions, to relay messages (see Figure 6.2). In serial communication, person 1 sends a message to person 2; person 2 then communicates his or her perception of person 1's message (not person 1's message itself) to person 3, who continues the process.

serial communication
a chain-of-command transmission

Whenever one person speaks or delivers a message to a second person, the message occurs in at least four different forms:[16]

1. message as it exists in the mind of the speaker (his or her thoughts)
2. message as it is spoken (actually encoded by the speaker)
3. message as it is interpreted (decoded by the listener)
4. message as it is ultimately remembered by the listener (affected by the listener's personal selectivity and rejection)

In traveling down this unwieldy chain of command from person to person, ideas can become distorted by as much as 80 percent. Several factors are responsible. First, because passing along complex, confusing information poses many problems, we generally like to simplify messages. As a result, we unconsciously (and consciously) delete information from the messages we receive before transmitting these messages to others. Second, we like to think the messages we pass along to others make sense. (We feel foolish if we convey a message we ourselves do not understand or deliver a message that appears illogical.) Thus, we try to make sense of a message before communicating it to someone else. We do this by adding to, subtracting from, or otherwise altering what we have heard. Unfortunately, as we see in Figure 6.2, once we make sense of the message, it may no longer correspond to the message originally sent. Such errors occur even though we have had years of practice in listening. Estimates are that a 20-year-old person has practiced listening for at least 10,000 hours; a 30-year-old, at least 15,000 hours; and a typical 40-year-old, 20,000 or more hours.[17] These figures are mind-boggling, but have we in reality been practicing listening or unlistening? Research suggests that we have been practicing unlistening.

By listening accurately and ethically, you help avoid communication difficulties and breakdowns and increase your chances of

Gossip is a form of serial communication.

How do you use your body and eyes to demonstrate readiness to listen?

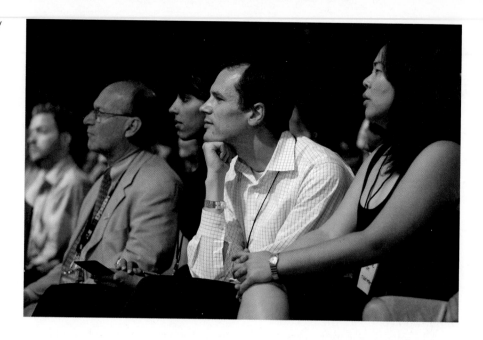

being well liked and appreciated by others.[18] Who has the primary responsibility for clear and effective communication—the speaker or the listener? An old proverb says, "Nature gave us two ears and one mouth so that we can listen twice as much as we speak." Actually, since everyone functions as both sender and receiver, everyone must assume 51 percent of the responsibility for communication. This practice might not be mathematically sound, but it would certainly increase the effectiveness of our interpersonal, small-group, public, and mediated communication.[19]

Review, Reflect, & Apply

Recall

Distinguish between listening and hearing.

Analyze

Describe your role in the listening process.

Apply

Consider the concepts of mindfulness and attentive listening, and use them to develop a personal listening improvement plan.

ARE YOU A RECEPTIVE LISTENER?

There is a relationship between a speaker's acts and a listener's responses. Typically, speaker gaze coordinates this relationship. While listeners usually look more at the speaker than the reverse, at key points a speaker will look directly at the listener, signaling that the speaker is seeking a response. If the listener is attentive, this creates a period of mutual gaze known as "the gaze window." When this occurs, the listener responds with a nod, a "mhm," or another verbal or nonverbal reaction that lets the speaker know she or he is listening and collaborating in the dialogue or conversation.[20]

Phrases like "I'm listening," "I hear you," and "I get it" are affirmations listeners can use to signify their respect, understanding, and acceptance.[21]

ARE YOU READY TO LISTEN BEYOND WORDS?

We need to listen to more than the words spoken. We need to listen to the tone and cadence of a speaker's words. We need to interpret the speaker's gestures and facial expressions. We need to pay attention to what speakers don't tell us. Sometimes, what speakers omit is more important than what they say.

Types of Listening

The type of listening we engage in should relate to our purpose for listening. Theorists identify four different types of listening: appreciative, comprehensive, critical, and empathic.

LO**2**

Distinguish among the four types of listening: appreciative, comprehensive, critical, and empathic.

APPRECIATIVE LISTENING

Do you spend time listening to music on your iPod, on your CD player, or at concerts? Why? Is it because you enjoy it? When our primary motivation for listening is pleasure or relaxation—to unwind, to escape, or to be entertained—we listen appreciatively. Listening to music, a movie, or a comedy routine are just a few examples of the kinds of **appreciative listening** we engage in. Courses in music or film appreciation teach us how to listen appreciatively. Unlike the next three types of listening we define, appreciative listening usually does not require us to focus on organizing or remembering what we have listened to.

appreciative listening
listening for enjoyment or relaxation

COMPREHENSIVE LISTENING

In contrast to appreciative listening, when we listen to gain knowledge, we listen comprehensively. Examples of **comprehensive listening** include listening to directions, a lecture, a job description, or a person's position on an issue of concern, such as whether abortion should be legal.

comprehensive listening
listening to gain knowledge

CRITICAL LISTENING

Often, however, we seek not only to gain knowledge, but also to evaluate the worth of what we have listened to. When we listen critically, we listen to determine the usefulness, soundness, and accuracy of messages. During **critical listening** our critical thinking skills also come into play as we decide whether to accept or reject a message. We talk more about comprehensive and critical listening later in this chapter.

critical listening
listening to evaluate the worth of a message

EMPATHIC LISTENING

The last type of listening, and the focus of this section, is **empathic listening.** The goal when we listen empathically is to understand the feelings and point of view of another person. Perhaps you serve as a relative's sounding board, listen to the troubles of a friend, or help a co-worker talk through problems. You also help restore that person's sense of emotional balance because you understand him or her as he or she desires to be understood, interpreting the situation he or she is facing as if it were your own. Thus, imagining yourself in another's place is essential in empathic listening.[22]

empathic listening
listening to help others

According to author Daniel Goleman, empathic listeners are effective at *decentering*—placing the focus on others rather than on themselves. They listen from the speaker's point of view, using three different skills to accomplish this: *empathic responsiveness* (the experiencing of an emotional response that corresponds to the emotions of another person),[23] *perspective taking* (placing yourself in another person's shoes)[24] and *sympathetic responsiveness* (feeling concern and compassion for the situation the other person faces). If you use only sympathetic responsiveness, however, your listening will fall short of empathic listening. If you only *feel for* a person, without using perspective taking and empathic responsiveness, you cannot succeed in *feeling with* the person.[25]

Review, Reflect, & **Apply**

Recall

List the activities associated with each type of listening.

Understand

Explain how you can you tell when someone is listening empathically.

Apply

Practice paraphrasing as a way of improving your empathic listening skills.

paraphrasing
restating in your own words what another person has said

Empathic listeners rely heavily on two communication skills: the ability to read the nonverbal cues of others, including their eye contact, physical contact (touching), and facial expressions; and the ability to use the active listening tool—*the paraphrase*—to let those they listen to know that they care enough to listen, understand what is said, and respond to the expressed feelings. When you paraphrase, you engage in listening actively, which means you put yourself in the speaker's place in an effort to understand the speaker's feelings and send back to the speaker what you believe the speaker communicated when delivering his or her total message; that is, you internalize and reflect the message's verbal content as well as the speaker's feelings.

How do you paraphrase? **Paraphrasing** is a three-step process in which you do the following:

1. make a tentative statement that invites correction—for example, "If I'm not mistaken . . ."
2. repeat the basic idea or ideas in your own words.
3. check your interpretation with the other person, saying something like, "Is that correct?"

For example:

Person 1: I am so mad at my professor. He's making me rework my entire paper. I worked forever on it.

Person 2: If I'm not mistaken, your professor is asking you to rewrite the paper you turned in. You're feeling frustrated because you worked hard. Is that right?

Empathic communication and paraphrasing have roles to play in both our personal and our professional lives. Research reveals that listening to family stories and reminiscing about the past may be both physically and emotionally healing for both the teller and the listener, contributing to their sense of overall well-being.[26] Findings from medical research also underscore the importance of effective listening. Medical school curricula now include courses that teach medical students how to listen, ask open-ended questions, and establish productive, caring, and empathic relationships with patients.[27] Doctors who do not practice empathic listening frequently interrupt their patients. This keeps them from eliciting relevant background on the patient's life circumstances and symptoms. The result? Costly mistakes.[28] Far too often doctors fail to paraphrase what a patient says, cutting off the patient's words after allowing only a scant 18 seconds for the patient to reveal what is troubling him or her.[29]

As we make our way through this chapter, we will see that, in addition to being a tool used in empathic communication, the paraphrase is of value in other listening venues as well.

HURIER model
a model of listening focusing on six skill areas or stages

Use the HURIER model to explain the six stages of listening.

The Stages of Listening: More Than Meets the Ear

A model of listening developed by listening researcher Judi Brownell, called the **HURIER model,** takes a behavioral approach to listening, suggesting that listening is composed of both mental processes and observable behaviors.[30] The model focuses on six skill areas, or listening stages: *hearing, understanding, remembering, interpreting, evaluating,* and *responding* (see Figure 6.3).

THE HEARING STAGE

As the model indicates, the first stage of the listening process is *hearing*. Sounds fill our world and compete to be noticed. Usually, however, we hear what we listen for, meaning that we choose to attend to some aspects of what we hear while ignoring the rest. Once we *attend* to a message—demonstrate our willingness to organize and focus on what we are hearing—if the message holds our attention, we will also seek to understand it.

THE UNDERSTANDING STAGE

During stage two, *understanding*, or listening comprehensively, we relate what we have listened to, to what we already know. We do not judge the message until we are certain we comprehend it. We might, for example, ask questions about or paraphrase what we believe another person said during the understanding stage.

According to Ralph Nichols and Leonard Stevens, the authors of *Are You Listening?*, words that cause listeners to react emotionally interfere with understanding. Nichols calls these red-flag words. **Red-flag words** produce emotional deafness, sending listening efficiency down to zero.[31] Among the words known to function as red flags for some listeners are *AIDS, spastic,* and *income tax.*

Other factors that interfere with understanding are the environment (for example, it could be too hot, too cold, too messy) and people themselves (speaking too fast, too slow, too loudly, or too softly). We also think faster than others speak. This is called the **speech-thought differential.** A person usually speaks at a rate of 125 to 150 words per minute. We think, however, at over 500 words per minute, meaning that we have time left over to take mental excursions and to daydream. To use the speech-thought differential to enhance understanding, we need to internally summarize, question, and paraphrase what is being said.

red-flag words
words that trigger emotional deafness, dropping listening efficiency to zero

speech-thought differential
the difference between speaking and thinking rates

THE REMEMBERING STAGE

Once our brain assigns meaning to a message, the next stage is *remembering*, in which we try to retain what we have listened to for future use. We personally decide how much of what we have listened to is worth storing in memory and how much we can forget. Intense feelings or the reinforcement of a message increases our chances of remembering. Once we remember a message, we should be able to recall it when necessary. However, we cannot possibly remember everything. Some forgetting is necessary for mental health.

We have two kinds of memory, short-term memory and long-term memory. Most of what we listen to we store briefly in our short-term memory. Unless we use and apply what is stored in short-term memory, we forget it before being able to transfer it into long-term memory. This helps explain why we remember only 50 percent of a message immediately after listening to it, and approximately 25 percent after a period of time has passed. Long-term memory, our more permanent memory bank, plays a key listening role by connecting new experiences to past ones.

Stages of Listening

Hearing
Understanding
Remembering
Interpreting
Evaluating
Responding

FIGURE 6.3
The HURIER Model (Stages of Listening).

We use three key tools to enhance recall. The first is *repetition*. The more we repeat an idea, the more likely we are to recall it later. The second tool is the now-familiar three-step *paraphrase*. By restating in your own words what a person just told you, you not only check on your understanding of what was said, but also help yourself recall it. The third tool is *visualization*. By picturing what someone has said to you—connecting a visual image to a name, a place, or numbers—you can help improve your recall. For example, you might picture a person named John Sanderson as standing atop a large sand pile. Many memory problems are due not to faulty memory, but rather to people's losing their ability to pay attention. Attention and focus build memory.[32]

THE INTERPRETING STAGE

During the fourth stage, *interpreting*, we make sense of a message, using *dual perspective taking*—considering the message from the sender's perspective as well as our perspective. If we are successful, we do not impose our personal meaning onto another person's message.

THE EVALUATING STAGE

During stage five, *evaluating*, we weigh the worth of a message and critically analyze it. (Evaluating is a type of listening referred to earlier in this chapter as critical listening.) During the evaluating stage we distinguish facts from inferences, weigh the evidence provided, and identify any prejudices or faulty arguments that could slant meaning. We stay mindful rather than mindless, listening between the lines and being careful not to jump to conclusions.

THE RESPONDING STAGE

During the last stage, *responding*, we react to what we have listened to and offer feedback to let the speaker know our thoughts and feelings about the message. We become the speaker's radar. (We cover feedback in more depth later in this chapter.)

The HURIER model provides a foundation for us to consider key aspects of the listening process and our own listening behavior.

THE ETHICS OF LISTENING: PROBLEM BEHAVIORS

LO4

Describe the factors that contribute to ineffective listening.

Of course, we do not—probably, we cannot—listen at full capacity all the time. But we should be aware of our ineffective listening behaviors if they prevent us from understanding what could be important to us or to someone else. Many factors contribute to ineffective listening, and the following kinds of ineffective listeners are certainly not the only ineffective listeners we can identify. However, we have probably interacted with most of those identified here at some point in the past.

- **Fraudulent listeners.** Fraudulent listeners are pseudolisteners; they are also nodders. Persons who practice fraudulent listening and engage in nodding pretend that they are listening. They look at the speaker, nod their heads appropriately in agreement or disagreement, and utter remarks such as "mm" or "uh-huh" that imply they are paying attention. In actuality, the words are falling on deaf ears.

© William Haefeli/The New Yorker Collection/www.cartoonbank.com

"Go ahead. Tell me your troubles. I promise to say 'Awww' in all the right places."

- **Monopolistic listeners.** Monopolistic listeners want you to listen to them, but they have neither the time nor the desire to listen to you. Frequently egocentric, and as a result, intrigued and obsessed with their own thoughts and ideas, monopolizers deny your right to be listened to while defending their right to express themselves, no matter what the cost.[33]

    According to researcher Alfie Kohn, men are more likely than women to be monopolistic listeners, or "ear hogs." Kohn finds that men interrupt women's statements more frequently than women interrupt men's statements; in fact, in his research 96 percent of the interruptions in male-female interactions were initiated by men.[34] Do you believe this finding is still valid?

- **Completers.** Completers are gap fillers; they never quite get the whole story when they listen. To make up for what they have missed or misinterpreted, they manufacture information to fill in the gaps. While the impression is that they got it all, nothing could be farther from the truth.

- **Selective listeners.** Selective listeners are like bees going after the honey in a flower; they zero in on only those portions of a speaker's remarks that interest them or have particular importance to them. Everything else the speaker says is considered irrelevant or inconsequential and thus is rejected. Selective listeners, in their search for just the honey, often miss the flower.

- **Avoiders.** Avoiders figuratively wear earmuffs; they close their ears to information they would rather not deal with. Sometimes they pretend not to understand what you tell them or act as if they did not hear you at all. Sometimes they simply forget, in short order, what you have told them.

- **Defensive listeners.** Defensive listeners tend to perceive the remarks of other persons as personal affronts or attacks. Usually insecure, they are apt to pounce when another person asks a simple question, or they are likely to perceive a threat in the comments of another, when none actually exists. When

We wear earmuffs when we close our ears to information we would rather not listen to.

MediaWise

Talk radio, a mediated form of interpersonal communication that is growing in influence, allows callers a higher level of psychological comfort than does face-to-face interaction, because they can remain relatively anonymous while interacting with another person. Programs featuring argumentative hosts, such as Guardian Angels founder Curtis Slewa and pundits Rush Limbaugh, and Rachel Maddow, often become either yelling matches between the host and a caller who openly disagrees with the position the host has taken or love fests between the host and a caller who support each other's views.

Why is this? In her book *The First Word: The Search for the Origins of Language,* Christine Kenneally offers a rationale for such poor listening behavior. She describes an experiment in which two apes, skilled in sign language, were thrown together and encouraged to interact. Rather than engaging in meaningful communication, however, they had an arm-waving, sign-shouting match, with neither ape willing to listen to the other.[35] Is there a lesson in there for us? Are we hardwired to prefer listening to ourselves rather than others?

---

we listen defensively, we assume others are going to criticize or belittle us; we assume that they do not like, trust, or respect us. As a result, an innocent question, such as, "Did you do your report?" may be interpreted as criticism for having spent too much time playing Angry Birds.

- **Attackers.** Attackers wait for you to make a mistake, so that they can undercut and challenge what you have to say. They lie in wait, hoping to gather ammunition they can use to diminish your effectiveness. They also are not above distorting your words to advance their personal goals. Attacking listeners are apt to precipitate defensiveness in the person they are listening to. Rather than working to understand your meaning and conducting a discussion with you that is open and fair, they compete with you in an effort to outdo you.

FEEDBACK: THE LISTENER'S RESPONSE

LO5

Summarize the kinds of feedback listeners can provide.

The feedback process is intimately connected with the listening process. Developing an understanding and appreciation of the way feedback works is essential to improving your listening skills.

What Is Feedback?

The term *feedback* implies that we are feeding someone by giving something back to him or her. Feedback consists of all the verbal and nonverbal messages that a person consciously or unconsciously sends out in response to another person's communication. As students, you continually provide your instructors with feedback. Many of you, however, are probably not completely honest when you send feedback. At times when you are confused or bored, you may nevertheless put on an "I'm interested" face and nod smilingly, indicating that you understand and agree with everything your instructor is saying. Unfortunately, such behavior tends to encourage the sending of unclear messages.

Types of Feedback

We constantly provide others with feedback, whether we intend to or not. Everything we do or fail to do in a relationship or interaction with others can be considered feedback. Sometimes we send feedback consciously, intending to evoke a particular response. For example, if you laugh or chuckle at a speaker's joke or story, you may be doing so because you want the speaker to feel that you enjoyed the story and hope he or she will tell more jokes. In contrast, some of the feedback we transmit is sent unconsciously and evokes unintended or unexpected responses. Often, when our words or behaviors prompt a reaction that we never intended, we respond with useless phrases such as "That's not what I meant!" or "I didn't mean it that way!" or "What I meant was . . ."

What we intend to convey by feedback, then, may not be what others perceive. Sometimes others intentionally choose not to perceive our messages. At other times, confusion results because feedback that we mean to be nonevaluative in tone is interpreted as evaluative. Distinguishing between these two categories of feedback will help us use both types effectively and appropriately.

Evaluative Feedback When we provide another person with **evaluative feedback**—that is, an evaluative response—we state our opinion about a matter being discussed. For example, "How did you like my speech?" will almost always evoke a response that will be perceived as evaluative. A slight hesitation before the words "I loved it" might be perceived as a negative response. When we give evaluative feedback, we make judgments—either positive or negative—based on our own system of values. As we go about the business of daily life, judgments about the relative worth of ideas, the importance of projects, and the classification of abilities are a necessity. By its very nature, the effect of evaluative feedback is either positive and rewarding or negative and punishing.

Positive Evaluative Feedback Positive evaluative feedback tends to keep communication and its resulting behaviors moving in the direction they are already heading. If a company places an advertisement and achieves a tremendous growth in sales, the company will tend to place the same or a very similar ad in the same or very similar media in the future. If a person wearing a new hairstyle is complimented, he or she will tend to keep that hairstyle.

Negative Evaluative Feedback Negative evaluative feedback serves a corrective function in that it helps extinguish undesirable communicative behaviors. When we perceive feedback as negative, we tend to change our performance accordingly. For example, if you were to tell a number of off-color stories that your listeners found in bad taste, they might send you negative responses. They might turn away, attempt to change the subject, or simply maintain a cold, lengthy silence. Each cue would indicate that your message had overstepped the bounds of propriety; as a result, you would probably discontinue your anecdotes.

Skill Builder

Looking at Faulty Listening

Describe your experiences with the kinds of faulty listeners depicted in this section: fraudulent listeners, monopolistic listeners, completers, selective listeners, avoiders, defensive listeners, and attackers. Explain what would have to happen for each situation discussed to be replayed more successfully. Finally, identify which of the faulty listening behaviors you personally have been guilty of exhibiting, and describe the steps you will take to prevent these behaviors from interfering with your exhibiting effective listening behaviors in the future.

Review, Reflect, & Apply

Recall
Identify some of the problem behaviors that faulty listeners exhibit.

Understand
Describe some helpful listening habits that put speakers at ease.

Apply
Invent a dialogue in which a monopolistic listener interacts with an avoider.

evaluative feedback
a positive or negative judgment

formative feedback
timed negative feedback

Formative Feedback **Formative feedback** is timed negative feedback. Don Tosti, an industrial psychologist, used timed negative feedback with some interesting results.[37] Tosti discovered that, in a learning situation, it is best to provide positive feedback immediately after someone has displayed a desired behavior. Thus, comments such as, "You did a good job" and "Keep up the good work" should be offered immediately, because these responses give people a sense of pride and pleasure in themselves and their work. However, Tosti suggests that what he calls "formative negative" feedback should be given only just before an undesired behavior (or a similar behavior) is about to be repeated. Tosti believes that withholding negative feedback until the person can use it constructively makes the feedback seem more like coaching than criticism. Comments such as "OK, team, let's eliminate the errors we made last time" and "When you go out there today, try to . . ." reduce the extent to which negative feedback is perceived as harmful rather than helpful. Thus, giving formative feedback just before an activity is to be performed again can help eliminate the feelings of rejection that sometimes accompany negative feedback. (In contrast, it should be remembered that immediate positive feedback can do wonders for people's self-image and morale.)

nonevaluative feedback
nondirective feedback

Nonevaluative Feedback In contrast to evaluative feedback, **nonevaluative feedback,** or nondirective feedback, makes no overt attempt to direct the actions of a communicator. Thus, we use nonevaluative feedback when we want to learn more about a person's feelings or when we want to help another person formulate thoughts about a particular subject. When we offer nonevaluative feedback, we make no reference to our own opinions or judgments. Instead, we simply describe, question, or indicate an interest in what the other person is communicating to us.

Despite its nonjudgmental nature, nonevaluative feedback is often construed as being positive. That is, other people's behaviors may be reinforced when we probe, interpret their messages, and offer support as they attempt to work through a problem. Nonevaluative feedback reaches beyond positive feedback, however, by providing others with an opportunity to examine their own problems and arrive at their own solutions. For this reason, carefully phrased nonevaluative feedback

Exploring **Diversity**

Feedback in Japan

Are you culturally sensitive when giving feedback? For example, many Japanese—unlike Americans—use an indirect style of communication. Thus, when interacting with someone from Japan, if you give feedback directly (for example, telling someone outright, "You are not working hard enough"), the feedback, instead of being viewed as helpful, might be viewed as a threat. And if it is perceived as a threat, it could well be ineffective. An American giving feedback to another American, however, can give feedback more directly.

Do you believe we ought to change the way we provide feedback to conform to the preferences of another culture? Explain.

---

can be enormously helpful and sustaining to people who are going through a difficult period.

We consider four kinds of nonevaluative feedback here. Three—probing, understanding, and supporting—were identified by David Johnson. The fourth—"I" messages—was identified by Thomas Gordon.[38]

Probing Probing is a nonevaluative technique in which we ask people for additional information to draw them out and to demonstrate our willingness to listen to their problems.[39] Suppose that a student is concerned about his or her grades in a particular course and says to you, "I'm really upset. All my friends are doing better in geology than I am." If you use probing, you might ask, "Why does this situation bother you?" or "What do you suppose caused this to happen?" Responding in this way gives the other person the chance to think through the overall nature of the problem while providing him or her with an opportunity for emotional release. In contrast, comments like "So what? Who cares about that dumb class?" or "You really were dumb when you stopped studying" would tend to stop the student from thinking through and discussing the problem and, instead, would probably create defensiveness.

probing
a nonevaluative technique in which we ask for additional information

Understanding A second kind of nonevaluative response is what Johnson calls **understanding.** When we offer understanding, we seek to comprehend what the other person is saying to us, and we check ourselves by restating what we believe we have heard. Doing this shows that we care about other people and the problems they face.

Examine the following paraphrases to develop a feel for the nature of this kind of response:

understanding
a nonevaluative response that uses restatement to check comprehension

Person 1: I don't think I have the skill to be picked for the team.

Person 2: You believe you're not good enough to make the team this year?

Person 1: I envy those guys so much.

Person 2: You mean you're jealous of the people in that group?

If we use understanding early in a relationship, in effect, we communicate that we care enough about the interaction to want to be certain we comprehend what the other person is saying to us. Such a response strengthens the relationship because it encourages the other person to describe and detail his or her feelings.

Supportive Feedback A third kind of nonevaluative feedback is what Johnson calls **supportive feedback.** This response indicates that a problem the other person

supportive feedback
a nonevaluative response indicating that the receiver perceives a problem as important

deems important and significant is also viewed by the listener as important and significant.

Suppose a friend comes to you with a problem she feels is extremely serious. Perhaps your friend has worked herself into a state of extreme agitation and implies that you cannot possibly understand the situation. In offering supportive feedback, you would attempt to calm your friend down by assuring her that the world has not ended and that you do understand the problem.

Offering supportive feedback is difficult. We have to be able to reduce the intensity of other people's feelings while letting them know that we consider their problems real and serious. Such comments as "It's stupid to worry about that" and "Is that all that's worrying you?" are certainly not supportive. A better approach might be to say, "I can see you are upset. Let's talk about it. I'm sure you can find a way to solve the problem." A friend who is upset because he or she has just failed an exam needs supportive feedback: "I can see you are worried. I don't blame you for being upset." This is certainly not the time to suggest that there is no valid reason for being upset or that your friend's feelings are inappropriate. When we use supportive feedback, we judge the problems to be important, but we do not attempt to solve them ourselves; instead, we encourage people to discover their own solutions.

According to Doris Iarovici, a medical student at Yale, "One of the best things you can do for any patient is to listen and show that you care."[40] This, in a nutshell, is supportive feedback.

"I" Messages Certain nonevaluative feedback messages are called **"I" messages,** a term coined by Thomas Gordon. When we deliver an "I" message, we do not pass judgment on the other person's actions but simply convey our own feelings about the nature of the situation.

According to Gordon, when people interact with us, they are often unaware of how their actions affect us. We have the option of providing these people with either evaluative or nonevaluative feedback. Neither type is inherently good nor bad. However, far too often, the way we formulate our evaluative feedback adversely affects the nature of our interactions and the growth of our relationships. For example, do any of these statements sound familiar? "You made me angry!" "You're no good!" "You're in my way!" "You're a slob!" What do these statements have in common? As you have probably noticed, each one contains the word *you.* Each also places the blame for something on another person. When relationships experience difficulties, people tend to resort more and more to name-calling and to blaming others. Such feedback messages create schisms that are difficult and sometimes even impossible to bridge.

To avoid this situation, Gordon suggests that we replace **"you" messages** with "I" messages. If, for example, a parent tells a child, "You're pestering me," the child's interpretation will probably be "I am bad," and this interpretation will evoke a certain amount of defensiveness or hostility toward the parent ("I am not bad!"). But if the parent tells the child, "I'm really very tired and I don't feel like playing right now," the child's reaction is more likely to be "Mom is tired." Such an approach is more likely to elicit the type of behavior the parent desires than would name-calling and blaming ("You are a pest"). Using "I" messages as feedback will not always evoke the behavior you want from the other person, but it will help prevent the defensive, self-serving behaviors that "you" messages frequently elicit.

"I" messages
nonevaluative responses that convey our feelings about the nature of a situation

"you" messages
responses that place blame on another person

"I" messages have one other aspect you should be aware of. It is quite common to say "I am angry" to another person. Anger, however, is a secondary emotion. We are angry because of a stimulus or stimuli. In actuality, we develop anger. For example, if your child or a child you are watching ran into the street, your first response would probably be fear. Only after the child was safe would you develop anger, and then you would probably share your anger—rather than your fear—with the child. When formulating an angry "I" message, be certain to look beyond or beneath your anger and ask yourself why you are angry. Try to identify the forces that precipitated your anger—these are the feelings that should be expressed. Thus, if someone says something that hurts you, find ways to express the initial hurt rather than the resulting anger.

Review, Reflect, & **Apply**

Recall

Define feedback.

Understand

Compare and contrast the following types of feedback: positive evaluative, negative evaluative, formative, probing, understanding, and "I" messages.

Evaluate

Consider what makes some feedback more valuable than other feedback. Give examples.

The Role of Critical Thinking: Assessing the Credibility of What You Listen To

While you listen to information, you interpret and assign meaning to the spoken words. Your primary focus is on gaining and retaining information. When you go the next step and engage in **critical thinking,** you think carefully about what another person has said to you, and you evaluate the believability of the spoken message. Just as speakers can get carried away with their message's urgency and importance, so listeners can end up believing false or dangerous ideas that have been made to appear reasonable. Consequently, it is essential for you as a listener to stay alert, so that you are ready to challenge and raise questions about what you are listening to. When functioning as a critical thinker, you make a commitment to think for yourself. Thus, your primary goal is no longer only to understand information, but also to evaluate the person you are listening to and his or her ideas, deciding whether that individual is credible and ethical and whether he or she is drawing a reasonable conclusion.

LO6

Discuss critical thinking and its impact on listening.

critical thinking
the careful and deliberate process of message evaluation

WHAT CRITICAL THINKERS THINK ABOUT

What do critical thinkers think about? Critical thinkers seek to identify the unstated assumptions that underlie a speaker's message, the strengths and weaknesses of the speaker's viewpoint, if the message contains distortions or suggestions of bias, and the implications, positive and negative, of accepting that message. Critical thinkers also check themselves by asking if they are being fair-minded in their assessment of the speaker's message.[41] In other words, as a critical thinker, you determine if there is a logical connection between ideas and feelings. Rather than falling prey to strong emotional appeals, you examine the evidence on which conclusions are based and establish if they are valid or contain weaknesses and inconsistencies. Critical thinkers listen carefully in an effort to determine if what they are listening to makes sense and is worth retaining or acting upon.[42] Thus, when engaging in critical

What advice would you give Dilbert?

thinking, you raise questions that will help you draw well-reasoned conclusions. You consciously avoid thinking in egocentric or self-serving ways. You don't accept or reject what you hear simply because you want to or feel you have to. Instead, you live up to the obligation to question the basis for your beliefs and your response.

THE CRITICAL VERSUS THE UNCRITICAL THINKER

The following characteristics differentiate a critical thinker from an uncritical one.

The Critical Thinker

1. knows what he or she does not know
2. is open-minded and takes time to reflect on ideas
3. pays attention to those who agree and disagree with him or her
4. looks for good reasons to accept or reject expert opinion
5. is concerned with unstated assumptions and what is not said, in addition to what is stated outright
6. insists on getting the best evidence
7. reflects on how well conclusions fit premises and vice versa

The Uncritical Thinker

1. thinks he or she knows everything
2. is closed-minded and impulsive; jumps to unwarranted conclusions
3. pays attention only to those who agree with him or her
4. disregards evidence as to who is speaking with legitimate authority
5. is concerned only with what is stated, not with what is implied
6. ignores sources of evidence
7. disregards the connection or lack of connection between evidence and conclusions[43]

Critical thinkers do not rush to judge another's words. Instead of prejudging or evaluating the words of another prematurely, they exhibit a willingness to reexamine ideas. Thus, they withhold their evaluation until they have had sufficient opportunity to assess the information being given to them.

QUESTIONS TO FACILITATE CRITICAL THINKING

You can ask yourself a number of questions to facilitate the critical-thinking process:

1. Is the speaker's message plausible? Could it have reasonably occurred? Does it have a high probability of being true?
2. Does the support provided by the person speaking back up his or her claims? Are the claims he or she makes verifiable?
3. What do I know of the speaker's credibility or authority? Is the speaker reliable; that is, is she or he someone I should trust?
4. Is the speaker's message free of inconsistencies or contradictions?

When you think critically about what other people say to you, you do much more than merely hear their words.

Review, Reflect, & **Apply**

Recall
Compare and contrast the characteristics of critical and uncritical thinkers.

Understand
Identify the signals an educated observer looks for to determine whether a listener is practicing critical thinking skills.

Evaluate
Provide examples from your life, or the media, of instances that could have benefited from the critical thinking process.

Gender and Listening Style

Women and men are likely to exhibit different listening styles. Women tend to search for relationships among message parts; they rely more on their feelings and intuition. They listen to enhance their understanding as well as to establish personal relationships. Women also demonstrate a greater ability to switch between competing messages; unlike men, who tend to focus on their reactions to only one speaker at a time, women appear able to split their focus. They are more receptive, in general, than are men to what is happening around them. Thus, women are more likely than men to be engaged in conversation with one person and still pick up on the words of another person who is conversing with someone else nearby. In contrast to men, women listen to confirm the relationship as well as the person.[44] They also use head nodding and facial expressions to indicate their interest in a conversation. Because they view talk as a relationship developer, women also provide more vocal and verbal feedback when speaking with others. Women consider it important that

LO7

Explain how gender, culture, and media and technology influence listening.

Ethics & Communication

Would You Ask for and Listen to Directions?

Research reveals sex differences when it comes to navigation ability. Women prefer directions containing landmarks to guide them in getting from one place to the next (start at Grove Street and then go until you see a bookstore), whereas men typically prefer receiving Euclidean information, instructions that tell them where to start and how far to go (start at Grove Street and go east for three blocks).[45] But which sex finds it easier to ease into the listening mode and ask for directions? Before answering, consider this:

Is it possible that men do not like to put themselves into a listening mode? Can it be that the male need for independence and control actually makes it harder for men to listen? What are the chances that women, used to seeking help from others, are better than men at listening to advice?

According to Deborah Tannen, author of *You Just Don't Understand: Women and Men in Conversation,* men desire dominance so strongly that they would prefer to drive right past a police officer than to stop and ask for directions. For men, listening to directions implies inferiority. But, according to Tannen, American women are so used to asking for help that they tend to ask strangers for directions even when they are well aware of where they are going.

What do you think? Do men and women listen differently? Should they? Explain.

SIX CHIX © 2006 Isabella Bannerman. King Features Syndicate.

others perceive them as receptive and open.[46] Thus, they use more listening cues than men and excel at empathizing and at identifying moods.

Men, in comparison, are more at home with comprehensive listening and less at home with the emotional content of messages. Men are more likely to focus on a message's structure or pattern. Their tendency is to direct their listening efforts toward a goal. Men listen to solve problems.[47] As a result, they listen primarily to get the facts; they want to get to the bottom line. Men will also play up their expertise and use it to control or dominate conversations. Their goal is to have others respect them. In addition, in contrast to women, who exhibit more eye contact when listening than men do, men are more likely than women to survey the environment and direct their gaze away from the person they are conversing with.[48] While past research reported that men did not listen to provide emotional support, more recent research finds that men and women alike place a value on this listening style.[49]

Of course, gender differences continue to be redefined. In your experience, have the observations made above changed? Which do you believe are still valid?

Influence of Culture on Listening

As the psychological distance between people who live in different countries shrinks, our need to listen to others who neither live in the country we live in nor have the same native language increases. The globalization of business and our personal thirst for traveling to diverse geographical locations demands that we become more aware of cultural differences in listening styles and behavior.

When listening to another person, depending on our purpose and preferences, we tend to favor using one of four primary listening styles: people-oriented, content-oriented, action-oriented, or time-oriented. Those of us who are **people-oriented** listeners display a strong interest in others and concern for their feelings. People-oriented listeners are *we*-, not *me*-oriented, likely to focus on emotions, and seek to connect with others. As a result people-oriented listeners are often considered empathetic. Those of us who are **content-oriented** listeners are more concerned with what is said than with the people involved or their feelings. Instead, content-oriented listeners care about facts, evidence, and credibility. **Action-oriented** listeners are focused on task and concerned with outcomes—what will be done, by whom, and when. Sometimes their particular interest in action and outcomes is interpreted by others as impatience. Listeners who are **time-oriented** let the clock direct their listening. Concerned with time management, they limit the time they have available for listening, having brief or hurried interactions that tend to annoy others. Most of us use more than one style depending on the circumstances. What we need to keep in mind is that we can make the conscious effort to change listening styles. We can become more people-, content-, action-, or time-oriented depending on the situation and our partner's needs. Interestingly, individuals from different cultures are likely to use different styles.

According to C. Y. Cheng, the Chinese place greater emphasis on the receiving process and less emphasis on the sending process, reflecting the East Asian concern for interpretation and anticipation.[50] In Japan anticipatory communication is the norm. Speakers rarely tell or ask directly for something they want, leaving receivers to guess and accommodate speakers' needs. This communication style helps speakers and receivers save face in case what the speaker wants done cannot be accomplished.[51] In comparison, Germans practice action-oriented listening. They are inquisitive and exhibit a direct style. Israelis, who carefully analyze information, prefer the content style of listening. Collective in orientation, they tend to de-emphasize the personal aspects of interactions. The individually oriented Americans, on the other hand, exhibit a people-oriented style, focusing more on the feelings and concerns of the people involved in an interaction and emphasizing the interaction's social aspects. At the same time, however, they are focused on the time that interaction consumes—a time-oriented style.[52]

Dialogic listening focuses on what happens between people as they respond to each other, work toward shared understanding, and build a relationship.[53] Too frequently, life's pressures keep us from adopting open-ended, tentative approaches to conversation. We seem to prefer certainty, closure, and control. Whereas persons from Eastern cultures practice more speculative, metaphoric thinking, believing that people should listen more than they talk, members of Western cultures are less open and tentative in their listening behaviors, preferring specifically focused and concrete thinking instead.[54]

people-oriented listener
focused on emotions and connections

content-oriented listener
focused on what is said

action-oriented listener
focused on task and outcomes

time-oriented listener
focused on time limitations

dialogic listening
listening that focuses on what happens to people as they respond to each other

Within the United States, listening rules vary depending on the racial group to which you belong. African Americans, in general, display a more participative listening style than do European Americans. When listening to a speaker, African Americans are likely to shout out responses as a means of demonstrating their interest and involvement. By acknowledging that people from different regions and countries differ in both how they listen and respond, you are less apt to misinterpret someone's words or actions.[55]

Influence of Media and Technology on Listening and Thinking

How are media and technology changing the listening landscape? What roles are they playing in challenging our abilities to listen?

MEDIA INFLUENCES

Is television viewing shortening attention spans? If young children watch more than an hour of television each day, research reveals they are at risk for developing attention deficit problems, as compared with children who watch less TV. Blame is placed on television's quickly changing visual images, which researchers believe may overstimulate and permanently rewire a brain in the process of developing.[56]

Television and radio together account for significant amounts of what we listen to. Increasingly, segments on both television and radio programs are being shortened for fear we will not pay attention to them if they are long, discuss complicated information, or contain descriptions of complex feelings. In the place of complex information, television substitutes more and more graphics. Radio fills in with music and talk shows with guests who, too often, shout over each other, unwilling to listen to another person's point of view, and denying the show's listeners the opportunity to listen to and/ or participate in a meaningful discussion.

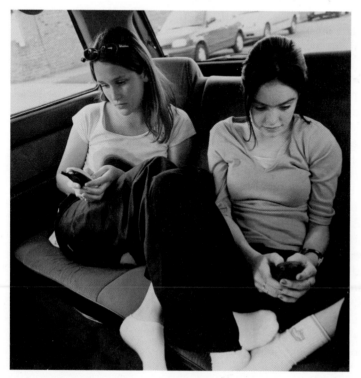

TECHNOLOGY INFLUENCES

Although they have been working on it for about two decades, scientists have yet to devise a computer that functions as a virtual best friend—one that is able to listen sensitively and empathically to a user.[57] Diametrically opposed to the efforts of these scientists are people who believe that our connections to computers, e-mail, and the Internet are impeding our ability to listen. Focusing our attention on the visual rather than the aural, critics contend, causes us to emphasize the eye over the ear. Despite this perceived failure of the scientists (we wonder if not

Listening Gains and Losses

New technologies are changing our listening landscape. On-line users spend less time listening to the radio, for example, than do nononline users. They also spend less time watching television. Consider this: How much more reading do you do today than in years past? Are you now reading more and listening less than you used to? In your opinion, what are the chances that texting ultimately will wipe out voice contact?

On the other hand, we can now listen to radio over the Internet or via podcasts. We can now personalize our listen-ing stimuli. In effect, we direct our own listening experi-ences. Is being able to control what you listen to a good thing? Or did having your listening experience determined for you by others make it impossible for you to filter out what you didn't want to listen to and enable you to develop skills that will now deteriorate? Explain your responses by describing how technology is enhancing or limiting your lis-tening opportunities and abilities.

succeeding is really a benefit) and the objections of critics, our technological listening landscape continues to evolve rapidly.

For one thing, texting has made it easy for deaf people to communicate with others. Wives now text their deaf husbands as a hearing wife might call to a husband in the basement. And deaf teens now blend in with other teens in the mall. Texting has made the deaf more independent.[58]

Today, in addition to technology providing us with perpetual linkages to others, we also have an expanding listening environment, tuning in and listening globally—using radio, television, CDs, cell phones, texting, podcasts, blogs, and other computer-assisted means of communicating.[59] Indeed, our appetite for traditional media as well as for the computer and the Internet is eating into time spent listening to other people in face-to-face settings. In fact, even when we are face-to-face with another person, perhaps when at lunch, on a walk, or out for a drive, one of us may be conversing with a third person via a cell phone. Texting during classes appears to be a habit, causing instructors to wonder how many students are actively listening. Fifty-two percent of students say they text friends in the same classroom.[60] Interpersonal etiquette appears to be at an all-time low. The world has become our phone booth. Perhaps we need cell-free zones, so that we can listen more attentively to the person we are with.[61] Perhaps we need cell-free zones for other reasons as well. More and more state legislatures have passed bills restricting car cell-phone use to hands-free rather than handheld models. However, merely listening on a phone has been shown to distract drivers. Listening while driving decreases driver accuracy by causing drops in function in the parts of the brain associated with visual and spatial processing, leading to more accidents.[62] Thus, although multitasking has become a way of life, driving and texting probably should not be part of our multitasking repertoire. Perhaps, listening is too complex an activity for us to multitask at all, if we want to do it well.

In addition to being surrounded by cell-phone users, according to David Shenk, author of *Data Smog*, we are being inundated with information that envelopes us within a toxic environment of continuous overstimulation[63] and supersaturates our minds.[64] It is probable that one outcome of this overload is a decrease in listening effectiveness.

Advances in technology will continue to add listening wrinkles. For example, in the past when we listened, we were generally face-to-face with the speaker; we engaged in real-time, synchronous listening. Then came the telephone, and we had the option of not having to share the same space when we exchanged a real-time conversation. Then we entered the era of voice mail; we could have serial

Exploring **Diversity**

Is having someone listen to you online the same as having someone listen to you in person? Even when cyber-communicators are using the same online language, because of the Internet's global reach, that language may not be their native language. As a result, the meanings given to the words used may differ drastically. As in face-to-face interaction, not all online listeners receive the same message. As you interact with persons from different cultures in cyberspace, ask yourself these questions:

1. Do they favor a direct or indirect style?
   While some cultures, including those in the United States, tend to exhibit a direct style in communicating—communicators tell it like it is—many Asian cultures use an indirect style, preferring to emphasize politeness and face-saving strategies rather than truth telling. Which style do you prefer?

2. Do they offer hard evidence or tell stories?
   In the United States, our decision making is influenced by logical reasons and credible testimony. In contrast, members of other cultures tend to be influenced by stories other sources tell convincingly. What kind of substantiation do you tend to offer? Receive?

3. What kind of feedback do they offer?
   In the United States, we expect to receive honest feedback that reveals the feelings of those with whom we communicate. In Asian cultures, however, communicators believe it is more important to offer positive reactions than truthful ones. Not every culture perceives feedback the same way. What kind of feedback do you prefer?

4. How do opportunities for anonymity influence online listening behavior?
   Because we may remain anonymous, some of us tend to exhibit less ego involvement when listening online than when interacting face-to-face. How does the change in ego involvement affect you?

conversations (asynchronous listening) with a person who is in a different location and does not hear our words as we speak them. More and more of our conversations are occurring asynchronously.[65] Continuing advances add to the listening challenge. In fact, people are reporting having little time to concentrate and reflect on what they're receiving. With all the texting and tweeting going on, they're also finding it hard to be "present" and responsive to family and friends in their immediate environment.[66] So everyone uses cell phones, but is anyone really "talking" or "listening"? Research reveals that talking on cell phones is now less than half of the traffic on mobile networks. Users see talking as intrusive and time-consuming, with many reporting no patience for talking to only one person at a time. They would rather multitask conversations.[67] There are other questions to ask when it comes to Twitter: Are the people who follow others on Twitter "listening" to them? Is following someone on Twitter and listening to him or her in person the same thing? What we do know is that we can now be more selective about our willingness to listen at all. Caller ID and the ignore choice on cell phones allow us to see who is calling and to decide whom we want to listen to. Call waiting makes it possible for us not to miss a call from someone important to us. We can now line up our listeners.

We now even have gadgets that listen and obey our commands. For example, we can ask our phones to play songs, direct us to a local bakery, or convert voice mail into e-mail. Maybe one day we will be able to yell out the name of our favorite program at the television set, and it will appear on the screen.[68] How might being able to speak our minds to our machines and have them obey alter the expectations we have when people and not machines are listening to us?

With the exception of films shown in theaters, media or computer-generated messages are usually processed by individuals viewing or listening to them alone or in small groups. Because we now process messages, CDs, and videos from around the world, our ears, habitually crossing national boundaries and opening wider and wider, are helping to erase cultural, informational, and personal barriers.

The real-time transmission of voice is possible over the Internet. Skype enables you to use your computer as a telephone with pictures. You can talk with and see another person anywhere in the world for as long as you want without the cost of a long-distance phone call. Videoconferencing programs make it possible to chat across the Internet while both hearing and seeing each other.[69]

Thus, we have to ask the following questions: While we may be listening more to the sounds of new media, are we listening less to each other? How actively can we listen to another human being in our immediate environment when technological advances are absorbing our attention and propelling us across national boundaries and into settings far removed from the ones with which we are most familiar?

Communication Skills

PRACTICE LISTENING SKILLS

LO8

Demonstrate effective listening.

✅ Use Your Listening Time Wisely

Rather than assume you know what another person is going to say, fully tune in and listen attentively to understand what the other person says. Summarize and ask yourself questions about the substance and meaning of what you are hearing. Use thinking time to identify the other person's major points and reasons given to justify or support them.

✅ Give Real, Not Pseudo, Attention

Too many of us fake attention when listening. Although our external cues— we make eye contact, smile, nod our heads—say that we are listening, we are only pretending. Instead, focus on interpreting the meaning contained in the other person's words.

✅ Withhold Judgment

When we prejudge a person or his or her message, we uncritically accept or reject both the person and his or her ideas. Understanding needs to precede evaluation.

✅ Maintain Emotional Control

Sometimes we distort the ideas of others merely because we do not like or agree with them. Listening involves processing, not manufacturing information. Rather than allow an emotional eruption to cause a listening disruption, we need to work harder when our emotions cause us to feel overly aroused, defensive, alienated, elated, or outraged. Feelings of rapture and hero-worship can limit understanding as much as can anger or hostility.[*]

✅ Be Willing to See Another Person's Viewpoint

A willingness to look at a situation from another's perspective increases the likelihood that you will be able to see and feel what the other person is experiencing. You do not have to agree with another individual, but it helps to understand where thoughts and feelings come from.

> ✔ **Listen with Your Whole Body**

Listening is an active, not passive process. By displaying an attentive posture and making meaningful eye contact, your body helps your mind increase its readiness to listen.

The Wrap-Up

SUMMARY

LO1 **Define** listening and explain its role in communication.

Listening is a deliberate process through which we seek to understand and retain aural (heard) stimuli. Unlike hearing, which occurs automatically, listening depends on a complex set of skills.

LO2 **Distinguish** among four types of listening: appreciative, comprehensive, critical, and empathic.

When we listen appreciatively, we are listening for pleasure. When we listen comprehensively, we listen to gain knowledge. When we listen critically, we seek to determine the usefulness, soundness, and accuracy of a message. When we listen empathically, we listen to understand the feelings and point of view of another person.

LO3 **Use** the HURIER model to explain the six stages of listening.

The HURIER model takes a behavioral approach to listening. Using it can help you to develop listening skills. The model focuses on the six key stages of listening: hearing, understanding, remembering, interpreting, evaluating, and responding.

LO4 **Describe** the factors that contribute to ineffective listening.

Behaviors we adopt can enhance or impede true understanding and critical reflection. The following are examples of problematic listeners: fraudulent listeners, monopolistic listeners, completers, selective listeners, avoiders, defensive listeners, and attackers.

LO5 **Summarize** the kinds of feedback listeners can provide.

Feedback is a prerequisite of effective listening. Feedback consists of all the verbal and nonverbal messages that one person consciously or unconsciously sends out in response to another person's communication. There are two main types of feedback: (1) Evaluative feedback gives an opinion, positive or negative, and attempts to influence the behavior of others; (2) nonevaluative feedback gives emotional support. Probing, understanding (or paraphrasing), supportive feedback, and "I" messages are all forms of nonevaluative feedback that help sustain interpersonal relationships.

LO6 **Discuss** critical thinking and its impact on listening.

When you engage in critical thinking you think carefully about what another person is telling you, and you evaluate the believability of the message. You also seek to determine if there is a logical connection between ideas and feelings.

LO7 **Explain** how gender, culture, and media and technology influence listening.

Recognizing how gender, culture, and media and technology influence listening skills may further enhance your ability to develop more effective listening practices. Women, men, and persons from different cultures are apt to exhibit different listening preferences. New technological advances, while giving you the ability to listen globally, also compete for your listening time.

LO8 **Demonstrate** effective listening.

By using your listening time wisely, offering real attention, being willing to withhold judgment, controlling your emotions, displaying a willingness to see from another's perspective, and listening with your whole body you increase your listening effectiveness.

KEY CHAPTER TERMINOLOGY

action-oriented listener 161

appreciative listening 147

comprehensive listening 147

content-oriented listener 161

critical listening 147

critical thinking 157

dialogic listening 161

empathic listening 147

evaluative feedback 153

formative feedback 154

hearing 141

HURIER model 148

"I" messages 156

listening 141

mindfulness 143

nonevaluative feedback 154

paraphrasing 148

people-oriented listener 161

probing 155

red-flag words 149

serial communication 145

speech-thought differential 149

supportive feedback 155

time-oriented listener 161

understanding 155

"you" messages 156

Looking Back and Ahead

CONSIDER THIS CASE: FIRST IMPRESSIONS

Stacey couldn't believe her luck. She'd been offered the summer internship of her dreams, working for Ángel de la Música, a new, independent record label with offices downtown. The company was small but growing, and Rick Sanchez, the founder and president, hadn't wasted any time setting up a company Web site in Spanish and English and contacting music distributors in Latin America. Rick had told Stacey that one of her assignments as a summer intern would be to help him and the marketing manager choose a list of 10 U.S. cities in which to hold promotional events over the next year, such as contests sponsored by local radio stations, music store appearances by the label's newest artists, and even a couple of free concerts. It all sounded exciting, and Stacey couldn't wait to begin.

"*Hola*, Stacey!" Rick greeted her cheerfully on her first day. "I was hoping I could introduce you to everyone, but I'm going to be gone most of the day meeting with some agents and promoters. There's a couple of new bands I want to sign, and I've got to get to them before anyone else does." He grinned at Stacey as he grabbed his jacket and headed for the door. "Listen, can you take a tour of the office, meet everybody, and then check in with me around four? I'll be back by then and we'll talk, OK?"

"Sure," said Stacey, hiding her surprise. "Perfect!"

"Great—thanks!" said Rick, and he was gone.

Stacey stood in the middle of Rick's office for a minute, thinking. Finally, she flung her coat over a chair and headed back to the reception area.

"*¿Puedo ayudarle?*" the receptionist asked.

"Hi," Stacey replied. "I don't speak Spanish very well; I'm sorry. I'm Stacey and I'm the new summer intern." She held out her hand. "How do you do?"

The young man at the desk shook hands. "I'm Luis," he said. "Rick run out on you already?"

"Oh!" said Stacey. "No, not really. That is, he had a meeting to go to, and . . ."

"Yeah," said Luis. "But you're still wondering what to do with yourself today, aren't you?"

"Well," said Stacey, "I'm not, actually. I want to meet everyone, introduce myself." She tried to smile.

"OK," said Luis, smiling back. "Maybe I can help you with that. Here's the company telephone list. This will tell you who everybody is. See how it's organized by department, with everybody's title next to their name?"

"Hey, thanks! This looks great," said Stacey in relief. She studied the list for a minute while Luis took a phone message in Spanish for Rick. "Where would I find María Lopez? She's the head of marketing."

"Down the hall to the left," said Luis as the phone rang again. Stacey waved her thanks and set off to find the marketing manager. Given her assignment for the summer, she figured María was someone it would be important to meet. She was already imagining herself giving Rick a brief but impressive account of her day when she felt herself bump hard into someone coming quickly around a corner.

"Oh! I'm so sorry!" Stacey cried. The middle-aged woman she'd walked into sighed, adjusted her glasses, and walked away without a word. As Stacey turned the corner to the left, she heard Luis greet the woman in Spanish. Stacey understood only one word, the woman's name. *María.*

Red-faced, Stacey scurried around the corner and buried herself in the phone list, looking for someone else she could meet.

By four that afternoon she was exhausted but pleased. Sitting in Rick's office waiting for him to return, she mentally reviewed her day. She'd met Lourdes, who managed the contracts department; Joe, the head designer for the label; Tina, Rick's part-time assistant; and Timotéo, who was Ángel de la Música's tech expert and Webmaster. Stacey had expected the company's tech people to be young, but Tim had pictures on his desk that he proudly pointed out were of his grandchildren. Tim had shown her the company's Web site for music downloads and asked her opinion about the pricing strategy the company was considering. Victoria, the financial officer, had found Stacey in

Tim's office and offered to take her to lunch, where she teased Stacey for not knowing much Spanish and then talked endlessly about her boyfriend.

Stacey hadn't seen María again, but she had met Greg, the advertising manager, and the heads of manufacturing and the warehouse, who had both been expecting to find Rick in the office. All in all, thought Stacey, smoothing out her crumpled phone list, it had been a day well spent. Suddenly she heard voices speaking Spanish outside Rick's office.

"Sorry, María," Luis, the receptionist, was saying. "Rick's not back yet. I haven't heard from him all day."

"That son of mine!" María exclaimed. "Late again! I'll wait for him in his office."

DISCUSSION QUESTIONS

1. How do you think Stacey's self-concept changed throughout the day? Why?
2. Do you think Stacey's poor Spanish skills will be a handicap during her internship? What does she have to offer Ángel de la Música?
3. Did Stacey make any prejudgments about the staff of Ángel de la Música? How well do you think she dealt with them on her first day?
4. Are there any potential self-fulfilling prophecies at work in this case? How can Stacey avoid them?
5. How can Stacey use communication skills to ensure that her internship is a success for her and for Ángel de la Música?

The Speaker and the Audience:
The Occasion and the Subject

11

After completing this chapter, you should be able to demonstrate mastery of the following learning outcomes:

LO1 **Define** *public speaking* and *public speaking anxiety.*

LO2 **Explain** how to approach public speaking systematically.

LO3 **Explain** why conducting a thorough self-analysis facilitates the speech-making process.

LO4 **Analyze** your audience and tailor your speech to them.

LO5 **Explain** how the nature of the occasion influences a speech.

LO6 **Identify** criteria for topic selection.

LO7 **Narrow** your topic and formulate a thesis statement.

Our technologically rich environment depends on user-generated content. Today, we create, send, and receive countless messages using blogs, Podcasts, YouTube, or Facebook. We send texts, tweets, and e-mail, sharing our thoughts and feelings. The chapters in this part of the text call on you to apply your skill at developing user-generated content and your understanding of and familiarity with technology to a different communication venue: the public speech—another means of opening minds, sharing information, and advocating for ideas.

In the United States there are more than twenty thousand different ways of earning a living, and effective speech is essential to every one.

—Andrew Weaver

In our age of abundant electronic connections, public speakers are in demand, and the number of platforms open to them is increasing. In fact, many venues seek speakers these days. From corporate meetings to trade shows, from educational conferences to political rallies, from town meetings to your classroom, speakers play important roles. Public speaking is like a form of currency, only instead of providing access to the marketplace of goods and services, it provides access to the marketplace of ideas. From Mark Zuckerberg to Sergey Brin, from the local school superintendent to a concerned parent, from Oprah to Bono, from us to you and your peers, we share the responsibility to make our voices heard. And there is no shortage of advice on how to improve the ability to speak so that others listen. From blogs to self-help books, from DVDs to this text, resources exist to help you become more effective and at ease speaking in public. Are you able to stand before an audience without fear? Can you personalize a message so that others believe your words are meant for them? Do you know how to organize your ideas and stay on course without derailing your objective? Can you deliver your message and not become unnerved, so that audience members leave the experience richer for having listened to you? And can you have fun doing it?

No matter your age, sex, or ethnic or racial background, becoming effective at speaking in public is an important skill to develop. Since public speaking is likely to play an important role in your future, let's prepare to meet that challenge.

Public Speaking Defined

Public speaking—these are two seemingly harmless words. **Public speaking** is the act of preparing, staging, and delivering a presentation to an audience. We speak every day. Under ordinary circumstances, we rarely give speaking, or our skills in speaking, a second thought—that is, until we are asked to deliver a speech or simply to speak in public. Once we know that is what we are going to have to do, if we are like most Americans, we fear it more than we fear bee stings, accidents, heights, or our own death.[1] (See Figure 11.1.) Examine the accompanying cartoon. Did you feel similarly after your instructor told you that as part of this course, you were going to have to give a speech? Is the day you've been assigned to give that presentation drawing closer? Experiencing stress at the thought of

SALLY FORTH © 1994. King Features Syndicate.

speaking in front of other people is not restricted to students—indeed, kings, presidents, actors, and professors experience it as well. Some people fear stuttering (as did King George of England whose experiences were dramatized in the film *The King's Speech*). Others fear saying the wrong thing, or putting their audience to sleep. You may feel so anxious that you wonder if you will really be able to gather the courage to stand and speak before an audience. The answer is, of course, you will! You can overcome whatever anxiety you feel by understanding its sources, learning to cope with your fears, using strategies to handle both the physical and mental symptoms of anxiety, and preparing and rehearsing thoroughly. When the speaker is energetic and passionate about a speech, the audience reciprocates, as illustrated by one prominent motivational speaker who begins his presentations as follows:

> I couldn't sleep last night. I finally got up at 4 this morning. I got dressed and went through this presentation 37 times. And guess what? You loved it. [Gentle laughter.] And let me tell you one thing I'll never forget about this group. That is, when I got introduced, everyone was standing. [More laughter.] Tell you what I'm going to do. I'm going to reintroduce myself, and what I want you to do is just give me the welcome you gave me this morning. Just pump it up, OK? Are you ready? [Music pulses.] Ladies and gentlemen, all the way from Atlanta, GA. If you forget everything I say, don't forget this. . . . You are the best at what you do because of one main thing: Attitude. [The audience stands and cheers.][2]

What attitude do you have toward speaking in public? Fear, or anxiety, is something that affects most public speakers.[3] It is so common that, when queried, many persons answer that they would rather be in the casket at a funeral than be delivering the eulogy. Thus, if you experience a certain amount of apprehension before, during, or after presenting a speech, rest assured that you are not alone.[4] Students sometimes allow their fears to get the better of them. Instead of using anxiety as a positive force, they let it overwhelm them. To combat this, let's look at how to make **public speaking anxiety** (fear of speaking to an audience), a form of **communication apprehension** (fear of communicating with others no matter what the context), actually work for you.

Approximately 20 percent of the U.S. population is "trait" communication apprehensive. This means that they exhibit a predisposition to being apprehensive and display escalated nervousness levels in most, if not all, communication situations. On the other hand, nearly all

FIGURE 11.1

Activities Adults Say They Dread.

public speaking anxiety
fear of speaking to an audience

communication apprehension
fear of communication, no matter what the context

Review, Reflect, & **Apply**

Recall
Distinguish between public speaking anxiety and communication apprehension.

Understanding
Identify techniques you can use to control speech anxiety.

Apply
Prepare advice you would give a speaker regarding how to control public speaking anxiety.

Create
Develop a visualization experience to use when preparing to speak in public.

Rehearsal is an integral part of speech preparation. It also helps decrease anxiety.

of us experience occasional "state" communication apprehension. This means that when facing a specific situation, such as public speaking, we display a somewhat elevated nervousness level.[5] To determine your communication apprehension score, you can take the self-analysis quiz included in the section "Self-Analysis: How Anxious Are You?" or access the Perceived Report of Communication Apprehension (PRCA) developed by James McCroskey, cited on his Web page (www.jamesmccroskey.com) under Communication Research Measures.

UNDERSTANDING YOUR FEARS

Self-Analysis: How Anxious Are You?

How anxious are you about delivering a speech? Use the following inventory to find out. Although this inventory is not a scientific instrument, it should give you some indication of your level of fear. Note that you must display some level of anxiety to be categorized as "normal." If you had no anxiety about speaking in public, you would not be considered normal; what's more, you would probably not be a very effective speech maker.

For each statement, circle the number that best represents your response:

1. I am afraid I will forget what I have to say.
   Not afraid   1 2 3 4 5   Extremely afraid

2. I am afraid my ideas will sound confused and jumbled.
   Not afraid   1 2 3 4 5   Extremely afraid

3. I am afraid my appearance will be inappropriate.
   Not afraid   1 2 3 4 5   Extremely afraid

4. I am afraid the audience will find my speech boring.
   Not afraid   1 2 3 4 5   Extremely afraid

5. I am afraid people in the audience will laugh at me.
   Not afraid   1 2 3 4 5   Extremely afraid

6. I am afraid I will not know what to do with my hands.
   Not afraid   1 2 3 4 5   Extremely afraid

7. I am afraid my instructor will embarrass me.
   Not afraid   1 2 3 4 5   Extremely afraid

8. I am afraid audience members will think my ideas are simplistic.
   Not afraid   1 2 3 4 5   Extremely afraid

9. I am afraid I will make grammatical mistakes.
   Not afraid   1 2 3 4 5   Extremely afraid

10. I am afraid everyone will stare at me.
    Not afraid   1 2 3 4 5   Extremely afraid

> The human brain is a wonderful thing. It operates from the moment you're born until the first time you get up to make a speech.
>
> —Howard Goshom

> *We are largely the playthings of our fears.*
>
> —Horace Walpole

Is Compulsory Speech Making Fair?

Studies show that many people fear public speaking more than they fear death. When informed they must give a speech, their bodies do all kinds of unpleasant things to them: hands sweat; mouths go dry; knees shake; voices quiver; hearts race; heads pound. All people with extreme fear of public speaking want to do is get out of the spotlight and sit down. Is it fair to demand that all students face up to their fear and take a course that requires them to deliver at least one speech? Are there other options that could provide the same skills without actually involving standing in front of an audience? Explain your answers.

Next, add the numbers you chose and rate yourself as follows:

41–50 Very apprehensive
31–40 Apprehensive
21–30 Normally concerned

11–20 Overconfident
10   Are you alive?

Sources of Public Speaking Anxiety

Why are we afraid to speak in public? Why do many of us fear speaking before an audience more than we fear snakes, heights, bee stings, or death? Before we can cope with our fears, we need to understand what causes them. The sections that follow discuss some of the more common causes of public speaking apprehension.

Fear of Failure Many of us fear failing. The idea of speaking in public makes us feel inadequate. We worry that we won't be able to cope with the challenges. This concerns us even more if we suffer from ESL (English as a second language) anxiety, the kind of anxiety experienced by ESL students. Visualizing ourselves failing, rather than succeeding, we try to maintain a low profile. Do you ever avoid risks because you imagine your performance will not be good enough? When you disagree with something you have read or heard, are you more comfortable swallowing hard and sitting quietly than speaking up for what you think is right? Do you find it easier to go along with a group than to voice your objections? If you fear failure, you are more likely to play it safe, trying not to put yourself in situations that might cause you to feel even more inadequate.

Fear of the Unknown A new job may cause us to feel fearful because our co-workers, the situation, and our responsibilities are unfamiliar, unknown, or still unclear. We may fear delivering a speech for the same reasons. Each new event has a threatening, unknown quality—a quality that many people prefer not to deal with. When such an event involves speaking, we may be afraid because we do not know how people will react to what we say. Although we have a cognitive understanding of what is and is not likely to happen before an audience, we let our feelings take charge, causing us to react emotionally and behave irrationally.

Fear of Being Judged How sensitive are you to the judgment of others? Are you concerned about a friend's opinion of or judgment about you? An instructor's? Do you believe that what an audience, a reader, or an instructor concludes about

Exploring **Diversity**

According to researcher Deborah Tannen, men are more comfortable speaking in public than women are, while women are more comfortable speaking in private. Tannen finds that men excel at "report talk," while women excel at "rapport talk."

Do your experiences confirm or contradict this finding? If this disparity exists, what, if anything, do you think should be done to change it? Men, she believes, are more focused on status, jockeying for position, while women like to refer one thing to another in an effort to reinforce relationships.

you is necessarily true? Sometimes we become so sensitive to the judgments of others that we try to avoid judgment altogether. Public speaking is one situation in which such an attitude is common.

Fear of Consequences Basically, one of two things can result from giving a speech: The audience may like it or may dislike it. That is, it will be a success or a failure. This basic result may then have further consequences. In the classroom, for example, an unsatisfactory speech may result in a failing grade. In a business situation, it may result in the loss of an important account. Whatever the consequences, the speaker needs to prepare to deal with them.

What advice would you give to a speaker about how to control fear and anxiety?

LEARNING TO COPE WITH YOUR FEARS: CONTROLLING ANXIETY

One of the best ways to cope with the fear of speech making is to design and rehearse your presentation carefully. The systematic approach suggested in this chapter covers both design and rehearsal and should—at least in theory—decrease your anxiety by increasing your self-confidence. However, theory and reality do sometimes diverge and, preparation notwithstanding, you may still find that you experience some anxiety about your speech. Let us now see how such anxiety can be controlled.

The first thing you need to do is recognize the actual bodily sensations and thoughts that accompany and support your feelings of nervousness. Make a list of the physical symptoms and fear-related thoughts that contribute to your anxiety. Then examine the symptoms and thoughts that you and others in your class identified. Do the lists include any of these physical symptoms?

rapid or irregular heartbeat	stiff neck
stomach knots	lump in the throat
shaking hands, arms, or legs	nausea
dry mouth	dizziness

When people are asked about fear-related thoughts, they often make statements like the following. Were any of these included on your lists?

Tense and Relax

1. Imagine that your body is divided into four basic sections:

   a. hands and arms
   b. face and neck
   c. torso
   d. legs and feet

2. Sit comfortably. In turn, practice tensing and relaxing each of these four sections of your body.

   a. *Hands and arms.* Clench your fists. Tense each arm from shoulder to fingertips. Notice the warm feeling that develops in your hands, forearms, and upper arms. Count to 10. Relax.

   b. *Face and neck.* Wrinkle your face as tightly as you can. Press your head back as far as it will go. Count to 10. Relax. Roll your head slowly to the front, side, back, and side in a circular movement. Relax.

   c. *Torso.* Shrug your shoulders. Count to 10 in this position. Relax. Tighten your stomach. Hold it. Relax.

   d. *Legs and feet.* Tighten your hips and thighs. Relax. Tense your calves and feet. Relax.

3. Work through the procedure described in the text for releasing tension.

4. As soon as you experience the warm feeling throughout your body, say to yourself, "calm." Try this several times, each time working to associate the "de-tensed" feeling with the word *calm.*

5. The next time you find yourself in a stress-producing situation, say "calm" to yourself and attempt to achieve the de-tensed state.

"I just can't cope."

"I'm under such pressure."

"This is a nightmare."

"I know something terrible is going to happen."

Once you have identified the physical and mental sensations that accompany fear, your next step is to learn how to control these reactions.[6] The next sections describe behavior modification techniques that can help you.

DEEP-MUSCLE RELAXATION: OVERCOMING PHYSICAL SYMPTOMS

Muscle tension commonly accompanies fear and anxiety. However, a muscle will relax after being tensed. Deep-muscle relaxation is based on this fact.

Try this: Tense one arm. Count to 10. Now relax your arm. What feelings did you experience? Did your arm seem to become heavier? Did it then seem to become warmer? Next, try tensing and relaxing one or both of your legs. When you examine what happens, you'll see why it is reasonable to expect that you can calm yourself by systematically tensing and relaxing various parts of your body in turn.

Try using the Skill Builder "Tense and Relax" several times before you actually present a speech. Many students report that butterflies or tensions tend to settle in particular bodily sections. Thus, it can be helpful to check the bodily sensations you feel when anxious, and personalize "Tense and Relax" to deal with your individual symptoms.

THOUGHT STOPPING: OVERCOMING MENTAL SYMPTOMS

Anxiety is not simply a physical phenomenon; it also manifests itself cognitively—that is, in thoughts. Thus it is important to work to eliminate the thoughts associated with anxiety, as well as the bodily symptoms.

Think you can or think you can't; either way you will be right.

—Henry Ford

Many people use the word *relax* to calm themselves. Unfortunately, *relax* doesn't sound very relaxing to some people. You can substitute the word *calm*. Try the second part of the Skill Builder "Tense and Relax."

A variation on the "calm technique" is to precede the word *calm* with the word *stop*. When you begin to think upsetting thoughts, say to yourself, "Stop!" Then follow that command with "Calm"—for example,

"I just can't get up in front of all those people. Look at their cold stares and mean smirks."

"Stop!"

"Calm."

You may find that you can adapt this thought-stopping technique to help you handle symptoms of anxiety in interpersonal situations.

VISUALIZATION: A POSITIVE APPROACH

Sports psychologists use a technique called visualization to help athletes compete more effectively. The athletes are guided in visualizing the successful completion of a play or a game. They are asked to imagine how they will feel when they win. Eventually, when they go out on the field to compete, it is almost as if they have been there before—and have already won.

You may want to try this technique to boost your confidence as a speaker. Sit in a quiet place. Picture yourself approaching the podium. See yourself delivering your presentation. Then hear your audience applaud appreciatively. After you have delivered the speech, answer these questions: Did the experience help you control your anxiety? Did it help you succeed?

Like athletes, speakers can use a variety of techniques to reduce apprehension.

OTHER TECHNIQUES

Speakers report that other techniques can also help reduce speech apprehension. Some try to include a bit of humor early in the speech to get a favorable response from the audience right away. They say that such a reaction helps them calm their nerves for the remainder of the presentation. Others look for a friendly face and talk to that person for a moment or two early in the speech. Others use charts, graphs, and other visuals to help them organize the material. In this technique, the visual shows the next major point to be covered, eliminating the necessity for the speaker to remember it or refer to notes. Still others report that they rehearse a speech aloud, standing in front of an imaginary audience and "talking through" the material again and again. What other techniques have you found helpful?

Remember, no matter how you choose to deal with it, fear is a natural response to public speaking and can probably never be eliminated completely. But you do need to learn to cope with fear; only in this way will you be able to deliver a successful, well-received presentation.

Just as we can learn to handle ourselves more effectively in our interpersonal and group relationships, if we take the time that is needed to analyze and practice successful behaviors, we can also learn to handle ourselves more effectively as public speakers. With practice, we can develop the understanding and master the skills that will make us articulate speakers who are organized, confident, and competent, and can communicate ideas in such a way that others will be interested in them and persuaded by them.

We start our examination of public speaking by putting the entire speech-making process into a logical format that you can examine and follow in detail. The process serves as a road map—one you can use to prepare every public presentation you will ever make. In this chapter, as well as Chapter 12, we explore factors involved in preparing a speech. In Chapter 13 we shift our focus from preparation to presentation and analysis. Then, once we have a handle on how the process works, in Chapters 14 and 15 we investigate two essential speech-making models: the informative speech and the persuasive speech.

APPROACHING SPEECH MAKING SYSTEMATICALLY

People respond to the challenge of public speaking in a variety of ways. Some believe that speech making is an inborn skill: "I talk a lot, so this public speaking business poses no difficulty for me." Others view it as torture: "I'm scared stiff! This will be traumatic!" These attitudes represent two extremes, and both can cause problems. Overconfident people run the risk of being inadequate speakers because they conduct little research and thus are ill prepared. People who are overly anxious or fearful may find it terribly trying and nerve-racking to stand before an audience and deliver a talk. The most effective speakers are those who display a healthy respect for the challenges involved in speaking before others and who work systematically to create, prepare, and deliver an admirable presentation.

Most likely, you will be assigned a speech before you have had the chance to finish reading and applying all the relevant information contained in subsequent chapters, so here we offer a preview of the speech preparation you need as you get ready to speak before your class for the first time.

The staircaselike chart in Figure 11.2 reveals a systematic, step-by-step approach. As you make your way up the staircase, you move from one speech-making phase into another. There is a logical order to speech making that reduces the process to four landings: (1) topic selection and self and audience analysis; (2) speech development, support, and organization; (3) presentation practice and delivery; and (4) postpresentation analysis. Although this chapter focuses only on the steps leading to the first landing of the speech-making staircase, we briefly review each of the tasks you need to accomplish as you climb to the top of the staircase, successfully completing and evaluating a speech. Before we look at these tasks, let us remind you that the staircase is

FIGURE 11.2

Systematic Speaking Process.

LO2

Explain how to approach public speaking systematically.

only as strong as its foundation. Each time you speak, ask yourself: Are you handling your topic as *ethically* as possible? Are you applying principles of *critical thinking*? Are you as sensitive as you can be to the challenges posed by the *diversity* inherent in receivers?

First Landing: Topic Selection and Audience Analysis

To reach the first landing of the speech-making staircase, *topic selection and self and audience analysis*, you need to ascend five steps, completing each of the identified tasks: (1) Analyze yourself to assess your confidence and identify your interests, concerns, and areas of special knowledge; (2) analyze your audience to identify ways their interests, needs, and knowledge could affect your selection; (3) identify the occasion for speaking, including any special requirements assigned by your instructor or the nature of the event that calls for the speech; (4) choose a general subject area; and (5) concentrate on making that subject increasingly specific, by narrowing its scope so that you can cover it in the allotted time and preparing a clear thesis statement.

Second Landing: Speech Development, Support, and Organization

To reach the next landing of the speech-making staircase, *speech development, support, and organization*, you research your topic and then gather supporting materials that clarify your speech's purpose. You also select presentation aids. Finally, you organize all the materials you decide to use in your speech into a logical sequence that facilitates the communication of your message.

Third Landing: Presentation Practice and Delivery

You complete a series of tasks to reach the third landing of the speech-making staircase. Each task helps you to deliver your speech as effectively as possible. First, you rehearse your presentation, taking pains to revise it during the rehearsal process as needed. Your ultimate goal is to deliver a presentation that flows, has maximum impact, and is readily comprehensible. You should also anticipate and prepare for questions audience members may ask and reactions they may have. You can then focus the energy produced by any anxiety you may be experiencing and put it to work for you during the actual delivery of your speech.

Fourth Landing: Postpresentation Analysis

After delivering your speech, compare and contrast your expectations with what you actually experienced during the delivery of your speech.

Effective speakers critique their performances. They know that they and their receivers will be changed in some way by every speech event; they know that their words, once spoken, leave an indelible impression, and they want to be certain that they learn as much as possible from the experience so that they can apply the lessons learned to the next speech.

The speech-making staircase is one you will climb again and again, working your way from one speech experience to the next. In time, you will master the ins and outs of public speaking. Answering questions such as the following can help prepare you to work your way systematically through the speech-making process:

> There is just no way around it—you have to do your homework. A speaker may be very well informed, but if he hasn't thought out exactly what he wants to say today, to this audience, he has no business taking up other people's valuable time.
>
> —Lee Iacocca,
> *Iacocca: An Autobiography*

Review, Reflect, & Apply

Recall

List the four stages involved in preparing and presenting a speech.

Understanding

Consider the first stage of the speech maker's ladder, and explain how you might go about analyzing an audience.

Apply

Using your peers as an example, identify the interests, needs, and knowledge of your audience.

What kind of presentation are you going to make? _____

What will be its central message? _____

Why are you giving it? _____

Where and when will you deliver it? _____

How much time will you have? _____

Who and how many people will be in your audience? _____

How much do audience members know about your topic? _____

What do you want your audience to think, do, feel, or remember? _____

What are your speech-making goals? _____

What will you do to capture the audience's attention? _____

What will you include in the presentation's body? _____

How will you close? _____

Let us continue our climb up the ladder together.

For the remainder of this chapter, we look more specifically at the steps involved in ascending to the first landing, topic selection and audience analysis, beginning with your need to analyze yourself.

Analyze Yourself

Thorough self-analysis is a prerequisite for effective speech making. Although at times topics may be assigned, under many circumstances the choice will be left to you, the speaker. Even when a topic is specified, it is recommended that you conduct a self-analysis to help you uncover aspects that you may find particularly interesting or appealing. Such an analysis can also become the basis for personal stories or anecdotes that can eventually be integrated into your presentation.

There are more topics for speeches than you could possibly exhaust in a lifetime. According to Elie Wiesel, holocaust survivor and Nobel Prize winner, "I don't know what to say," is an all-too-familiar lament:

> But where was I to start? The world is so vast, I shall start with the country I know best, my own. But my country is so very large. I had better start with my town. But my town, too, is large, I had best start with my street. No: my home. No: my family. Never mind, I shall start with myself.[7]

At the outset of your preparation, you should take some time for what corporate trainers call a front-end analysis—a preliminary examination of possibilities. The following sections describe four useful forms that a front-end analysis can take.

REVIEW YOUR LIFE: YOUR AUTOBIOGRAPHY

You can begin by reviewing your life in terms of potential topics:

1. Divide your life (thus far) into thirds: early, middle, more recent. Compose one sentence to sum up what your life consisted of during each segment (for example, "I lived in Gary, Indiana, with my two brothers and mother, and went to elementary school").

LO3

Explain why conducting a thorough self-analysis facilitates the speech-making process.

Speech . . . preserves contact—it is silence which isolates.

—Thomas Mann

From the Listener's Point of View

1. Describe the behaviors exhibited by the most effective speaker you have had the good fortune to hear.

2. Contrast that description with a description of the most ineffective speaker you ever had the misfortune to hear.

2. Under each summary statement, identify your main interests and concerns at that time of your life.

3. Examine the interests and concerns you listed. Which of them recur? Which have you left behind? Which have you developed only recently?

CONSIDER THE MOMENT: THIS MOMENT

A second approach is to consider this very moment as a source of potential topics:

1. On the left side of a sheet of paper, list sensory experiences; that is, list everything you are able to see, hear, taste, smell, or touch from your present vantage point.

2. When you have listed 10 to 15 items, go back over the list and note topics that might be suggested by each observation or experience. Arrange these in a corresponding list on the right side of the paper. For example, if you list "passing train" in the left column, you might enter "mass transportation" in the right column. Note: If you are not satisfied with the topics you have identified, move to another location and begin the process again.

SEARCH THE NEWS: NEWSPAPERS, NIGHTLY NEWS, AND NEWSMAGAZINE SHOWS

A third approach is to work with a newspaper to find potential topics:

1. Take today's newspaper and, beginning with the front page, read a story and compile a list of topics suggested by it.

2. Do not prejudge your ideas. Simply work your way through the paper, looking for possibilities. For example, the April 26, 2011, issue of *The Wall Street Journal* featured an article on how authors of novels are turning to product placement to help fund publishing costs.[8] Imagine the possible speech topics that this article could suggest: how product placement works, the current uses of product placement in film and other entertainment media, the ethics of product placement, or the relationship between product placement and other forms of advertising.

A variation on this approach calls on you to view a nightly local or national news broadcast or newsmagazine program with pen and paper in hand. Divide the paper into two columns. Label the first column "Stories Presented." Label the second column "Ideas Generated by This News Story." Work your way through the program, looking for possibilities. The same methodology will work for newsmagazine programs such as *60 Minutes, 20/20,* and *Nightline.*

USE TECHNOLOGY

Explore online sites such as About.com, Quamut.com, eHow.com, ExpertVillage.com, Squidoo.com, and YouTube.com to find examples of presentations on a vast array of subjects, from the basics of football, to how to make sushi, to how to do your hair like a rock star, and on and on. Such sites are likely to include advice from both experts and amateurs.

A number of other Web sites can also help with topic generation. Try using the following topic generators:

www.speech-topic-help.com

www.tallmania.com/topicgenerator/topicgenerator.htm

Review, Reflect, & **Apply**

Recall

Identify four approaches to conducting a self-analysis in preparation for giving a speech.

Apply

Choose two of the four approaches to generate possible speech topic ideas.

Analyze

Compare both approaches and describe the degree to which they were helpful in generating ideas.

Analyze Your Audience

Having conducted a search of yourself, it is now time to determine where your audience fits in. A pitfall for many speakers is speaking to please themselves—approaching speech making with only their own interests and their own points of view in mind and neglecting the needs and interests of their audience. These speakers will often choose an inappropriate topic, dress improperly, or deliver a presentation that is either too simple or too technical for the audience. We have all heard medical experts address general audiences using such complex language that their listeners were baffled and bored. We have also heard speakers address highly educated groups in such simple language and about such mundane topics that everyone was not only bored but insulted. There is a catchy acronym for describing speeches that bore or confuse audience members; it is **MYGLO,** for "my eyes glaze over"—which is exactly what happens when you lose the audience's attention.[9]

LO4

Analyze your audience and tailor your speech to them.

MYGLO
an acronym for "my eyes glaze over"

Poor preparation may cause audience members to stop paying attention—a direct result of MYGLO—"my eyes glaze over."

Ethics & Communication

The Magic Bullet of Speech Making

What is the magic bullet of speech making? Practitioners and consultants offer varied answers to this question. One analyst says that to deduce the answer, listen to and view masters of speech making such as Winston Churchill and Martin Luther King Jr. on YouTube.[10] Another believes the answer lies in embodying both style and substance, that leadership and communication go hand-in-hand.[11] A third, Roger Ailes, president of Fox News, writes that the magic bullet of communication is being likable: "With it, your audience will forgive just about everything else you do wrong. Without it, you can hit every bull's eye in the room, and no one will be impressed."[12]

What do you think the magic bullet is? Is it being emotionally involving, likable, or something else? Is being able to emotionally arouse receivers more or less important than having something significant to say? Should it be? Is being likable more or less important than giving receivers information they need to have but may not enjoy hearing? Should it be? What happens when you have something significant or necessary to say but you fall short when it comes to involving receivers or motivating them to like you? What hurdles does a speaker whom you dislike have to overcome or who fails to involve you emotionally have to overcome?

Your focus during the initial stages of speech preparation should not, therefore, be solely on yourself. Be prepared to consider a potential topic from the point of view of your audience. Just as you bring your own background and experiences to a presentation, the audience members will bring theirs. Thus, it is important to consider what your listeners are thinking about, what their needs and hopes are.

To pay proper attention to your audience, you must know something about it. For example, how familiar are the audience members with what you are going to talk about? What is their attitude toward your topic? What are they anxious about? What would they like to know? What are their expectations? If you do not find out the answers to questions like these, you run the risk of having your words fall on deaf ears. Unfortunately, of all the steps in the process of public speaking, audience analysis is most often overlooked.

BEGINNING YOUR AUDIENCE ANALYSIS: WHO ARE THEY?

Of the three elements in speech making—speaker, subject, and person addressed—it is the last one, the hearer, that determines the speech's end and object.

—Aristotle

How can you know, or how can you try to determine, precisely who will attend your presentation? For example, can you expect certain interested groups or individuals to come? Will others whom you do not expect surprise you by showing up?

Information about your audience should come from two key sources: (1) your personal experience with the group and (2) original research.

Personal Experience

The best source of information about your audience is your personal experience with the group—either as a speaker or as an audience member. If you have attended several functions or are a member of the class or organization you are expected to address, you have personal knowledge of the audience members. Thus, you will probably be able to formulate reasonably accurate predictions about the appropriateness of your material for that group.

Research

What if you have had no previous contact with the group you are to address? If that is the case, you might ask the program planner to provide you with relevant information. For instance, if you have been asked to speak at a professional convention, you would be concerned with specific information about the makeup of the audience: How many will attend the lecture? Will there be students present? These and other factors would have to be taken into account in preparing and customizing the presentation.

Speakers sometimes access the Internet to discover how to reach an audience.

Another way to gather information about a group is to obtain copies of public relations material. Recent news releases highlighting the organization may help put you on the same track as your audience. Corporate newsletters and Web sites can also be valuable, as can a trip to the local library for information describing the organization.

The library and the Internet also hold clues to the backgrounds and interests of potential audience members. You can use these resources to discover what local, regional, and national opinion polls reveal about the views potential audience members might have on a variety of social and political issues.

To further enhance your knowledge, you might also directly survey potential receivers. You can use the results of a well-thought-out questionnaire to help estimate how much your listeners already know about your subject and their attitudes toward it. Questionnaires usually contain the following types of questions: closed ended, scaled, and open ended. Closed-ended questions are highly structured, requiring respondents only to indicate which of the provided responses most accurately reflects their own. The following are examples of closed-ended questions:

Please indicate your marital status:

❑ married ❑ single ❑ divorced ❑ widowed ❑ separated

Do you think prayer should be permitted in public schools?

❑ yes ❑ no ❑ undecided

In contrast, scaled questions allow respondents to indicate their views along a continuum ranging by degree from polar extremes such as strongly agree to strongly disagree. The following is a scaled question:

To what extent do you agree or disagree with the following statement? Condoms should be dispensed in public high schools.

Strongly agree　　Agree　　Neutral　　Disagree　　Strongly disagree

Open-ended questions allow respondents even more answering freedom. For example:

Respond to this statement: A politician's private life is not the public's business.

Original research also takes the form of direct discussions with members of the potential audience.

Robert Orben, a speech consultant and writer for former president Gerald Ford, tells the following story.[13] A presidential address had been planned for a college campus in Minnesota. The speechwriters knew that many of the students were not supporters of the president. They therefore spent a great deal of time on the telephone with students and school officials in an effort to obtain specific bits of information that could be included in the speech to help create a bond between the president and his audience. Finally, a somewhat disgruntled student provided the writers with the "gem" they felt they needed. They completed the speech, confident that they had done their job well—and they had. Ford began his address by saying, "Washington may have the new subway, Montreal may have the monorail, but this campus has the Quickie!" The students in the audience laughed and applauded warmly. Why? The drinking age was 21 in Minnesota but 18 in a neighboring state. And the 15-mile trip students often took to get to the first bar across the state line was known as "the Quickie." In this instance, talking at length to potential members of the audience provided information that helped establish an atmosphere in which the listeners, although not necessarily in agreement with the speaker, were at least rendered friendly enough to listen to his views.

DEMOGRAPHICS OF AUDIENCES: WHAT ARE THEY LIKE?

Since the background and composition of your audience are important factors to consider in planning a speech, every effort must be made to determine audience demographics: age, gender, family orientation, religion, cultural background, occupation, socioeconomic status, educational level, and additional factors (such as membership in organizations). Despite the fact that no one audience will be entirely uniform in all these categories, you should consider each one during your initial planning sessions.

Age

Would you give precisely the same presentation to a group of children that you would give to your class? Almost certainly not. How might your presentations differ? Could you even deal with the same subject? The adult students would bring many more years of experience to your presentation than the children would. Adults may have been through economic hassles and even a war, for instance—experiences that children probably have not yet faced. Of course, the maturity of the two audiences would also differ. These contrasts may seem obvious, but age is a factor often overlooked in planning speeches. You might choose to speak on abortion or birth control to a college audience, but you might fail to realize that the same material would probably have less intrinsic appeal to an audience of senior citizens.

It's also wise to consider how your own age will affect your presentation. How close are you to the mean, or average, age of your anticipated listeners? If you are about the same age as the audience members, your job may be a little easier. If you are much older or much younger than the audience members, you will need to attempt to see your topic through their eyes and adjust it accordingly.

Your goal is to be sensitive to the references you employ, the language you use, and the rate at which you speak so that you shrink rather than enlarge the age gap that may exist between you and your receivers. Only if the receivers are able to comprehend your words, identify with your examples and illustrations, and recognize the persons and events you refer to will they be in a position to respond as you hope. When you close whatever age gap exists, you increase the likelihood of audience understanding. The point is that the average age of your audience matters. Research shows that, while younger listeners are more open to new ideas,

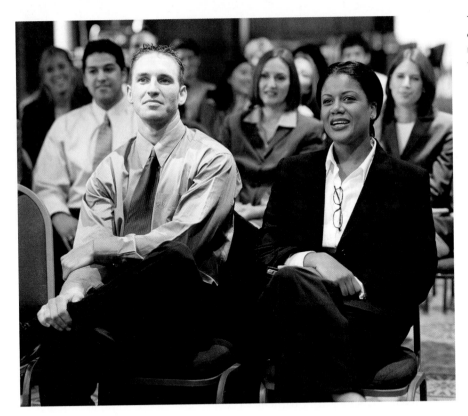

The background and composition of the audience need to be taken into account when planning a speech.

older ones are less receptive to change. You can use information like this to judge how difficult it will be for you to attain your speech-making goal.[14]

Gender

Gender can also influence an audience's reaction to your speech. There are, admittedly, some myths and misconceptions about the effects of gender. (For example, in the past, researchers believed that women could be more easily persuaded than men.[15] Do you think this is a valid viewpoint today?) Still, you need to consider gender differences, especially if you speak to an audience composed entirely or mainly of one sex. Study your potential audience before drawing any conclusions. Although the same topics may appeal to both men and women, gender may affect the ways male and female audience members respond. For example, a discussion of rape may elicit a stronger emotional reaction from the women in your class, whereas a discussion of vasectomy may elicit a stronger response from the men. Be aware, though, that the so-called traditional roles of men and women are changing and that stereotypes once attributed to both groups are crumbling.

Family Orientation

Are most of the members of your audience single? Married? Divorced? Widowed? From one-parent or two-parent homes? These factors might influence your audience's reactions to your presentation. The concerns of one group are not necessarily the concerns of another.

Religion

If you are speaking to a religious group with which you have little familiarity, make a point of discussing your topic in advance with some group members. Some groups have formulated very clear guidelines regarding issues such as divorce, birth control, and abortion. It is important for you to understand the audience and its feelings if you are to be able to relate effectively to its members.

Cultural Background

Use your knowledge of an audience's culture and mind-set to bond with listeners. Because our society is increasingly multicultural, it is very important that you attune yourself to beliefs audience members hold, perhaps seeking sources and interviewing experts with different cultural orientations to ensure your speech accurately reflects a diversity of thinking rather than one knowledge system.[16] Your analysis of receivers will also influence your speech's style. For example, receivers from low-context cultures expect a speaker to explicitly explain his or her message, while persons from high-context cultures prefer more indirection. So, as you plan your speech, keep cultural preferences in mind. By identifying racial, ethnic, religious, or cultural differences, you can prevent potential misunderstandings. Being aware of audience makeup helps you predict how audience members will respond to your topic or the position you are advocating. Take time to consider how the presence or absence of receiver diversity might influence how receivers react to you and your speech.

Occupation

People are interested in issues that relate to their own work and the work of those important to them. Consequently, if possible, relate your subject to the occupational concerns of your audience. Also, if you are speaking before an audience whose members belong to a particular occupational group, you must attempt to find or create examples and illustrations that reflect their concerns.

Socioeconomic Status

Researchers have found that there are psychological as well as economic differences among different socioeconomic classes. Having or lacking discretionary income, power, and prestige evidently influences our attitudes and beliefs. Since our society is socially mobile, with a "move-up" philosophy, as a speaker, you can usually assume that your audience members want to get ahead and improve their position in life, and you can adjust your presentation to appeal to that desire.

Educational Level

Although it is important to determine your listeners' educational level, you cannot let your findings trap you into making unwarranted assumptions—either positive or negative—regarding their intellectual ability. Still, in general, you will probably find that the higher people's level of education, the more general their knowledge and the more insightful their questions. In addition, the more knowledgeable members of your audience may have specific data to dispute your stand on controversial issues. An educated and sophisticated audience may be far more aware of the impact of various political and social programs than, say, a group of high school dropouts. A less educated audience may need background information that a more educated audience may consider superfluous.

Whatever the educational level of your listeners, the following are three precepts to keep in mind:

1. Don't underestimate the intelligence of your listeners; don't speak down to them.

2. Don't overestimate their need for information; don't try to do too much in the time that is available to you.

3. Don't use jargon if there's a chance that your listeners are unfamiliar with it; listeners will quickly tune out what they don't understand.

Additional Factors

You may find that you need to consider several additional variables as you prepare your presentation. For example, if your audience is your class, do class members belong to a particular campus organization? Do members of the class involve themselves in any particular types of projects? Do the interests of the class relate in any way to your speech? Do class members have any identifiable goals, fears, frustrations, loves, or hates that could be tied in? How has their environment influenced their perception of key issues?

When delivering a toast, what should you know about receivers?

Summary

If used wisely, your knowledge of audience demographics can help you achieve your purpose as a speech maker. It can permit you to draw inferences about the predispositions of audience members and their probable responses to your presentation.

ATTITUDES OF AUDIENCES: WHAT DO THEY CARE ABOUT?

Once you have considered audience demographics, your next step is to try to predict the attitudes your listeners will have toward you and toward your presentation. You should consider whether or not the audience members are required to attend, whether the audience is homogeneous or heterogeneous, and whether the audience members favor your stand or are actively opposed to it.[17]

Motivation: Is Attendance Optional or Required?

People may attend a presentation because they want to (that is, they do so willingly), because they have to (they are required to do so), or simply because they are curious. You might attend a town council meeting because a proposed increase in property taxes is being considered, or you might attend a parents' meeting at school out of a sense of duty or because your spouse insisted that you go.

Try to rate your audience on the following scale with respect to audience members' overall motivation:

Required to attend   1   2   3   4   5   Strongly desire to attend

Since the audience's willingness to attend can affect how your presentation is received, it is important to make an educated guess regarding its probable level of enthusiasm. (Of course, it is also important to remember that audience members will not necessarily agree with what you have to say just because they want to attend your talk.)

Values: Is the Audience Homogeneous or Heterogeneous?

A second factor for consideration is the degree of homogeneity—that is, the extent to which everyone in the audience has similar values and attitudes. Of course, it is easier to address a homogeneous audience than a heterogeneous one. In addressing heterogeneous groups, speakers need to vary their appeals to ensure that all segments of the audience spectrum are considered.

Use the following scale to measure the extent to which the members of your audience share similar characteristics and values:

Homogeneous   1   2   3   4   5   Heterogeneous

Level of Agreement: Does the Audience Agree with Your Position?

We like to hear what makes us feel comfortable and self-assured. Yet this is exactly what we have no need of hearing; only those who disturb us can improve us.

—Sydney J. Harris

Whatever your topic, you must attempt to predict your audience members' reaction to the stance you take. For example, they may oppose you, they may support you, or they may be neutral or uninterested. The accuracy of your prediction will determine to some extent how your presentation is received.

Use the following scale to help you assess your audience's position in terms of its similarity or dissimilarity to your own:

Agrees with me   1   2   3   4   5   Disagrees with me

Your objective when speaking to an audience that agrees with your position is to maintain its support. Your objective when speaking to a neutral audience is to gain your listeners' attention and show them how your presentation can be of value to them. When facing an audience that disagrees with you, you need to be especially careful and diplomatic in your approach. In this case, your objective is to change your listeners' minds—to move the audience closer to the "agrees with me" side of the continuum. This task becomes easier if you establish a common ground with audience members—that is, if you first stress values and interests that you share. Keep in mind that your goal is to increase the likelihood that a voluntary audience will attend to your message and that a captive audience will give you a fair hearing.

Level of Commitment: How Much Do They Care?

Finally, you need to consider how much the audience members care about your topic. Is it very important to them? Do they feel strongly enough to be moved to action? Or are your concerns irrelevant to your listeners?

Use the following scale to represent your audience's commitment:

Passive   1   2   3   4   5   Active

Together, the four attitudinal scales will indicate how much background and motivational material you need to include in your presentation.

PREDICTING THE AUDIENCE'S REACTION

Once you have completed your audience research, you will be in a position to predict your listeners' reception of any topic you select. Consider the following questions:

1. What do the audience members now know about my topic?

2. To what extent are they interested in my topic?

3. What are their current attitudes toward this topic?

As you develop your presentation, you must keep in mind the audience's knowledge of, interest in, and attitude toward the subject matter. These important factors will help you select and shape material specifically for the audience members. If you have been unsuccessful at gathering information about how your audience feels about your topic, you may find it helpful to take the pulse of public opinion, in general, by familiarizing yourself with the results of several public opinion polls on your chosen subject. Log on to a Web site that features public opinion polls, such as www.gallup.com or www.washingtonpost.com, and www.norc.uchicago.edu (The National Opinion Research Center) in an effort to get information you need. These are well-known and respected polling organizations that conduct polls on a broad array of topics, from attitudes toward the presidency and government to attitudes toward the trustworthiness of the press and the military.

In addition to focusing on yourself and your receivers, whenever you give a speech, you should also have a clear idea of the nature of the speech-making occasion and how your topic relates to it. Both the occasion and your subject will affect the way you develop your presentation, stage it, and deliver it. We focus on these considerations next.

Review, Reflect, & **Apply**

Recall
Identify key sources for researching your audience.

Understand
Explain how analyzing audience demographics and attitudes can help you prepare your speech.

Analyze
Explain how the age demographic of your audience would affect your approach to choosing a topic.

Consider the Occasion

If asked to speak before a group—including your own class—your first response might well be "Why? What's the occasion?" Identifying the occasion and your role in it is also an essential step in the process of preparing a speech. Fortunately, much, if not all, of what you need to know about the occasion is relatively easy to determine. Essentially, only the following need to be specified:

LO5

Explain how the nature of the occasion influences a speech.

  date and time of the presentation

  length of the presentation

  location of the presentation

  nature of the occasion

  size of the audience

DATE AND TIME: WHEN AND HOW LONG?

Date and time are the most obvious—and among the most important—bits of information you need to acquire. On some occasions, student speakers and professional speakers have arrived an hour early, an hour late, and even a day early or a day late.

Timing can influence a speaker's effectiveness. For example, one well-known speaker arrived late at a New York college and found a hostile audience that had waited nearly an hour. Some professional speakers schedule their engagements so close together—two or three a day—that they must rush out the door rudely, almost before they have completed their talks. In a situation like that, the audience may react angrily.

The length of the presentation can also influence its effectiveness. For instance, one student speaker was supposed to deliver a 10-minute informative speech, "The History of the Corvette." Although it was suggested that he limit his consideration of the topic to two or three major model changes, he attempted to discuss every minute body and grill alteration in the Chevrolet Corvette from 1954 to the present. The instructor made several attempts to stop him, but 40 minutes into the speech he was still going strong. At this point, the instructor announced a class break. The student responded, "That's fine. I'll just continue." And he did—although the majority of his audience had departed.

Are you able to plan a presentation to ensure that you will not run over or under your time limit?

LOCATION AND PARTICIPANTS: WHERE AND WHO?

Reminding yourself of the location of your presentation and of the people directly connected with it is an important aspect of preparing a speech. This may seem obvious, but it is sometimes neglected, with absurd and embarrassing results. For example, at a speech by a world-famous psychologist whose audience consisted of members of the host college and the surrounding community, early in his speech, the eminent Dr. M_____ mumbled what seemed to be the name of another college, although most of his listeners failed to notice. The second time, however, he clearly announced how happy he was to be at X_____, mentioning the wrong college again. (Doubly unfortunate was the fact that college X was a rival of the host college.) By then, some members of the audience appeared embarrassed for the speaker, and others appeared hostile. The third time, the psychologist mentioned not only the wrong school but the wrong town as well. At this point, there was sufficient commotion in the audience for him to realize his error, and in evident confusion he turned to the college president to ask where he was.

How can you avoid such a problem? The minister who officiated at this book's authors' marriage had a possible solution. During the wedding rehearsal, a page in his Bible was marked with a paper clip that held a slip of paper, and later we asked him about it. The minister showed us that it had our names clearly written on it. He explained that, because he was somewhat nervous when conducting a wedding, he frequently tended to forget the names of the bride and groom, even if they had belonged to the congregation for years. The slip of paper provided an unobtrusive reminder. Taking our cue from this experience, we now attach a slip of paper to the first page of our notes whenever we address a group. The slip bears the name of the organization, its location, the name of the person introducing us, the names of the officers, and other important information. Thus, we have at our disposal the data we need, to be integrated as appropriate. You may also want to adopt this simple procedure to avoid unnecessary embarrassment or loss of credibility.

TYPE OF OCCASION: WHY AND HOW MANY?

Why have you been asked to speak? Although every occasion is unique, you can ask some general questions to clarify the situation in your own mind. For example, is it a class session? Right now it probably is, but in the future it could

Speakers need to be prepared to address sales meetings and management planning sessions.

well be a sales meeting, a management planning session, a convention, or a funeral. Is your presentation part of the observance of a special event? For example, is the occasion in honor of a retirement? A promotion? Is it some other type of recognition? Who else, if anyone, will be sharing the program with you? Factors like these can affect the nature of your presentation. An appropriate topic for a retirement party, for instance, might be considered inappropriate for a more formal occasion. Similarly, a speech delivered at a celebratory luncheon will have a different tone than a speech delivered on Memorial Day to honor fallen soldiers. What is important to remember is that the occasion for your speech influences audience expectations.

Speakers also need to consider how large or small their audience will be. Determining how many people will show up to listen to any particular presentation is difficult. In a classroom situation, for example, on one day the room may be filled, but on another day a speaker may arrive and find that a number of students are out sick or off on a special project for another course. The same problem confronts the professional speaker. It is a good idea to multiply and divide the sponsor's estimate by 2. Thus, you can be prepared to speak to a small group—that is, possibly 20—if 40 are expected—or to a large group—possibly 100—if 50 is the estimate.

Since you are not likely to have an advance person at your disposal when preparing to deliver your presentation—at least not yet—you must do all the advance thinking for yourself. Make it a habit to complete an analysis of both your audience and the occasion before completing work on any presentation. The predictions you make will serve you well as you continue preparing your speech.

Review, Reflect, & Apply

Recall
Identify the factors you should consider regarding the occasion for a speech.

Understand
Summarize the specific criteria by which you would evaluate your ideas for a topic.

Evaluate
Using this criteria, create two lists: one of topics you would consider worthwhile and of interest, and another you would not.

Select Your Subject Area

Carefully examine the list of possible topics you generated thus far. To continue preparing your speech without having selected a subject—on the basis of self-analysis, audience analysis, and occasion analysis—would be like trying to buy an airline ticket without knowing your destination. During this examination, you evaluate your ideas according to specific criteria: (1) apparent worth, (2) appropriateness, (3) interest, and (4) availability of material. When you keep these criteria in mind, selecting a topic will be easier—if only because few of your choices will meet each of the criteria equally well with regard to the needs of particular audiences.[18]

IS THE TOPIC WORTHWHILE?

You need to determine if the topic is important to you and to the people who will listen to you. Many speakers—including college students and businesspeople—often fall into the trap of choosing topics that are of little value to the audience. One of the authors recalls a time in a military training institute when he heard one colonel tell another, "After 25 years as an officer, I'm expected to waste my time hearing how to inspect a fork!" To that audience of high-ranking officers, the topic "Fork Inspection Techniques" was clearly trivial. You may also find that some topics chosen by others are trivial from your perspective. They may be so commonplace—how to set a table, for example—that they do not merit the time and energy you must expend in listening to them. Many subjects that are acceptable for interpersonal discourse may be inconsequential when presented in a public setting where the speaker's purpose is to inform or persuade. Which topics do you judge to be worth your time? Which, in your opinion, are unworthy of consideration?

IS THE TOPIC APPROPRIATE?

We have already discussed how important it is to determine if a topic is appropriate to you and your personal interests. Two additional facets of this criterion must also be considered: (1) Is the topic appropriate to the audience? (2) Is it appropriate to the occasion? Let's examine each in turn.

By this time, you should have developed an audience profile. That is, you have either determined precisely or made educated guesses about the age, gender, and educational level of the majority of the people who are going to hear your speech. It then becomes imperative for you to ask which of your possible topics is most appropriate for such a mix of people. Sometimes this determination is easy. For instance, you would not ordinarily give a talk about the evils of television to a group of network representatives. Nor, ordinarily, would you opt to speak on the advantages of a women's college to an audience already attending a women's college. Every subject area must be seen through the eyes of its intended audience. Just as an automobile is customized for a particular owner, so a subject area must be customized to reflect the needs of a particular group of listeners. Just as the automobile is painted, detailed, and upholstered with an owner or a type of owner in mind, so you as a speaker must "outfit" your topic to appeal to the audience members you hope to reach. This takes work, but it can be done.

The appropriateness of the topic to the occasion must also be considered. For example, you can probably think of any number of occasions on which a humorous topic would be ill-conceived. Can you think of occasions when a humorous topic would be an asset?

IS THE TOPIC INTERESTING?

Speech makers often make the mistake of selecting topics they think they should speak about rather than topics they want to speak about. Student speakers, for instance, will sometimes turn to a newspaper or newsmagazine and, without further thought, select a story at random as the basis for a speech. One student insisted on talking about labor-management relations. Why? He thought it sounded like an important subject. Unfortunately, he had spent little time in the labor force and no time in management. And because he did not care enough to do much—if any—research, the entire subject remained foreign to him. Not surprisingly, the speech he delivered was dull and disjointed.

John Silverstein, a spokesman for General Dynamics, put it this way: "You need to believe in your idea. This is very important. What a listener often gauges is how convinced the speaker is. If he has lived it, breathed it, and is himself really sold on it, it generally is enough to sell the argument."[19] Of course, selecting a topic that is appealing to you is a personal matter and can be relatively simple, but determining what will interest your audience can be somewhat more challenging.

Here, students have an advantage. As a student, you know your fellow students, and you should be able to identify topics that will interest them. When addressing less familiar audiences, however, you should feel free to return to your audience analysis and make some educated guesses. Determining an audience's interests is a never-ending challenge—one that some unadventurous speech makers prefer not to tackle. One corporate executive, for example, once delivered a speech that was gratifyingly well received. Unfortunately, he then delivered essentially the same speech for the next five years, although times and needs kept changing. Needless to say, his current audiences are not interested in his topic. Topics must be updated to match the moods, needs, and concerns of listeners; only by updating can you ensure that your topic treats an issue of interest to your audience.

When considering the interests of your audience members, ask yourself how your subject relates to them. Ask yourself what they stand to gain from listening to you. Create an inventory for each of your possible subjects. If you are unable to identify significant ways your audience will benefit from hearing about a topic, there is good reason for you not to speak on that topic.

IS SUFFICIENT RESEARCH MATERIAL AVAILABLE?

Before choosing a topic, be certain that material on the subject exists and that you can find it readily—on the Internet, in a library, or somewhere else. Many speakers fall into the trap of requesting material that is unavailable in a school or local library, only to have it arrive too late or turn out to be unpromising. Such an experience can cause last-minute panic, and the result is an inadequately prepared speech maker and an inadequate presentation. Avoid this pitfall by giving careful attention to your library and other nearby sources during the selection phase of your preparation.

Review, Reflect, & **Apply**

Recall

Summarize the criteria to use when choosing a speech topic.

Evaluate

Select a topic and demonstrate how it meets the following criteria: apparent worth, appropriateness, interest, and availability of material.

Narrow the Topic and Clarify Your Purpose

LO7

Narrow your topic and formulate a thesis statement.

It is essential to consider how much time is available for your speech. For example, an army chaplain more than once demonstrated how adept he was at handling time constraints. The chaplain's job was to address groups of recruits during basic training, and on each occasion he was given only three minutes to get his message across. One day his objective was to persuade soldiers not to use foul language. (It was his belief that such a practice degraded both individuals and the service.) Realizing that he could accomplish only so much in the time permitted, he chose to focus on a single word—the particular word that he found most offensive. During his three-minute talk, he suggested that the troops avoid using just that one term. By doing this, the chaplain demonstrated that he understood how important it is to narrow a topic to manageable proportions and, incidentally, succeeded in realizing his objective. (After his speech, the abused word was heard much less frequently around the base.)

Far too many speakers attempt to give audiences "the world" in five minutes. It is essential to narrow your topic to fit the constraints imposed by the situation. Do not try to take on too much. Five minutes is not sufficient time to discuss the history of Russia, the industrial revolution, or even pedigreed dogs.

There is a strategy you can use to avoid biting off more than you can chew—or talk about. Select a topic and place it at the top of a topic cone. Then subdivide the topic into constituent parts; that is, break it down into smaller and smaller units, as shown in Figure 11.3. The smallest unit should appear on the lowest step of the ladder. This process is like whittling or carving a stick of wood. The more you shave off, the narrower the topic becomes. Like the carver, you decide what shape to give your topic and when to stop shaving.

Let's say that you want to speak on the need to save the rain forest. One way to narrow your topic would be to focus on how indigenous people can save the rain forest. Your topic could be focused even further. You might explore how their harvesting of native plants can stop deforestation or, more specifically, how their harvesting of fruit can help preserve the ecological balance. Here's another example: If you want to talk on the current technology revolution, you might focus on how the use of multimedia has revolutionized education or, more specifically, on how computers are used to teach writing skills.

FIGURE 11.3

Topic Cone Technique for Narrowing a Topic.

FORMULATE A PURPOSE STATEMENT AND BEHAVIORAL OBJECTIVES

Once you have identified a topic and narrowed its scope, reexamine exactly why you are speaking. What is your purpose? What do you hope to accomplish? What kind of response would you like from your audience? What do you want your listeners to think or do as a result of your presentation? What is your ultimate objective?

Most speakers have one of two general objectives when they prepare to deliver a speech: They aim either to inform listeners (to share new information or insights with the audience) or to persuade listeners (to convince audience members to believe in or do something). However, in actual speaking situations, the purpose is not always so clear. Persuasive speeches usually contain informative material, and informative speeches may sometimes include elements of persuasion.

This chapter introduces you to both the informative and the persuasive speech. In Chapters 14 and 15, respectively, we look at each format in greater depth.

The Informative Speech

If your purpose is to inform, your primary responsibility is to relay information to your audience in an interesting, well-organized, and professional manner. Informative speakers may explain something, demonstrate how something functions, or describe how something is structured. When speaking informatively, you hope to provide a learning experience for your listeners, sharing information they did not possess before your talk. In other words, if your main goal is to inform an audience, you must be certain that the data you provide will enhance your listeners' understanding, and you must find ways to help the audience remember what you say.

To ensure that your purpose is clear—initially to yourself and ultimately to your listeners—you will find it helpful to develop a purpose statement. What this means is that you commit to writing a summary of what you want to accomplish; you describe what you hope to do with your speech. The purpose statement of an informative speech often contains such words as *show, explain, report, instruct, describe*, and (not surprisingly) *inform*. The following are examples of purpose statements for various kinds of informative speeches:

To explain how selected Chinese character letters evolved

To describe how a tornado forms

To instruct class members on how to reduce personal debt

To report on the health effects of bisphenol-a or BPA.

Notice that each example takes the form of an infinitive verb phrase; thus, each begins with *to*. Notice also that each statement contains only one idea and that it is written from the speaker's perspective.

Sometimes, in addition to developing a purpose statement, it is helpful to view the speech from the perspective of the listeners. To facilitate this process, you can formulate behavioral objectives. Objectives identify what you want the audience to take away after hearing your presentation; that is, they describe the behavior or response you want the audience to exhibit as a result of listening to your speech. For instance, you may want your listeners to be able to list, explain, summarize, state, or apply certain information. The following are examples of behavioral objectives:

After listening to this speech, the audience will be able to name three kinds of questions that are unlawful in employment interviews.

After listening to this presentation, the audience will be able to discuss the three main reasons college students fail to graduate.

The Persuasive Speech

The same principles used for an informative speech may be applied in formulating a purpose statement and behavioral objectives for a persuasive speech. In a persuasive speech, your main goal is to reinforce or change an audience's beliefs or to make the

Subject Evaluation

Answer each of the following questions about your subject by awarding yourself a score from 1 to 10, where 1 represents "poor" and 10 represents "excellent." The highest score is 100.

1. Is your subject worthwhile?

    _____ From your perspective?

    _____ From your audience's perspective?

2. Is your subject appropriate?

    _____ From your perspective?

    _____ From your audience's perspective?

3. Is your subject interesting?

    _____ From your perspective?

    _____ From your audience's perspective?

4. Is sufficient information available?

    _____ Information exists.

    _____ Information can be obtained in time.

5. Have you narrowed your topic to fit the situation? _____

6. What is your overall assessment of your preparation at this time? _____

TOTAL SCORE _____

audience behave in a certain way. The words *convince, persuade, motivate,* and *act* commonly turn up in purpose statements for persuasive speeches. The following are some examples:

> To motivate listeners to contribute money to the American Cancer Society

> To persuade class members to become actively involved in the conservation of global resources

> To convince class members that racist speech should be exempt from First Amendment protection

With regard to behavioral objectives, you might want your audience to support a plan or take an overt action. The following are examples of behavioral objectives:

> After listening to my presentation, audience members will write their representatives, asking them to seek legislation requiring an increase in student loan programs.

> After listening to my presentation, students will sign up to will their eyes to an eye bank.

> After listening to my speech, students will boycott stores that sell products made using child labor.

In summary, formulating precise purpose statements and behavioral objectives makes good sense. Both can help you focus your efforts and clarify your goals.

FORMULATE THE THESIS STATEMENT

In recent years, public speaking theorists have begun to look more closely at guidelines for writing. As a result, speakers are now often encouraged to develop theses for their speeches, just as writers do for papers. A thesis simply divides a topic into its major components. Thus, once you have formulated a specific purpose, the next step is to prepare a declarative sentence that summarizes the thesis of your speech. When your speech is an informative one and not intended to persuade, the thesis statement is phrased in a relatively objective and neutral manner and is sometimes referred to as the central idea or topic statement of your speech. Its focus is on what you want audience members to understand or learn—for example, "Nuclear power plants have three major parts: the reactor core, vessel, and control rods." When your speech is persuasive, it is simply called the thesis statement or the claim. A thesis for a persuasive speech expresses an arguable opinion or point of view; for example, a thesis for a persuasive speech against the use of nuclear energy plants might be, "Nuclear power plants should be decommissioned." Whether your speech is informative or persuasive, the thesis statement can be a powerful rhetorical device for setting your agenda as a speaker.

The thesis statement is the core idea or bottom line of your speech; it is your speech in a nutshell. It is a statement of the overriding concept of your speech that all the facts, quotations, and ideas in your speech are designed to support. In effect, the specific statement is the steering wheel of your speech; it directs the course of your speech and determines the content in it. The thesis helps you derive the main ideas or major propositions your speech will explore. Everything you say should support the thesis. In and of itself, the thesis statement does not present all the information you will offer in your speech; instead, it efficiently focuses that information into a brief summarizing statement.

An effective thesis statement fulfills three guidelines. First, it is a single sentence that conveys the essence of the speech. Second, it focuses the attention of the audience members on what they should know, do, or feel after experiencing your speech. Third, it supports the specific purpose. The following are examples:

Thesis: Sleep deprivation costs business billions of dollars a year in employee accidents and avoidable mistakes.

Thesis: Criminalizing eating when driving will decrease accidents and save lives.

Thesis: Getting a good night's sleep will enhance your personal and professional life in four key ways.

Thesis: Community efforts to censor the books we read are an infringement of our individual right of freedom of expression and will limit our ability to think critically about important issues.

Thesis: Decreases in state funding to colleges will result in cuts in educational programs, extracurricular offerings, and financial aid.

As you can see from these examples, the thesis brings you a step closer to the structure of the speech itself.

Review, Reflect, & **Apply**

Understand

Explain the functions of a topic cone.

Apply

Develop a topic cone that narrows down your idea to a clear objective, or thesis.

Communication Skills

PRACTICE TIPS FOR IMPROVING SPEECH ANALYSIS

Effective speech makers do not approach their task haphazardly. As we have seen, careful thought precedes the actual speech. Every speaker, from novice to professional, can benefit from following these suggestions:

✅ Conduct a Systematic Self-analysis as a Preparation for Speech Making

Take the time you need to survey your own likes, dislikes, and concerns. Effective speakers know themselves well. They know what they care about, and they know what ideas they would like to share with others.

✅ Analyze Your Audience

Effective speakers adapt their ideas to reflect the needs and interests of their listeners. Speeches are delivered with the specific purpose of informing or persuading others—of affecting others in certain specific ways. The degree to which you will succeed is directly related to how well you know your listeners and how accurately you are able to predict their reactions.

✅ Analyze the Occasion

It is essential that you learn why, when, where, and for how long you are expected to speak. Without this information, your preparation will be incomplete and insufficient.

✅ Determine if Your Topic Is Supported by Your Own Interests, Your Audience's Interests, and the Demands of the Occasion

Be certain to evaluate your subject according to the following criteria: Is the topic worthwhile? Is the topic appropriate? Is the topic interesting? Is sufficient research material available?

✅ Narrow and Clarify Your Topic

Ask yourself: Have I sufficiently narrowed my focus? Is my thesis clear?

The Wrap-Up

SUMMARY

LO1 **Define** public speaking and public speaking anxiety and use techniques to assess your confidence and control speech-making anxiety.

Public speaking is the act of preparing, staging, and delivering a presentation to an audience. Anxiety, or fear, affects all speech makers. One of the best ways to cope with speech fright is to plan and rehearse your presentation carefully. In addition, you should learn to recognize the causes of fear, as well as the physical and mental sensations that accompany it, so that you can learn to control your reactions using a variety of techniques including deep muscle relaxing, thought stopping, and visualization. These techniques help eliminate the tension, thoughts, and symptoms associated with fear—the first by eliminating stress, the second by stopping the fear-inducing process, and the third by boosting confidence.

LO2 **Explain** how to approach public speaking systematically.

There is a logical order to speech making that speakers follow: (1) topic selection and audience analysis; (2) speech development, support, and organization, (3) presentation practice and delivery; and (4) postpresentation analysis.

LO3 **Explain** why conducting a thorough self-analysis facilitates the speech-making process.

Self-analysis is a prerequisite for preparing an effective speech. A self-analysis lets you take your interests, strengths, and limitations into account when selecting a topic.

LO4 **Analyze** your audience and tailor your speech to them.

You should conduct demographic and attitudinal analyses of your receivers. By keeping in mind the background, needs, and interests of audience members, and by considering potential topics from their point of view, you focus attention and adopt the speech to the people you hope to reach.

LO5 **Explain** how the nature of the occasion influences a speech.

Identifying the occasion and your role in it is another essential step in speech preparation. Once you determine the date, time limit, and location of the speech, as well as the nature of the occasion, you can continue thinking about a suitable topic.

LO6 **Identify** criteria for topic selection.

You need to carefully examine the list of possible topics generated during self, audience, and occasion analyses in an effort to identify which topics best reflect the following criteria: apparent worth, appropriateness, interest, and availability of material.

LO7 **Narrow** your topic and formulate a thesis statement.

Once you choose your topic, you need to reexamine your purpose for speaking. Most speakers have one of two general objectives when they prepare to deliver a speech: to inform listeners (to share new information or insights) or to persuade listeners (to convince audience members that they should believe or do something). To ensure that your purpose is clear, you should formulate a purpose statement—a summary of what you want to accomplish, expressed as an infinitive phrase. For example, you may want to inform your audience about something, describe something, or explain how something is done. You can also list behavioral objectives—what you want the audience to have internalized after listening to your presentation. The thesis statement is the central idea or claim of your speech. It is your speech in a nutshell. A declarative sentence, the thesis statement directs the course of your speech, helping you determine the main ideas or major propositions your speech will explore.

KEY CHAPTER TERMINOLOGY

communication apprehension 293   public speaking 292
MYGLO 303   public speaking anxiety 293

COMMUNICATING TO THE PUBLIC

Researching, Supporting, and Outlining Your Speech

12

After completing this chapter, you should be able to demonstrate mastery of the following learning outcomes:

LO1 **Research** your speech topic using materials found both on- and offline.

LO2 **Define** and conduct primary research.

LO3 **Explain** how to use various types of support to enhance a presentation.

LO4 **Explain** the speech framework and outlining stages and principles including the identification of main and subordinate ideas.

LO5 **Summarize** the types and features of traditional speech formats and the reasons for using them.

LO6 **Compare** and contrast nontraditional and traditional speech formats.

LO7 **Discuss** characteristics of effective introductions and conclusions.

LO8 **Use** a checklist to evaluate a speech's supporting materials, organizational format, and outline.

Now that you have considered your choice of subject from both your point of view and the point of view of your audience, and you have taken the nature of the speech-making occasion into account, it is time for you to focus on researching, selecting support, choosing an organizational approach, and outlining the speech, the next steps you take on your way up the speech-making staircase (see Figure 12.1). When engaged in research, you investigate your subject, both online and offline. Your research will lead you to an array of supporting materials, including illustrations, statistical evidence, expert opinions, and quotations, to use in your speech. Why are such materials valuable? They answer the questions of audience members. As you

Speech development, support, and organization

Outline your speech.

Select an organizational approach.

Select support.

Research your topic.

FIGURE 12.1

On Your Way to the Halfway Point

Research is the process of going up alleys to see if they are blind.

—Marston Bates

The world is already full of speakers who are too busy to prepare their speeches properly; the world would be better off if they were also too busy to give them.

—William Norwood Brigance

deliver your speech, audience members listen, silently asking themselves: What do you mean? Why should I accept what you say? Why should I care? If you develop your speech with care, being certain to research, support, and organize your ideas, you will make the answers to these questions clear to receivers. Accordingly, once we complete this chapter, we will have climbed to the halfway point of the ladder—speech development, support, and organization. We will then be ready to ascend to the third landing, presentation practice and delivery, and the fourth landing, the postpresentation analysis. Let's continue climbing.

If you are like many people in America today, you are fascinated with crime scene investigation (CSI) television programs and films that demonstrate the painstaking effort that goes into solving crimes. Like forensic pathologists, whose task it is to take nothing for granted and to leave no stone unturned in the search for clues and the analysis of evidence, so the public speaker also needs to investigate a topic carefully in an effort to discover appropriate supporting material with which to build the substance of a speech.

Research Your Topic

LO1

Research your speech topic using materials found both on- and offline.

Like most people, when you want to see a movie or try a new restaurant, you might start by accessing Fandango online. Or you might decide to drive by the theater to see what films appear on its marquee. When it comes to choosing a new restaurant, you might ask your friends for their advice, or review Zagat and restaurant home pages on the Internet. What does this have to do with public speaking? The research we do when preparing to speak in public is much like the personal research we conduct daily. However, because a speech is likely to be shared with others in a somewhat more formal setting, we use a more formal research approach.

Research sources available to you include published works, other people, and of course, yourself. If you are discussing some aspect of sports medicine, for instance, you may rely on your experience of being injured when playing a sport. If your topic has to do with business or technology, you may use examples from your work in an industry that relates directly to your topic. Far too often, speakers fail to realize that they can use their personal experiences to establish credibility and add interesting and pertinent examples.

Basic research is what I am doing when I don't know what I am doing.

—Wernher von Braun

CONDUCT RESEARCH ONLINE AND OFFLINE

Suppose you were going to speak on the role of framing in our society, and you wanted to focus on how both government supporters and dissenters used framing during the waging of the war on terror. Where would you go for information? What sources would you turn to in order to learn what framing is, how it functions, why it is used, what its effects are, and whether it is ethical and/or legal, as well as to find examples of it in action? For example, both adherents of the wars in Iraq and Afghanistan and those opposed to them framed their stories of the wars' successes and failures. Would these stories serve as good examples to use in your speech? Through conducting research, you become able to answer such questions.

Libraries contain information storage and retrieval systems—resources that are invaluable for every type of research. The library is one of the few real bargains left in our society. A huge array of material is available free; other materials and services (those available through a variety of photographic and electronic systems) are yours for only a minimal cost. In addition, every academic and public library has on its staff knowledgeable people who have been trained to aid you with your investigative work. In addition to your college library, you can also consult the following Internet libraries: the Internet Public Library (www.ipl.org), the Library Spot (www.libraryspot.com), and the Reference Desk (www.refdesk.com).

When you begin library research, consult an array of reference sources to compile a preliminary bibliography. Your first stop may well be the library's electronic catalog. Next, you may move on to a variety of newspaper, magazine, and journal indexes. Depending on your subject, you may also consult bibliographical sources, encyclopedias, and almanacs. And you will almost certainly use online searches.

Use the Library's Online Catalogs

In lieu of the card catalog system, now banished from most libraries, today's libraries usually contain a computerized catalog. Libraries, in increasing numbers, now offer computer or online catalogs that enable you to run more productive Boolean searches. When you run a **Boolean search,** instead of needing to know a specific author or title, you can merely enter two or three keywords into the computer and it will search the library's collection for you. No longer do you need to go from card catalog drawer to card catalog drawer, searching for source materials. The computer makes the search process much more efficient.

Boolean search
a keyword search

Use Reference Works

Since magazines, newspapers, and scholarly periodicals may contain information valuable to you, indexes are critical resources. One of the first indexes you will consult will probably be the *Reader's Guide to Periodical Literature*. It can lead you to a variety of popular, mass-distribution magazines, including *Time, Newsweek,* and *U.S. News & World Report*, all of which may contain information relevant to your subject. The *New York Times Index* and the *Wall Street Journal Index* are also high on the list of indexes you should consider. If your topic warrants it, you may also need to explore issues of *Education Index, Psychological Abstracts,* and *Sociological Abstracts*. These sources will offer you leads to articles that have appeared in a number of scholarly journals.

The *World Almanac, Statistical Abstract of the United States,* and *Information Please Almanac* are only three of many such reference works that can provide the speech maker with interesting factual and statistical evidence.

Biographical materials can be located in the *Dictionary of National Biography*, the *Dictionary of American Biography*, and even the *New York Times Obituary Index*. Similarly, *Current Biography* can help you research the lives of contemporary public figures.

Use Online References and Databases

Libraries are user friendly. You can visit yours in person or access it from afar. You also can conduct much of the research for your speech online by using your library's computerized systems when in the library or by using passwords and following logon procedures that give you access when at home or in another more remote location. In preparation for conducting online research, your first step should be to attend a live orientation session in your library or to take an online tutorial. Meet the reference librarian and find out what research databases your college library subscribes to. At the same time, familiarize yourself with the library's electronic catalogs and reference room.

During your research, you will want to consult a variety of online references and databases, including the Reader's Guide to Periodical Literature (www.hwwilson.com), Facts on File (www.fofweb.com), Academic Search Premier (www.ebscohost.com), and LexisNexis (www.lexisnexis.com). Of course, you can also use Google and Google Scholar, popular online databases, or access newspapers such as the *New York Times* and the *Wall Street Journal* online (see Figure 12.2).

Among other databases you may want to consult are ERIC, a comprehensive research system that indexes published and unpublished materials on a wide array of educational topics, and American Statistics Index (ASI).

You may want to consult the online encyclopedia Wikipedia, but be wary of using it as a speech source. Wikipedia may offer a quick basic overview of a subject, but because of its penchant for inaccuracy, many instructors question its validity when it comes to students citing it in research. Many people in higher education simply do not view it as a definitive source.

FIGURE 12.2

Sample Google Search.

SOURCE: Used by permission of Google.

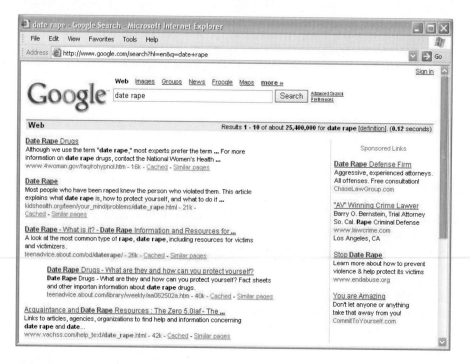

Among the major Internet resources you will want to use when researching your speech are e-mail, newsgroups, and the World Wide Web.

E-Mail You can use e-mail to write to knowledgeable potential sources, a group, or a **listserv,** an e-mail list of several to over hundreds of people who have interest in and knowledge of a particular topic—potentially one that you are researching. Go to Catalist.us, a directory containing information about numerous listservs and whether new members are welcomed, to explore potentially useful listservs. Before joining a listserv, try to identify the types of messages members send and their usefulness to you. Also read the frequently asked questions (FAQ) file so that you do not ask questions that have already been answered.

listserv
an e-mail list of people who have interest in and knowledge of a particular topic

Using e-mail, you can also create a listserv for your class. Once you have one in place, you can use it to ask your potential audience members to fill out questionnaires that reveal their attitudes toward your chosen topic. You can also use the class listserv to seek and receive feedback after your speech.

Newsgroups Newsgroups facilitate the exchange of ideas on a broad array of topics through discussion forums. The Internet contains a multitude of newsgroups, also known as Usenet. In a newsgroup, you can post messages, read the posts of others, and respond to them. Like listservs, newsgroups bring together people interested in sharing ideas about a topic. As with a listserv, before joining a newsgroup, be sure you read through the FAQ file; doing so will ensure you receive maximum benefits from the newsgroup.

You can use binsearch.info or giganews.com to search newsgroups for information on requested topics. Newsgroups that receive news feeds from news services such as the Associated Press are especially useful. You can also use the newsgroup to ask questions and poll people for opinions for a speech.

World Wide Web Almost any kind of content you can find in print is also available on the World Wide Web. You can subscribe to various special interest groups or use a search engine to browse for information on your selected topic. While browsing, you might visit CNN or the Associated Press online, peruse copies of historical documents or the *Congressional Record*. With the Internet, you have easy access to the information that exists on numerous campuses and every continent.[1]

A number of widely used search engines are available, including Google (www.google.com), the most popular search engine; Bing (bing.com), a search engine from Microsoft; Yahoo! (www.yahoo.com), the next most popular; followed in popularity by MSN Search (www.msn.com), AOL Search (www.aolsearch.com), and Ask (www.ask.com).[2] Each of these is a search engine as well as a directory. Other Web sites gaining in popularity are Dogpile (www.dogpile.com), Mamma (www.Mamma.com), Vivisimo (www.vivisimo.com), and Go (www.go.com). Among the most useful metasearch engines, these simultaneously search the databases of an array of search engines.

You can also search for relevant video on the Internet using video search engines such as Google, Blinkx, Truveo, and Fooooo. Google, for example, uses speech recognition technology to create searchable transcripts of videos.[3]

It is possible to predict the Web site addresses of potential sources. When you know an address, or a uniform resource locator (URL), you are able to access the Web site by simply entering it in your Web browser. Corporate Web sites, for example, usually accessed by www.nameofcorporation.com, will provide you with access to annual reports, copies of speeches, and other information. Remember to bookmark your favorite sites to facilitate future access.

While the information contained in traditional research sources, including books, magazines, and journal articles, is typically reviewed and checked by others before being published, virtually anyone can post information in a Web site or to a newsgroup. Thus, verifying and thinking critically about the quality of the information you find online is a serious responsibility. As you decide what and what not to include in your speech from your Web search, ask yourself who a site's sponsor is. For example, CNN, MSNBC, and Fox are established news organizations, and you can weigh the information you find on their sites in the same way as you would weigh the information you use from their cablecasts. The same goes for major newspapers that also operate Web sites. As you evaluate Web-based information from other sources, it is important to determine if the source has an apparent or hidden bias. Ask yourself if postings are specific or general. Do the claims they make seem justifiable? Do not value a source simply because it is published on the Internet. Seek out confirming sources for what you discover.

Your college library most likely also has criteria for you to use when checking the accuracy and validity of online sources. Compare your library's suggestions with the evaluative criteria we offer:

1. Evaluate the author. Who is the author? How credible is she or he to write about your topic?

2. Evaluate the publisher. Who sponsors the site? What does the extension at the end of the site's URL reveal about its sponsor? For example, *.edu* refers to a college or university, *.com* refers to a commercial venture, *.org* tells us the publisher is a nonprofit or trade association, while *.gov* refers to a governmental agency, official, or organization, and *.biz* refers specifically to a business.

3. Evaluate the timeliness of information on the site. When was the site created and last updated?

4. Pursue the links identified on the site. Do they connect you to sources that are credible or questionable? What connections exist between the site and its links?

5. Evaluate the site's purpose. Why does the site exist? Is its primary function to inform, persuade, sell, or entertain? Recall that the end of a site's URL offers clues to its purpose. Sites ending in *.edu* typically having an informational function, *.org*, an advocacy function, and *.com*, a sales function.

6. Determine if the information contained in the site can be confirmed. Compare the site's contents with the contents of other available sources to see if there are any major disagreements or discrepancies.

Review, Reflect, & Apply

Understand

Give some examples of online and offline research.

Analyze

Compare and contrast the nature of investigating a crime scene and researching a speech.

Create

Demonstrate how people on two sides of an issue or from different backgrounds might frame a topic of your choosing.

CONDUCT PRIMARY RESEARCH

LO2

Define and conduct primary research.

Primary research involves the collection of information that does not already exist. It enables you to give your audience members a firsthand report based on (1) your personal observations and experience, (2) informal surveys you conduct, and/or (3) interviews you hold.

Personal Observation and Experience

primary research
collection of information that does not already exist

One of the best ways to research a topic is to examine what you know about it. Search your own background and experiences for materials you might want to integrate into your presentation.

If your topic is one for which direct observation of an event, a person, or a stimulus would be appropriate, then by all means go out and observe. An observational excursion might take you to a biology laboratory, an airport, a supermarket, or a construction site, for example. When conducting a direct observation, be sure to take careful notes. If possible, ask the interviewee's permission to arrive at the location with tape recorder or video recorder in hand. Sit down immediately after the experience and record your thoughts and feelings. File your firsthand notes with the materials gathered during your library research.

Informal Surveys

Developing a reliable scientific survey instrument is complicated. However, informal surveys can provide the speech maker with useful and often entertaining information. Let's say you are investigating the possibility of adding online courses to the curriculum; a survey at your school may produce data you can use. (For instance, you may be able to discover the percentage of students interested in enrolling in such courses.)

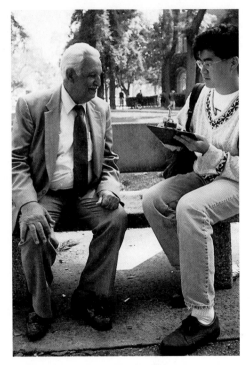

Informal surveys and formal interviews provide a speaker with statistical information, testimonials, and examples to use in his or her speech.

Informal surveys normally consist of no more than 5 to 10 questions. To conduct an informal survey with a prospect, you need to identify yourself first and state the purpose of your survey: "Hello, I'm _____. I'm investigating the feasibility of incorporating online courses into the regular curriculum of the college." The survey can be conducted either orally, in writing, or over the Internet. A sample of 25 to 50 people and some simple mathematical calculations should provide adequate statistical information to integrate into your presentation. When you conduct an informal survey, you may gain more than expected. While running the survey or examining the results, you may find interesting off-the-cuff remarks to incorporate in your speech.

Interviews

An interview is similar to a survey except that it is usually more detailed and assumes that the person being interviewed is in some way an expert on the topic under consideration. On your campus, in your community, or in an online Usenet discussion group, you will probably find knowledgeable people to interview about current issues and many other topics. Political, business, and religious leaders, for instance, can often be persuaded to talk to student speakers. And, of course, faculty members of a college are often eager to cooperate.

Be sure to record accurately the information gathered during an interview. Take careful notes and repeat or verify any direct quotations you intend to use in your presentation. Also be certain during the speech to credit the interviewee as your source, unless he or she has asked not to be mentioned by name.

RECORD INFORMATION DERIVED FROM RESEARCH

The information you gather during your research should be easy for you to retrieve. Either buy a pack of 4- by 6-inch or 6- by 8-inch note cards to record your information or use a laptop computer to compile your notes. When the time comes, either

> **Raymond Robinson, Mayor of Ourtown, NJ**
>
> "During the storm, many people had to be evacuated. Otherwise they would have been caught in grave danger. This was a storm that caught us completely by surprise."
>
> Interview 1/16/11, 4 p.m.

FIGURE 12.3

Notecard Derived from an Interview.

approach will let you move information around to wherever you need it or want to use it in the speech. Try this approach:

- Use a bibliography card or page for each basic article or source you reference.
- Record the title, author, and subject on the top of each card or page.
- Record one bit of information per card.

For examples of what note cards and pages look like, see Figures 12.3 and 12.4. Notice how each one contains either a direct quotation from the material or paraphrased information.

FIGURE 12.4

Sample Note Cards.

Using bibliography, direct quotation, and paraphrase cards will increase the speed and accuracy of your information gathering.

> **Bibliography Card**
>
> Mark Hosenball, "Airplanes: Dangerous Descents," Newsweek January 10, 2005, p. 6.

> **Direct Quotation Card**
>
> From Hosenball, "Airplanes: Dangerous Descents," p. 6.
>
> "A series of mysterious incidents in which powerful laser beams were flashed into the cockpits of low-flying passenger planes has jolted the air-travel system."

> **Paraphrase Card**
>
> From Hosenball, "Airplanes: Dangerous Descents," p. 6.
>
> Commercial airliners landing at airports reported laserbeams flashed into the cockpit. A pilot could suffer eye injury from laser beams. Homeland Security has been concerned but feels the incidents are probably either accidental or mischievous in nature.

Whenever you research, be sure to give each source correct attribution to avoid plagiarizing. The word *plagiarism* derives from the Latin word *plagiarius*, meaning "kidnapper." When you plagiarize, you kidnap or steal the ideas and words of another and claim them as your own. Plagiarism is a growing problem. An increasing percentage of students are guilty of "cut and paste plagiarism," in which the student takes sections from the works of a number of other people and weaves them together into a "new" work that the student then claims to be his or her own. Here are three simple steps to follow to avoid passing off someone else's ideas or words as your own:

1. Attribute the source of every piece of evidence you cite in your speech. Never borrow the words or thoughts of a source without acknowledging them.

2. Tell receivers when you are quoting a statement, or paraphrase it.

3. Use and credit a variety of sources.

Following these guidelines will demonstrate your respect for the audience and will also help you earn their respect. The unique expression of ideas matters. Giving sources the credit due them not only protects you but also increases your credibility.

Audience members do not expect you to be the sole source of ideas in your speech, but they do expect you to provide oral citations (also known as oral footnotes) when referring to the ideas of others. Such citations are easy to include in your presentation as long as you have done your research and recorded your information carefully. What do you say in an oral citation? If you are citing a speech or article, you might say,

> In his speech given to honor those killed and wounded on January 8, 2011, in Tucson along with Representative Gabrielle Giffords, President Barack Obama told those assembled. . . .

If you are using a direct quotation, state the name of the author and the source:

> In her book *Confidence*, researcher and Harvard Business School Professor Rosabeth Moss Kanter tells readers. . . .

If you are paraphrasing a book or article, you might tell your audience,

> Howard Gardner, author of the best-seller *Changing Minds*, feels that most of us change our minds gradually. The notion that mind change happens suddenly is wrong.

As you build your speech, the experts you bring onto your team give your speech more impact. Be sure to include each source you use in a Works Cited page (for sources actually mentioned during your speech) or in a Works Consulted page (for all the sources you referred to when conducting your research). When preparing your Works Cited or Works Consulted page, use a consistent referencing style. The MLA (Modern Language Association) or APA (American Psychological Association) formats are the most popular. For examples, see the Works Consulted sections of the sample speech outlines included in Chapters 14 and 15, on informative and persuasive speaking.

Review, Reflect, & Apply

Recall

Define primary research.

Understand

Describe three kinds of primary research.

Apply

Prepare and conduct a short interview with a classmate, friend, or relative on basic biographical info, a personal interest or hobby, or some other topic of your choosing.

Select Support: Types of Supporting Material

LO3

Explain how to use various types of support to enhance a presentation.

Taken together, your research and your experiences should yield a wealth of information to integrate into your presentation. But making your research and experiences come to life for an audience is not an easy task; in fact, it is a key challenge facing the speech maker. Following are some major ways to make research and experience understandable and believable for an audience.[4]

DEFINITIONS

definitions
explanations of what a stimulus is or what a word or concept means

It is especially important to use **definitions** when your listeners are unfamiliar with terms you are using or when their associations for words or concepts might differ from yours. Only if you explain how you are defining a term can you hope to share your meanings with your listeners. Thus, the purpose of a definition is to increase the audience's understanding.

For example, in a speech on exercise-anorexia, one student specifically defined the disorder as "the obligation or compulsion to continually exercise."[5] In contrast, in a speech on the curability of anorexia, one student attempted to explain the difficulty she was having in defining what recovery from anorexia meant by saying, "There is surprisingly little agreement as to what 'recovery' means for people with anorexia."[6] Both speakers convey vital information about the disorder by addressing its defining characteristics (or lack thereof).

statistics
facts expressed in numerical form

In a speech on post-traumatic stress disorder and soldiers serving in Iraq and Afghanistan, speaker Megan Solan defined *psychological injury* as "that which soldiers suffer when they lose their peace of mind, their ability to function in society and their belief in the existence of human virtues."[7] The student went on to flesh out this definition with specifics: "soldiers learn skills such as the art of deception; the capacity to respond instantly with violent, lethal force; and the suppression of such emotions as compassion, horror, guilt, tenderness, grief, and disgust, all necessary skills for combat, but all skills with dangerous potential within civilian society and severe consequences for the human psyche."[8]

STATISTICS

Statistics are simply facts expressed in numerical form. They may be cited to explain relationships or to indicate trends. To be used effectively as support, statistics must be honest and credible. If used appropriately, they can make the ideas you are presenting memorable and significant.

In a speech on why criticisms of what it costs the United States to support the United Nations are unjustified, U.S. Permanent Representative to the United Nations, Susan E. Rice, said, "Let me provide a bit of perspective. Out of every tax dollar you pay, 34 cents goes to Social Security and Medicare, 22 cents to national security and our amazing military, and a nickel to paying interest on the national debt. Just one-tenth of a single penny goes to pay our UN dues."[9]

Review, Reflect, & **Apply**

Recall

Identify six kinds of verbal support.

Understand

Define and give an example of the following kinds of verbal support: definition, statistics, examples and illustrations, testimony, comparisons and contrast, and repetition and restatement.

Analyze

Compare and contrast a bar graph, pie graph, line graph, and pictograph.

Evaluate

Discuss criteria to use when evaluating testimony.

Create

Select a word for which people have different associations—for example, an abstract concept such as honesty, jealousy, freedom, justice or love—and define it.

In a speech on problems with our organ donor system, Amy Solomito of Lafayette College used statistics to emphasize the failure of the current organ donation system: "The Web site of the United Network for Organ Sharing, *unos.org*, reports that as of this morning, 96,201 Americans are waiting for healthy organs. . . . Only 15 percent of these people can expect to receive the organs they need."[10]

Even using the simplest of statistics can prove effective. The following research tidbit was used by a student in a speech on the distraction powers of the Internet: "Last year a joint study of Microsoft and the University of Illinois found that it takes, on average, 16 minutes and 33 seconds for a worker interrupted by an e-mail to get back to what he or she was doing."[11]

EXAMPLES AND ILLUSTRATIONS

Examples are representative cases; as such, they specify particular instances.[12] **Illustrations,** on the other hand, tell stories and thus create more detailed narrative pictures. Both examples and illustrations may be factual or hypothetical. When used effectively, they turn the general into the specific, the unfocused into the focused, and the dull into the interesting, breathing life into a speech.

examples
representative cases

illustrations
stories; narrative pictures

Solomon D. Trujillo, chairman, president, and CEO of US West, Inc., used a series of examples to demonstrate for audience members that one idea can make a difference:

> We've seen how the idea that all people are created equal can find expression in an African-American woman on a bus in Alabama, or [in] a student on a soda-fountain stool in North Carolina, or even in a young Hispanic businessman in Cheyenne, Wyoming.
> A few weeks back, I was at the University of Colorado talking to a group of business students, and I told them that I would not be in the job I have were it not for Affirmative Action.
> When I joined the old Bell system, AT&T had just entered into a consent decree with the government. Before I joined the company, people like me . . . for some reason . . . weren't likely to get hired. Those who were hired . . . for some reason . . . weren't in management jobs.
> But people with courage and foresight knew that our nation's promise of freedom and justice for all was an empty one if you had the wrong color of skin, if you were female, if you spoke with an accent, or if your last name ended in a "z" or a vowel.[13]

Illustrations are more detailed than examples. Built like a story, they open, reveal a complication, contain a climax, and describe a resolution. Emotionally compelling, illustrations add a sense of drama to a speech as they focus attention on the issue at hand.

In a speech on the power of "positive deviance," Risa Lavizzo-Mourey, M.D., the Alvin M. Poussaint Visiting Lecturer at Harvard Medical School, used the following illustration to demonstrate the importance of Alvin M. Poussaint to her career:

> When I showed up here for medical school in the 1970s, only 12 black physicians had graduated from Harvard Medical School in the preceding two decades. Nationally in that era annually there were only 300 African Americans out of about 10,000 first-year med students in the entire country—and half of them were at Howard or Meharry. The other half made up only 1.4 percent of all first-year students in the more mainstream medical schools like Harvard. Not long afterward, I added to that statistic. I was young, naïve, and consumed with a passion to become a physician. Not just any physician—but one educated and trained at the best of the best, by the best of the best. There was only one hang-up. Some of the school's old guard was still unhappy

about admitting either minorities or women. They questioned the capability of our brains. Complained we were not good enough. "Not Harvard material." In my second year, a senior faculty member—a biochemist renowned in his field—attacked us in an article in the *New England Journal of Medicine*. "Faculty lowered standards," he said, so we could pass. Our medical degrees were awarded on a "charitable basis." The professor scolded that we were like airline pilots who'd flunked landing. Patients, like passengers, might die in our care and on our watch. He even suggested it could be considered "criminal." We were furious. Frustrated. Maybe even a little bit frightened. That's when Doctor Poussaint became our hero. Right from day one, he was there for us.[14]

TESTIMONY

testimony
someone else's opinions or conclusions

Whenever you cite someone else's opinions or conclusions, you are using **testimony,** or a testimonial. Testimony gives you an opportunity to connect the ideas in your speech with the thoughts and attitudes of respected and competent people. The testimony you include in a presentation need not be derived exclusively from present-day sources; words of people from the past may also be used to tie today and yesterday together. When using testimonials, be sure to consider whether the people you cite as authorities are credible sources, whether their ideas are understandable, and whether their comments are relevant to your purpose.

In a speech on life after graduation from college, best-selling author and motivational speaker Harvey Mackay used testimony to emphasize the importance of listening, telling his audience,

> Bill Marriott, chairman and CEO of Marriott International, the world's largest hotel chain, described the biggest lesson he has learned through the years: "It is to listen to your people. I find that if you have senior managers who really gather their people around them, get their ideas, and listen to their input, they make a lot better decisions."[15]

As we see, testimony reinforces a speaker's claims. It may be quoted directly, as in the preceding example, or it may be paraphrased, as illustrated by Theresa McGuiness in her speech advocating that fraternities be abolished:

> Bernice Sandler, executive director of the Project on the Status and Education of Women at the Association of American Colleges, said that 90 percent of the gang rapes reported to her office involved fraternity members. According to Sandler, fraternity members have a word for gang rape: they call it "pulling train." She adds that charts of how many beers it took to seduce sorority women are common in fraternity houses. And if a woman actually does press charges against a fraternity, Sandler says, "Their excuse is, 'she asked for it'—even if she was unconscious."[16]

Use direct quotations when you believe that the language and the length of an expert's remarks are appropriate for your audience. Use a paraphrase when you need to summarize an expert's opinion in fewer words, or when you need to simplify its language.

COMPARISONS AND CONTRASTS

Comparisons stress similarities between two entities; contrasts stress differences. Both are employed by speakers to help audiences understand something that is unknown, unfamiliar, or unclear.

William L. Laurence combined comparison and contrast when he described the atomic bombing of Nagasaki:

> As the first mushroom floated off into the blue, it changed its shape into a flowerlike form, its grand petals curving downward, creamy white outside, rose-colored

Experts and Cultural Groups

If the testimony of others influences us in making decisions and assessing situations, then an audience's judgments about a public speaker—and about his or her speech—ought to be influenced by people the speaker quotes or refers to, who presumably have special knowledge or experience relevant to the topic.

Does it matter whether a speaker uses experts from the same cultural group as the audience, or would experts from other cultural groups serve just as well in adding strength and impact to the speaker's ideas? Explain your position.

inside. . . . Much living substance had gone into those rainbows. The quivering top of the pillar was protruding to a great height through the white clouds, giving the appearance of a monstrous prehistoric creature with a ruff around its neck, a fleecy ruff extending in all directions, as far as the eye could see.[17]

In a speech supporting the right of gays to serve openly in the military, Lady Gaga used comparison and contrast to make clear that she wants the "don't ask, don't tell" policy to end:

I'm concerned that homophobia is being used as a defense for "don't ask, don't tell." At the nexus of this law, openly gay soldiers affect unit cohesion, like it's OK to discriminate or discharge gay soldiers because we are homophobic, we are uncomfortable, and we do not agree with homosexuality, and I can't focus on the field of duty when I am fighting. "We have a problem with you." Wasn't that the defense of Matthew Shepard's murderers? When they left him to die on a fence in Laramie, they told the judge, "Oh, Matthew's gay, and it made us uncomfortable, so we killed him." "Oh, he's gay, it makes me uncomfortable, send him home." As a side note, both Matthew Shepard's killers have life sentences in prison, and laws have since been passed that homophobia cannot be used as a defense anymore in hate crimes in our judicial system. Doesn't it seem to be that "don't ask, don't tell" is backwards? Doesn't it seem to be that, based on the Constitution of the United States, that we're penalizing the wrong soldier?[18]

REPETITION AND RESTATEMENT

When a speaker uses repetition, the same words are repeated verbatim. When a speaker uses restatement, an idea is presented again, but in different words. If used sparingly, these devices can add impact to a speech maker's remarks and thereby increase memorability.

One of the most famous examples of successful use of repetition is the speech delivered by Martin Luther King, Jr., in 1963 at the Lincoln Memorial:

I say to you today, my friends, so even though we face the difficulties of today and tomorrow, I still have a dream. It is a dream deeply rooted in the American dream. I have a dream that one day this nation will rise up . . . live out the true meaning of its creed—we hold these truths to be self-evident, that all men are created equal. . . .

I have a dream that my four little children will one day live in a nation where they will not be judged by the color of their skin but by the content of their character. I have a dream today. . . .

I have a dream that one day every valley shall be exalted, and every hill and mountain shall be made low, the rough places shall be made plain, and the crooked places shall be made straight and the glory of the Lord will be revealed and all flesh shall see it together.[19]

Outlining Your Speech: Building a Speaking Framework

Explain the speech framework and outlining stages and principles, including the identification of main and subordinate ideas.

Every speech ought to be put together like a living creature, with a body of its own, so as to be neither without head nor without feet, but to have both a middle and extremities, described proportionately to each other and to the whole.

—Plato

speech framework
a skeleton for speech development

What is your goal when organizing ideas? Primarily, you want to facilitate communication with your audience. How can you accomplish this? You must plan. Just as an architect develops a plan for a building, so you must develop a plan for your speech. Your plan shows the structure you will adhere to—the developmental sequence you think will work best. Communication theorists have developed guidelines to help you with this phase.

An audience has to be able to follow your speech for it to be effective. Without good organization, a speech's message remains fuzzy and hard to follow. Since receivers rarely interrupt speakers during a speech to seek clarification, and because they do not usually have access to transcripts or tapes of presentations, speakers need to organize the ideas of their speeches so that receivers comprehend them the first time they hear them. Receivers have no rewind button to push if they become distracted or confused. Thus, speakers must structure their messages so that confusion is kept to a minimum.[20]

As we saw in Chapter 6, not everyone is a skillful listener. For this reason, you should base your organization on the *principle of redundancy*. In other words, to ensure comprehension, you will need to build a certain amount of repetition into your speech. Only if this is done will listeners be able to follow your ideas easily. This basic developmental principle is often expressed as follows: *Tell them what you are going to tell them, then tell them, and finally, tell them what you have told them.*

One of the best ways to organize a speech is the introduction-body-conclusion format (see Figure 12.5), called a **speech framework** because it provides a frame, or skeleton, on which any speech or other formal presentation can be built.

Any speech you develop should be organized according to this framework. Your introductory remarks and your concluding statements should each take up approximately 10 to 15 percent of the total presentation. That leaves 70 to 80 percent of your time for developing the ideas contained in the body of your speech. Since the body will be the main portion of your presentation, it is often advisable to begin by preparing this part of the speech; once the body is set, you can move on to develop the introduction and the conclusion. Let's consider the three key parts of a speech in that order: body, introduction, and conclusion.

FIGURE 12.5

Framework for a Speech.

Introduction
Body
Conclusion

Creating Your Outline

As you begin to organize the body of your speech, you will want to build a suitable structure onto which you can place your ideas. You develop this structure in stages. During the first stage of outline development, you create a *preliminary working outline*. This sparse outline has points containing one or two words that eventually will achieve fuller form in the second stage, the full sentence outline. You develop the *full sentence outline* only after you have researched and fully developed the ideas of your speech. Ultimately, during the third stage of outline preparation, you will transform your full sentence outline into an *extemporaneous outline*, or *speaker's notes*, that you will then use as your guide when you deliver your speech.

OUTLINING PRINCIPLES: IDENTIFYING MAIN AND SUBORDINATE IDEAS

Let's imagine that you have created the following working plan, or outline, for a speech about affirmative action:

I. Definition

II. Purposes

III. Outcomes

IV. Why under attack

Your next task is to develop those topics. As you begin the development process, keep in mind that your audience is unlikely to recall a long, wandering, unstructured collection of data. Thus, after you have conducted your research, you will need to develop a full sentence outline that distinguishes between your **main ideas**—your speech's subtopics that directly support your thesis—and your **subordinate ideas**—those ideas that function as support or amplification for your main ideas or subtopics.

In many ways, subordinate ideas are the foundation on which larger ideas are constructed (see Figure 12.6). Consequently, you should begin the organizational process by arranging your materials into clusters of main and subordinate ideas. As you do this, you will be able to determine which evidence supports the main ideas and which supports the subordinate ideas. Your main ideas will be, say, two to five major points that you want the audience to remember.

If you are developing a speech on affirmative action programs, you might begin as follows:

Purpose: To inform the audience about affirmative action

Behavioral objective: After listening to my speech, audience members will be able to define affirmative action, identify its uses and results, and explain why it is a policy under fire.

Thesis: The definition, uses, and results of affirmative action have contributed to its being a policy under fire. (See Figure 12.7.)

main ideas
the main points of a speech; the subtopics of a speech

subordinate ideas
ideas that amplify the main ideas or subtopics of a speech

FIGURE 12.6
Construction of an Idea.

I	II	III	IV
Definition of affirmative action	Uses of affirmative action	Results of affirmative action	Reasons affirmative action is under fire as a policy

FIGURE 12.7
Dividing a Thesis into Major Points.

You are now off to a good start. Next, you need to develop these major points into complete sentences using parallel structure—that is, using sentences with similar or matching styles.

I. Affirmative action can be defined as any action taken to ensure or affirm equal opportunity for oppressed or previously disadvantaged groups.

II. Affirmative action is used in hiring and college admissions decisions.

III. Affirmative action has benefits and drawbacks.

IV. Affirmative action is under fire for being reverse discrimination.

Many people find it helpful to pull together clusters of information that support their main ideas, as follows:

I. Main idea
   A. Subordinate idea
      1. Support for subordinate idea
      2. Support for subordinate idea
   B. Subordinate idea
      1. Support for subordinate idea
      2. Support for subordinate idea

When you take the time to prepare an easy-to-follow structure for your speech, in addition to enhancing receiver perceptions of your competence and adding to the personal credibility you have in their eyes, your efforts also help fulfill receiver expectations. That is, the main points of a speech alert receivers to listen for supporting information. Because they are not struggling to give order to a disordered array of information, they can focus instead on the thesis of your speech and the support you offer to build your presentation. Taking time to develop an outline has a third benefit, as well. Because you know what information you are using to support each main point of your speech, your delivery of the speech will be improved. Since your ideas are carefully laid out before you, instead of having to concentrate on what to say next, you free yourself to focus on establishing a good relationship with your receivers.

If you have taken notes on cards, you can lay out or pattern the body of your speech in the following way:

Purpose:

I. Main idea
   A. (Supports I)   B. (Supports I)
      1. (Supports A)   1. (Supports B)
      2. (Supports A)   2. (Supports B)
      3. (Supports A)

II. Main idea
   A. (Supports II)
   B. (Supports II)

Notice that the outline you develop indicates the relative importance of each item included in it. The main points—roman numerals I, II, III, and so on—are the most important items you want your audience to remember. Your subpoints—capital letters A, B, C, and so on—are supportive of but less important than the main points. Likewise, items beginning with arabic numerals 1, 2, 3, and so on are supportive of but less important than subpoints. Remember to line up the entries in your outline correctly. Locate the main ideas closest to the left margin. The subpoints underlying the main points should begin directly underneath the first letter of the first word of each main point. Keep in mind that a traditional rule of outlining is that at least two subpoints must support every main point.

Items that support the subpoints begin directly underneath the first letter of the first word of each subpoint. Indicate the supporting materials for these with lowercase letters (a, b, c, and so on). In this way, the full sentence outline functions as a visual representation of the supportive underpinnings for ideas. In general, there should be at least a 3 to 1 ratio between the number of words in your speech and the number of words in your outline.

An outline on avian flu, using the symbols and indentions just discussed, might be built as follows:

Purpose: To inform audience members about the fears and questions concerning the H5N1 avian flu (bird flu)

I. Several fears about H5N1 avian flu are prevalent in society today.

II. Many questions remain regarding future efforts to protect against a pandemic strain of avian flu.

Looking at this example, we have in plain sight the central features of what will become a speech. Because the speaker identifies two aspects of the subject, there will be two main points in the speech. It is important for the ordering of main points to flow logically if receivers are going to be able to follow the presentation easily. In this speech, to guide the receiver in processing the speech, the speaker chose to first confront existing fears about the avian flu, and then to discuss the questions revolving around the disease's control and potential treatment should it develop into a pandemic. Here is how the speaker developed the speech's main points:

I. Several fears concerning the H5N1 avian flu are prevalent in society today.
   A. Many people fear that H5N1 avian flu is the next pandemic.
      1. Cases of human infection of H5N1 avian flu have been reported in a number of countries, including China, Cambodia, Turkey, and Iraq, among people who handled infected birds.
      2. There is concern that the H5N1 avian flu virus will mutate spontaneously, giving it greater ability to jump from human to human.
      3. There is concern that travel, especially by air, will accelerate transmission of the disease around the world.
   B. Currently, chances of contracting H5N1 avian flu are small for people who do not have intimate contact with birds.
      1. Not a single bird in the United States has been found to suffer from avian influenza.
      2. Casual contact with birds will not spread flu because of the species barrier.

II. Many questions remain regarding future efforts to protect against a pandemic strain of avian flu.
   A. Developing a vaccine to attack a pandemic avian flu virus is problematic.
      1. Whether Tamiflu and Relenza will be effective against the pandemic version of the avian flu virus is unclear.

Review, Reflect, & Apply

Understand

Describe the basic framework of a speech.

Apply

Explain how distinguishing main from supporting ideas facilitates the building of a speech outline.

Analyze

Distinguish between a preliminary, full sentence, and extemporaneous outline.

Create

Develop the following outlines on a speech topic of your choosing: preliminary, full sentence, and extemporaneous.

2. Because scientists do not know what the pandemic flu virus will look like, a vaccine cannot yet be made.
3. Scientists hope that the H5N1 vaccines now in trials will provide at least some protection in a pandemic.

B. Improving international cooperation is critical.
   1. We need to increase awareness of the threat.
   2. We need to improve surveillance and diagnosis of the disease in birds.

C. Biosecurity is key.
   1. The president signed an executive order adding pandemic influenza to the list of quarantinable diseases.
   2. The N95 mask provides aerosolization protection from the droplets that spread the virus.
   3. Discouraging personal stockpiling, the government is calling for the maintenance of national and regional supplies.

GIVING ORDER TO YOUR IDEAS USING TRADITIONAL AND NONTRADITIONAL FORMATS

LO5

Summarize the types and features of traditional speech formats and the reasons for using them.

Speeches have either a linear or a nonlinear format. Western cultures favor a linear organization, while non-Western cultures favor organizational nonlinear formats. As Richard Nisbett notes, there appears to be a geography of thought when it comes to both the development of a worldview and the frameworks of thinking that support it.[21] In his book *The Geography of Thought: How Asians and Westerners Think Differently . . . and Why*, Nisbett notes that human cognition and reasoning preferences differ, depending on whether you were brought up in a Western or an Eastern culture. According to Nisbett, East Asians are more holistic and contextual in their perceptions, while Westerners have more of a tunnel-vision perceptual style that depends more on identifying with what is prominent in a situation and remembering it. Persons from Eastern cultures tend to tolerate subtleties and deal in relationships (the stress is placed on intuitive thinking and informal logic, not the use of categories—for example, the practice of feng shui is not atomistic but extraordinarily complex). On the other hand, persons from Western cultures tend to be analytic, prefer absolutes, and deal in categories (the stress is placed on categorization and rational, logical thinking—for example, delivering a speech entitled "Six Ways to Increase Your Self-Esteem"). East Asian persons start out by focusing on the context, not zeroing in on an object of interest. Westerners begin by focusing on a central object.

These preferences affect how persons from Eastern and Western cultures prefer to organize their ideas. According to Nisbett, in the West, we start out with a general statement and give suggested solutions. We present the evidence in favor of our position. We argue against the reasons that others might not accept the position we have taken. We summarize and offer a conclusion. In the East, they do not do it this way. Instead, they cycle back into the same topic from different directions.[22] Nisbett suggests that the following example—offered by an English professor, which focuses on writing but could equally focus on public speaking—reveals this difference in methodology:

> I was surprised when one of my students who had been a teacher in China before coming here told me that she didn't understand the requirements of essay structure. I told her to write a thesis statement and then prove its three points in the following paragraphs. She told me if she wrote this way in China she would be considered stupid. "In China," she said, "essays were written in a more circular fashion moving associated ideas closer and closer to the center."[23]

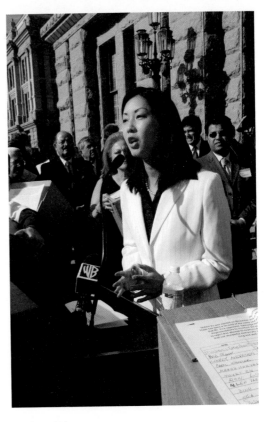

While we need to be cautious about overgeneralizing, especially since persons from one culture who spend time in another culture tend to tune their thinking style into the culture in which they are interacting, we will see these differences surface as we explore both linear and nonlinear organizational formats. You need to order the ideas in your speech in a way that will make sense to your audience.

Traditional Organizational Formats

Traditional organizational formats display a linear logic and are typical of the prototypes many North American speakers use to make sense of information. A speech has a linear organization if its main points develop and relate directly to the thesis or topic sentence that comes early in the presentation. We will look at five traditional approaches to ordering material: (1) chronological, or time, order; (2) spatial order; (3) cause-and-effect order; (4) problem-and-solution order; and (5) topical order.

Chronological Order **Chronological, or time, order** involves developing an idea or a problem in the order it occurs or occurred in time.

chronological, or time, order
an organizational format that develops an idea using a time order

One student, for example, used chronological order to inform receivers about the evolution of the right to privacy in the United States:

> *Purpose:* To inform the audience about the evolution of the right to privacy.
>
> *Thesis:* Americans believe they have a fundamental right to privacy.

I. More than a century ago, Justice Louis D. Brandeis called privacy "the right to be let alone."

II. Within a decade, the courts began to recognize the right to privacy.

III. The Supreme Court relied on a privacy rationale in reaching its famous and controversial decisions on birth control and abortion.

IV. Threats to privacy abound today.

As you can see, this student has considered the steps leading to the present situation in the order they occurred. In addition, each main point the speaker used covers a particular time period. Since the main points describe a sequence of happenings, they help the audience keep track of where the speaker is in time.

Any event that has occurred in time can be examined chronologically. When using a time-ordered presentation, you decide where to begin and end your chronology and what events to include. As you might expect, time order is used most often

Visuals, like the one held by this attorney, reinforce presented information— would you find this visual effective if you were on the jury?

spatial order
an organizational format that describes an object, a person, or a phenomenon as it exists in space

in informative speeches. Why do you think the following speaker decided to use a reverse chronology? Do you find it more or less effective than a chronology proceeding from earliest to latest?

Purpose: To inform the audience about the development of euthanasia. *Thesis:* Euthanasia has an interesting history.

I. Today euthanasia is considered mercy killing.

II. During the nineteenth century, the concept of euthanasia was associated with the acceleration of the death process.

III. The ancient Greeks were the first to espouse euthanasia as a concept.

Spatial Order **Spatial order** describes an object, a person, or a phenomenon as it exists in space. An object, for example, might be described from

top to bottom

bottom to top

left to right

right to left

inside to outside

outside to inside

With spatial order, you must select one orientation and carry it through.

One student used spatial order to explain the appearance and functioning of a beehive:

I. Outside the hive

II. Inside the hive

Another student used a spatial pattern to discuss the different kinds of natural disasters that plague different sections of the United States:

I. States along the East Coast of the United States are hurricane-prone.

II. States in the central region of the United States are tornado-prone.

III. States along the West Coast of the United States are earthquake-prone.

Like chronological order, spatial order is used most frequently in informative speeches.

Here is an example of how a speaker used a spatial pattern in talking about Stonehenge.

Purpose: To inform the audience of the appearance of the mysterious monuments of Stonehenge.

Thesis: The mystery of Stonehenge is revealed in its five circles of stones.

I. The outermost circle of Stonehenge is called the Outer Sarsen Circle.

II. The first circle is called the Outer Bluestone Circle.

III. The second circle is the Inner Sarsen Trilithons.

Speaker's Choice

1. Find a rock, a shell, a piece of driftwood, or some other natural object.

2. How would you describe the object to a partner, a group of students, or the entire class, using spatial order?

3. Explain why your spatial ordering took the form it did.

4. Would approaching the object from a different angle have altered your audience's understanding and appreciation? How?

IV. The third circle is the Inner Bluestone Horseshoe.

V. The innermost circle is the Altar Stone.

Cause-and-Effect Order Cause-and-effect order requires you to categorize your material into things related to the causes of a problem and things related to its effects. It is then up to you to decide which aspect you will explore first. Thus, in a speech on drunk driving, you might begin by discussing the percentage of drivers during a certain period who were drunk when involved in car accidents (cause). You might then discuss the number of deaths each year that are attributed directly to drunk driving (effect). You might, for example, use cause-and-effect order when speaking about the causes and effects of high blood pressure, the causes of Alzheimer's and its impact on the victim and family members, or the causes and consequences of metal fatigue in airplanes.

You can vary this approach by discussing the effect before the cause. In the following example, a student used effect-and-cause order to reveal the causes of excessive stress among students:

I. The number of students suffering from stress-related ailments is increasing at an alarming rate.

II. Experts on such ailments have identified four major explanations for this increase.

Cause-and-effect order and effect-and-cause order are quite versatile. They are used in both informative and persuasive speeches.

cause-and-effect order
an organizational format that categorizes a topic according to its causes and effects

Problem-and-Solution Order Problem-and-solution order requires you to (1) determine what problems are inherent in a situation and (2) present a solution to remedy them. Thus, you might discuss the problems that develop when many students entering college are deficient in writing skills. The second portion of your speech can then suggest a number of ways the identified problem might be alleviated (perhaps, for example, by expanding tutoring programs or offering noncredit remedial courses).

One student who focused on carjackings in shopping mall parking lots used a problem-solution order, beginning her speech by referring to the number of carjackings that had occurred recently in local malls. She then discussed a solution that combined increased lighting with additional security patrols. The next example also illustrates a problem-solution pattern. Notice how the emphasis is on how the problem can best be resolved.

problem-and-solution order
an organizational format that identifies the problems inherent in a situation and presents a solution to remedy them

Ethics & Communication

Sound Bites

Are sound bites—public presentations of positions that usually last no more than 90 seconds—an effective way of informing the electorate? Why or why not?

How organized must a speaker be to present ideas or urge action in this manner? What organizational format do you believe lends itself best to this type of presentation? Is 90 seconds or less enough time to deliver a message designed not just to inform but also to influence? Explain your position.

© Jack Ziegler/The New Yorker Collection/www.cartoonbank.com.

"Hey, do you want to be on the news tonight or not? This is a sound bite, not the Gettysburg Address. Just say what you have to say, Senator, and get the hell off."

Purpose: To convince my audience that national health insurance can help solve our health care problems.

Thesis: National health insurance will solve many of the problems caused by rising health care costs.

I. Rising health care costs have resulted in an uninsured class of people.

II. Implementing national health insurance will solve this problem.

When using a problem-and-solution format, you may discuss the advantages of the solution as well. In that case, the body of the speech would include three main points:

I. The problem

II. The solution

III. The advantages of adopting the solution

The following example demonstrates how to develop the problem-and-solution format.

Purpose: To convince my audience that we should act now to revise the way we report poverty statistics

Thesis: We should act now to solve the problem caused by the way we currently report poverty statistics.

I. The poverty level is currently understated to keep people off welfare rolls.
   A. Poverty levels for families of four are absurdly low.
   B. Poverty levels for single-parent families are even more outrageous.

II. Minimally acceptable income levels must be raised.
   A. Government levels must be raised for families.
   B. Additional help must be given for single parents.

III. These increases will solve some of the problems of the poor.
   A. They will make life easier for families.
   B. Additional aid to single parents will help them help themselves and their children.

Problem-and-solution order is most frequently employed in persuasive speeches.

Topical Order At times, a speech may not fit neatly into any of the patterns described previously. When this happens, you may choose to develop or cluster your material by arranging it into a series of appropriate topics. This is **topical order.** Examples of topical order include the following categorical arrangements: advantages and disadvantages of a proposal; social, political, and economic factors that contribute to a problem; perceptions of upper-class, middle-class, and lower-class people on an issue. When you use topical order, you may find that you can intermingle cause-and-effect, time, problem-and-solution, or spatial order within the topical order.

One student used topical order to speak about the pros and cons of using animals for medical and product research.

topical order
an organizational format that clusters material by dividing it into a series of appropriate topics

Purpose: To inform audience members of the advantages and disadvantages of using animals for medical and product research.

Thesis: Using animals for medical and product research presents both advantages and disadvantages.

I. There are two advantages to using animals as research subjects.
   A. Using animals is more effective than simply using results of test tube experiments.
   B. During the early stages of research, using animals is more effective than using human subjects.

II. There are two disadvantages to using animals in research.
   A. Animals are often mutilated and experience pain.
   B. Animals do not respond in precisely the same manner that human subjects do.

Support All Main Points In a developed outline, each point is supported by information, including examples, definitions, and visuals aids pertaining to the subject in the main point they support, enabling the audience to understand why the main point is true. Usually, two to four subpoints are offered in support of a main point.

Connecting Your Ideas: Using Internal Previews and Summaries, Transitions, and Signposts

Audience members who rely on linear logic will expect you to transmit your ideas with clarity and fluidity. They will count on your using transitional tools as you move from one idea to the next. The devices that speakers using linear logic use to create a sense of presentation coherence and unity are internal previews, **internal summaries,** transitions, and signposts.

An *internal preview* precedes information the speaker will discuss, helping to prepare the audience for important information to follow as well as what to look for as the speech progresses. For example, in a presentation on genetic engineering, a speaker told her audience: "We will next consider a technique that allows biologists to transfer a gene from one species to another. It is called recombinant DNA technology."

Internal summaries follow information the speaker has presented and are designed to help receivers remember the content. The following are examples: "Thus far we have examined two key housing problems. Let us now consider a third" and "The four characteristics we have discussed thus far are. . . ." Besides helping the audience recall the material, **transitions**—connective words and phrases—facilitate the speaker's movement from one idea to another; in effect, they bridge gaps between ideas so that there are no abrupt switches.[24]

Speakers use *signposts*, signaling cues such as "equally important" or "furthermore," to indicate that additional information is forthcoming. They also use them to make receivers aware that they are about to explain something, share an important idea, or let the audience know where they are in the progression of a speech. Commonly used signposts include the words *first, second,* and *third*; phrases that focus attention, such as "you'll especially want to keep this in mind" or "above all else, remember this"; phrases that indicate an explanation is forthcoming, such as "for example" or "to illustrate what I mean"; or rhetorical questions (questions you ask and also answer), such as "What steps can we take to make things better?" To signal that you will be discussing a cause-and-effect relationship, you can use the expressions "as a result" and "consequently." To indicate that there is a contrasting view to the one being elaborated, you could use "after all," "and yet," "in spite of," and "on the other hand." Signposts also signal the end of a speech. When a speaker says something like "finally," or "to sum up," he or she is signaling that the speech is about to conclude. So, in addition to moving a speech forward, signposts also draw it to a close.

internal summaries
rhetorical devices designed to help listeners remember content

transitions
connective words and phrases

Review, Reflect, & Apply

Recall

List the kinds of organizational formats available to speakers.

Understand

Explain when to use an internal preview, internal summary, transition, and signpost in a linear speech.

Apply

Think of three topics you could develop using chronological order. Why do they lend themselves to that arrangement?

LO6

Compare and contrast nontraditional and traditional speech formats.

Nontraditional Formats

In developing an outline, you can use a number of organizational patterns in place of a linear framework. You should use one of the nontraditional patterns discussed in this section if you believe the cultures and dispositions of the persons in your audience warrant it. While a number of us prefer to use **linear logic** to develop our ideas, others of us—including some persons from Native American, Asian-American, or Latino cultures—do not. As we deduce from the preceding prototypes, linear logic develops ideas step-by-step, relying on facts and data to support each main point. In contrast to formats that depend on linear logic are formats that are more indirect and less explicit in offering hard evidence and proof in defense of a point. These patterns are called **configural formats.**

linear logic
the step-by-step development of ideas; the reliance on facts and data to support main points

Instead of previewing, spelling out, and discussing each key point, one at a time, persons who prefer configural thinking approach their subject from a variety of perspectives and rely on examples and stories to carry the crux of their message; they also rely on receivers to understand the messages implied by the examples and stories used. Because they believe the explicit stating of a message is unnecessary, speakers who use a configural style do not bluntly tell receivers their conclusion or call on them to make a specific response; instead of ensuring that the conclusion is obvious to receivers, the speakers lead them to their conclusion indirectly and by implication. Thus, configural frameworks require receivers to do more work.

configural formats
organizational patterns that are indirect and inexplicit

While persons in cultures who favor the use of configural patterns might not categorize them in this way, Westerners do identify three kinds of configural systems of organization. First is the *deferred-thesis pattern*, in which the main points of a speech gradually build to the speaker's thesis, which he or she does not indicate until the speech is nearly over. Second is the *web pattern*, in which threads of thought refer back to the speaker's central purpose; while to Western ears the speaker may seem to be "off topic" at points, to receivers in other cultures the tangents the speaker explores are connected to the speaker's topic and make it more meaningful. Third is the *narrative pattern*, in which the speaker tells a story without stating a thesis or developing it with main points. When using a narrative pattern, the speaker uses a series of illustrations and parables to uncover or help receivers discover the speech's main points. The speaker uses indirection and implication rather than bridges or transitions to circle and connect ideas, establish their point, and ultimately help the audience members arrive at their conclusion.[25]

The following speech outline is organized configurally. As such, it requires the audience to participate more actively in interpreting what the speaker implies.

Purpose: To persuade my audience that E. coli presents problems for our food supply

I. A hypothetical food worker, Jake, who is employed in a meat-packing plant, inadvertently infects the plant's meat supply with E. coli.

II. Jake's carelessness contributes to the infection of a number of persons in an array of cities across the United States.

III. The plant is closed because of E. coli contamination.

IV. Today, members of the families of those who were sickened by E. coli ask the federal government, "How can our food supply be made safe?"

Looking at the preceding example you can see that it has four main points, a format typical of narration. First, the speaker sets the scene for receivers, introducing the subject and the situation. The speaker next describes the sequence of

Exploring **Diversity**

Edward T. Hall suggests that "culture . . . designates what we pay attention to and what we ignore." If this is so, how can speakers ensure that audience members who belong to other cultural groups will pay attention to the right things? In other words, how can speakers target crucial ideas and emphasized points? How can a speaker be sure that listeners are not paying attention to the wrong thing and screening out what they should be concentrating on?

_____

Source: Edward T. Hall. *The Hidden Dimension.* New York: Doubleday, 1966.

events as they occurred. Then, she or he discusses the situation's effects. Finally, the narrator points to a solution. If you choose to use narration, tell a solid story, use descriptive language, intersperse dialogue when possible, build interest or suspense, and help your audience identify with the people involved. When serving as a narrator, you can place yourself there and tell the story in the first person, use the second person and help audience members imagine themselves in such a situation, or use the third person, as the speaker in the provided example did, and describe what happened.

As the speaker embellishes each of the ideas identified in the outline during his or her presentation, it is up to the receivers to interpret the meaning of the speaker's narrative from the stories, examples, and testimony offered. The speaker will not state directly what receivers should think or do but will rely on them to draw their own conclusions and come up with their own solutions.

Recall from Chapter 2 that members of low-context cultures, such as the United States, are usually more direct in how they convey information to others than are members of high-context cultures, such as Latin America, Japan, and Saudi Arabia. To low-context receivers, the speaker from a high-context culture may come off as vague or deceptive because of his or her reluctance to be direct, explicit, or obvious. In contrast, high-context receivers prefer to receive information through examples, illustrations, and other indirect means of expression.[26]

According to most intercultural communication theorists, English is primarily a speaker-responsible language, but other languages, including Japanese, Chinese, and Arabic, are more listener responsible. Native users of speaker-responsible languages typically believe it is up to the speakers to tell receivers exactly what they want them to know. In contrast, native speakers of listener-responsible languages typically believe that speakers need indicate only indirectly what they are speaking about and what they want receivers to know. They believe it is up to audience members, not the speaker, to construct the message's meaning.[27]

Review, Reflect, & **Apply**

Recall

Name three configural systems of speech organization.

Understand

Outline what distinguishes a nontraditional format from a traditional one.

Apply

Think of three topics you could develop using a configural format. Why do they lend themselves to that arrangement?

Beginnings and Endings

Once you have outlined the body of your speech and considered the need for transitional devices, you are ready to "tell them what you are going to tell them" and "tell them what you have told them." In other words, it is time to develop your introduction and conclusion.[28]

LO7

Discuss characteristics of effective introductions and conclusions.

THE INTRODUCTION

All too frequently, the introduction is overlooked or neglected because speakers are in too much of a hurry to get to the heart of the matter. However, in public speaking, just as in interpersonal communication, first impressions count. Thus, it is essential that you make the first few minutes of your speech particularly interesting.

Functions of the Introduction

The functions of your introduction are to gain the attention of the audience members, to make them want to listen to your speech, and to provide them with an overview of the subject you will be discussing. The art of designing introductions is much like any other art; that is, it requires creative thinking. You will need to examine your purpose, the speech itself as you have developed it, your analysis of the audience, and your own abilities.

The opening moments of contact, with one person or with a multitude, can affect the developing relationship either positively or negatively. Unquestionably, the first few moments of your speech—the introduction—will affect your audience's willingness to process the remainder. It is at this point that people will decide whether what you have to say is interesting and important or dull and

> A bad beginning makes a bad ending.
>
> —Euripides

In the introduction, one of the speaker's goals is to build rapport with the audience.

inconsequential. If your introduction is designed poorly, your audience may tune you out for the remainder of your speech. On the other hand, a well-designed introduction can help you develop a solid rapport with the audience and thus make it easier for you to share your thoughts.

The material you include in your introduction must be selected with care. Since in all likelihood your listeners have not been waiting in line for several days to hear you speak, you will need to work to spark their interest; you will need to motivate them to listen to you. Student speakers sometimes go overboard in trying to accomplish this objective. Some have been known to yell or throw books across the room. Such devices are certainly attention-getters, but startling an audience can turn your listeners against you. Other speakers look for a joke—any joke—to use as an attention-getter. Unfortunately, a joke chosen at random is seldom related to the topic and thus can confuse or even alienate listeners rather than interest and involve them. (A well-chosen anecdote, however, can be very effective.) Some speakers insist on beginning with statements like "My purpose here today is . . ." or "Today, I hope to convince you. . . ." Such openings suggest mainly that the speech maker has forgotten to consider motivation and attention.

Years ago, television shows began simply by flashing the title of the program onto the screen. Today, however, it is common to use a teaser to open a show. The teaser usually reveals segments of the show designed to arouse the interest of potential viewers—to encourage them to stay tuned. Without this device, many viewers would probably switch channels. Your listeners, of course, cannot switch speakers, but they can decide not to listen actively to what you have to say. Therefore, you, too, must design a teaser to include in your introduction—material that will interest and appeal to your audience.

Types of Introductions

Effective speech makers begin in a number of different ways. They may relate an unusual fact, make a surprising statement, or cite shocking statistics. Or they might ask a question, compliment the audience, or refer to the occasion. Sometimes they use a humorous story or an illustration as a lead-in. Sometimes they rely on a suspenseful story or a human interest story to capture their listeners' attention. Audiences respond to stories about people. For this reason, the plight of a family left homeless by a fire might be used effectively to open a speech on fire prevention, and a description of people severely injured in an automobile accident might introduce a speech supporting the use of air bags. If you have selected a topic because you have a personal interest in it, you can use a personal anecdote to begin your presentation. Let us examine a few examples of these approaches.

Some of the most effective introductions use *humor*, as in the following example from a speech about changes the U.S. army has made, delivered by David H. Petraeus, then Commander, United States Central Command, and now the head of the CIA:

> Earlier today, as I was talking with my wife about tonight's speech, she reminded me of a story about a young schoolboy's report on Julius Caesar. "Julius Caesar was born a long time ago," the little boy explained. "He was a great general. He won some important battles. He made a long speech. They killed him. . . ." I'll try to avoid Caesar's fate. But this is the Irving Kristol lecture—and I do need to say something meaningful.[29]

When used in introductions, *illustrations*, more detailed than examples, can add even more drama, as is seen in the following introductory remarks of Brittany Young of Shepherd University:

> Tarek Dergoul, a British citizen raised in east London, sustained shrapnel wounds when a bomb exploded while he was on business in Afghanistan. He lay among the ruins for at least a week, drinking from a tap that still worked, and living on biscuits and raisins he had in his pocket. Exposed to the freezing weather, his toes turned black from frostbite. At last, he was found by troops loyal to the Northern Alliance who took him to a hospital where he received food and three operations. After five weeks, he was driven to an airfield and handed over to Americans who arrived by helicopter. They flew him to the U.S. detention camp at Bagram airbase, near Kabul. While imprisoned, Dergoul said that violence and sexual humiliation was routine. Then in February, Dergoul was taken south to another camp at Kandahar. Due to his treatment, his memories of this time are hazy. On May 1, he was dressed in goggles and an orange jump suit, injected with a sedative and flown to Guantanamo Bay, where he sustained further abuse. Dergoul was one of the fortunate ones. He was able to go home. . . .[30]

Students Erin Gallaher and Adrienne Hallett both used *suspense* to make their points. Which of the introductions do you think is more effective? Erin's speech began this way:

> Flip through any furniture catalog, and you'll be sure to note descriptions of color, style, fabric, and texture. When deciding to purchase a new sofa or armchair, most likely you'll carefully weigh options like "to recline or not to recline"—that is the question.
>
> But there is something that most people never even consider when they're shopping for upholstered furniture. What is this hidden feature? It's the extremely flammable polyurethane foam found in the cushions of virtually every piece of upholstered furniture in your home.[31]

Adrienne's speech began this way:

> He showed all of the classic symptoms. His response time was slowed, his judgement was impaired, but he thought he could handle it. As he drove home along the Interstate, his car swerved onto the shoulder of the road, running over and killing a man who was trying to change a flat tire. When the police questioned him later, he didn't remember a thing. What caused this Ohio man's actions is something we have all been guilty of, yet we won't readily admit it. Although the U.S. Department of Transportation estimates that it kills 13,000 people annually, no one will be taking the keys, calling a cab or taking a stand on this issue. Whenever we get into the driver's seat, we must be prepared for the risk presented by an impaired driver—surprisingly, not from alcohol but from a lack of sleep.[32]

Another student began a speech by asking a rhetorical question:

> Do you know who you voted for in the last presidential election? I bet you don't. I bet you think you voted for the Democratic, Republican, or Independent candidate. But you didn't. You voted to elect members of the electoral college. In the course of my speech, I will explain why this practice is undemocratic, un-American, and unacceptable.

Another student used *frightening facts* to jolt her audience:

> In the time it takes me to complete this sentence, a child in America will drop out of school. In the time it takes me to complete this sentence, a child in this country will run away from home. Before I finish this presentation, another teenage girl will have a baby.

> We have a country [that] is gripped by a lost generation. This is an invisible group of kids lost and alone on the streets. On their own, they are hungry, sick, and scared. They are victims of our society. They are victims who desperately need help. In this presentation I will show you how we can all help these kids.

Finally, many speakers use *startling statistics* to capture the audience's attention. The following example from a speech by the president of the AFL-CIO on the problems of working people demonstrates the speaker's use of statistics to spark interest:

> We have to begin the conversation by talking about jobs—the 11 million missing jobs behind our unemployment rate of 9.7 percent.[33]

THE PREVIEW

If your speech is organized in a linear fashion, after you have used your introduction to spark interest and motivate your audience to continue listening, it is necessary for you to preview your speech. That is, you need to let your audience know what you will be discussing. Consider the following example of a preview:

> There are three "weight classes" of people in our society: the overweight, the underweight, and those who are the right weight. Unfortunately, many people fail to understand the role weight plays in their lives. Your weight affects how your body functions. Let's explore how.

Your preview should correspond to your purpose statement. It should let your audience know what to listen for. Additionally, by presenting it after you have gotten your listeners' attention and motivated them to continue paying attention, you ensure that your purpose statement will get a fair hearing.

THE CONCLUSION

The conclusion summarizes the presentation and leaves your listeners thinking about what they have just heard. It provides a sense of completion.

Functions of the Conclusion

A speech is like a love affair. Any fool can start it, but to end it requires considerable skill.

—Lord Mancroft

The conclusion's summary function may be considered a preview in reverse. During your preview, you look ahead, revealing to your listeners the subject of your efforts. During the summary, you review for them the material you have covered. For example, a summary might begin, "We have examined three benefits you will derive from a new town library." During the remainder of this summation, the three benefits might be restated, to cement them in the minds of the listeners.

Inexperienced speech makers sometimes say that the summary appears to be superfluous ("After all, I've just said all of that not more than two minutes ago"). However, it is important to remember that you are speaking for your listeners, not for yourself. The summary provides some of the redundancy mentioned earlier; it enables audience members to leave with your ideas freshly impressed on their minds. In addition to refreshing your listeners' memory, the conclusion can help clarify the issues or ideas you have just discussed.

Besides serving as a summary, your conclusion should be used to heighten the impact of the presentation. You can do this in a number of ways. One popular technique is to refer to your introductory remarks; this gives your speech a sense

An effective conclusion heightens the impact of a presentation.

of closure. If, for example, you are speaking about child abuse and you begin your presentation by showing pictures of abused children, you might paraphrase your opening remarks and show the pictures again, to arouse sympathy and support. Quotations and illustrations also make effective conclusions. For example, if you are speaking about the problems faced by veterans of the war in Iraq, you could provide a moving conclusion by quoting some veterans or retelling some of the challenges they face. You are also free to draw on your own experiences when designing a conclusion. Keep in mind that, as they do with introductions, audiences respond to conclusions that include personal references, surprising statements, startling statistics, or relevant humor.

Types of Conclusions

Let's examine how some conclusion techniques work in practice. The director of the New Jersey School Boards Association used this illustration in her conclusion to a speech on why public schools must thrive:

> One of the students being honored as an unsung hero in Ocean County had suffered through a childhood filled with taunts and ridicule, because he had a birth defect that affected his balance and made him fall down. As a teen, he had major surgery and is now described as a handsome young man who you'd never know suffered from such problems. In his freshman year, he accompanied to the prom a girl with such crippling health issues she could barely stand to three feet tall. Yet this empathetic young man treated her with such respect, he spent the evening dancing with her on his knees so that he was her height.[34]

In a speech on skin cancer, University of Northern Iowa student Jesse Ohl concluded with a startling statistic:

> And finally, be informed patients. Regularly examine your body for skin cancer. Skin cancer usually begins in oddly shaped moles that often bleed or don't heal. If you see something like this, do yourself and your family a favor, and ask your physician. Be the first line of defense, and do not assume that your doctor will check for skin

What advice would you offer this speaker?

cancer. The *Journal of Dermatology* reports that, unless asked, physicians provide skin cancer examinations to only 1.5 percent of patients.[35]

Recognizing the effectiveness of statistics and *rhetorical questions*, Brian Swenson, a student at Dakota Wesleyan in South Dakota, ended a speech on guns and children with these words:

> Today we have looked at a few cases of child shootings, some facts and statistics about child shootings, and what you should do if you own a gun to prevent this from happening to your children or other children. Now, maybe you still think that you don't need to lock up your gun and that this won't happen to you; but I have one more figure for you. One child is killed every day with a handgun, and for every child killed ten others are injured. Now, I have a question for you. Is your child going to be one of the ten that are injured, or is it going to be the one that is killed? The choice is yours.[36]

Quotations can increase the impact of a conclusion. Former attorney general Robert Kennedy often ended his speeches with the following words by the playwright George Bernard Shaw.

> Some men see things as they are, and ask, "Why?" I dare to dream of things that never were, and ask—"Why not?"[37]

Humor, when used appropriately, can help keep people on your side. One student ended a speech directed at first-year students with the following "letter":

> Dear Mom and Dad:
>
> Just thought I'd drop you a note to clue you in on my plans.
>
> I've fallen in love with a guy named Buck. He quit high school between his sophomore and junior years to travel with his motorcycle gang. He was married at 18 and has two sons. About a year ago he got a divorce.
>
> We plan to get married in the fall. He thinks he will be able to get a job by then. I've decided to move into his apartment. At any rate, I dropped out of school last week. Maybe I will finish college sometime in the future.
>
> Mom and Dad, I just want you to know that everything in this letter so far is false. NONE OF IT IS TRUE.
>
> But it is true that I got a C in French and a D in math. And I am in need of money for tuition and miscellaneous.
>
> Love, _____

Review, Reflect, & Apply

Recall

List the functions of speech introductions and conclusions.

Understand

Identify the techniques a speaker could use to introduce you to an audience.

Evaluate

Assess factors that limit or enhance the effectiveness of speech introductions and conclusions.

Apply

Brainstorm ways to introduce Lady Gaga, your state senator, and a local philanthropist to an audience of your peers.

A Sample Outline

The following is a student's full sentence outline, containing an introduction, body, transitions, and a conclusion. What do you think are its strengths and weaknesses?

Granny Dumping

Specific purpose: To explore why "granny dumping" is on the rise

Thesis: Increased family stresses and a lack of government assistance are causing families to abandon their older relatives.

Introduction

I. Over 45 years ago playwright Edward Albee wrote *The Sandbox*, a play in which a family brings their grandmother to a playground and dumps her in a sandbox.

II. Over 45 years ago this idea was labeled as absurd.

III. Now this idea is all too real.

IV. Today, I would like to talk to you about the growing problem of granny dumping, a form of elder abuse.

(Transition: Let's begin by examining the plight of growing numbers of older Americans.)

Body

I. Older Americans are being abandoned by their families.
  A. John Kingery, 82, was abandoned outside a men's room in Post Falls, Idaho.
    1. His clothes were stripped of their labels.
    2. An Alzheimer's sufferer, Kingery was not able to remember his name.
  B. Thousands of older Americans face similar situations.
    1. The American College of Emergency Physicians estimates that 70,000 people are abandoned each year.
    2. Most are from families that cannot pay for the necessary care.
    3. Many have suffered financially in the recent recession, making them vulnerable to predators who too often are also family members.

(Transition: In addition to the pain that is being inflicted on the elderly, pain is also being inflicted on those who should care for them.)

II. Caregivers are overwhelmed by their responsibilities.
  A. Millions of Americans carry the burden of caring for one or more older adults.
    1. One in five families takes care of an older adult.
    2. Caregivers are besieged with bills.
    3. Caregivers receive little government assistance.
  B. When caregivers fall on hard times, physical abuse of elder relatives increases.
    1. Job losses lead to escalating tensions in the home.
    2. Feeling desperate, stress leads caregivers to take desperate action.

(Transition: So much for the problem; what about solutions?)

Would you have phrased the thesis similarly? Why or why not?

What do you think of the speaker's introduction?

Can you come up with an alternative transition?

What strategies did the speaker use to develop the first main idea?

How do you assess this transition?

How did the speaker develop the second main idea?

What functions does this transition serve?

III. There are a number of solutions.
   A. Families themselves can work together more effectively.
      1. They can avoid placing all of the responsibilities on one person.
      2. Relatives can help out with the nonending stack of paperwork required by government agencies.
   B. The government needs to do more.
      1. Programs need to be added so that patients can be cared for outside the home at least part of the time.
         a. This would provide variety for the patient.
         b. Such programs would also give a rest to the family so they could avoid burnout.
      2. A holistic approach to elder care needs to be adopted.
         a. Caregivers need help in coping with the increased stresses that caring for an aged relative creates.
         b. Patients need help so that they are treated with respect.
         c. Both caregivers and patients need help to maintain their dignity.

To what extent, if any, do you think the speaker developed the last main idea of the outline?

Conclusion

I. We have seen that there is much that can be done to help people who must help their aging parent.

II. While Edward Albee's *The Sandbox* was labeled as an example of absurdism 45 years ago, granny dumping has become an all too real and all too tragic way of life for tens of thousands of American citizens.

What functions does the conclusion serve?

Works Consulted

"Abuse Underreported in Many States," *USA Today*, April (from The Society for the Advancement of Education) 2004, p. 3.

Edward Albee, *The Sandbox* (New York: New American Library, 1961).

"Avoiding 'Granny Dumping'," *Daily Utah Chronicle*, January 10, 2008, accessed at www.dailyutahchronicle.com/news/2008/01/10/News/Avoiding.Granny.Dumping3148735.shtml.

Rachel Boax, "Why Do Some Caregivers of Frail Elderly Quit?" *Healthcare Financing Review* 30(2): winter 1991, pp. 41–47.

Robert Butler, "Health Care for All: A Crisis in Cost Access," *Geriatrics* 47(9), September 1992, pp. 34–48.

"Elder Abuse: A Hidden Tragedy," *Biotech Week*, October 20, 2004, p. 195.

"Granny Dumping by the Thousands," *The New York Times*, March 29, 1992.

Chris Harris, "Elder Abuse Caught on Video," *The Record*, March 5, 2011, pp. A1, A6.

Paul Krugman, "Does Getting Old Cost Society Too Much?" *New York Times Magazine*, March 9, 1997, pp. 58–60.

What do you think of the outline's Works Consulted?

Review, Reflect, & Apply

Understand

Explain criteria used to evaluate support, organizational format, and outline.

Evaluate

Assess the effectiveness of the support, organizational format, and outline for your speech.

National Center on Elder Abuse, "2004 Survey of Adult Protective Services: Abuse of Adults 60 Years of Age and Older."

National Committee for the Prevention of Elder Abuse, "What Is Elder Abuse?" www.preventelderabuse.org/elderabuse.

Cynthia Ramnarace, "Tempting Targets," http://bulletin.aarp.org, July–August 2009.

Communication Skills

LO8

Use a checklist to evaluate a speech's supporting materials, organizational format, and outline.

PRACTICE TIPS FOR SPEECH DESIGN AND ORGANIZATION

At this point, in order to review your progress in designing and organizing your speech, answer these questions:

- Is the specific purpose of my speech clear? If not, how can I increase its clarity?

- Have I expressed the main idea or thesis of my speech as effectively as I can? Does everything I include in my speech support my thesis? If not, what alterations should I make?

- Does my speech contain an introduction that includes both an attention-getter and a preview? Is each one of my introduction's components expressed as effectively as possible? If not, what can I do to enhance its expression?

- Have I developed a clear outline of my presentation, one that clearly delineates each one of my main points? If not, how can I make my outline clearer?

- In developing each main point, do I present sufficient verbal or visual support? Which of my main points is currently the most fully developed? What can I do to bring the others up to its level?

- Have I taken the cultural backgrounds of receivers sufficiently into account? If not, what can I do to broaden my speech's interest and appeal?

- Do I offer sufficient internal previews and summaries, as well as transitions and signposts, to facilitate comprehension and recall in my audience members? If not, what can I do to accomplish this?

- Does my speech contain a conclusion that summarizes it? Does the conclusion also use psychological appeals to promote receiver interest and heighten my speech's impact? Is each of my conclusion's components as effective as it can be? If not, what changes should I now make?

By assessing your progress toward your goal and making whatever revisions you discover are needed now, you will save yourself time and extra work during rehearsal, a topic we explore in Chapter 13.

The Wrap-Up

SUMMARY

LO1   **Research** your speech topic using materials found both on- and offline.

Researching the content of your speech using online and offline resources is among your first tasks in preparing a speech. For example, when working offline, you may consult published works, including books, journals, magazines, and newspapers. When working online you have the Internet and its many resources at your disposal.

LO2   **Define** and conduct primary research.

In addition to making personal observations, speakers conduct informal surveys or personal interviews to gather information for their speeches. Informal surveys consist of approximately 5 to 10 questions that you ask people affected by or familiar with your topic. Interviews are similar to surveys excepts that they are more detailed and assume that the persons whom you interview are experts on your topic.

LO3   **Explain** how to use various types of support to enhance a presentation.

Among the kinds of verbal support that speakers use to make their research interesting and understandable to audience members are: definitions (explanations of what words or concepts mean), statistics (facts expressed in numerical form), examples (representative cases), illustrations (stories and narrative pictures), and testimonials (someone else's opinions or conclusions; quotations). They also use comparisons that express similarities and contrasts that express differences, repetition (the same words repeated verbatim) and restatement (the same idea in different words), to increase the impact and memorability of their speeches.

LO4   **Explain** the speech framework and outlining stages and principles including the identification of main and subordinate ideas.

A speech framework or outline is composed of an introduction, body, and conclusion. An outline is developed in stages. First the speaker creates a preliminary outline, then a full sentence outline, and ultimately an extemporaneous outline or speaker's notes. Main ideas are the primary points of the speech. Subordinate ideas amplify the main ideas.

LO5   **Summarize** the types and features of traditional speech formats.

There are five generally accepted ways based on linear logic to order the ideas in a speech: (1) chronological order, (2) spatial order, (3) cause-and-effect order, (4) problem-and-solution order, and (5) topical order. When you use linear logic, the body of your presentation contains internal previews and summaries. Internal previews prepare receivers for important information to follow. Internal summaries help receivers recall content. Transitions facilitate movement from one idea to another. Signposts indicate that additional information is forthcoming. Together, these devices help listeners follow and recall the speech's content.

LO6   **Compare** and contrast nontraditional and traditional speech formats.

Nontraditional speech formats often use implication, examples, stories, and different perspectives to bring across a message. Speakers from a number of cultural groups prefer to use configural logic to structure their ideas. They may use a deferred-thesis pattern, a web pattern, or a narrative pattern to organize a speech.

LO7   **Discuss** characteristics of effective introductions and conclusions.

The introduction should gain the attention of audience members, make them want to listen to your speech, and provide them with an overview of the speech. Devices used to enhance introductions include humor, illustrations, questions, surprising statements, and statistics.

The purpose of the conclusion is to summarize the speech, heighten its impact, and enable the audience to leave the occasion with ideas from the speech freshly impressed on their minds. Devices used to increase the effectiveness of conclusions include surprising statements, rhetorical questions, quotations, and humor.

LO8   **Use** a checklist to evaluate supporting materials, organizational format, and the speech outline.

Speakers select supporting materials by evaluating them for currency, accuracy, reliability, sufficiency, appropriateness, and effectiveness. They build a framework for their speech and prepare a detailed outline to ensure the parts of the speech have coherence and will be easy for receivers to follow and digest.

KEY CHAPTER TERMINOLOGY

Boolean search 325
cause-and-effect order 343
chronological, or time, order 341
configural formats 347
definitions 332
examples 333
illustrations 333
internal summaries 346
linear logic 347
listserv 327
main ideas 337

primary research 328
problem-and-solution order 343
spatial order 342
speech framework 336
statistics 332
subordinate ideas 337
testimony 334
topical order 345
transitions 346

COMMUNICATING TO THE PUBLIC

Preparing Presentation Aids and Delivering Your Speech

13

After completing this chapter, you should be able to demonstrate mastery of the following learning outcomes:

LO1 **Explain** how to use visual and audio aids, including PowerPoint, to enhance the content and delivery of a speech.

LO2 **Distinguish** among four styles of delivery: manuscript, memorized, impromptu, and extemporaneous.

LO3 **Identify** speech rehearsal and delivery strategies including the effective use of nonverbal cues.

LO4 **Analyze** a speech maker's performance (including your own) in terms of content, organization, language, and delivery.

Let's continue on the road to making your speech. You are almost prepared to present—just a few steps stand between you and success. By now, you have chosen a topic and adapted that topic to your audience. You have also conducted research, selected support, chosen an organizational approach, and outlined your speech. What happens next? You shift your focus and begin thinking about how to illustrate the content of your speech, that is, whether adding audio and visual aids to your speech will enhance it (see Figure 13.1).

FIGURE 13.1
The Third Landing.

Presentation, practice, and delivery

Deliver the presentation.

Rehearse the presentation.

Choose a delivery option.

Select audio and visual aids.

If all my talents and powers were suddenly taken from me by some inscrutable providence, and I were allowed to keep only one, I would unhesitatingly ask to be allowed to keep my power of speaking for with that one, I would quickly regain all the others.

—Daniel Webster

The human brain is a wonderful thing. It operates from the moment you're born until the first time you get up to make a speech.

—Howard Goshom

Select Presentation Aids: Illustrate Your Speech

LO1

Explain how to use visual and audio aids, including PowerPoint, to enhance the content and delivery of a speech.

The first question to ask yourself about audio and visual aids is, Do I need them? Many speakers make the mistake of not using such aids when the content really demands them. Other speakers use too many audio and visual aids; they clutter the content so much that the presentation becomes confusing and loses momentum. Visual aids have become a tool of choice of speakers in the public arena. In fact, at congressional hearings, it is common for senators and representatives to use aids with text large enough to be seen by the cameras.

In this section, we consider (1) how to determine whether adding audio and visual aids to your presentation will enhance it and (2) how to select and prepare such aids when you decide to use them.

WHY USE PRESENTATION AIDS?

Presentation aids have several functions. Ideally, they make it easier for the audience to follow, understand, respond to, and remember your speech. Thus, when deciding whether to use an audio or visual aid, begin by asking yourself if it will serve at least one of those purposes:

- Facilitate the communication of highly technical information, increasing understanding and reducing confusion
- Highlight or add emphasis to one or more points
- Increase listeners' motivation
- Generate more interest
- Enhance recall
- Dramatize data

For example, using a three-dimensional model of the molecular structure of a virus might create more interest than your words alone could provide. Visuals depicting the damage that cigarette smoke does to human lungs or sound effects that recreate the breathing of lung-cancer victims can similarly add impact. A chart dramatizing the number of infants who fall prey to sudden death syndrome each year, or one symbolizing a decline in real income can also reinforce the spoken message. By providing audience members with an additional channel, audio and visual aids

Visual aids reinforce a speaker's spoken message. A visual that is tangible can add drama to a presentation.

impel them to use their ears and their eyes, pay attention, and care about a speech in ways they otherwise might not.[1]

Once you decide to use audio or visual aids, you have to make a number of serious decisions. Initially, you will need to identify precise points in your presentation when aids will be effective. One way to prepare yourself to make such judgments is to examine how producers of newscasts select audio and visual aids to complement the work of on-camera reporters. After all, in many ways you are the "producer" of your speech.

Another strategy is brainstorming. Examine your outline, consider the information you have, and repeatedly ask yourself the following question: Which specific pieces of information could be improved with audio or visual aids? Keep a record of each idea that comes to mind, being sure to indicate how you would actually use the audio or visual aid.

TYPES OF VISUAL AIDS

Let's now examine a sampling of visual aid choices.

Objects and Models In your brainstorming session, you may have decided that you would like to use an object to illustrate a certain concept. The object you choose can be the real thing—for example, a set of earphones, a food processor, or a computer.

However, using an actual object is often impractical: Objects like automobiles are obviously too large, and objects like microelectronic chips may be too small. In such cases, it may be necessary to use a model instead. A model can be made of clay, papier-mâché, wood scraps, or other materials. If used creatively, inexpensive materials can serve your purpose very well. Your aim is simply to make a reasonable facsimile of the object—something that will enable you to share information more meaningfully.

The photograph above shows celebrity spokesperson Sean "P. Diddy" Combs using himself as a model and wearing the message he sought to share with receivers. Do you think a speaker's dress should become part of the speaker's message?

Objects and models make it easier for you to pull your audience into your speech. Since they are tangible, they can make your points more realistic, and they can add drama to your presentation.

Graphs You can use graphs to make an effective presentation even more successful. The most commonly used graphs are pie, or circle, graphs; bar graphs; line graphs; and pictographs.

A **pie, or circle, graph** is simply a circle with the various percentages of the whole indicated by wedges. By focusing on relationships, pie graphs show how items compare with each other and with the whole. Since the entire circle represents 100 percent, the pie graph is an effective way to show percentage relationships or proportions. In a speech on how to meet the challenges posed by diversity on the job, one student used a pie graph to provide a snapshot of the extent to which employees perceive diversity in the workplace to have changed in a decade (see Figure 13.2).[2]

Sean "P. Diddy" Combs is wearing a message he wants others to accept. In your opinion is wearing a message an effective means of communicating? Why or why not?

pie, or circle, graph
a circle with the various percentages of the whole indicated by wedges; a means of showing percentage relationships

Workplace diversity

Has the level of diversity in your workplace changed from 10 years ago?

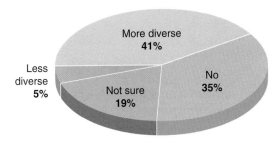

FIGURE 13.2

Pie Graph.

SOURCE: *USA Today* August 13, 2008. Reprinted with permission.

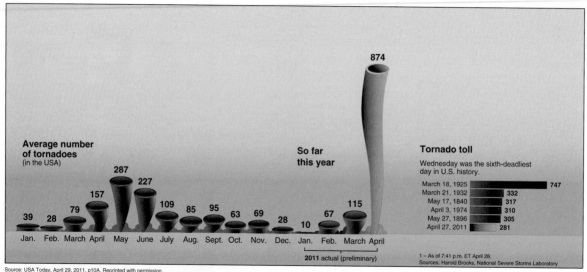

Source: USA Today, April 29, 2011, p10A. Reprinted with permission.

FIGURE 13.3

Average Number of Tornadoes.

bar graph
a graph used to show the performance of one variable over time or to contrast various measures at a point in time

line graphs
graphs used to illustrate trends, relationships, or comparisons over time

pictographs
graphs that use sketches to represent concepts

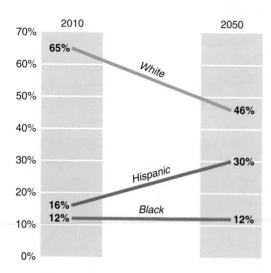

FIGURE 13.4

Growing Minority Influence.

SOURCE: *USA Today* August 14, 2008. Reprinted with permission.

If your goal is to show the performance of one variable over time, a **bar graph** might be appropriate. A bar graph is used to compare quantities or magnitude.

In a speech on how tornadoes form, a student used the bar graph in Figure 13.3 to compare and contrast the average number of tornadoes with the huge number that occurred in April 2011. Thus a bar graph can also be used to show the performance of a variable over time.

Like bar graphs, **line graphs** can illustrate trends, relationships, or comparisons over time. In a speech on incarceration in the United States, one student used a line graph to make the point that while violent crime has abated, harsher sentencing for less serious crimes has caused a dramatic increase in the national prison population.[3] The line graph, in addition to showing the numbers of people in the prison population, also illustrates a perceptible upward trend. If a line graph contains more than one line, the presenter should color-code each line for clarity, as did the speaker in a speech on the growing influence of minorities in the United States (see Figure 13.4). When well designed, the line graph is one of the easiest types for audiences to read and follow.

Pictographs use sketches of figures to represent concepts. During your research, you may discover sketches or pictures that could be integrated into a pictograph to help vitalize your content.

In a speech on incarceration, the speaker incorporated a pictograph (see Figure 13.5) to compare and contrast the percentages of males and females, Whites, Hispanics, and Blacks currently in prison. As you work on your speech, keep a lookout for material you can turn into pictographs that may help audience members visualize your message, as did a

Of every 100 inmates in prison or jail:

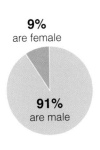

9%
are female

91%
are male

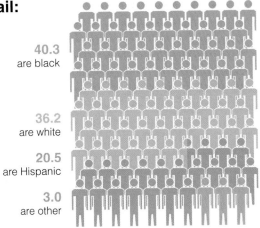

40.3
are black

36.2
are white

20.5
are Hispanic

3.0
are other

1 in 9

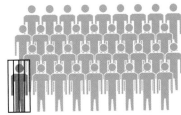

are black men age 20 to 34

1 in 36

are Hispanic men age 18 or older

1 in 106

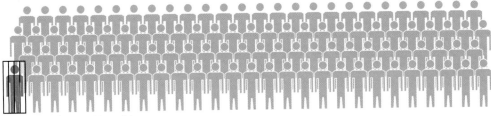

are white men age 18 or older

1 in 100

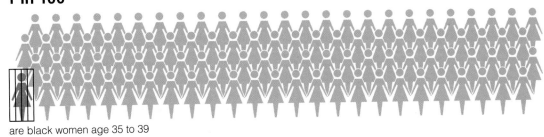

are black women age 35 to 39

1 in 355

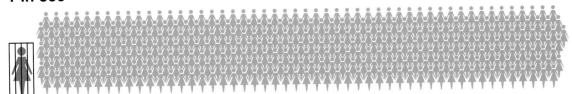

are white women age 35 to 39

FIGURE 13.5

Pictograph of Who Is in Prison.

SOURCE: Time March 17, 2008.

FIGURE 13.6

Pictograph of
Percentage of Nuclear
Power Plants Globally.

SOURCE: *USA Today* July 17, 2008.
Reprinted with permission.

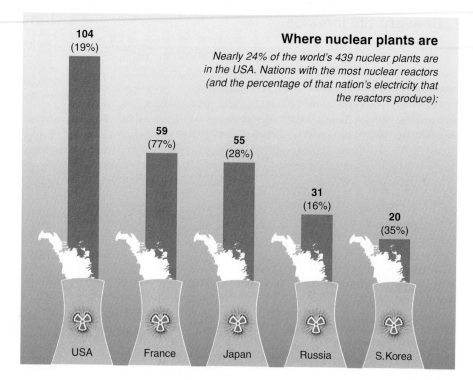

Where nuclear plants are

*Nearly 24% of the world's 439 nuclear plants are
in the USA. Nations with the most nuclear reactors
(and the percentage of that nation's electricity that
the reactors produce):*

speaker delivering a speech on the global implications of nuclear power plants
(see Figure 13.6).[4]

The general rule to follow in making and using graphs is that a single graph
should be used to communicate only one concept or idea. Consider the line graph
in Figure 13.7. This graph is far too cluttered for an audience to read easily and
quickly. Your goal in devising a graph is to eliminate extraneous information and
to focus, rather than diffuse, the audience's attention. Emphasize the essentials.

Photographs and Drawings Drawings, like photographs, can help generate a
mood, clarify, or identify. In explaining a sequence of plays that led to a success
for his football team, one speaker used a drawing like the one in Figure 13.8.
Would you recommend simplifying this sketch?

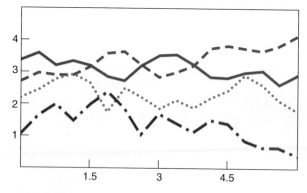

You may find photographs or drawings that can
add interest to your presentation and provide greater
reality. For example, one student used drawings taken
from her local newspaper to help illustrate her speech
on the danger of rip currents (see Figure 13.9).[5]

If possible, use a variety of dark, rich colors, such
as red, black, blue, and green, to add contrast to a
drawing. But remember, unless a drawing is large
enough to be seen, it will not increase your audience's
attention or strengthen your presentation.

FIGURE 13.7

Poorly Designed Line Graph.

Computer Graphics Speech makers commonly use
computer-generated visual aids in their presentations.
Years ago the tradition was for college speakers to use

poster board and marking pens to enlarge charts and graphs so that audience members could see them easily. Now, however, computer graphics make it possible for students to develop professional-looking charts and graphs.

To prepare a computer graphic, begin by organizing your data. Then select the type of graphic you want—for example, pie chart, bar chart, or some other graphic. Many programs automatically generate legends for the visual.

The leading graphics program available is PowerPoint. Figure 13.10 shows a sample of a computer-generated graph. You can use Power-Point to produce such a graph. When using PowerPoint to strengthen or help communicate ideas, the presenter is free to select or create backgrounds, colors, formats, layouts, and sounds. The speaker can also animate text and graphics to fade in or out or to dissolve, as he or she desires. In

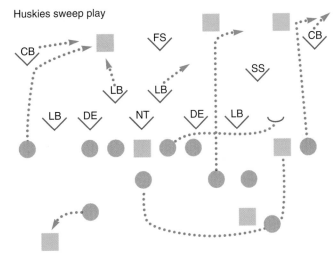

FIGURE 13.8

Drawing.

Rip currents are powerful, channeled currents of water. They typically extend from the shoreline, through the surf zone and past the line of breaking waves. They can extend as far as 3,000 feet offshore, reach 90 feet in width and travel up to 8 feet per second.

How rip currents are formed*

1. Incoming waves cause the water to pile up between the shore and sandbars.

2. A section of a sandbar collapses from the increased water pressure.

3. The excess water is forced through the gap created by the collapsed sandbar and creates a strong, narrow current that can take a swimmer away from the shore.

*They also can occur when the longshore current is diverted by a groin, pier or jetty, or when longshore currents moving in opposite directions meet.

How to escape a rip current

- Stay calm to conserve energy and think clearly.
- Never fight the current.
- Swim out of the current in a direction following the shoreline. When out of the current, swim at an angle away from the current and toward shore.

- If you are unable to swim out of the rip current, float or calmly tread water. When out of the current, swim toward shore.
- If you are still unable to reach shore, draw attention to yourself by waving your arm and yelling for help.

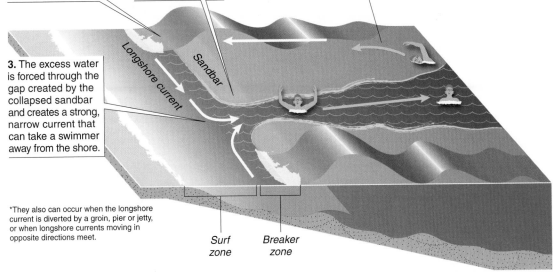

FIGURE 13.9

Drawing.

SOURCES: National Weather Service, U.S. Coast Guard.

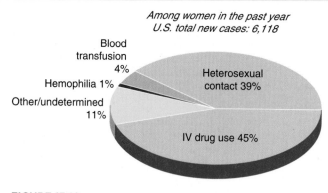

Who Gets AIDS, and Where?

Among women in the past year
U.S. total new cases: 6,118

- Blood transfusion 4%
- Hemophilia 1%
- Other/undetermined 11%
- Heterosexual contact 39%
- IV drug use 45%

FIGURE 13.10

Computer-Generated Graph.

addition, the presenter can scan in other appropriate photographs or relevant visuals, including film clips. (We discuss PowerPoint-assisted presentations in greater detail a little later in this chapter.) You can also use graphics generated by a professional, as one student did when delivering a speech on stages of melanoma (see Figure 13.11), and as another student did when explaining how the Ebola virus works (see Figure 13.12).[6]

Guidelines for Using Visual Aids

When evaluating visuals, remember that they must be appropriate to the audience, the occasion, the location, and the content of your speech—and to you yourself.

In developing and selecting visual materials, keep four criteria in mind: (1) simplicity, (2) clarity, (3) visibility, and (4) authenticity. *Simplicity* means that the visuals should be as transportable as possible (so that you can easily take them with you to the presentation) and as easy as possible to use. Give careful consideration

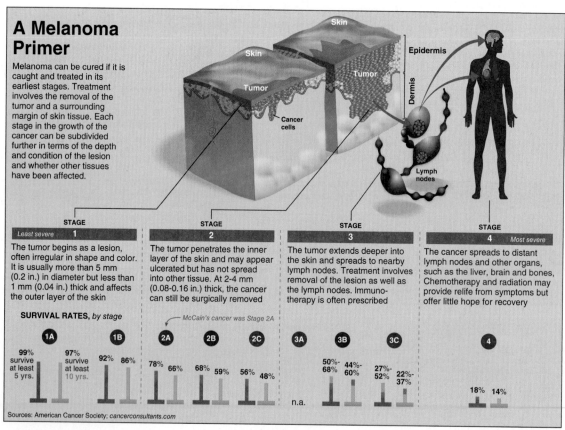

FIGURE 13.11

A Melanoma Primer.

to the size and weight of large items. Ask yourself if you will be able to display the visual without disrupting the environment. Ask yourself if you can set it up and take it down in a minimal amount of time. With regard to clarity, remember that the purpose of a visual aid is to enhance understanding, not to cause confusion. Ideally, each visual should depict only one idea or concept, or at least should be displayed so that only the relevant portions are visible at the appropriate point in your speech. Visibility is the third criterion. Since a visual aid obviously serves no purpose if it cannot be seen and read, you must determine if your audience will be able to see and read it. Make sure that the lettering is tall enough (3 by 4 inches high or larger) and that photographs or pictures are large enough.

FIGURE 13.12

Speakers Often Use Professional Graphics.

The Ebola virus at work.

Authenticity means that the visual is a true depiction of what you are illustrating, that it has not been doctored or "Photoshopped" in the effort to misrepresent evidence and deceive receivers. For example, in May 2012, after the Navy SEALS killed Bin Laden, fake death photos of the terrorist leader spread on the Web. In one, a frame from the film *Black Hawk Down* was used to create a fake photo of Navy SEALS carrying Bin Laden's body. Fabrications like this one succeeded in fooling some newspapers that published them.[7] Too often insatiable hunger for images fuels the use of unauthenticated photographs, causing journalists to have to issue retractions, and harming the credibility of their reporting in the process. When you use a visual, your goal is to enhance your credibility, not detract from it. Unless giving a presentation on the nature or effects of fake photos or fake footage, avoid using such visuals.

When using DVDs, you will need to cue up the DVD before you begin your speech. Far too many speakers press the Play button only to find that they have no picture or sound on the monitor. One speaker had scarcely begun his presentation before he had to call a coffee break while repairs were done on the video equipment. Audiences today are simply not willing to sit while you and others tinker with electronic gadgetry. Prepare it carefully in advance, and rehearse.

Photoshopped images can be deceiving. In the top set of photos, Secretary of State Hillary Clinton was removed when a photo of the Situation Room during the Bin Laden raid ran in the Hasidic newspaper, Der Tzitung. Below, a faked image of Bin Laden's corpse was released by several media outlets.

What is this cartoon suggesting about the use of visuals? Visuals should enhance a presentation.

AUDIO AIDS

Audio is readily available and easy to use as an accompaniment to a speech. CD and MP3 players are very portable. Since speech makers often find it advantageous to integrate a brief excerpt from a song or a segment from an interview or a newscast into their presentations, sound has become a popular support medium. One student, for example, reinforced an informative presentation entitled "The Speech Capabilities of Dolphins" with a few moments of dolphin sounds that she had recorded during a visit to an aquarium.

If you decide to use sound, cue the CD player to the precise point at which you want to begin. Do this before you arrive at the front of the room, so that finding the right spot on the tape will not bring your presentation to an untimely halt.

COMPUTER-ASSISTED PRESENTATIONS: POWERPOINT

Of all the visual aids mentioned, computerized presentations have increased the most in popularity.[8] You can use your outline to build an effective PowerPoint presentations integrating video clips, text, animation, photographs, drawings, and charts in it. PowerPoint contains a clip art library that enables you to select images that enhance the meaning of your words. It also allows you to generate backgrounds, formats, layouts, and colors that you believe best reflect your presentation's purpose. The computer-generated visuals you create can be run directly from a computer projector, printed out in handout form, or blown up for display to the audience. To deliver an effective PowerPoint presentation you need to think visually. By connecting the right words with the right visuals, you can succeed in unifying thought and emotion in audience members. For this to happen, the pictures or images you use need to be the right ones and the message needs to be succinct. Try using the *glance test:* Your receivers should be able to process the message contained in each of your slides in two to three seconds. Receivers should not be distracted from what you are saying to read a slide that is designed more like a technical manual.[9] (See the sample computer-assisted slide presentation on page 372.)

When planning a PowerPoint presentation, think in bullets (see sample slide presentation). Supporting, not replacing your spoken speech, PowerPoint slides illustrate your talk.

Although computerized presentations are the standard in business and education, you do need to be selective when deciding whether or not to create one. If not prepared with care or if allowed to upstage the speaker and overpower the message, computer presentations can drain a speech of its vitality.[10] Reflecting the

Using Many Eyes

Do you currently share videos on YouTube or photos using Flickr? Now an experimental Web site designed to help people publish and discuss graphics in a group, Many Eyes (www.many-eyes.com), lets people share graphs, charts, and other visuals with one another to help interpret data. The theory is that collaborative interpretation of visual information will spur insight and protect against bias.

Access the Many Eyes Web site. Identify the different ways data are presented. Which visuals do you find particularly interesting? Which do you think a public speaker might find useful? Discuss a visual that you believe could be used to tell at least two different stories.

growth in PowerPoint presentations, a chairman of the Joint Chiefs of Staff issued the following order, although not in these exact words, to U.S. military bases around the globe: "Enough with the bells and whistles—just get to the point."[11] To what extent do you agree or disagree with this advice? Whatever your position, the point is that a technological tool that is supposed to facilitate communication should not be used in such a way that it becomes an obstacle to it.

When effective, PowerPoint helps tell a story, working much like scenes from a movie. When it runs smoothly, PowerPoint improves audience member recall by showing why your message should matter to them.

Critics warn that dazzling PowerPoint presentations can be used to cover up weak content.[13] The role of technology is not to elevate format over content but to facilitate communication. Although fiddling with fonts may be fun, it is more important to do adequate research. Another criticism is that by enabling speakers to rely on fuzzy bullet points—bullet points that are deliberately vague or lacking specificity in the information they contain—PowerPoint stifles critical thinking and thoughtful decision making.[14] One blogger, for example, who pointed out that there is nothing inherently visual about bullet points. Imagine, the blogger wrote, if Winston Churchill had used PowerPoint:

Where We Will Fight Them:
- beaches
- hills
- trenches[12]

Another fear is that you will use too many slides and fill them with too many words. In fact, one U.S. computer company has distributed guidelines to its employees about PowerPoint presentations that require them to adhere to the "Rule of Seven": seven bullets or lines per slide, seven words per line.[15] PowerPoint gets a bad rap when a speaker forgets that its role is to *enhance* a speech, not to *be* the speech. By limiting the number of slides you use, taking pains to ensure that your spoken words are not merely what receivers see on your slides—that nothing that comes out of your mouth is replicated word for word in the slides that you display—your slides will enhance rather than overshadow you and your presentation.[16] According to MIT psychology professor Steven Pinker, when used effectively PowerPoint gives visual shape to an argument. Says Pinker, "Language is a linear medium: one damn word after another. But ideas are multidimensional. . . . When properly employed, PowerPoint makes the logical structure of an argument more transparent. Two channels sending the same information are better than one."[17]

SAMPLE COMPUTER-ASSISTED SLIDE PRESENTATION

PowerPoint has been dressing up ideas and contributing to the delivery of crisp presentations for over 20 years.[18] For an example of one such PowerPoint presentation, see below.

1.

Whirlwinds

Tornadoes in Your Life

2.

What Is a Tornado?

The National Weather Service defines a tornado as a violently rotating column of air in contact with the ground. It is a pendent from a thunderstorm.

3.

How Tornadoes Work

- Vortex of air rises into a cloud.
- Vortex becomes a funnel.
- Vortex wind speed can reach 300 mph.

4.

A spinning tube of air formed by low-level wind shear is lifted into the supercell thunderstorm, causing it to rotate.

Downdraft

Supercell storm

Updraft

5.

A downdraft splits the tail end of the tube into two columns — one spinning clockwise, the other spinning counterclockwise.

Downdraft

Supercell storm

Updraft

6.

The updraft stretches the counterclockwise spinning column into the rotating storm; when the storm and column connect, a tornado often is formed.

Tornado forms

7.

Tornado Warnings

- A major storm approaches.
- The atmosphere feels unsettled.
- Wind becomes more and more violent.

1. The first slide introduces the topic to the audience. Speakers usually keep the title slide simple but provocative to draw receivers into the presentation. The speaker's task is to find a background for the slide that reflects the tone of the presentation. What do you think of the background provided here?

2. The second slide introduces the first main point of the speech. The speaker uses the slide to ask and answer a question, clarifying the subject for receivers. How did the speaker add credibility to the definition provided? In your opinion, should the speaker have done more to orient receivers visually to the topic prior to defining this key term?

3. The third, fourth, fifth, and sixth slides introduce the second main point of the speech by summarizing how tornadoes work. In your opinion, will these slides help sustain receiver interest? Why or why not?

4. The seventh slide introduces the third point of the speech by revealing the warning signs of an approaching tornado.

5. In the eighth, ninth, and tenth slides, the speaker develops the fourth main point of the speech by describing how tornadoes are rated, explaining the size of the average tornado, and offering dramatic examples of tornado damage.

6. In the eleventh and twelfth slides, the speaker develops the fifth main point of the speech by summarizing where and when tornadoes are likely to occur

Review, Reflect, & Apply

Recall

Identify the kinds of audio and visual aids speakers can use.

Evaluate

Provide an example of an effective and ineffective visual aid.

8.

The Fujita Scale
Wind Speed

- F0–Up to 72 mph. Broken tree limbs and signs.
- F1–Up to 112 mph. Trailer homes flipped.
- F2–Up to 157 mph. Roofs torn off; trailer homes demolished.

9.

The Fujita Scale
Wind Speed

- F3–Up to 206 mph. Roofs and walls torn down; trains thrown from tracks.
- F4–Up to 260 mph. Frame homes leveled.
- F5–Over 260 mph. Homes and buildings completely destroyed.

10.

How Large Are Tornadoes?

- Average 500 feet in width
- Travel 5 miles on ground
- Last only a few minutes

11.

Where Do Tornadoes Occur Most Often?

- South in early spring
- Midwest in May
- The Texas and Oklahoma Panhandles are sometimes known as Tornado Alley in the spring and early summer.
- Later in the summer, tornadoes are found in the eastern part of the country.

12.

Who Chases Tornadoes?

- People who work for the National Weather Service
- Tourists
- A travel agency in Amarillo, Texas, plans two-week tours every summer for amateur tornado chasers.

13.

Protection from Tornadoes

- Listen to weather reports.
- Get inside a building away from glass.
- Basements are the safest places.

14.

AVOID!

- TRAILER HOMES
- OVERPASSES ON THE HIGHWAY
- TRYING TO CHASE A TORNADO

15.

WHIRLWINDS

DON'T LET THEM CAUSE
TURBULENCE IN YOUR LIFE!

and the kind of people who track them. In your opinion, are any of these slides too wordy? What should the speaker do to enhance receiver involvement in this phase of the speech? For example, should the speaker have included a slide like this showing a tornado's devastation?

7. The thirteenth and fourteenth slides focus on the speaker's last main point—what receivers can do to protect themselves from tornadoes.

8. The final slide wraps up the speech by supporting the speaker's concluding words. It also provides a sense of closure by reflecting the first slide the speaker used in the presentation. In your opinion, did the speaker need to use a slide prior to this one, summarizing what the speech had accomplished? If so, what should that slide have contained?

Would you use this photo in a speech on tornados?

Ethics & Communication

Visual Manipulation

We used to say a photo was worth a thousand words. We used to consider it proof of reality. In fact, there was a time we considered photographic images better than eyewitness accounts. Does that still hold true today? As countless events and scandals have shown, computer programs make is very easy for someone to distort an actual image or fabricate something that never happened. Like a magician creating an illusion, unethical speakers manipulate their audience by altering their visuals to fit the point they are trying to make. For example, after the Japanese tsunami that devastated Japan's coast on March 11, 2011, images appeared on Twitter and Facebook purporting to be photographic evidence of the event. Unfortunately, many were fakes. Fake charity-relief organizations post fake footage on social media to solicit money. Today, receivers are wise to expect speakers to substantiate the visuals they show. For example, a university admitted to doctoring a photo on its brochure cover by inserting Black students into a crowd of White football fans because it was seeking an image of diversity in its recruitment literature.[19] Because speech makers now have the technological ability to doctor their visuals to make their points, the question that needs to be answered is, At what point does the touching up or alteration of a visual put a speaker on ethical thin ice?

9. Are there any other slides you think the speaker should have added to this presentation, or are there any that you feel the speaker could have done without?

10. How many slides did the speaker use that you believe contain too many words or bullets? Shorten these slides to make them more effective.

Preparing to Speak

LO2

Distinguish among four styles of delivery: manuscript, memorized, impromptu, and extemporaneous.

After selecting audio and visual aids, and indicating where in your speech you will integrate them, it's time to take another look at your wording. You want to be certain that you are using an oral rather than a written style, that you have prepared your speech to be heard, not merely read. In what ways do the two styles differ?

First, an oral style is more *personal*. When you deliver a speech, you are able to talk directly to your audience, invite participation, and adapt to reactions in ways a writer typically cannot. Second, an oral style is more repetitive. Because listeners cannot rehear or replay what you have said, you will need to use repetition and reinforcement, repeating and restating important ideas. Third, an oral style is *less formal*. Whereas written discourse often contains abstract ideas, complex phrasing, and a sophisticated vocabulary, simpler sentences and shorter words and phrases characterize the oral style.

The public speaker's language is less like the language of an essayist and more like the language of a skilled conversationalist. Filling your speech with everyday colloquial expressions, clear transitions, personal pronouns, and questions that invite participation is more effective than using abstract language, complex sentences, and impersonal references.

Thus, when wording your speech, remember to do the following:

- Speak in short units.
- Avoid using jargon or technical language when talking to audience members unfamiliar with your subject.
- Keep your words simple, concrete, appropriate, and vivid.

By following these guidelines, you won't sound as if you are reading an essay or a manuscript, which as you will soon see, under most circumstances, you will not be doing.

Four general styles of delivery are available to you as a speech maker: (1) manuscript, (2) memorized, (3) impromptu, and (4) extemporaneous. We briefly examine all four options.

MANUSCRIPT SPEECHES

A **manuscript speech** is written out word for word and then read aloud by the speech maker. Manuscript speeches are most common when it is imperative that precise language be used. For example, since presidential addresses are likely to be under close scrutiny not only in this country but also throughout the world, they often are read from a typed page or a TelePrompTer.

Unfortunately, the use of a manuscript tends to reduce eye contact between speaker and audience. Furthermore, speakers reading aloud often sound as if they are reading to, rather than talking to, the audience, and thus it is difficult to establish the much-needed conversational tone.

manuscript speech
a speech read from a script

MEMORIZED SPEECHES

A **memorized speech** is a manuscript speech that the speaker commits to memory. It often takes on a canned tone. Also, speakers who memorize their lines are less able to respond to audience feedback. Additionally, of course, there is the problem of retention. Speech makers who insist on memorizing their presentations word for word often find themselves plagued by memory lapses, leading to long, awkward silences, during which they valiantly attempt to recall forgotten material. You may want to memorize certain key words, phrases, or segments of your speech, but at this point in your career there is little reason for you to commit the entire presentation to memory.

memorized speech
a manuscript speech committed to memory

IMPROMPTU SPEECHES

An **impromptu speech** is a speech you deliver spontaneously, or on the spur of the moment without formal preparation. An impromptu speaker often has no more than a few seconds or minutes to gather his or her thoughts. An impromptu speaking situation may arise, for example, when a boss unexpectedly asks an employee to discuss the status of a project that is still in its developmental stages. If you are faced with such a request, you will need to rely on what you have learned about patterning your ideas; using the introduction-body-conclusion format will facilitate your task.

impromptu speech
a speech delivered spontaneously, or on the spur of the moment

EXTEMPORANEOUS SPEECHES

An **extemporaneous speech** is researched, outlined, and then delivered after careful rehearsal. Extemporaneous speaking is more audience centered than any of the preceding options. Since the speaker prepares and rehearses in advance, she or he is free to establish eye contact with the members of the audience and to respond to feedback. In addition, because extemporaneous speakers may use notes, they are not constrained by a need to commit the entire presentation to memory. Nor are they handicapped by a manuscript that must be read word for word, inhibiting their adaptability.

extemporaneous speech
a speech that is researched, outlined, and delivered after careful rehearsal

```
    I. Smoking is harmful
        A. Animal studies
            (show visual of animal tests)
        B. Human studies
            (show visual of human lungs)

    II. Smoking must be banned
            (the surgeon general says)
        A. Current laws
        B. New laws needed
```

FIGURE 13.13
Sample Speaker's Notes.

Thus, before delivering an extemporaneous speech, take time to create speaker's notes, also known as an *extemporaneous outline*. The extemporaneous outline contains brief reminders of the key parts of your speech as well as references to support you will use to develop each of your main points.

The extemporaneous outline you prepare should include reminder phrases for your speech's introduction; a statement of your central idea or thesis; brief notes on your main points and subpoints, including the complete names of sources or citations for references; transition reminders; and reminder phrases for your speech's conclusion. Also feel free to include delivery cues in the margins of your outline, such as "emphasize" or "hold up the visual aid," much as an actor marks up a script to facilitate speaking smoothness.

Keep the extemporaneous outline as brief as possible so that you will not be tempted to read your notes instead of maintaining eye contact with your audience. A key to using the extemporaneous outline effectively is to begin practicing your speech using the more detailed outline you developed previously. Once you rehearse a few times using that outline and are comfortable and familiar with the content of your speech, make the switch and rely only on the extemporaneous outline during remaining practice sessions. (For a sample of a card containing brief speaker's notes, see Figure 13.13.)

Unfortunately, many speakers confuse manuscript, memorized, and impromptu speeches with extemporaneous speeches. Although asked to give an extemporaneous speech, they may insist on writing it out word for word and then either memorizing or reading it. Or they may spend too little time preparing the speech and deliver what is essentially a poorly developed impromptu presentation. Such misconceptions defeat the speakers' purpose and decrease their effectiveness as speech makers. The extemporaneous speech has been found most effective for most public speakers. Above all, do not turn extemporaneous speaking into something it is not.

Review, Reflect, & Apply

Recall

Define four delivery styles: manuscript, memorized, impromptu, and extemporaneous.

Apply

For each delivery style, give one example of an occasion in which that style of speaking would be most appropriate.

Analyze

Compare and contrast the speaker's challenges when speaking (1) from a manuscript, (2) from memorization, (3) impromptu, and (4) extemporaneously.

Rehearsing: Using Tryouts and Speakers' Tools

LO3

Identify speech rehearsal and delivery strategies including the effective use of nonverbal cues.

In the theatre, playwrights, producers, directors, and performers never open an important show without first holding a series of tryouts or preview performances. These performances give the cast and backers an opportunity to experience audiences' reactions and, if necessary, make needed alterations in the script or actors' performance. As a speech maker, you can benefit by giving yourself the same opportunities. At your disposal are three basic speech-making tools—(1) visual, (2) vocal, and (3) verbal—which, if mastered during rehearsals, will reinforce your message.

In addition to your ideas, what qualities in you do you want to communicate to your audience? If you are like most speakers, you want your audience to accept you as a credible source. As we will see in Chapter 15, this means that you want your listeners to consider you competent, trustworthy, and dynamic.

How is credibility communicated? Obviously, it is conveyed, verbally, through the content and structure of language. However, far too frequently, speakers forget that credibility is also conveyed through visual and vocal cues. As we noted in Chapter 5, the nonverbal components of a message account for at least 65 percent of the total meaning transmitted to listeners. Thus, during rehearsals, the visual and vocal dimensions of your speech merit careful attention. You want to ensure that the sound of your voice, your appearance, and your demeanor add to your presentation. This calls on you to rehearse.

CONDUCT TRYOUTS: REHEARSE, REHEARSE, REHEARSE

Your extemporaneous outline is complete. It is now time for you to become your own audience and explore the sound and feel of your speech before you present it to others. You will need three essential ingredients for your first tryout: (1) your speaker's notes, (2) a clock or wristwatch, and (3) a recording device (audio or visual) so that you can review the exact words you use to express your ideas. Before starting, check the time and turn on the recorder. Then stand up, face an imaginary audience, and begin delivering your speech. In effect, you are now in the process of preparing an oral rough draft of your presentation. Many speakers find it helpful to commit the first and last sentences of the speech to memory. If you do not memorize your opening and closing sentences, you should at the least become very familiar with them. (As one student put it, "That way I know that I'll be able to start and stop the speech.") Present the entire speech a number of times, conducting a series of tryouts or rehearsals over several days, sometimes alone, at other times before a small group of friends or relatives. During your rehearsals be sure to practice using your audio and visual aids. Also practice delivering the speech in several locations. This will help you get used to the foreign feel of the room where the speech will be given. Your goal is to develop a flexible delivery—one that will enable you to meet the unique demands of the live audience.

What will you discover and do during rehearsals? First, you want to know if your presentation consumes too much or too little time. If your run-through takes 25 minutes and your time limit is 5 minutes, you have to make some serious revisions. If, on the other hand, you have designed a "60-second wonder," you may find that you need to go back to the library for more material. Second, as you listen to your speech, be alert for ideas that you have not expressed as clearly as you would like. This is your opportunity to fix them. Third, you may find that you express the same thoughts again and again and again—more than is necessary for redundancy. This is your opportunity to edit. Fourth, you may realize that your speech's structure is confusing because of missing or inappropriate transitions, or that you need to remind yourself to stress certain points because of their importance. Add needed transition and delivery reminders to your notes.

Just as a playwright reworks a scene, you may also rework sections of your speech. If, when conducting a tryout, you find that your main attention getter is not as effective as it could be, improve it. If the supporting material under, say, the second main point in the body of your speech is confusing, rewrite it. If an illustration is

The clothing a speaker wears should reinforce, not detract from, the presentation.

too long and drawn out, shorten it. Your goal during tryouts is to refine your speech until it is as close as possible to the one you will present to your audience.

CONDUCT A VISUAL TUNE-UP

Let's consider visual cues. How do you think a speech maker should look standing before an audience? Close your eyes and picture his or her clothing, posture, gestures, movements and facial expressions, and use of eye contact.

CLOTHING

In deciding what to wear when you deliver your speech, you should consider the topic, the audience, and the occasion. Sometimes speakers make thoughtless errors in dress. For example, one student delivered a very serious tribute to a well-known leader while wearing a shirt emblazoned with a huge Mickey Mouse emblem. (When asked why he wore that shirt, he responded, "I didn't think anyone would notice.") The clothes you wear should not distract receivers from focusing on the ideas of your speech.

Be aware that it is up to you to choose what you will wear. Your clothing does not choose you.

Posture

As a public speaker, you will almost always be expected to stand when addressing your audience. Thus, unless you are physically challenged, you should expect to be on your feet. Although this may seem obvious, the problem is that standing is something many of us do not do very well. Your posture communicates; it sends potent messages to the audience. Speakers often seem to forget this, assuming a stance that works against them rather than for them. For example, some speakers lean on the lectern or actually drape themselves over it as if unable to stand without its assistance. Some prop themselves against the wall behind them, giving the impression that they want to disappear into it.

To prepare yourself to stand properly in public, assume your natural posture and ask others to evaluate it. Are you too stiff? Do you slouch? Do you appear too relaxed? Feedback can help you put your best posture forward when you rise to speak.

Gestures

As we noted in Chapter 6, gestures are movements of a speaker's hands and arms. The gestures you use when speaking in public may be purposeful, helping reinforce the content of your speech, or purposeless, detracting from your message. Gestures can also be cultural. For example, people in the United States point with one finger while the Chinese point with a open hand. A problem most of us encounter is that we have certain favorite gestures that we are unaware of doing—things like scratching our neck, putting our hands into and out of our pockets, jingling our keys or jewelry, or smoothing our hair. Such mannerisms often become intensified when we find ourselves faced with a stressful situation such as speaking in public. In fact, when people are nervous, it is not unusual for them to add new gestures to their repertoire of annoying mannerisms. Speakers will sometimes tap a pencil or ring on the lectern or even crack their knuckles—things they would never do in normal circumstances.

Gestures can, however, serve a number of useful purposes. They can help you emphasize important points, enumerate your ideas, or suggest shapes or sizes. Thus, your job with regard to gestures is really twofold. First, you need to work to eliminate annoying gestures; second, you need to incorporate appropriate gestures that can be used to enhance the ideas contained in your speech.

Movements and Facial Expressions

It is important to understand that your presentation begins as soon as you are introduced or called on to speak—that is, before you have spoken your first syllable. The way you rise and approach the speaker's stand communicates a first impression to your listeners. Similarly, your facial expressions as you complete your speech and your walk as you return to your seat also send important signals to your audience. Far too many speech makers approach the lectern in inappropriate ways. For example, they may walk in a way that broadcasts a lack of preparation. Some even verbalize this by mumbling something like "I'm really not ready. This will be terrible." Others apologize for a poor showing all the way back to their seats.

Consider carefully your way of moving to and from the speaker's stand. The way you move communicates whether or not you are in control. You may have noticed that confident people walk with head erect, follow a straight rather than a circuitous path, proceed at an assured rather than a hesitant or frenetic pace, and use open rather than closed arm movements.

Eye Contact

Eye contact also communicates. Unfortunately, some speakers "talk" to walls, chalkboards, windows, trees, or the floor rather than to their listeners. Some speakers seem embarrassed to look at any audience members; others seek the attention of one person and avoid looking at anyone else. Some student speakers avoid meeting the eyes of the instructor during a speech; others focus on him or her exclusively.

Be sure that your gaze includes all the members of the audience. Look at each individual as you deliver your speech. Such contact will draw even the most reluctant listeners into your presentation. Remember that in the United States, direct eye contact conveys sincerity.

CONDUCT A VOCAL TUNE-UP

Obviously, the voice is one of our main tools in speech making. In Chapter 5, we considered four basic vocal dimensions: volume, rate, pitch, and quality. Review this material during your rehearsals, keeping in mind that your goal is to use your voice to reinforce the content of your speech.

To respond to your ideas, your audience must, of course, first hear them. Maintaining your voice at an appropriate volume is your responsibility. If you are to address a group in a large auditorium, a public-address system will probably be provided. If you are addressing a group in a smaller room, you will probably be expected to speak without amplification. By observing the people in the rear, you should be able to determine if you are speaking loudly enough for them to hear you easily. If you notice that any of the audience members look confused or upset, speak up. On the other

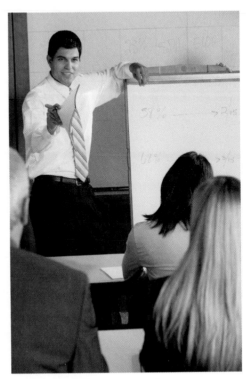

Eye contact draws receivers into a presentation.

hand, if your voice is normally loud and you notice that those seated nearest to you are cringing, turn down your volume a bit.

With regard to pitch, try not to fall into the monotone trap. If you maintain one predominant tone throughout your presentation, you will create a sense of boredom in the audience. Use pitch to reflect the emotional content of your material; use it to create interest.

Like volume and pitch, rate also communicates. Speaking too quickly or too slowly can impede understanding. Thus, respond to feedback from your audience and speed up or slow down your pace as appropriate.

Nonfluencies are a problem every public speaker needs to consider. "Uhs" and "ums" are normal in communication encounters, but they are not expected in speech making. During person-to-person conversations, we realize that people are thinking about or planning what they are going to say next. In contrast, we expect public speakers to have prepared their remarks carefully, and thus we are less tolerant of their nonfluencies. Attempt to eliminate nonfluencies from your delivery as much as possible.

CONDUCT A VERBAL TUNE-UP

Although we have already focused on developing the verbal aspects of your speech (see Chapter 12), when rehearsing, be sure to use language that is clear and vivid.

As you rehearse your speech, ask yourself if it contains any unnecessary or confusing words or expressions. If so, eliminate them. For example, instead of saying "a sufficient supply of," say "enough." In general, choose simpler and more familiar words over those that could cause audience members difficulty in deciphering their meaning. Thus, say "plan" rather than "strategize." This especially holds true for idioms when addressing audiences composed of people from diverse cultures. Also remember to use transitions to guide your audience from one point to the next.

How do you make your words live in the minds of audience members? As you rehearse, ask yourself if your speech contains vivid words, including strong and

What would you tell this speaker about his approach to speech making?

© Mike Twohy/The New Yorker Collection/www.cartoonbank.com.

"It's a good speech—just a couple of points that need obfuscation."

Culture and Delivery

Cultural background and conditioning affect a speaker's nonverbal repertoire and how members of the audience interpret nonverbal cues. Consider the following:

When it comes to eye contact, we know that speakers of Arabic, Latino, and Southern European descent tend to look directly into the faces of audience members, while Chinese, Japanese, Northern European, and Pakistani speakers are more likely to avoid focusing directly on receivers' faces. Similarly, in Native American culture, direct eye contact could be construed as insulting, whereas Caucasian Americans consider it a sign of respect. What is more, while in the West a speaker placing his or her hands on his or her hips may suggest confidence, among Asians it reflects obstinacy. Similarly, Asians are likely to interpret a speaker's folding his or her arms across the chest as arrogant. And whereas scratching one's lip in the United States probably means it itches, in China, it is an invitation to sexual intimacy.

Cultural norms also govern the intensity of a speaker's nonverbal cues. For example, speakers from Mediterranean cultures are known to amplify emotional displays, whereas Asians are likely to conceal emotional intensity by masking it with a smile. Asian speakers also tend to make less use of their arms and hands to underscore a point than do Westerners. Their constrained use of nonverbal cues may suggest a lack of involvement when that is not the case.

Vocal cues also vary from culture to culture. For example, Asians are likely to use a lower voice to express emphasis rather than a louder one. Additionally, the higher pitch and intonation pattern used by Arabic speakers is apt to convey extreme emotion to North Americans. Thus, some North American audience members may conclude that Arabic speakers are angry or agitated when neither is the case. And for similar reasons, an Arabic receiver may interpret the speech patterns and emotions of North American speakers as indicating a lack of commitment to expressed positions when this also is untrue.

Given these cultural practices, in your opinion, what adaptations in the use of nonverbal cues, if any, should a speaker from a culture different from most members of an audience make when delivering a speech?

active verbs, and figures of speech and images to enliven your presentation by helping audience members form mental pictures. Avoid using tired words such as "very interesting," or "world-class" or clichés such as "cool as a cucumber" or "sly as a fox." Phrases like these are used so often that audiences find them trite and meaningless. Language that helps audience members not only understand but also see, hear, and feel your message is your goal.

THE REHEARSAL-CONFIDENCE CONNECTION

Rehearsal—careful practice of your presentation—gives you the confidence you need to deliver an effective speech. Now that you have prepared and tried out your extemporaneous outline, integrating appropriate presentation (both visual and audio) aids, do you find that you are more confident? Rehearsal is your key to synthesizing all you have done into a polished presentation. During rehearsals you make final revisions based on whether

- your speech is the right length or you need to delete or add material to it
- the words of your speech flow smoothly or you need to spend more time on phrasing
- your visual and audio aids work effectively or you need to troubleshoot technical problems
- you control your apprehensiveness or need to use more relaxation techniques
- you master using speaker's notes or need even more practice

> *If you have eight hours to cut down a tree, you should spend six hours sharpening your saw.*
>
> —Joey Ashner, Speaking Consultant

Review, Reflect, & **Apply**

Recall

Describe procedures for rehearsing a speech.

Understand

Identify criteria for assessing the speaker's use of visual and vocal cues.

Apply

Keep a log of your progress during rehearsals.

Giving the Speech: Some Final Tips

If you follow the developmental plan outlined in this book, you should find your-self ready and eager to deliver your speech. Not only will you have carefully prepared and rehearsed your address, you will also have at your disposal tested techniques to help you control your nerves. At this juncture, you should need only a few additional pointers:

1. Arrive at your speaking location with ample time to spare. Be sure that you have prepared equipment to hold your notes and presentation aids.
2. If you are going to use a public-address system or other electronic equip-ment, test it so that you will not have to adjust the volume or replace bulbs or batteries unnecessarily during your presentation.
3. Give ample consideration to your clothing and appearance. Your confi-dence and believability will increase if you look the part. (But do not distract yourself with worries about your appearance while you are speaking.)
4. Let your audience know you are prepared by the way you rise when introduced and by walking confidently to the podium.
5. While speaking, work to transmit a sense of enthusiasm and commitment to your listeners.
6. Complete your speech before returning to your seat. You have worked hard to communicate your credibility to audience members; don't ruin it in the last few seconds. Last impressions, like first impressions, count.

After the Speech: Evaluating Your Effectiveness

LO4

Analyze a speech maker's performance (including your own) in terms of content, organization, language, and delivery.

As soon as you have completed your presentation, the first question you will ask yourself is, How did I do? No doubt you will also want to know what your peers and your instructor thought of your performance. You and your listeners can eval-uate your speech by analyzing how effectively you were able to handle each of the following: content, organization, language, and delivery.

CONTENT

Was the subject of your speech appropriate? Was it worthwhile? Was your purpose communicated clearly? Did you research the topic carefully? Were your audiovisual aids helpful? Did you use a variety of support? Were your main points adequately developed? Were the main divisions of your speech effectively bridged by transi-tional words and phrases?

ORGANIZATION

How effective was your organizational approach? Did you begin with material that gained the attention of the audience? Did you preview each main point? Were your main points arranged in a logical sequence? Was the number of main points appropriate for the time allotted? Was your organizational design easily discern-ible? Did your conclusion provide a logical wrap-up of your main parts? Did it motivate listeners to continue thinking about your presentation?

LANGUAGE

Did you use clear language to explain your ideas? Was it vivid? Did your speech sound as if it should be listened to rather than read? Could any of the words or phrases you used have been considered offensive to any audience members?

DELIVERY

Did you maintain effective eye contact with the members of the audience? Did you approach the speaking situation confidently? Were you able to use an extemporaneous style of delivery? Could you be heard easily? Was your speaking rate appropriate? Did you articulate clearly? Were you able to convey a sense of enthusiasm as you spoke? Did your gestures help reinforce your content?

Review, Reflect, & **Apply**

Recall
Define what is meant by postpresentation analysis.

Understand
Explain how you might go about evaluating a speech and its delivery.

Evaluate
Assess your own performance as a speechmaker.

Communication Skills

PRACTICE TIPS FOR SELF-EVALUATION

When it is time for the audience members to comment on your presentation, they, like you, should consider the positive dimensions of your performance before making recommendations for improvement. Speaker and audience alike should remember that analysis is designed to be constructive, not destructive. It should help build confidence. It should not destroy the speaker's desire to try again.

Your instructor will probably provide you with a more formal analysis of your work, using an evaluation form similar to the one shown in Figure 13.14.

FIGURE 13.14

Evaluation Form.

Name: _____ Speech: _____

Specific purpose: _____

1. Content
    ___ Based on accurate analysis of speaking situation.
    ___ Specific goal of speech was apparent.
    ___ Subject appropriate, relevant, and interesting to intended audience.
    ___ All material clearly contributed to purpose.
    ___ Had specific facts and opinions to support and explain statements.
    ___ Support was logical.
    ___ Handled material ethically.
    ___ Used audio and/or visual aids when appropriate.
    ___ Included a variety of data—statistics, quotations, etc.
    ___ Moved from point to point with smooth transitions.
2. Organization
    ___ Began with effective attention-getter.
    ___ Main points were clear statements that proved or explained specific goals.
    ___ Points were arranged in logical order.
    ___ Each point was adequately supported.
    ___ Concluded with memorable statement that tied speech together.
3. Language
    ___ Ideas were clear.
    ___ Ideas were presented vividly.
    ___ Ideas were presented emphatically.
    ___ Language was appropriate for intended audience.
4. Delivery
    ___ Was prepared to speak.
    ___ Stepped up to speak with confidence.
    ___ Maintained contact with audience.
    ___ Sounded extemporaneous, not read or memorized.
    ___ Referred to notes only occasionally.
    ___ Sounded enthusiastic.
    ___ Maintained good posture.
    ___ Used vocal variety, pitch, emphasis, and rate effectively.
    ___ Gestured effectively.
    ___ Used face to add interest.
    ___ Articulation was satisfactory.
    ___ On finishing, moved out with confidence.
    ___ Fit time allotted.

    Additional comments:

Whether or not your instructor uses the form in Figure 13.14, you will find it helpful as a personal guide.

Another means of evaluating your own effectiveness as well as the effectiveness of other speakers is to evaluate the credibility of the evidence included in a presentation. See the evaluation checklist at the end of Chapter 15.

The Wrap-Up

SUMMARY

LO1   **Explain** how to use visual and audio aids, including PowerPoint, to enhance the content and delivery of a speech.

Integrating visual images and sound effects in a speech helps to reinforce, clarify, and dramatize its content. Among the visual and audio aids speakers can use in a speech are objects, models, graphs, photographs, drawings, slides, DVDs, and sound from CDs or MP3s. If used to enhance rather than overpower a presentation, PowerPoint can also be an effective speech-making tool.

LO2   **Distinguish** among four styles of delivery: manuscript, memorized, impromptu, and extemporaneous.

A manuscript is written out word for word and then read aloud by the speech maker. A memorized speech is one the speaker commits to memory. An impromptu speech is a speech a speaker delivers on the spur of the moment without formal preparation. An extemporaneous speech is one the speaker researches, outlines, and then delivers after careful rehearsal.

LO3   **Identify** speech rehearsal and delivery strategies including practicing the effective use of nonverbal cues.

During rehearsals or speech tryouts speakers time their presentation, refine the clarity and vividness of their words, edit out unnecessary redundancy, and add needed transition and delivery reminders. They also consider how to dress for the presentation, and work on supporting their speech with appropriate posture, gestures and body movement, facial expressions, and vocal cues. On the day of their presentation, they arrive prepared, and make sure any equipment they will use is working.

LO4   **Assess** a speech maker's performance (including your own) in terms of content (including the integration of audio/visual aids), organization, language, and delivery.

The speaker and the audience evaluate the speech's effectiveness. Among the factors they consider are its content, organization, language, and delivery.

KEY CHAPTER TERMINOLOGY

bar graph 364	manuscript speech 375
extemporaneous speech 375	memorized speech 375
impromptu speech 375	pictographs 364
line graphs 364	pie, or circle, graph 363

COMMUNICATING TO THE PUBLIC

Informative Speaking

14

After completing this chapter, you should be able to demonstrate mastery of the following learning outcomes:

LO1 **Define** *informative speaking.*

LO2 **Distinguish** among four types of informative discourse.

LO3 **Explain** how to create information hunger and increase listeners' comprehension.

LO4 **Develop** and present an informative speech.

Life is different today than it was even a decade ago. Now computer screens surround us. When walking on the street, people no longer look straight ahead. Instead, they gaze downward, looking at smart phone screens in the effort to connect with another person or to find information they seek. While we literally are awash in connections to more and more information, can we ever thoughtfully process all the information we gather?

How does it feel to have more access to information than ever before? Information not only has value today, it also confers power. Once in possession of the *right* information, we can understand things we otherwise might not have been able to, and accomplish things we otherwise would not have done. But is it possible that we now have *too much* information? According to *Living in the Information Age,* because our capacity to absorb information has not increased while we daily face deluges of new and sometimes conflicting data, we have a greater need to filter, process, and edit the information we receive.[1] We also have an increasingly important need to conceptualize. In fact, while information remains essential, we are now transitioning—moving out of the information age and into the *conceptual age*—a time when people with the ability to understand and interpret meaning, think

We now face the pros-
pect of information
obesity.

—David Shenk

There are things that
are known and things
that are unknown; in
between are doors.

—Anonymous

differently, detect patterns, recognize opportunities, and edit and put the pieces together in new ways will be in demand.[2] Do you have these skills?

Informative speakers face three primary challenges: (1) to identify information important to others; (2) to put themselves in the position of their receivers and make the information they deliver understandable to them; and (3) to communicate information in ways that create interest, enhance learning, and help audience members remember their message.

Being able to convey information and meaning to others is among the most useful skills you can acquire. That is what this chapter prepares you to do—to share information you have with people who lack it but need it, or who possess it but do not fully understand it. Let's get started.

Speaking Informatively

LO1

Define informative speaking.

informative speech
a speech that updates and adds to the knowledge of receivers

What's happening? How does it work? What's going on? What is it? What does it mean? These are the kinds of questions that an **informative speech** answers. Whenever you prepare an informative speech, your goal is to offer your audience members more information than they already have about a topic. Your objective is to update and add to their knowledge, refine their understanding, or provide background.[3]

How does the informative speech relate to your life? Our world is filled with informative messages that we depend on. Many of these messages are informal, but others are carefully planned, structured, and rehearsed to achieve maximum impact.

In today's world, it is important to develop the ability to share information with other people. Some three-quarters of the U.S. labor force hold jobs that require the production, storage, or delivery of information. Educators in schools and businesses, sales professionals, medical practitioners, and consultants and managers in a wide array of fields depend on their skill in giving and receiving information for their livelihoods. They all share the need to make their messages clear, relevant, and useful to receivers.

Review, **Reflect,** & **Apply**

Recall

Identify the purposes of an informative speech.

Understand

Give examples of informative speeches, either real or hypothetical.

Types of Informative Presentations

LO2

Distinguish among four types of informative discourse.

Let's now consider four types of informative speeches: (1) messages of explanation (speeches of demonstration that explain the how or how-to of a subject), (2) messages of description (speeches that describe what a person, an object, or an event is like), (3) messages of definition (speeches that define what something is), and (4) narrative messages (speeches that tell a story).

EXPLANATIONS

If your purpose is to explain how to do something (for example, how to motivate employees), how to make something (for example, how to make glass), how something works (for example, how a slot machine works), or how something develops or occurs (for example, how tornadoes form, how insider trading works), then you are preparing to deliver an explanation of a process. Your primary goal is to share your understanding of the process or procedure with your listeners and, in some instances, to give them the skills they need to replicate it. A speech of explanation deepens understanding by answering an interesting question, helping receivers get the answer(s) they need to facilitate their understanding or skill development.[4]

What techniques is this coach using to share information with his players?

When organizing a message of explanation, be especially careful to avoid overcondensing the data. It is not uncommon for an inexperienced speaker to merely enumerate the steps involved in a process. This kind of perfunctory outline is hard for an audience to follow. Instead, use meaningful information groups. For example, grouping information under such headings as "Gathering Ingredients," "Blending Ingredients," and "Adding the Garnish" would be considerably more effective than simply relaying 15 steps involved in preparing a chocolate mousse. Besides facilitating understanding, this grouping system also helps the audience retain the material.

It is also important to consider the length of time it will take to accomplish your objectives in a process speech. Take a tip from televised cooking shows. Notice how an on-the-air chef always demonstrates some parts of the process live but has other parts of the dish prepared in advance to save time. This technique can be of great value to you, too.

DESCRIPTIONS

One of your responsibilities as a speaker is to be able to describe a person, place, or thing for your listeners. For instance, if you were a site-location specialist for a fast-food chain, you would have to describe potential store locations to the management. If you were a spokesperson for a nuclear plant that had experienced a radiation leak, you would have to describe the location and extent of the mishap to the media. Your aim is to help your listeners form mental close-ups of places, people, or things. To do this, you need to find ways to describe condition, size, shape, color, age, and so on to make your subject come alive for your audience.

Speakers tend to use either a spatial or a topical organizational pattern when describing a person, place, or thing. Thus, a speaker might use a spatial pattern when describing the Newseum, but opt to use a topical organization when describing the scientific contributions of Galileo.

Of course, visual aids are particularly relevant to a descriptive presentation. For example, photographs, maps, and drawings can make it easier for you to describe a significant archaeological dig, the pathos of a homeless person, the appearance of a high-tech artificial limb, or the destruction caused by a tornado or tsunami.

Whatever your topic, you will want to ensure that your words and phrases evoke the appropriate sensory responses in your listeners. To do this, communicate how your subject looks, tastes, smells, feels, and sounds. In a descriptive speech, you paint with words.

Assessing Informative Speaking Skills

Daniel Shenk, the author of *Data Smog: Surviving the Information Glut,* observes, "With a majority of American workers now paid to churn out data, we have generated a morass of expert information that has started to undermine logical approaches to deliberation and problem solving."[5] Well over 100,000 studies now exist on depression. It has produced not only an overabundance of information, but also so many competing expert opinions that it becomes virtually impossible for the receiver of this magnitude of information to draw a conclusion, leading one to suffer the consequences of "paralysis by analysis." Therefore we must ask, how much information is too much information? Could endless information result in perpetual argumentation, but no decision? Does a speaker have an obligation to avoid overwhelming audience members with data? What advice would you offer a speaker regarding the steps to take to minimize the effects of "data smog"?

DEFINITIONS

"What do you mean?" is a common question. In most cases, the questioner asks it when seeking clarification or elaboration of ideas from a speaker. Sometimes a satisfactory answer can be supplied in a sentence or two. At other times, however, it takes a speech, or even a book, to define a concept adequately. For example, books with titles such as *Data Smog, The Age of Paradox, Emotional Intelligence, Leader Effectiveness Training, Loyalty,* and *Happiness Is . . .* are actually extended definitions: The authors are discussing their meaning for a particular concept or idea. An informative speech of definition likewise provides an audience with an explanation of a term. "Shyness," "The Grief Cycle," "ESP," and "Bullying" are among the topics for which a definitional presentation would be appropriate.

Can you think of others? Many students find that topics such as "Racial Profiling," "The Meaning of Obscenity," "Prejudice," "Friendship," and "Sexual Harassment" give them the freedom they need to develop effective speeches of definition.

Since many of the concepts you may choose to define will have connotative, or subjective, meanings not traditionally found in dictionaries, not all members of your audience will agree with the definition you present. On one television talk show, for example, two experts on shyness were unable to agree on what it means to be shy. It is necessary, therefore, to organize a definitional speech in a way that will be clear and persuasive. For example, how would you define *shyness?* To explain your meaning for the term, you might offer examples of what it feels like to be shy, describe how a shy person behaves, and then go on to discuss the consequences of shyness. Perhaps you would explain shyness by comparing and contrasting a shy person with an extrovert. Or you might choose to discuss the causes of shyness and then focus on different types or categories of shyness. No matter how you choose to order your ideas, your organization should be suggested by the topic and grow out of it.

NARRATIVES

Extended stories, or narratives, function as "teaching moments" and are an alternative means of providing information. They are often more entertaining and involving than more traditional approaches to informative speaking. Speakers who use the narrative format need to convey clearly the message contained in the story they tell so that audience members perceive its relevance. "Post-Traumatic Stress Syndrome: A Soldier's Story," "The Story of My Brother's Death: My Travels through the Cycle of Grief," "My Adoption," and "How I Used a Defibrillator to Save a Life" are the titles of informative speeches in which speakers could benefit from using a narrative approach to tell audience members more about their subject. Personal stories interest receivers who are drawn to someone they can relate to. Stories help audience members identify with your topic. When delivering a narrative, fill your story's plot with action and conflict—opposing ideas or forces in opposition—with one side pitted against another. Your story may also contain humor or drama to hold the audience's attention, and suspense to heighten and maintain interest. Speakers can use temporal, topical, and spatial patterns to develop informational personal narratives.

Review, Reflect, & Apply

Recall

List four types of informative speeches.

Analyze

Compare and contrast the speech of explanation, description, definition, and narrative speech.

Apply

Identify a process you feel equipped to speak about and prepare a short speech to explain it.

Effective Informative Speeches: Increasing Your Listeners' Interest and Comprehension

An effective informative speech accomplishes several tasks: (1) makes your listeners want to learn more about the topic; (2) communicates the information clearly by providing information balance; (3) emphasizes key points; (4) involves audience members in your presentation; and (5) provides information in ways that make it memorable, perhaps through novelty, creativity, and audiovisuals. Let's look at these tasks.

LO3

Explain how to create information hunger and increase listeners' comprehension.

CREATE INFORMATION HUNGER

Your primary goal in an informative speech is to deliver a message of explanation, description, definition, or narrative, but it is equally important that audience members find your presentation interesting, intellectually stimulating, and relevant (that is, significant or personally valuable). In other words, you need to work to increase each listener's need to know and hunger to receive your message.

You will be more adept at creating information hunger if you have analyzed your audience carefully (see Chapter 11). Then, by using appropriate vehicles, you will be able to generate the interest that will motivate audience members to listen to the information you want to share. Remember to use the attention-getting devices discussed in Chapter 13. For example, you can relate your own experiences or the experiences of others; you can ask rhetorical questions; you can draw analogies for your listeners to consider. You can also arouse the audience's curiosity, and you can incorporate humor or use eye-catching visual aids.

Obviously, your effectiveness as a speaker will increase to the extent that you present your information creatively and succeed in arousing the desire and the need to know among audience members.

Exploring **Diversity**

Conveying Information across Cultures

When preparing to deliver an informative speech, should the information you include depend on the cultural makeup of your audience? Should you always work to exhibit divergent thinking by approaching your topic from a variety of perspectives? Before answering, consider this.

An African proverb says, "The earth is a beehive; we all enter by the same door, but live in different cells," meaning that people share a basic capacity to look at the same world of ideas (a hive), focus on a particular topic (a door), and strive for a similar goal (a cell). Yet in spite of having similar access to the same information, people are individually motivated and they head for different destinations. Thus the same information can take a different course when delivered to several audiences.

Consider an informative topic such as how to avoid contracting AIDS. The scientific and social information on this topic are the same everywhere in the world, yet no two groups will have the same approach to it. An informative talk on the subject addressed to a group of prison inmates might be aimed at specific remedies for a high-risk group. (The speech would contain very basic biological data regarding channels of transmission and specific physical methods of preventing exposure.) The same talk addressed to a group of apprehensive parents in a middle-class suburb might focus on the effects of presenting such information to children of various ages. A speech on the subject to a group of Chinese health professionals visiting the United States might aim at their concerns for minimizing the impact of the disease in their country.

The question: Should a speech be a global mosaic that cuts across cultures to develop common understandings, or should a speaker who belongs to a specific racial or ethnic group speak to the interests of his or her own group? What advantages and disadvantages do you see in each approach?

Thus, if you addressed an audience on how the changing demographics in the United States will affect the workforce in the next decade, your speech would likely interest them because it would add to their knowledge and better prepare them to respond to changing times.

SEEK INFORMATION BALANCE

Your speech will inform receivers only if they are capable of processing the information you deliver. A common danger in informative speaking is that the audience experiences information overload. **Information overload** occurs when (1) the speech maker delivers far more data about the topic than the audience needs or wants, confusing listeners and causing them to tune out what is being communicated; and (2) the speech maker presents ideas in words the listeners do not understand. Instead of using clear language and speaking at a level the audience comprehends, the speaker creates frustration among audience members by using unfamiliar jargon or words that soar beyond the reach of the listeners' vocabulary.

information overload
the situation that occurs when the amount of information provided by a speech maker is too great to be handled effectively by receivers

A speaker who tries to avoid information overload will often overcompensate and create a situation of information underload. **Information underload** occurs when the speaker underestimates the sophistication or intelligence of the audience members and tells them little that they do not already know.

information underload
the situation that occurs when the information provided by a speech maker is already known to receivers

As a speech maker, you need to strike a balance, providing neither too little information nor too much. As a rule, effective speech makers neither underestimate nor overestimate the capabilities of the audience. Instead, they motivate their listeners to want to fill in any information gaps.

Remember this: Pace, don't race. When you are delivering an informative speech, your task is to communicate so that audience members understand you, not to race to see how much new information you can cram into their brains in

5 or 10 minutes. Your real challenge is to know not only what to include but also what *not* to include.

EMPHASIZE KEY POINTS

As we discussed in Chapter 12, emphasis can be created through repetition (saying the same thing over again) and restatement (saying the same thing in another way). As long as you do not become overly repetitious and redundant, these devices will help your listeners process and retain the main points of your speech.

The organization of your speech can also reinforce your main ideas. Remember that you can use your introduction to preview ideas in your conclusion and to help make those ideas memorable. Transitions and internal summaries also help create a sense of cohesiveness.

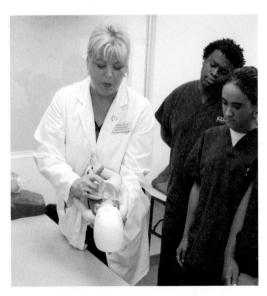

Receivers learn more when directly involved in a presentation.

INVOLVE YOUR LISTENERS

The relationship between audiences and speakers is changing. Contemporary audiences are restless. Public speakers need to work to channel the nervous energy of their audience members, who will learn more if they become involved with the material presented to them.[6] Effective speech makers do not view the audience as a passive receptacle; rather, they work to find ways to let the audience take an active part in the presentation. For example, the audience may be called on to perform an activity during the presentation. If you are giving a speech on how to reduce stress, you might have your listeners try one or two stress-reducing exercises. Or if your speech topic is "How to Read an EKG," you might pass out sample EKGs for audience members to decipher.

PROVIDE INFORMATION MEMORABLY

Remember that people want to understand and remember information that they perceive as relevant to their own lives. Few of us would have much interest in a speech on the development of bees. If, however, we found that the bees we are hearing about are a new species of killer bee that is extremely resistant to common insecticides, and that droves of these bees are on the way to our community and will arrive within the next two weeks, we would develop an intense interest very quickly.

Audiences also want to listen to new information. In this case, the term *new* means "new to them." A historical blunder may be new in this sense, and it may be relevant to a college or business audience today. The cable television industry has found that weather is worthy of its own channel; the weather forecast is constantly being updated and is therefore considered new.

Repetition can help as well; audiences respond to information that is repeated. Martin Luther King, Jr.,

Review, Reflect, & Apply

Understand

Explain how speakers can create information hunger, achieve information balance, emphasize key points, involve receivers, and provide information memorably.

Analyze

Identify a speaker who increased your information hunger and what they did to accomplish this.

Apply

Give an example of how to do this in an informative speech on a topic of your own choosing.

Create

Come up with ideas for involving an audience composed mainly of people under age 65 in a speech on the Medicare prescription drug plan.

understood the value of repetition in his "I have a dream" speech. As you prepare your informative speech, look for ways to let repetition augment your message by adding emotional involvement.

Novelty and Creativity

An effective speaker looks constantly for ways to approach information from an unusual direction. If you are the fifth speaker that your audience will hear on the homeless, you must find a different slant or approach to the topic, or the audience may be bored from the outset. You might try taking a different point of view—through the eyes of a child, for example. Look for analogies that bring topics home to an audience: "The number of people entering teaching today is diminishing. The teaching profession is like a stream drying up." Try other ways to complete this analogy. As you prepare your presentation, remember that you are looking for creative ways of bringing your topic to life for the audience.

Audiovisual Aids

You will want to include audiovisual aids in an informative presentation. Remember first, though, that you are your primary visual aid. The way you stand, walk, talk, and gesture is extremely important to the effectiveness of your presentation.

Take objects, or make simple models if you cannot take the objects themselves. Use PowerPoint charts, graphs, and drawings when appropriate as a speaker did when delivering a speech on hands-only CPR (see Figure 14.1.)

In addition, consider using video and audio clips to create or sustain interest. You can use tiny camcorders to conduct interviews or show processes at work. You can also use online video and audio clips. One student, for example, showed a brief YouTube segment of a chemical reaction that could not have been demonstrated safely in the classroom. Keep in mind that you can find abundant images, charts, and graphs on the Internet and incorporate them into your presentation to help communicate your message.

How to perform hands-only CPR

Target area for compressions

Repeat until help arrives.

Source: American Heart Association

By Robert W. Ahrens, USA TODAY

FIGURE 14.1

How to Perform Hands-Only CPR.

Sample Informative Speech Outline

FULL SENTENCE OUTLINE

Topic: Food contamination

Purpose: To inform the class about four sources of contamination in the human food chain.

Central idea: It is important to understand the sources of contamination in the human food chain.

Introduction

I. Are you familiar with the food pyramid? (Hold up visual of food pyramid.) It's a nutritional advisory prepared by the government containing suggestions of foods we should eat to ensure a healthy diet. Of course, grains, vegetables, fruits, cheese, and meat all have their place on the food pyramid. Over the past few years, however, tainted food products have formed their own peculiar food pyramid. In the United States, food increasingly is coming under suspicion and has even sickened thousands. If you are like me, you put food in your mouth every day without much thought. But according to the movie *Food Inc.*, what we put in our mouths could be dangerous to our health—even deadly—whether because of filthy conditions on farms, warehouses, supermarkets, and kitchens, the chemicals farmers use, or the antibiotics they give to the animals and poultry. What foods have recently made people like you and me ill? I'll name just a few: tomatoes, peppers, beef, scallions, and spinach. These ingredients don't just comprise parts of the food pyramid—they make a great salad. (Show salad bowl.)

II. 76 million people in the United States come down with cases of foodborne disease annually.

III. Today I would like to tell you about the nature, means of transmission, and effects of four sources of contamination in our human food chain: salmonella, E. coli, staph germs, and mad cow disease.

(Transition to main point I: First let's explore the nature of each of these sources of food contamination.)

Body

I. Salmonella, E. coli, and mad cow disease are food contaminants.
    A. According to the U.S. Department of Agriculture, salmonella is a rod-shaped bacterium that leads to foodborne illness.
        1. Two types of salmonella bacteria, Salmonella enteritidis and Salmonella typhimurium, are the most common, contributing to over half of all human infections.
        2. The salmonella bacteria live in the intestinal tracts of infected animals and humans.
        3. Salmonella contributes to about 1.4 million cases of illness, causing approximately 600 deaths in the United States each year.

The purpose statement and central idea guide the speaker in developing the outline.

A number of rhetorical questions and a visual aid draw receivers into the speech.

The speaker reveals the speech's purpose.

The speech's body is organized into three main points, each with a number of subpoints. Note that every entry in the body is a complete sentence and contains only a single idea.

continued

B. E. coli is a bacterium that lives in the digestive tracts of animals and humans.

   1. The most common type of E. coli is E. coli O157-H7, the kind contributing to most human outbreaks.

   2. E. coli afflicts approximately 70,000 people a year in the United States.

C. The staph germ is a germ found in meat and poultry.

   1. *Staphylococcus aureus* is a strain of the staph germ that makes people sick.

   2. Roughly 240,000 people come down with staph every year.

   3. Fifty percent of the animals sampled had a drug-resistant form of staph.

D. Mad cow disease, formally known as bovine spongiform encephalopathy, is a fatal disease that enters and destroys the brains of cattle, sheep, deer, and elk and then us if we eat an afflicted animal.

   1. The disease's cause is a deformed prion, a mutant protein that kills the brain by literally poking holes in it, causing the brain to look like a Swiss cheese.

   2. Though few mad cow cases exist in the United States, the incubation period for the disease could extend for decades.

(Transition to main point II: Now that we have discussed the nature of each of the four food contaminants, let's explore their means of transmission.)

II. Salmonella, E. coli, and mad cow disease are transmitted through the food supply.

A. Salmonella is usually transmitted to humans when they eat foods contaminated with animal feces or by the unwashed hands of an infected food handler.

   1. Salmonella can originate in meat, poultry, milk, dairy products, eggs, seafood, and fruits and vegetables that carry the bacteria.

   2. Salmonella survives if the product is not cooked to a safe minimum internal temperature.

   3. It can also be transferred through cross-contamination.

B. E. coli are transmitted to humans when they consume food containing tiny amounts of human or animal feces—including milk that has not been pasteurized; water that has not been disinfected; soft cheese; undercooked meat; seafood including lobster; or contaminated lettuce, green onions, or spinach—or through contact with people infected with the disease.

   1. E. coli gets into food during processing.

   2. E. coli gets into lakes, pools, and water supplies if the water has not been properly treated.

   3. E. coli also spreads from food to food when they are combined before shipping.

   4. E. coli spreads from person to person when an infected person fails to wash his or her hands.

   5. Because there are so many potential sources, often the infection source remains unknown.

C. Staph germs are transmitted to humans in many settings including meat packing plants, grocery stores, and kitchens.

   1. Staph germs were found in meat at 26 grocery stores in five major cities.

2. Staph germs were found in 77 percent of turkey samples, 42 percent of pork samples, 41 percent of chicken samples, and 37 percent of beef samples.
   3. Staph germs spread to humans when they eat or fail to handle staph-infected meat correctly.
D. Mad cow disease is spread through infected feed, blood transfusions, and infected food.
   1. Mad cow is caused by healthy cows eating ground-up parts of deceased animals.
   2. Mad cow spreads to humans when they eat infected cows, receive a transfusion from an already infected person, or ingest a dietary supplement or receive a vaccine containing ingredients from infected cows.

(Now that we have looked at the means of transmission of these food contaminants, let's discuss how you know if you're afflicted with the disease.)

III. Salmonella, E. coli, and mad cow disease sufferers present symptoms.
   A. Salmonella's symptoms include diarrhea, abdominal cramps, and fever within 8 to 72 hours after eating the contaminated food.
      1. Most people recover quickly.
      2. Some develop Reiter's syndrome.
   B. E. coli's symptoms include bloody diarrhea, stomach cramps, nausea, and vomiting.
      1. Children are more likely to experience the bacteria's effects.
      2. Some people never notice any symptoms.
      3. Serious cases can affect the blood or kidneys.
   C. The staph germ can cause serious infections in people.
      1. Staph germs can spread to the bloodstream, urinary tract, lungs, and heart.
      2. MRSA, a superbug, can be fatal.
   D. Mad cow disease symptoms show up in both cows and humans.
      1. Cows lose weight, are skittish, behave belligerently, appear confused, and may not be able to walk.
      2. People experience paranoia, suffer from lack of coordination, and lapse into a coma.

Personalizing symptoms for receivers helps the speaker develop the third main point of the speech.

Conclusion

I. Today we have explored the nature, means of transmission, and symptoms of four food contaminants: salmonella, E. coli, staph germs, and mad cow disease.

II. Food safety experts believe regulation will allow better tracking of contaminants in the food chain.

III. From killer tomatoes of a recent salmonella outbreak, to spinach and fresh vegetables tainted with E. coli, to that juicy hamburger you ate yesterday—eating has become a challenge. So study the food pyramid, and prepare that well-washed salad, well-cooked hamburger, or tasty snack, and all the while, think carefully about what you're eating, and critical links in the food chain, including where the food came from, how it was shipped, whose hands may have touched it, and most important, how it was prepared and may affect you. Salad anyone? (Refer again to visual of the food pyramid and hold up salad bowl with steak.)

The speaker summarizes what the speech has accomplished and uses a visual that refers receivers to the speech's introduction, providing a sense of closure.

Sample Informative Speech

Topic: Food contamination

Purpose: To inform the class about three sources of contamination in the human food chain.

Central idea: It is important for us to understand the sources of contamination in the human food chain.

Does the speaker succeed in gaining your attention? Do you believe the topic of the speech has relevance?

Do you find the use of this visual effective? Is there any other visual you might have considered using in the introduction?

Are you familiar with the United States Department of Agriculture's food pyramid? Do you follow its guidelines and try to eat healthy foods? The food pyramid (hold up visual of food pyramid) is a nutritional advisory prepared by the government containing suggestions of foods we should eat to ensure a healthy diet. Of course, grains, vegetables, fruits, cheese, and meat all have their place on the food pyramid. Over the past few years, however, tainted food products have formed their own peculiar food pyramid. In the United States, food increasingly is coming under suspicion and has even sickened thousands. If you are like me, you put food in your mouth every day without much thought. But according to the movie *Food Inc.*, what we put in our mouths could be dangerous to our health—even deadly—whether because of filthy conditions on farms, warehouses, supermarkets, and kitchens, the chemicals farmers use, or the antibiotics they give to the animals and poultry. What foods have recently made people like you and me ill? I'll name just a few: tomatoes, peppers, beef, scallions, spinach, and peanut butter. Foods like these don't just comprise key parts of the suggested food pyramid—they also make great salads or snacks. (Show salad bowl.)

How effective do you find the speaker's orientation? Does it prepare you for what is to come?

How effective is the speaker's change in tone? Does the speaker provide an effective transition?

On a serious note, this is not a joke. Unfortunately, according to the Centers for Disease Control and Prevention, increasing numbers of us are being sickened by contaminated food. In fact, Centers for Disease Control estimates are that some 76 million people living in the United States come down with cases of foodborne disease annually. Here is an example of just one of those cases taken from an article by Michael Moss, titled "The Burger That Shattered Her Life," that appeared in the October 4, 2009, issue of *The Record*. Moss's article described the problems that a 22-year-old, Stephanie Smith, faced after eating contaminated food. Smith, a dance instructor, at first attributed the aches and cramping she felt to a stomach virus. Then, her diarrhea turned bloody. Her kidneys shut down. Seizures knocked her unconscious. She convulsed so violently and relentlessly that doctors put her in a coma for nine weeks. Her mother said, "Thanksgiving Day, I was sitting there holding her hand when a group of doctors came in, and one looked at me and just walked away, with nothing good to say. And I said, 'Oh my God, maybe this is my last Thanksgiving with her,' and I stayed and prayed." When Stephanie finally awoke, she could no longer walk. E. coli had ravaged her nervous system and left her paralyzed. Her kidneys are at a high risk of failure. Doctors say that the once energetic and vibrant dance instructor will most likely never walk again. E. coli is one food toxin, but it is

Do you believe the illustration helps spark receiver interest?

far from the only culprit. Unfortunately, there are many. I will focus on four of them. Today, I would like to tell you about the nature, means of transmission, and effects of four sources of contamination in our human food chain: salmonella, E. coli, staph germs, and mad cow disease.

First let's explore the nature of each of these sources of food contamination, starting with salmonella.

According to the U.S. Department of Agriculture, salmonella is a rod-shaped bacterium that leads to more cases of food-borne illness than any other bacteria. Microscopic living creatures, salmonella bacteria pass from the feces of people or animals to other people or animals. Two types of salmonella, Salmonella enteritidis and Salmonella typhimurium, are the most common forms of the bacteria, contributing to over half of all human infections. Where does salmonella reside? I'll give you a clue—somewhere very close to you. Salmonella lives in the intestinal tracts of infected animals and humans. The bacteria usually are transmitted to humans when they eat foods contaminated with animal feces. You eat it because you can't see it, smell it, or taste it. Could any salmonella be hiding inside of your intestinal tract right now? The Surveillance Report from the Food Diseases Active Surveillance (FoodNet) identifies salmonella as the most commonly reported bacterial infection. Centers for Disease Control and Prevention statistics reveal that salmonella contributes to about 1.4 million cases of foodborne illness annually and causes about 600 deaths in the U.S. every year. According to food safety expert Tom Chestnut, interviewed on the June 10, 2008, airing of National Public Radio's *Morning Edition,* simply cleaning food appropriately does not get rid of the salmonella bacteria. While cleaning food reduces bacteria on the outside, Chestnut affirms that "it's very difficult to get a total elimination" of the salmonella bacteria.

Salmonella, as I noted, is not the only source of food contamination. Like salmonella, E. coli, the second of the food contaminants we will discuss, is also a bacteria that lives in the digestive tracts of both animals and humans. The most common type of E. coli is E. coli O157-H7, the strain that causes the most human outbreaks of the disease. E. coli afflicts large numbers of us but fewer than salmonella, causing approximately 70,000 people a year in the U.S. to become ill. Thoroughly cooking meat kills E. coli. Washing produce contaminated with E. coli removes the surface bacteria. However, according to food toxicologist Michele Norris, who appeared on the September 26, 2006, airing of National Public Radio's *All Things Considered,* rinsing the bacteria out of some foods, like sprouts, is impossible.

In addition to salmonella and E. coli, the third foodborne illness we are exploring is staph. Staph germs are commonly found on the skin and in the noses of up to 25 percent of healthy people. The bacteria is also found in about half of the meat and poultry sold in supermarkets and can be spread in meat-packing plants, supermarkets, and kitchens. The form of the staph germ that makes people sick is called *Staphylococcus*

continued

What is the speaker aiming to accomplish with the first main point?

Is the speaker's use of rhetorical questions effective?

Is the speaker's choice of experts appropriate?

Does the speaker's use of statistics advance the speech's purpose?

aureus. According to the Centers for Disease Control, roughly 240,000 people come down with this form of staph every year. Much of the meat sold in stores contains staph germs, with some 50 percent of the animals sampled carrying a drug-resistant strain of the germ.

The last foodborne illness we are exploring, mad cow disease, formally known as bovine spongiform encephalopathy, does not just make its victims ill. Mad cow, in contrast to salmonella, E. coli, and staph germs, which cause more illnesses than deaths, is a fatal disease that enters and destroys the brains of cattle, sheep, deer, elk, and humans if we are so unfortunate as to eat food from an afflicted animal. The emergence of mad cow disease is traced to a deformed prion, a mutant protein, that kills the brain by literally poking holes in it, leaving it to look like a piece of Swiss cheese. So this is likely what your brain will look like if you end up sickened by mad cow disease. (Hold up visual of Swiss cheese.) Dr. Robert Gallo, a scientist who has researched mad cow disease, tell us that, unfortunately, nothing is as indestructible as a prion, an organism that can survive temperatures upwards of 600 degrees Centigrade. Thus, even cooking meat thoroughly does not kill the prion. Neither do antibiotics. Though few mad cow cases have afflicted people in the U.S., the incubation period for the disease could extend for decades, so we're really uncertain about how many people are actually at risk—not a very comforting thought.

Now that we have discussed the nature of each of these three food contaminants, let's explore their means of transmission. Salmonella, E. coli, staph germs, and mad cow disease are each transmitted through the food supply. Salmonella is usually transmitted to humans when they eat foods that have been contaminated with animal feces or by the unwashed hands of an infected food handler. Salmonella can originate in meat, poultry, milk, dairy products, eggs, seafood, and fruits and vegetables that carry the bacteria. Just a few months ago, as reported in the *New York Times* and other media outlets, a salmonella scare attributed to jalapeño peppers, cilantro, or some brands of salsa, made over 1,000 people in the U.S. ill. Salmonella is also a resilient bacterium and survives if the food product is not cooked to a safe minimum internal temperature. Fear of contracting salmonella is one reason that food experts offer advisories telling us to cook food thoroughly. Salmonella can also be transferred through cross-contamination that causes bacteria to spread beyond its original source.

As is true of salmonella, E. coli may be transmitted to humans when they consume food containing tiny amounts of human or animal feces. Among the prominent sources of E. coli are milk that has not been pasteurized and water that has not been disinfected, soft cheese, undercooked meat, seafood including lobster, lettuce, green onions, and spinach. E. coli is also spread through contact with people already infected with the disease. How does E. coli get into both the food supply and people? E. coli gets into food during processing, especially if meat is not cooked to at least 160 degrees Fahrenheit. E. coli

How do you respond to the speaker's choice of a visual aid? Does it advance the speaker's goal?

Would you alter this transition in any way?

What does the speaker do to add credibility to the information being provided to receivers?

gets into lakes and pools in which people swim, and into the water supply if the water is not properly treated. E. coli also spreads from food to food when a contaminated food is combined with one or more other foods before shipping. E. coli also spreads from person to person when an infected person fails to wash his or her hands after moving his or her bowels. Because there are so many potential sources of E. coli poisoning, often the infection source remains unknown.

Like salmonella and E. coli, staph germs are transmitted to humans in many settings including meat-packing plants, grocery stores, and kitchens. In fact, researchers at the nonprofit Translational Genomics Research Institute in Arizona found staph germs abundantly present in meat sold at 26 grocery stores in five major cities. Staph germs were found in 77 percent of turkey samples, 42 percent of pork samples, 41 percent of chicken samples, and 37 percent of beef. As with salmonella and E. coli, humans can contract food poisoning attributed to staph germs when they eat or fail to handle the already infected meat correctly. Livestock and poultry that are consistently fed low doses of antibiotics are likely a contributor to the antibiotic resistance found in some strains of staph, making it difficult to cure in humans.

In contrast to how salmonella, E. coli, and staph germs spread, mad cow disease is spread through infected animal feed, infected animals we consume, and blood transfusions. Caused by healthy cows eating the ground-up parts of deceased animals, mad cow spreads to humans when they eat beef from mad-cow-infected cows, receive a transfusion from an already infected person, ingest a dietary supplement, or receive a vaccine containing ingredients from mad-cow-infected cows. So if you've received a blood transfusion, take a dietary supplement, or been given a vaccine—you may be at some risk because, since 1986, over 200,000 cows are known to have been stricken with mad cow disease.

Now that we have looked at both the nature and the means of transmission of these four food contaminants, let's discuss how you'll know if you're unfortunate enough to become afflicted with one of the diseases attributed to them. Like the symptoms of a number of diseases, some of the symptoms of salmonella, E. coli, staph germ, and mad cow disease are similar, and some are unique, so listen carefully. Salmonella's symptoms include diarrhea, abdominal cramps, and fever within 8 to 72 hours after eating a contaminated food. Luckily, most people who come down with salmonella recover quickly. However, if you are among the unlucky minority of salmonella victims, you may develop Reiter's syndrome, a disease caused by salmonella acquired through the digestive tract that leads to inflammation throughout the body and could cause you to develop arthritis.

E. coli's symptoms, while akin to salmonella's, also include bloody diarrhea, stomach cramps, nausea, and vomiting. Children are more likely to experience this bacterium's effects. Fortunately, some people who have E. coli never notice any

continued

Does the speaker's warning enhance the speech's impact? Do you believe the speaker is exaggerating the dangers receivers face?

Does this transition work?

Is the speaker's description of symptoms vivid enough for you?

symptoms. So you may have had it, but not know it. However, serious cases can also affect the blood or kidneys.

Like salmonella and E. coli, staph germs can also cause serious infections in people. While staph infections usually only cause minor skin problems, infections can worsen, and then spread to the bloodstream, urinary tract, lungs and heart. A form of staph germ you may have heard of, MRSA, is a super-bug that is, according to the Centers for Disease Control, antibiotic-resistant and potentially fatal.

In contrast to salmonella, E. coli, and staph germs, the symptoms of mad cow disease present themselves differently, with symptoms manifesting themselves in both animals, typically cows, and humans. When afflicted, cows lose weight, become skittish, behave belligerently, appear confused, and may not even be able to walk. You've probably heard the term *downer cow,* referring to a cow that's no longer mobile. When humans come down with mad cow disease, they experience paranoia, suffer from lack of coordination like downer cows, and lapse into a coma.

Now that you are informed about salmonella, E. coli, staph germs and mad cow disease, you also have more knowledge of foodborne contaminants. As noted in the July 31, 2008, issue of the *New York Times,* food safety experts like Mike Doyle, director of the Center for Food Safety at the University of Georgia and former FDA official Michael Taylor, now a professor at George Washington University, believe that stronger regulation and a better system for tracking food throughout the food chain will facilitate the traceability of contamination and help segregate any sources of contamination.

In conclusion, today we have explored the nature, means of transmission, and symptoms of four increasingly common food contaminants: salmonella, E. coli, staph germs, and mad cow disease. From the killer tomatoes of a recent salmonella outbreak, to the spinach and fresh vegetables tainted with E. coli, to the antibiotic-laden chicken leg you had last night, to that juicy hamburger you ate yesterday that might have come from a mad-cow-suffering steer—eating food safely is increasingly becoming a challenge. So study the food pyramid, prepare that well-washed salad, well-done hamburger, or tasty snack, and all the while, think carefully about what you're eating, and the critical links in the food chain, including where the food came from, how it was shipped, whose hands may have touched it, and most important, how it was prepared and may affect you. After all, only time will tell if you become sick from what you eat. Is anyone hungry? How about a salad? (Visual: Hold up salad.)

How would you evaluate the speaker's use of research? In your opinion, does the research add to the speaker's credibility?

Does the speaker effectively summarize the speech? What does the speaker do to give the speech a sense of closure? How else might the speaker have ended the speech?

In your opinion, did the speaker provide you with information that you need and can use? Do you think the speaker sought to provide too much, too little, or just the right amount of information?

WORKS CONSULTED

Ken Alltucker, "Staph Germs Prevalent in Store Meat, Study Says," www.azcentral.com/news/, 4/15/2011.

Associated Press, "Taco Bell Removes Scallions Following Outbreak of E. coli," *Wall Street Journal,* December 7, 2006, p. D6.

Allison Aubrey, "Health Officials Track Salmonella, Suspect Tomatoes," *Morning Edition,* June 10, 2008.

Marian Burros, "You Are What You Eat: 2006 and the Politics of Food," *New York Times,* December 27, 2006, p. F2.

"E. coli Shouldn't Dampen Appetite for Vegetables," *All Things Considered,* September 26, 2006.

Morbidity and Mortality Weekly Report, 2006.

Amanda Gardner, "Home-Grown Problems Threaten U.S. Food Safety," *USA Today.*

"Human Mad-Cow Case Confirmed," *Wall Street Journal,* December 7, 2006, p. D6.

Melissa Jane Kronfeld and Andy Geller, "Attack of the Killer Tomatoes," *New York Post,* pp. 1, 5.

Paul Krugman, "Bad Cow Disease," *New York Times,* June 13, 2008, p. A29.

Michael Moss, "The Burger That Shattered Her Life," *New York Times,* October 4, 2009, pp. 1, 24–25.

"MyPyramid.gov access point," U.S. Department of Agriculture.

en.wikipedia.org/wiki/Food_guide_pyramid.

"New Test Scans Beef for Mad Cow Disease," *U.S. News & World Report,* health .usnews.com/articles/health/healthday/2008/08/12/new-test-scans-beef-for-mad-cow-disease_print.htm.

Eric Schlosser, "Has Politics Contaminated the Food Supply?" *New York Times,* December 11, 2006, p. A27.

Annys Shin, "Scientists Take on Food Poisoning's Long-Term Effects," *The Record,* September 17, 2008, p. F6.

Mike Stobbe, "Much Meat in Stores Contains Staph Germ," *The Record,* April 16, 2011, p. A-4.

Bina Venkataraman, "6 More States Report Illnesses from Tomatoes," *New York Times,* June 13, 2008, p. A21.

Bina Venkataraman, "Amid Salmonella Case, Food Industry Seems Set to Back Greater Regulation," *New York Times,* July 31, 2008, accessed at www.nytimes .com/2008/07/31/health/policy/31outbreak.html.

Jane Zhang, "Salmonella May Be Tied to a Death," *Wall Street Journal,* June 13, 2008.

www.cdc.gov/ncidod/dvrd/bse/.

www.about-salmonella.com.

www.aolhealth.com

www.cdc.gov

www.fsis.usda.gov/factsheets/salmonella_questions_&_answers/index.asp

Sample Speaker's Notes

Topic:	Food contamination
Purpose:	To inform the class about four sources of contamination in the human food chain.
Central idea:	It is important for us to understand the sources of contamination in the human food chain.

continued

Apply

Create an informative speech on a topic of your choice.

Evaluate

Agree or disagree with this statement using the sample speech at the end of chapter to support your position: *All information is persuasive. There is no such thing as a purely informative speech.*

Introduction

I. Foods in the food pyramid including tomatoes, peppers, scallions, spinach, and beef are increasingly coming under suspicion.

II. CDC statistic: 76 million cases of foodborne disease in U.S. Story of Stephanie Smith as told by Michael Moss on 10/4/09 in Record.

III. Today I'd like to tell you about the nature, means of transmission and effects of salmonella, E. coli, staph germ, and mad cow disease.

Body

I. What salmonella, E. coli, staph germ, and mad cow diseases are.
U.S. Dept. of Agriculture description of salmonella
Two types of salmonella—Salmonella enteritidis and Salmonella typhimurium; 1.4 million cases and 500 deaths
Where it lives
Refer to Tom Chestnut, Food Safety Expert, NPR, *Morning Edition,* June 10, 2008
E. coli—O157-H7; 70,000 people made ill
Michele Norris, Director of Food Safety Program on NPR, *All Things Considered,* September 26, 2006
Staph germ—240,000 people made ill—CDC
Mad cow disease, bovine spongiform encephalopathy—number of cases unknown.
Dr. Robert Gallo—resilience of prion

II. Means of transmission
Salmonella: contaminated food supply
food handlers
food preparation
E. coli: feces, food processing
shipping
handling
unknown sources, too
Staph germ: packing plants
handling in stores & kitchens
Mad cow: contaminants in feed
person-to-person transmission

III. Symptoms
Salmonella—diarrhea, abdominal cramps, fever, Reiter's syndrome
E. coli—bloody diarrhea, cramps, nausea, vomiting
Staph germ: bloody diarrhea, cramps
Mad cow—downer cows
lack of coordination

Conclusion

I. Now you have important information about salmonella, E. coli, staph germ, and mad cow disease; you are also more knowledgeable about foodborne contaminants.

II. Today we have explored the sources, nature of transmission, and symptoms of four kinds of food chain contamination.

III. Reference to killer tomatoes, spinach and fresh vegetables, and beef.

IV. Salad anyone??? (Visual: Food pyramid and a salad bowl with steak.)

The Wrap-Up

SUMMARY

LO1 **Define** *informative speaking.*

The goal of the informative speaker is to offer audience members more information than they presently have about a topic. Informative speaking aims to update and add knowledge, refine understanding, or provide background.

LO2 **Distinguish** among four types of informative discourse.

Four kinds of informative speaking with which you need to be familiar are (1) messages of explanation, which explain the what or how-to of a subject; (2) messages of description, which describe what a person, an object, or an event is like; (3) messages of definition, which define what something is; and (4) narrative messages, which tell a story.

LO3 **Explain** how to create information hunger and increase listeners' comprehension.

A primary goal of the informative speech is to increase each listener's need to know and hunger to receive a message. To do this, speakers need to analyze the audience and use appropriate attention-getting devices to generate receiver interest in their topics. At the same time that speakers work to create interest in receivers, they also need to avoid overloading or underloading receivers with information.

LO4 **Develop** and present an informative speech.

Being able to design and deliver an effective informative speech has important implications for both your career and your life. An effective informative speech makes listeners want to learn more about the topic, communicates information clearly, involves audience members, and delivers information in a way that makes the speech memorable.

KEY TERMS

information overload 392   informative speech 392
information underload 392

Persuasive Speaking

After completing this chapter, you should be able to demonstrate mastery of the following learning outcomes:

LO1 **Define** *persuasive speaking.*

LO2 **Explain** the purposes of persuasion.

LO3 **Distinguish** between types of persuasive speeches.

LO4 **Discuss** what it means to persuade responsibly, strategically, and credibly.

LO5 **Identify** guidelines for persuading effectively.

LO6 **Describe** Monroe's motivated sequence.

LO7 **Develop** and present a persuasive speech.

"Vote for me," demands the candidate. "Buy me," reads the ad. "Support my cause," cajoles the lobbyist. "Attend my rally," cries out the advocate. "Give money to our movement," pleads the fund raiser. How do you respond? Would you rally to protect freedom of speech on the Internet, or do you support government controls? Do you favor opening our borders to increased numbers of immigrants or closing them? Do you support a woman's right to choose, or are you an advocate of the right-to-life movement? Would you march against the death penalty, or do you believe in capital punishment?

Choice and change characterize our times.[1] With information and knowledge exploding, and multiple alternatives held out to us by persons competing for our attention and support, how we make decisions matters. Do we take shortcuts, or do we make reasoned choices? Do we look for easy answers, or are we skilled at seeing nuance and possibilities others may not notice? And most important, do we want to make a difference in our world (or in our community, our college, or the

n.org

like)? **Persuasion,** the attempt to change or reinforce attitudes, beliefs, values, or behaviors, permeates our lives. Advertisers, public relations professionals, politicians, religious leaders, and numerous others have the same primary goal—persuading you.

Our aim in this chapter is to increase your ability to prepare, present, and process persuasive speeches by showing you how to apply your general knowledge and skills to this special type of discourse.

Man is the only animal that laughs and weeps; for he is the only animal that is struck with the difference between what things are and what they ought to be.

—William Hazlitt

It is not enough to identify the gene that predetermines the prospect of Alzheimer's disease if we go through the prime of life with a closed mind.

—Tom Brokaw

Speaking Persuasively

LO1

Define persuasive speaking.

persuasive speech
a speech whose primary purpose is to change or reinforce the attitudes, beliefs, values, and/or behaviors of receivers

When you deliver a **persuasive speech,** your goal is to modify the thoughts, feelings, or actions of your audience. You hope that your listeners will change attitudes or behaviors you do not approve of and adopt attitudes and behaviors that are

© Arnie Levin/The New Yorker Collection/www.cartoonbank.com.

"I found the old format much more exciting."

compatible with your interests and the way you see the world. Persuasive discourse is becoming increasingly important; more than ever, we are concerned with being able to influence others.[2]

Today's communication environment demands effective persuasion skills. In fact, with the exception of class lectures, a majority of the presentations others direct at you are likely persuasive. So are the majority of presentations you make to others. When was the last time you tried to change someone's mind at home, at school, or at work? Maybe you wanted to be given the opportunity to improve a grade on a paper and had to develop reasons why your instructor should allow you a "do over." At work, you may have sought to persuade your employer to give you a raise or a more responsible position. Whatever your objective, it is the attitudes, beliefs, and values of the person(s) on the receiving end of your persuasive appeal that you use to frame and support your case. So, whether you are negotiating to buy property, arguing that the jury should acquit your client, working in support of Amnesty International, or making an appeal for any one of thousands of other causes, understanding your receivers enables you to decide how to approach persuasive discourse.

Review, Reflect, & **Apply**

Recall
List the goals of persuasive speakers.

Understand
Discuss the role persuasion plays in daily life.

Apply
Identify the attempts you make to persuade others in a single day.

Analyze
Compare and contrast attempts to influence your thoughts, feelings, and actions.

Evaluate
Explain how effective communication skills facilitate persuasion.

Create
Develop a list of things you would like to persuade others to think, feel, or do.

Purposes of Persuasion: Thought and Action

A speaker may believe that flying saucers exist, even though most of the audience may not; oppose bilingual education, while others support it; or want audience members to become organ donors, while audience members feel reluctant to make that commitment. The speaker's objective, sometimes referred to as the **proposition** of the speech, indicates what type of change the speaker would like to create in audience members. Typically, speakers want one or both of two general outcomes: They want to convince listeners that something is so (that is, to change the way audience members think), or they want to cause audience members to take an action (that is, to change the way they behave). Whatever the general nature of the proposition, it most likely will reflect at least one of the following persuasive goals: adoption, discontinuance, deterrence, or continuance.[3]

When your goal is *adoption*, you hope to persuade the audience to accept a new idea, attitude, or belief (for example, that genetically engineered food is hazardous to health), with the hope that in time, that belief will also be supported by action (your listeners will eliminate genetically engineered products from their diet). When your goal is *discontinuance*, you hope to persuade audience members to stop doing something they are now doing (stop drinking alcohol while pregnant, for example). When your goal is *deterrence*, you want to persuade the audience to avoid an activity or a way of thinking (for example, "If you believe that every woman has the right to exercise control over her own body, don't vote for

LO2

Explain the purposes of persuasion.

proposition
a statement that summarizes the purpose of a persuasive speech

Review, Reflect, & Apply

Recall

Name four persuasive goals.

Understand

Distinguish between the following persuasive goals: *adoption, discontinuance, deterrence,* and *continuance*.

Apply

Describe how others have used each of the four persuasive goals on you.

Create

Brainstorm topics for speeches that have goals focusing on adoption, discontinuance, deterrence, or continuance.

candidates who would make abortions illegal."). Finally, if your goal is the *continuance* of a way of believing or acting, you want to encourage people to continue to think or behave as they now do (for instance, keep limiting our sun exposure).

Adoption and discontinuance goals involve asking listeners to alter their way of thinking or behaving, whereas deterrence and continuance goals involve asking them not to alter the way they think or behave but, rather, to reinforce or sustain it. In general, persuaders find it easier to accomplish deterrence and continuance objectives. That does not mean, however, that accomplishing adoption or discontinuance goals is impossible. They may be more difficult to achieve, but if the speaker uses a variety of appeals and a sound organizational scheme and has credibility, these goals can also be realized.

Types of Persuasive Speeches

LO3

Distinguish between types of persuasive speeches.

proposition of fact
a persuasive speech with the goal of settling what is or is not so

proposition of value
a persuasive speech that espouses the worth of an idea, a person, or an object

proposition of policy
a persuasive speech on what ought to be

Persuasive speeches focus on questions of fact, value, or policy. Selecting which kind of speech to present is among the first tasks you need to complete. By choosing one type over the others, the speaker formally decides to speak on what is or what is not (**proposition of fact**), how good or bad something is (**proposition of value**), or what ought to be (**proposition of policy**).

PROPOSITIONS OF FACT

The following are sample propositions of fact:

Civility is teachable.

DNA is the ultimate fingerprint.

Education prevents poverty.

Internet use decreases interpersonal skills.

The United States is addicted to oil.

The federal deficit is a threat to our economic security.

Natalee Holloway was murdered in Aruba.

The last example was a proposition of fact that consumed the attention of commentators on a number of 24-hour news channels, such as Fox News and MSNBC. Various "experts" appeared on network programs in the effort to convince viewers of the persuasiveness of their evidence.

Good propositions of fact cannot be resolved with just a yes or a no answer. Instead, they are open to debate, and settling them typically requires close examination and careful interpretation of evidence, usually from a number of documents or sources. When speaking on a proposition of fact, the speaker must provide enough evidence to convince receivers of the factual nature of the statement.

PROPOSITIONS OF VALUE

The following are examples of propositions of value:

Same-sex high schools are better than co-ed high schools.

Sex education belongs in school.

Using persons in developing nations as guinea pigs for drug testing is unethical.

The use of chemical weapons is immoral.

Grade inflation decreases the value of a college education.

Finding alternative sources of fuel is a worthwhile endeavor.

Propositions of value explore the worth of an idea, a person, or an object. Like questions of fact, they require more than a simple answer, or in this case, a true or false response. When speaking on a proposition of value, the speaker must convince receivers that the evaluation contained in the proposition is valid. This usually requires that the speaker also explore one or more propositions of fact. For example, you probably will not be effective advocating for the premise that fetal tissue research is morally justifiable until you establish that such research is necessary.

PROPOSITIONS OF POLICY

The following are sample propositions of policy:

Gay and lesbian partners should be permitted to marry.

Alcohol should be banned at sporting events.

Colleges should limit financial support for athletes.

The United States should encourage investment in alternative fuel sources.

Consumers should boycott companies that use child labor to manufacture products.

The U.S. government should repudiate enhanced interrogation and torture as a means to fight terrorism.

National health insurance should be provided to all U.S. citizens.

When speaking on a proposition of policy, the speaker goes beyond questions of fact or value. Instead, the speaker must demonstrate a need for the policy and earn audience approval or support for the policy in question. When you ask audience members to support a proposition of policy, you ask them to support a course of action. Such a request often needs to be supported with statements of fact and value as well.

In conclusion, if given the option, we may approach a topic by speaking on a proposition of fact, value, or policy.

Review, Reflect, & Apply

Recall
List three types of propositions.

Understand
Distinguish between propositions of fact, value, and policy.

Apply
Identify how you might approach the same topic in different ways by formulating a proposition of fact, a proposition of value, and a proposition of policy.

Evaluate
Assess the kind of change and support elicited in audience members when delivering a speech on a proposition of fact, value, and policy.

Create
Your topic is civility on campus or another topic of your choosing. Explain how you would approach the topic using a proposition of fact, value, and policy.

For example, let's say we selected as our topic the effects of corporate influence on U.S. foreign policy. Our three options might read as follows:

Proposition of fact: Corporations influence U.S. foreign policy positively and negatively.

Proposition of value: It is wrong for corporations to influence U.S. foreign policy.

Proposition of policy: Write your representatives and express your displeasure regarding corporate influence over U.S. foreign policy.

Persuading Responsibly

Whenever we try to cause others to change their beliefs, attitudes, or behaviors, or whenever others try to influence us, we are participating in the persuasive process.[4] Understanding what persuasion *is not* will enable us to use it responsibly.

PERSUASION IS NOT COERCION

Imagine this: Someone puts a gun to your head and says, "Your money or your life." Such a person is acting illegally and coercively. You follow the individual's demands only because you fear for your life. Persuasion is different. When someone is successful at persuading you to do or believe what she or he asks, you choose to think or act differently because you *want to*, not because you think you *have to*.

PERSUASION IS NOT MANIPULATION

When someone manipulates you to do or believe something, he or she usually uses unethical means to take advantage of you so that you do what is in *his or her* but not necessarily *your* best interest. Ethical persuasion is honest and in the best interests of receivers. Its success does not depend on spreading false or misleading information. For example, one politician used deception to convince voters of his honesty by re-editing newspaper articles written about him so that receivers were manipulated into processing the information he presented about himself favorably, when in fact it was highly unfavorable.[5] When this unethical act was uncovered, it cast a cloud over the candidate.

LO4 Persuading Strategically and Credibly

Discuss what it means to persuade responsibly, strategically, and credibly.

logos
logical proof

pathos
emotional proof

What makes one person more persuasive than another person? Countless books and articles address this question. However, over 2,000 years ago, the Greek philosopher Aristotle first identified three tools that contemporary theorists still believe persuaders use to achieve goals: ethos, logos, and pathos.

Logos is logical proof. The more effective your proof—the more reasonable your arguments and the more convincing your reasons—the greater the chances your message will make rational sense to receivers and the more likely they are to accept it. **Pathos** is emotional proof. Pathos develops empathy and passion in receivers, touching them by arousing their feelings, often through the use of expressive and emotional language and the telling of stories high in human interest. Such stories may contain testimony; recount suffering; arouse fear, anger, or compassion; or use humor. When moved by pathos, audiences are more likely to agree with your message because they believe what you are sharing could also affect them or a loved one personally. **Ethos** is the audience's judgment of the speaker's character or credibility. The more credible your audience believes you to be, the greater your chances of having them accept you as a source and your message as true.

ethos
audience's judgment of speaker's character or credibility

Becoming a More Credible Persuader

According to attorney Gerry Spence, your success as a persuader will be determined in part by what your "targets" think of you—in other words, by your **credibility** (ethos).[6]

When we use the term *credibility*, we are talking not about what you are really like but about how an audience perceives you. If your listeners accept you as credible, they probably believe that you are a person of good character (trustworthy and fair) and are knowledgeable (trained, competent to discuss your topic, and reliable as a source of information) and personable (dynamic, charismatic, active, and energetic). As a result, your ideas are more likely to get a fair hearing. However, if your listeners believe that you are untrustworthy, incompetent (not sufficiently knowledgeable about your topic), and passive (lacking in dynamism), they are less likely to respond as you desire.

credibility
the receiver's assessment of the competence, trustworthiness, and dynamism of a speaker

It is entirely possible—even probable—that your listeners may consider you more credible about some topics than others. For example, the following are two pairs of imaginary statements. Which statement in each pair would you be more inclined to accept?

The United States must never negotiate with terrorists. Strength is the only language they will understand.

—Hillary Clinton

The United States must never negotiate with terrorists. Strength is the only language they will understand.

—Lady Gaga

****

The world of contemporary music has room in it for everyone. The message music sends is tolerance.

—Bono

The world of contemporary music has room in it for everyone. The message music sends is tolerance.

—Michael Bloomberg

If you're like most people, you find the first statement in each pair more credible. The

For some groups of people, the Dalai Lama is considered a highly credible speaker.

Exploring **Diversity**

Persuasion and Assumed Similarity

LaRay M. Barna, an intercultural communication theorist, points out that we are all influenced by our cultural upbringing, and, while we tend to assume that other people's needs, desires, and basic assumptions are the same as our own, often they are not. How can assumed similarity—the belief that we all have similar thoughts, feelings, attitudes, and nonverbal codes—cause problems for persuasive speakers? For example, while Americans tend to value materialism, success, and rationality, Arabs are more likely to value self-respect, courage, and honor. Arabs also value storytelling, eloquence, and the ability of words to spark emotional responses in others. To this end, they use emphatic assertions to convey their seriousness. When such assertions are missing, others may assume that an Arab speaker means the opposite of what was said.[7]

On the basis of this realization, is it more beneficial for a persuasive speaker to assume *differences* rather than similarity? Explain.

What should the speaker do if members of the audience come from a variety of cultures, some who expect a more formal style of delivery than the speaker is used to, some who expect the speaker to begin by humbling himself or herself and making respectful references to the audience, some who expect the speaker to be restrained rather than overly expressive, some who expect the speaker to rely on narratives rather than formal logic or standard inductive or deductive structures, and so on?

Review, Reflect, & **Apply**

Recall

Define *credibility, logos, pathos,* and *ethos.*

Understand

Explain how a speaker's use of logos, pathos, and ethos affects persuasion.

Apply

Imagine that you want to appeal a grade. Discuss how you would use logos, pathos, and ethos to convince your instructor.

Evaluate

Determine what you believe to be the most essential tool to a speaker's success and why: logos, pathos, or ethos.

Create

Your subject is obesity. Develop three examples, one focused on logos, the second on pathos, and the third on ethos.

initial credibility
a measure of how an audience perceives a speaker prior to the speech-making event

source cited for the first statement seems obviously more knowledgeable about the subject.

Regardless of the circumstances, however, it is up to you to build your credibility by giving audience members reasons to consider you competent, trustworthy, and dynamic.[8] To help them see you as competent, you can describe your own experiences with the subject and suggest why you feel you've earned the right to share your ideas. You can help receivers see you as trustworthy by demonstrating respect for different points of view and communicating a sense of sincerity. To help them see you as dynamic, speak with energy, use assured and forceful gestures, and create vocal variety.[9]

Note that the audience's assessment of your credibility can change during your presentation or as a result of it. Thus, we can identify three types of credibility:

Initial credibility is your credibility before you start to speak.

Derived credibility is your credibility during your speech.

Terminal credibility is your credibility at the end of your speech.

Of course, if your initial credibility is high, your task should be easier. But keep in mind that your speech can lower your initial credibility—and that it can also raise your initial credibility. What you say and how you say it are important determiners of credibility.

We will refer to these tools as we talk about the nature of effective persuasion.

Ethics & Communication

Big and Little Lies

1. What kinds of communication choices do you make when attempting to accomplish a goal? What would you do to get others to comply with your wishes? Would you lie? Would you cheat? Is it acceptable for a speaker to manipulate receivers?

   Our society has been criticized for being a "culture of cheating."[10] From the school yard to the White House, from the boardroom to the war room, from the ball field to the farm field, cheating appears to go on everywhere. We saw it with the presentation of the reasons for going to war against Iraq, and we saw it with the alleged "rescue" of Private Jessica Lynch, the lies about how football great Pat Tillman was killed, and the ensuing accusations that "the Pentagon tried to pull a fast one."[11] We saw it with Enron. We saw it with ImClone. We saw it with *A Million Little Pieces.* Politicians, CEOs, and some authors of books, such as James Frey, fudge statements, exaggerate the value of evidence, and fabricate claims. Some lies are told "to protect national security," some to protect the president's skin; some are just boasting. What is more, it appears that the "cheaters prosper until they get caught."[12]

   What damage, if any, do you believe is done to a speaker's credibility when receivers discover that he or she has lied to them? Is a speaker's tendency to exaggerate as harmful as committing a lie of omission or telling an outright lie? Do the ends ever justify the means? In other words, is it acceptable for a speaker to make up facts if his or her goal is a worthy one?

   Would you ever lie to receivers? Would you make up statistics, pass off as true a narrative you knew to be hypothetical, or tamper with visuals if you knew that doing so would help you realize the objective(s) of your speech?

2. To be considered ethical, should you have to reveal your motive for speaking to your receivers?

   For years, big drug companies have paid tens of thousands of dollars to doctors and medical professionals to speak at sponsored events to their colleagues. At such events, the paid speakers deliver presentations that, for the most part, were written for them by the drug companies. The goal of these speeches is to convince those in attendance to use the drug company's featured products. Speakers act as if they wrote these speeches, but they actually deliver canned presentations, and typically fail to disclose to audience members their remuneration by and relationship with the event's sponsor.

   In your opinion, do such speakers violate the principle that the words you speak should be your own? Should receivers be told when speakers are being paid to speak? Should receivers be informed of the speakers' relationship to event sponsors?

Guidelines for Persuading Effectively

Persuasion usually occurs in steps. Audience members do not usually surrender current ways of thinking and behaving easily or all at once. However, if you offer convincing arguments, solid evidence, and a clear message in persuasive messages that you plan incrementally and deliver over time, receivers may gradually alter their positions.

Your persuasive goal needs to be based on an accurate analysis of the current beliefs and attitudes of receivers. For example, if your goal is to convince members of the National Rifle Association (NRA) that the nation's gun-control laws need overhauling, rather than advocating against the sale of all guns to the public, you might start your persuasive campaign by working to convince receivers that there are some problems with existing gun laws. Simply reducing the strength of their current stance on gun control would be a step forward that repeated persuasive efforts could then build on. Let's examine what you can do to increase your persuasiveness as a speaker.

LO5

Identify guidelines for persuading effectively.

derived credibility
a measure of a speaker's credibility during a speech-making event

terminal credibility
a measure of a speaker's credibility at the end of a speech-making event

IDENTIFY YOUR GOAL

Acting on a good idea is better than just having a good idea.

—Robert Half

To be a successful persuader, you must have a clearly defined purpose. You must, in fact, be able to answer these questions:

What response do I want from audience members?

Would I like them to think differently, act differently, or both?

Which of their attitudes or beliefs am I trying to alter? Why?

Unless you know what you want your listeners to think, feel, or do, you will not be able to realize your objective.

KNOW THE RECEIVERS YOU ARE TRYING TO REACH

How do audience members feel about your proposal? Do they favor the change? How important is it to them? What is at stake? The more ego-involved the members of your audience are, the more committed they will be to their current position; hence, the harder it will be for you to reach them.[13] The information here builds on Chapter 11 (the second rung on the ladder).

UNDERSTAND THE FACTORS AFFECTING YOUR LISTENERS' ATTITUDES

To be able to influence others, you need to understand the favorable and unfavorable mental sets, or predispositions, that audience members bring to a speech; that is, you need to understand **attitudes**—how they are formed, how they are sustained, and how they may be changed by you. The following forces or factors are among the most important influences on our attitudes.

attitudes
predispositions to respond favorably or unfavorably toward a person or subject

Family

Few of us escape the strong influence exerted by our families. Many of our parents' attitudes are communicated to us and are eventually acquired by us. "It is the family that bends the tender twig in the direction it is likely to grow."[14]

If you say it enough, even if it ain't true, folks will get to believing it.

—Will Rogers

Religion

Not only believers but also nonbelievers are affected by religion. In fact, the impact of religion is increasing as religious organizations strive to generate and guide attitudes on politics and such social issues as abortion, civil rights, the death penalty, child abuse, and divorce.

Education

More people than ever are attending school; they start young (sometimes before the age of 5), and many attend until they are in or beyond their twenties. Moreover, the traditional role of the school has expanded, since large numbers of adults are now returning to complete their education. The courses taught, the instructors who teach them, the books assigned, and the films shown all help shape attitudes.

Socioeconomics

Economic status and social status also shape our attitudes. Our economic status helps determine the social arena we frequent. Our view of the world is likewise affected by the company we keep and the amount of money we have.

Culture

As seventeenth-century poet John Donne wrote, "No man is an island, entire of itself." From the crib to the coffin, we are influenced by others—in person and through the media. The groups we belong to, our friends, and the fabric of the society in which we find ourselves all help mold us. We shape our social institutions and are reciprocally shaped by them.

UNDERSTAND YOUR LISTENERS' BELIEFS

Your persuasive effectiveness will improve if you understand not only your listeners' attitudes but also their beliefs—and if you understand how audiences might respond when their important beliefs are challenged.[15]

Attitudes and beliefs are, of course, related—in fact, the two terms are sometimes used interchangeably—but they are not the same thing. Attitudes and beliefs are related to each other as buildings are related to bricks, beams, boards, and so on. That is, in a sense, **beliefs** are the building blocks of attitudes. Whereas we measure attitudes on a favorable–unfavorable scale, we measure beliefs on a probable–improbable scale. Thus, if you say that you think something is true, you are really saying that you believe it. According to psychologist Milton Rokeach, your belief system is made up of everything you agree is true. Your disbelief system, which is composed of all the things you do not think are true, develops along with your belief system. Together, the two significantly affect the way you process information.[16]

beliefs
confidence in the truth of something

The more central or important a belief is, the harder audience members will work to defend it, the less willing they will be to change it, and the more resistant they will be to your persuasive efforts.

USE TWO PRINCIPLES OF INFLUENCE: CONSISTENCY AND SOCIAL PROOF

When you are speaking persuasively, you should be aware of two significant principles. First, we all have a desire to be consistent with what we have already done. In other words, once we take a stand, consistency theory tells us that our tendency is to behave consistently with that commitment.[17] Therefore, it is important to determine how your speech can engage this tendency toward **consistency.** If you can find a way to get audience members to make a commitment (to take a stand or go on record), you will have set the stage for them to behave in ways consistent with that stand.

consistency
the desire to maintain balance in our lives by behaving according to commitments already formed

Second, we all respond to **social proof.** That is, one method we use to determine what is right is to find out what other people think is right.[18] You can use the actions of others to convince your listeners that what you are advocating is right. As motivation consultant Cavett Robert notes: "Since 95 percent of the people are imitators and only 5 percent initiators, people are persuaded more by the action of others than by any proof we can offer."[19]

social proof
the determination of what is right by finding out what other people think is right

REASON LOGICALLY

Rational or logical proof (logos) includes arguments, reasoning, and evidence that add substance to a claim. Evidence is quotations or testimony from authoritative sources, conclusions from relevant studies and reports (sometimes presented in the form of statistics), and examples and illustrations in support of a proposition. You increase your chances of persuading others if you offer logical reasons why they should support what you advocate.

Talk show hosts are known for taking a social or political issue and turning it into an argument with a guest. Although such transformations may entertain us, when we analyze them critically, the arguments made are often illogical and lack sound principles of reasoning.

Effective persuaders reason with the audience, presenting evidence and arguments to help receivers move closer to their point of view. In his book *The Uses of Argument*, Stephen Toulmin identified the elements of a persuasive argument:

claim
debatable conclusion or assertion

1. A **claim,** a debatable conclusion or assertion, the proposition or thesis you hope to prove and want receivers to accept (for example, "The Electoral College should be abolished.").

reasons
facts or evidence for making the claim

2. Data or good **reasons,** facts and evidence for making the claim (for example, "The Electoral College should be abolished because it makes it possible for a candidate for president of the United States to lose the popular vote but win the Electoral College vote and become president.").

warrant
explanation of the relationship between the claim and the data

3. A **warrant,** a logical and persuasive relationship that explains how you get to your claim from the data you offer (for example, "Democracy depends on all the people having their votes count rather than allowing the influence of small states to count more than the voices of a majority of the voters."). The purpose of the warrant is to legitimize the claim, making it more persuasive.

backing
support that answers concerns of others

4. The **backing,** support that gives the warrant more strength by answering other questions of concern.

qualifier
indication of the strength of the connection

5. The **qualifier,** an indication of the strength of the connection between the data and the warrant, usually containing words such as *most, sometimes,* or *always.*

rebuttal
potential counterarguments

6. **Rebuttal,** potential counterarguments, sometimes offered during the presentation of the initial argument.

In diagram form, the Toulmin model looks like this:

Thus, if you state your claim clearly and qualify it by limiting its applicability so that it is not overly broad, support it with reasons, and connect it to the evidence you offer via the warrant, you improve your chances of persuading the audience to accept your claim. By anticipating opposing arguments and preparing counterarguments that rebut them, you increase your chances of success. The most common forms of logical reasoning are deduction, induction, causal reasoning, and reasoning from analogy.

Deduction

When we reason deductively, we move from the general to the specific. When using **deduction,** you present a major premise (a generalization) and a minor premise (a specific instance) that leads you to deduce a conclusion. The argument you make looks like this:

Major premise: People who study regularly instead of cramming usually get better grades.

Minor premise: You want to get better grades.

Conclusion: Therefore, you should study regularly instead of cramming.

Wrong premises lead to faulty conclusions. For example:

All protestors are liberal.

James Dobson is a protestor.

James Dobson is a liberal.

If you choose to use deductive reasoning in support of your ideas, be sure your premises are true and defensible.

You can evaluate deductive reasoning by asking the following two questions:

1. Are the major premise and the minor premise (or minor premises) true?
2. Does the conclusion follow logically from the premises?

Be sure to give the necessary evidence to buttress your major and minor premises.

deduction
reasoning that moves from the general to the specific

Induction

When we reason inductively, we move from specific evidence to a general conclusion. Because we cannot examine the whole, we *sample* it by examining a number of specific instances and then drawing a generalization about them. The following is an example of **induction;** it moves from the specific to the general—from a series of facts to a conclusion:

Fact: One of every three children violates the "no drinking before the age of 21" law by the age of 12.

Fact: Businesses benefit from violations of the "no drinking before the age of 21" law.

Fact: Parents commonly violate the "no drinking before the age of 21" law.

Conclusion: The "no drinking before the age of 21" law is disregarded widely in our society.

Whenever speakers use what is true in particular cases to draw a general conclusion, they are reasoning by induction.

You can evaluate inductive reasoning by asking the following two questions:

1. Is the sample of specific instances large enough to justify the conclusion drawn from them?
2. Are the instances cited representative, or typical, ones?

induction
reasoning that moves from specific evidence to a general conclusion

Causal Reasoning

causal reasoning
speculation about the reasons for and effects of occurrences

When we reason from causes and effects, we either cite observed causes and hypothesize effects or cite observed effects and hypothesize causes. We use **causal reasoning** every day. Something happens, and we ask ourselves, Why? Similarly, we speculate about the consequences of certain acts; that is, we wonder about what effects they have. The following statements illustrate causal reasoning:

> The stereotype of the successful minority hurts Asian Americans.
>
> Focusing on *average* Asian Americans and their success stories hurts Asian Americans.
>
> The fact that many organizations no longer consider Asians a disadvantaged minority hurts Asian Americans.
>
> The problems faced by the majority of Asian Americans are not being taken seriously enough.

To evaluate the soundness of causal reasoning, ask the following questions:

1. Is the presumed cause real or false?
2. Is the presumed cause an oversimplification?

Reasoning from Analogy

In arguing that drugs should be legalized, John P. Walters, the former director of the Office of National Drug Control Policy, used this analogy:

> Just as ending Prohibition did not destroy organized crime in the U.S., legalizing drugs would not break the terrorist criminal groups in Mexico.[20]

reasoning from analogy
reasoning by comparison

When we use **reasoning from analogy,** we compare like things and conclude that since they are alike in a number of respects, they are also alike in some respect that until this point has not been examined. For example, if you wanted to argue that the methods used to decrease the high school dropout rate in a nearby city would also work in your city, you would first have to establish that your city is similar to the other city in a number of important ways—number of young people, number of schools, skill of personnel, financial resources, and so on. If you said that the two cities were alike except that your city had not instituted such a program, and that its dropout rate was therefore significantly higher, you would be arguing by analogy.

To check the validity of analogical reasoning, ask the following questions:

1. Are the two things being compared alike in essential respects? That is, do the points of similarity outweigh the points of difference?
2. Do the differences that do exist matter?

When you reason logically, you not only back up your persuasive arguments with solid evidence, but also cite your sources carefully. When quoting or using a source, share the source's credentials with audience members. Careful citation is critical to the development of well-reasoned arguments.

REASON ETHICALLY

Ethical speakers do not employ logical fallacies. A fallacy is an error in logic; it is flawed reasoning. When a speaker attempts to persuade using flawed reasoning, in addition to misusing the reasoning process, he or she is also abusing the persuasion process. The following are among the most common fallacies that speakers should avoid.

Argumentum Ad Hominem

When you present your audience with an **argumentum ad hominem,** you inject name-calling into your speech. It is literally an "argument against the man" (or woman). You appeal to receivers to reject an idea because of a flaw in a person associated with that idea. You attack a person's character instead of his or her stand on an issue. "She's just a left-wing liberal" and "He's just a member of the radical right" focus attention on the person and not his or her ideas.

Red Herring

The term **red herring** derives its meaning from an act performed during English fox hunts, in which hunt masters would drag red herrings across trails in an effort to divert the hunting dogs from chasing the foxes. When you use a red herring in your speech, your goal is to send the audience on a wild goose chase. By causing receivers to focus on one or more irrelevant issues, you prevent them from considering the issue under discussion. For example, in an effort to negate the right of women to have abortions, one speaker attempted to deflect the focus of receivers by concentrating instead on the cost of health insurance.

False Division

When you use a **false division** in your speech (a false dichotomy, dilemma, or either-or argument), you require audience members to choose between two options, usually polar opposites, when in reality there are many options in between. The following are examples of the false division at work: "If you believe in flag burning, you don't believe in the country." "If you don't like the policies of the United States, go back to your native country." "If you are not part of the solution, then you are part of the problem." "Either we eliminate gun control, or only outlaws will have guns."

The Hasty Generalization

When you are quick to jump to a conclusion, you hope receivers will disregard any other potential options and make the leap with you, however illogical. Hasty generalizations, often the result of emotional gut reactions, prevent careful examination of issues and contribute to deficient analyses of problems. Because they are based on insufficient evidence, they frequently lead to fatally flawed conclusions and solutions.

The Slippery Slope

When your argument asserts that one action will set in motion a chain reaction, you are on a slippery slope. You assert such a fallacy hoping that receivers will believe that one occurrence—without question—necessarily and inevitably follows another occurrence. One event, however, does not necessarily precipitate another event. Usually, there are a series of steps or options between one event and the next—because event X occurred doesn't automatically mean event Y will occur.

Ethics & Communication

Illogical Reasoning

When logic fails, speakers sometimes substitute logical fallacies in its place. Speakers may flaw their speeches with reasoning fallacies: Using the Internet, books of published speeches, or issues of *Vital Speeches of the Day,* locate examples of fallacious reasoning. Explain why you believe the logic is flawed in each example.

argumentum ad hominem
the use of name-calling in an argument

red herring
a distraction used to lead the receiver to focus on an irrelevant issue

false division
the polarization of options, when, in fact, many options exist

---

The following is an example of a slippery slope: "First, they ban pornography, then they'll ban comic books, and finally they'll ban all books."

The Appeal to Tradition or Novelty

If you tell receivers that things have always been done a certain way, you are appealing to their sense of tradition. The argument might go something like this: "Of course this form of management is best; we've had this structure for over a decade." The assertion is that because X has always been done, X is right. When times change, however, what once worked may no longer work. Sticking to what's "tried and true" is easy for people who fear change, but change can be healthy. On the other hand, the appeal to novelty is the opposite of the appeal to tradition. Here you assert that because something is new, it's better. That also is not necessarily true. Being new doesn't necessarily make something better.

Post Hoc, Ergo Propter Hoc (False Cause)

When your argument is based on the assumption of **post hoc, ergo propter hoc,** you identify a false cause; that is, you lead your receivers to assume mistakenly that one event causes another merely because they occur sequentially. For example, one speaker pointed out that a decrease in abortions in the United States began about the same time as increased opportunities in sports for women. While a causal link may exist, the speaker has to supply evidence to establish a definitive link between the two phenomena. Correlation is not causation.

Argumentum Ad Populum (Bandwagon Appeal)

An **argumentum ad populum** is a bandwagon appeal—that is, an appeal to popular opinion. The speaker who uses such a fallacy tells receivers that, because "everyone is doing or supporting it," they should, too. Widespread acceptance of an idea, however, does not mean the idea is sound. Rather than rush to judgment based on what everyone else is saying or doing, you should consider the facts carefully and decide for yourself.

Argumentum Ad Verecudiam (Appeal to Authority)

When you inject an **argumentum ad verecudiam** fallacy into your speech, you use the testimony of someone who is not an expert on your subject and does not possess the credentials that would permit him or her to make a claim or an endorsement. Name recognition and expertise are not synonymous. For instance, while Coldplay may be well-known performers and experts on music, when it comes to talking about U.S. foreign policy, their value as a source decreases.

GAIN YOUR LISTENERS' ATTENTION

Before you can persuade or convince other people, you must first get their attention. In his book *The Art of Persuasion,* Wayne Minnick relates how a 9-year-old girl succeeded in getting the undivided attention of a male guest at her party. It seems that all the boys had gathered at one end of the room, talking to each other and ignoring the girls. "But I got one of them to pay attention to me, all right," the little girl assured her mother. "How?" inquired the mother. "I knocked him down!" was the undaunted reply.[21]

The speeches of speakers from groups such as the Ku Klux Klan usually contain an array of logical fallacies.

post hoc, ergo propter hoc
the identification of a false cause

argumentum ad populum
a bandwagon appeal; an appeal to popular opinion

argumentum ad verecudiam
an appeal to authority

You should not knock down your listeners to get their attention, but you will need to find ways to encourage them to listen to you. It is your responsibility to put them into a receptive frame of mind. You can do this in several ways. You can compliment your listeners. You can question them. You can relate your message directly to their interests, or you can surprise them by relating to them in an unexpected way. Once you have the attention of your listeners, you must continue to work to hold it.

MAKE YOUR LISTENERS FEEL AS WELL AS THINK

Appeals to emotion (pathos) add to a speech's impact. Following is an excerpt from a student's speech on the issue of Palestinians jailed without trial in Israel. In it, the student quotes from a letter written by a Palestinian prisoner to an Israeli officer who was sentenced to jail himself for refusing to serve as a jailer for the political detainees because of his belief that the practice of administrative detentions was wrong. Why do you think that the use of this passage in the student's speech is effective?

> Who are you, officer?
>
> I want to write to you, but first I have to know who you are. I have to know the reasons that moved you to act as you did. I have to know how you arrived at this principled decision of conscience; how you chose such a unique rebellion, so unexpected.
>
> What's your name? Where do you live? What do you do? How old are you? Do you have children? Do you like the sea? What books do you read? And what are you doing now in the cell where you are held? Do you have enough cigarettes? Is there someone who identifies with you over there? Do you ask yourself, "Was it worth paying the price?"
>
> Can you see the moon and stars from the cell window? Have your ears grown accustomed to the jangle of the heavy keys, to the creak of the locks, to the clang of the metal doors? . . . Do you see in your sleep fields of wheat and kernels moving in the wind? Do you see expanses of sunflowers, and are your eyes filled with yellow, green and black hues, and the sun tans you, and you smile in your sleep, and the walls of the cell tumble and fall, and an unknown person waves his hand to you from afar? . . .
>
> Don't you have regrets? Didn't you have doubts when they told you: "They're dangerous; they belong to Hamas, to Islamic Jihad and the Popular Front? Don't you trust our security services? Do you really believe that we are ready to throw innocent people in jail?"
>
> Why do I feel as if I know you? . . .
>
> Anonymous lieutenant, whatever your name is, sleep well; sleep the peaceful slumber of someone whose conscience is clear.

Effective speakers develop emotional appeals designed to make audience members feel.

Many changes in human behavior have resulted from messages that combined emotional appeals with rational reasons. Since few people will change their attitudes or take action if they are unmoved or bored, effective speakers develop emotional appeals that are designed to make listeners feel.[22] Whether the feeling evoked is sadness, anger, fear, sympathy, happiness, greed, nostalgia, jealousy, pride, or guilt depends on the speaker's topic and the response desired.

As a speaker, you must appeal not just to your listeners' heads but also to their hearts. Thus, although your speech should be grounded in a firm foundation of logic and fact, it should also be built on feelings.

EVOKE RELEVANT NEEDS AND ISSUES

Balance is a state of psychological health or comfort in which our actions, feelings, and beliefs are related to each other as we would like them to be. When we are in a balanced state, we are content or satisfied. Thus, we engage in a continual

balance
a state of psychological comfort in which one's actions, feelings, and beliefs are related to each other as one would like them to be

struggle to keep ourselves in balance. What does this imply for you as a persuasive speaker? If you want to convince your listeners to change their attitudes or beliefs, you must first demonstrate to them that a current situation or state of affairs has created an imbalance in their lives and that you can help restore their balance. The simple introduction of imbalance, or dissonance (whether that imbalance, or dissonance, is experienced by receivers for real or created vicariously by the speaker) motivates change in receiver thinking or behaving. Thus, speakers may deliberately create dissonance in receivers and then suggest what receivers need to think or do in order to be able to alleviate their dissonance and restore their sense of balance. It is our inner drive for balance that helps explain our positive responses to an array of persuasive appeals.

Remember that human behavior depends on motivation. If you are to persuade people to believe and do what you would like them to do, you must make your message appeal to their needs and goals.

One popular device used to analyze human motivation is a schematic framework devised by the famous psychologist Abraham Maslow.[23] In **Maslow's hierarchy of needs,** motivation is seen as a pyramid, with our most basic needs at its base and our most sophisticated needs at its apex (see Figure 15.1). Maslow defined survival (physiological) needs as the basic necessities of life: shelter, food, water, and procreation. Safety needs include the need for security and the need to know that our survival requirements will be satisfied. At the third level are love and belonging needs. Once these are met, our esteem needs can be addressed. Esteem needs include self-respect and the respect of others. Our efforts to succeed are often attempts to satisfy our esteem needs, because success tends to attract respect and attention. At the peak of Maslow's hierarchy is the need for self-actualization. When we satisfy this, we have realized our potential; that is, we have become everything we are capable of becoming.

How does Maslow's hierarchy relate to you as a persuasive speaker? Find out by trying the Skill Builder "Climbing the Motivation Pyramid." Remember that salient needs make salient motives. Your goal is to make your receivers identify your proposal with their needs. Whenever you attempt to do this, you will probably have to involve personal feelings.

FIGURE 15.1

Maslow's Hierarchy of Needs.

From Abraham Maslow, *Toward a Psychology of Being.* Copyright © 1962. Reprinted by permission of John Wiley & Sons, Inc.

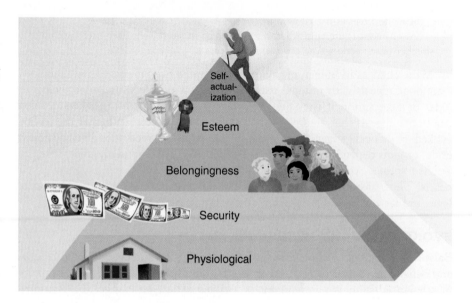

Climbing the Motivation Pyramid

For each of the following situations, identify the types of appeals you could use to persuade audience members to believe or behave as you would like them to. First, consider the nature of the particular audience. Second, aim a part of your persuasive effort at each level of Maslow's hierarchy pyramid. For each audience, which level and which appeal do you think would be most effective? Explain your reasons.

1. You want to persuade high school seniors not to drink and drive.

2. You want to convince college students to use debit, not credit, cards.

3. You want to persuade the members of your hometown to donate blood.

4. You want to convince veterans not to support an amendment making burning the flag unconstitutional.

5. You want to convince voters to support the passing of a law prohibiting former members of Congress or the president's cabinet from becoming lobbyists.

PROMISE A REWARD

When you are speaking persuasively, demonstrate how your listeners' personal needs can be satisfied by your proposal. You should stress how your ideas can benefit the people you are trying to persuade. Make them believe that your proposal will supply a reward.

Remember, however, that different audiences value different types of rewards. For practice, think of three different types of audiences and identify the most important needs of each. Imagine that you are a salesperson trying to persuade each of those audiences to buy one of the following items: (1) guitar, (2) plant, (3) dog, (4) hat, (5) attaché case. Describe the strategies you would use with each group. What adaptations would you make? To what extent would you display your awareness of individual differences?

It is important to remember that people are usually preoccupied with how something will benefit them personally. Your listeners, whoever they are, will want something in return for behaving as you would like them to behave.

Review, Reflect, & Apply

Recall
List guidelines for a speaker to follow when planning a persuasive speech.

Understand
Discuss factors affecting listener attitudes and beliefs.

Apply
Explain how you can use the Toulmin model to identify the elements in a persuasive argument of your choice.

Analyze
Identify the nature of reasoning used in a speech by a politician or public figure.

Evaluate
Assess the nature of logical fallacies in the speech of a radio or talk show host of your choosing.

Monroe's Motivated Sequence: A Framework for Persuasive Speaking

LO6

Describe Monroe's motivated sequence.

Monroe's motivated sequence
a speech framework composed of five phases—attention, need, satisfaction, visualization, and action

One organizational framework that persuasive speakers have found particularly effective in motivating receivers to respond positively to their purpose is **Monroe's motivated sequence.**[24] Based on the psychology of persuasion, Monroe's framework is composed of five phases, which sequentially move receivers toward accepting and acting on a speaker's proposition. Its persuasive structure especially meets the needs of speakers who desire to move audience members to action.

Phase One: Attention. At the outset of a speech, the speaker's primary task is to gain the audience's attention. (In effect, you say, "Pay attention." Perhaps you enhance receivers' interest by asking a question, referring to their experiences, using an illustration or a dramatic story, supplying startling statistics, or providing an eye-catching visual. As a result of what you say or do, your audience members should realize why your message is important to them and why they should listen to what you have to say.)

Phase Two: Need. The speaker demonstrates for receivers that the present situation poses serious problems. He or she explicitly states the need and illustrates it with a variety of supporting materials. By revealing what is wrong to receivers and relating the need to their interests and desires, the speaker prepares them for the problem's solution. (In this stage, you say, "This is wrong, and here is what we need to do about it." In addition to identifying the problem or need, you illustrate it with specific examples. In addition, you support the need's existence with illustrations, statistics, testimony, or other forms of support. Your objective is to show how the identified need has an impact on the lives of audience members and how it affects their personal or professional goals, health, happiness, and/or financial security, for example.)

Phase Three: Satisfaction. Having shown the audience members that a need exists, the speaker's next task is to satisfy their desire for a solution. (Here, you tell receivers, "I have a way to solve the problem." You present your plan, explain it fully to receivers, and help them recognize that solving the problem will satisfy their interests and desires. By using examples and illustrations to flesh out what you want audience members to believe or do, and explaining why you are asking them to believe or do this, you help them understand how they can satisfy the need you described previously.)

Phase Four: Visualization. The speaker visualizes the plan's benefits for receivers, describing how things will improve when the plan is put into action. (In this phase, you say, "This is how my plan will meet your needs, alleviate the problems you face, and help make things better." You demonstrate the benefits audience members will receive once they act upon your ideas; if desired, you also explore the negative effects receivers will suffer if they fail to act on your plan.)

Phase Five: Action. The speaker's next task is to move receivers in a particular direction by telling them what they should do to ensure that the need is satisfied. In effect, the speaker asks receivers to support the policy and act on it. (In this phase, you say, "Here's what I would like you to do." You conclude with an appeal that reinforces their commitment to putting your solution to work. You are telling them to act.)

The following outline illustrates how the motivational sequence can be used to design a presentation advocating that we should not drive when drowsy.

Review, Reflect, & **Apply**

Recall

Identify the five phases in Monroe's motivated sequence.

Understand

Explain how speakers can use each stage in Monroe's motivated sequence to move receivers toward their goals.

Apply

Discuss how a speaker used Monroe's motivated sequence to persuade you to act on his or her proposition.

Create

Use Monroe's motivated sequence to develop an outline for a persuasive speech that asks receivers to support the fund-raising efforts of your college or a local charity.

Introduction	I. It was after midnight when six students walking to a fraternity party were killed when Brandon Kallmeyer fell asleep at the wheel of the pickup truck he was driving, veered off the road, and hit them.
(Attention)	II. Over 100,000 accidents occur every year because drivers fall asleep at the wheel.
	III. The problem of people driving while drowsy is increasing.
	IV. Today I would like to explore why it is important to us to examine this problem, why it continues to escalate, and what steps we can take to help alleviate it.
Body	I. We have put sleep on the back burner.
(Need)	A. Everyone needs approximately eight hours of sleep a day to function effectively the next day, but we average only about six hours of sleep a day.
	B. The most important sleep hour is the REM stage, which occurs between the seventh and eighth hour.
	II. Sleep-deprived persons pose serious dangers on the road.
	A. Highway patrol officers report stopping motorists who appear drunk, only to discover they are fatigued.
	B. Drowsy driving is approaching a national epidemic.
	III. The drowsy driving problem can be alleviated once we fully understand its causes.
(Satisfaction)	A. We are poor judges of our own sleeplessness.
	B. Alcohol consumption contributes to becoming sleepy behind the wheel.
	C. Boredom is a contributing factor to becoming tired.
(Visualization)	IV. Tragedy can be prevented if we take the proper steps.
	A. Imagine what would happen if the Federal Highway Administration added more rumble strips designed to wake us up when we began to veer off the road.
	B. Imagine what would happen if cars were equipped with AutoVue cameras that emit rumble strip–like sounds when a driver drifts out of a lane.
	V. There are some steps we can take personally to protect ourselves.
(Action)	A. We can take naps to fight fatigue.
	B. We can sleep the recommended seven to eight hours a night.
Conclusion	I. Six innocent students were killed because someone didn't take action to avoid the tragedy.
	II. It is time to get the sleep that could save our lives and the lives of others.[25]

Delivering a Persuasive Speech

As a persuasive speaker, you must show a great deal of interest in and enthusiasm for your topic. At the moment of presentation, it must become the most important issue in the world for both you and your listeners.

LO7

Develop and present a persuasive speech.

Review, Reflect, & Apply

Apply

Create a persuasive speech on a topic of your choice.

Evaluate

Agree or disagree with the following statement using the sample persuasive speech at the end of the chapter to support your position: *All persuasive speaking is informative. There is no such thing as a purely persuasive speech.*

Be aware that audience members may object to what you say. As a persuader, you need to be able to handle objections in an effective manner. First, be prepared for opposing points of view. Anticipate your audience's concerns and rehearse possible answers. Second, consider the source of objections. For example, audience members may dispute your facts. If you make a statement about the number of millionaires in your state and an audience member has just completed a study on wealth in the United States and has up-to-date statistics, you will need to agree, restate your findings, or suggest that this is a good point, which you both should explore. An effective way to handle opposing views is to agree with them as much as possible. "I agree that life insurance may not be the best investment . . ." is a disarming technique often used by sales representatives to counter objections to purchasing insurance.

Answer any argument in a professional manner. Do not become angry that anyone would dare question your reasoning. Remember that your credibility is at stake while you are speaking in front of others. Respond to the question or objection in an authoritative manner and move on to other questions. Maintain control.

Sample Persuasive Speech Outline

By starting with a story involving undocumented students, the speaker attempts to draw receivers into the speech.

Having aroused the interest of receivers, and established that a problem exists, the speaker reveals the speech's subject and identifies clear objectives for the speech.

FULL SENTENCE OUTLINE

Topic: Undocumented students[26]

Purpose: To persuade the audience that undocumented students should be allowed to attend college.

Thesis: Undocumented students should be permitted to attend college.

Introduction

I. The scene is the third annual underwater robotics competition hosted by NASA.
   A. An unlikely team of four students from an inner-city high school was able to build a robot to compete against schools like MIT and do what was thought to be impossible—win.
   B. The four students were undocumented immigrants.

II. Undocumented students are regularly denied the opportunity to attend college.
   A. While the 1982 Supreme Court decision *Plyler v. Doe* established that K–12 elementary schools could not bar undocumented children, colleges and universities have no such obligation.
   B. The systematic exclusion affects a total of over one million students, most brought to the United States as children and who didn't intend to break the law.

III. To understand the problems facing undocumented students, we'll first explore the extent of institutional discrimination against undocumented students, next, address the criticism leveled against undocumented students, and finally put forth solutions to ensure undocumented students are allowed to enroll in college.

Body

I. Undocumented students are unable to attend college for two key reasons.
   A. Undocumented students face a legal obstacle.
      1. In a March 4, 2007, interview, college admissions counselor Carolyn Tweedie of St. Paul's Preparatory Academy noted that many universities and community colleges will not accept a student without a valid Social Security number.
      2. Undocumented students do not have valid Social Security numbers.
   B. Undocumented students face financial obstacles.
      1. Forty states prohibit undocumented students from paying in-state tuition rates, forcing them to pay the higher out-of-state tuition rates, and making it financially impossible for them to attend college.
      2. Undocumented students are barred from obtaining federal grants, loans, or institutional scholarships.
      3. A 2006 report by the U.S. Census Bureau reveals that the wage difference between high school and college graduates is $23,000, meaning that undocumented students will be condemned to legalized poverty.

II. The three criticisms leveled at undocumented students—involving taxes, displacement, and legality—are unwarranted.
   A. The belief expressed in the *Salt Lake Tribune* of February 8, 2007, that Americans will have to subsidize the education of undocumented students because they don't work and don't pay taxes is untrue.
      1. The *Los Angeles Times* of April 17, 2006, argues that many undocumented students obtain phony Social Security numbers and work.
      2. Many undocumented students also pay Social Security, Medicare, state, and federal taxes, along with sales, consumption, and property taxes.
   B. The argument made on March 8, 2007, in the *Denver Post* by the Federation of Americans for Immigration Reform, FAIR, that undocumented immigrants would displace American students by siphoning away critically needed financial aid is inaccurate.
      1. These students are not less American.
      2. Their identity and right to a better life should not be contingent on a label.
   C. The position criminalizing undocumented students, expressed by U.S. congressman J. D. Hayworth in his 2006 book *Whatever It Takes,* and withholding access to higher education for that reason is unfair.
      1. According to the 2006 book *Targeting Immigrants,* legality does not assume morality.

The speaker identifies the problems undocumented students face, explaining each problem with reasons.

The speaker identifies and refutes the criticisms leveled at undocumented students, supporting each position with references.

continued

The speaker explains how the undocumented student problem can be solved, supplying both institutional and personal solutions.

The speaker involves receivers by telling them their help is needed.

The speaker reminds receivers that sometimes unfair laws need to be broken to restore fairness.

2. The 13th Amendment, women's suffrage, and the civil rights movement show it is common to fight against things codified into law.

III. There are a number of solutions to the problem of undocumented students.

　A. Institutionally, our government needs to stop criminalizing children brought here by their parents by passing the DREAM Act.

　　1. The act would grant residency to undocumented students who seek to attend college.

　　2. The act would allow undocumented students to legally obtain employment upon graduation.

　　3. The act would also help the armed forces.

　B. Personally, we need to become involved by taking actions aimed at helping undocumented students.

　　1. I've started a blog, *breakingdownborders.org.*

　　2. I've partnered with on-campus organizations to collect over 3,000 letters addressed to Arizona representatives.

　　3. I'm soliciting your help in finding out if your admissions department requires a Social Security number.

　　4. We need to stop describing undocumented students as illegal.

　　5. We need to promote dialogue and discourse about the plight of undocumented students.

Conclusion

I. It's time to move beyond the shallow reasoning the law provides regarding undocumented students.

II. Today's law is often tomorrow's injustice. Should we call Susan B. Anthony "wrong" for illegally voting in the 1872 election? Rosa Parks "disorderly" for refusing to give up her seat? Gay couples "immoral" for coming together in marriage?

III. By looking at the problem and overcoming the objections, we see that all the most driven, dedicated, and patriotic Americans lack is the label and the title.

Sample Persuasive Speech

Speech Title:	Breaking Down Borders: Allowing Immigrants to Obtain a Higher Education[27]
Topic:	Undocumented students
Purpose:	To persuade the audience that undocumented students should be allowed to attend college.
Thesis:	Undocumented students should be permitted to attend college.

The scene is the third annual underwater robotics competition hosted by NASA. The players are teams from some of the top engineering universities across the nation and four inner-city high school students with a robot that they built. They called the robot "Stinky." This very unlikely team of engineers was able to build a robot to compete against schools like MIT and do what was thought to be impossible—win. But even more amazing than the underwater war the robots were waging was the political battle that the students faced even to enter the competition. You see, all four students were undocumented immigrants who didn't let their status dictate what they could do.

As undocumented students, they don't have citizenship, residency, or any sort of legal status and, because of current immigration laws, cannot be put on the path to residency—and that's just the start. The American Immigration Foundation Web site, updated daily, argues that these students are regularly denied the opportunity to attend college. While the 1982 Supreme Court decision *Plyler v. Doe* established that K–12 elementary schools couldn't bar undocumented children, colleges and universities have no such obligation. The *San Jose Mercury News* of March 3, 2007, reveals that this systematic exclusion affects the 65,000 undocumented immigrants who graduate from high school each year for a total of over one million students. The article further comments that the overwhelming majority were brought here as children. They didn't choose to break the law and yet they're still being punished. So today, we'll first explore the extent of this institutional discrimination. Next, we will overcome the objections associated with undocumented students. Finally, we will embrace solutions to ensure that these students are allowed to be just that—students.

So, why can't undocumented students attend college? Well, the issue is twofold: discriminatory admissions and a multitude of financial obstacles. First, in a March 4, 2007, interview with college admissions counselor Carolyn Tweedie of St. Paul's Preparatory Academy, she states that many universities and community colleges will not accept a student without a valid Social Security number. But even if they do, the *Pioneer Press* of February 29, 2007, puts forth that undocumented students are prohibited from obtaining in-state tuition in forty states even though most have lived in-state for most their lives. These students are forced to pay out-of-state tuition that regularly costs thousands of dollars more—making it financially impossible for them even to attend college. According to the National Immigration Law Center, passage of the National Dream Act (also known as the Development, Relief, and Education of Alien Minors Act) would have changed this, but in December 2010, that bill failed to pass and was allowed to die.

Second, regardless of your residency status, I've ingested enough ramen to know that college costs a lot of money. Traditionally, applicants can turn to financial aid to help defer the cost, but as the *Pioneer Press* further comments, undocumented students are barred from obtaining federal grants, loans, and even institutional scholarships. This lack of financial aid makes attending college a financial burden that many immigrant families simply cannot overcome. Even more sobering, a 2006 report by the United States Census Bureau states that

continued

Do you think that starting with a story is a good idea? Does the speaker's opening capture your attention and motivate you to want to hear more? How else might the speaker pull you in to the speech? Is there a visual aid that the speaker might use in the speech's opening?

How effective do you find the speaker's orientation? Does it clearly establish the major parts of the speech?

How would you describe the speech's structure?

Does this transition facilitate the speech's progression?

Do you find the speaker's use of contemporary sources effective?

Does a signpost work here?

the wage difference between college and high school students is an average of $23,000, which means that these prohibitions are condemning these students to legalized poverty.

Are the problems the speaker cites convincing? Is the speaker supplying sufficient evidence to build a case?

This past November, Arizona became the latest state to pass laws denying in-state tuition and financial aid to undocumented students. Now, this sentiment exists because of three main reasons: taxes, displacement, and legality. First, the *Salt Lake Tribune* of February 8, 2007, outlines a common argument—undocumented immigrants don't pay taxes, and Americans would therefore be subsidizing their education. The *Los Angeles Times* of April 17, 2006, argues otherwise: Undocumented immigrants can't legally work in America so most use made-up Social Security numbers. Here's the kicker—the government checks the validity of these numbers to dispense benefits but not to collect taxes. This means that Social Security, Medicare, and state and federal taxes are withheld from every check, regardless of residency status, leading to over $7 billion in surplus taxes every year. Undocumented immigrants also pay sales, consumption, and property taxes, all of which directly contribute to state funding for universities, and millions more even file tax returns using specially assigned IRS numbers.

Does the speaker do a good job of handling objections?

Next, the Federation of Americans for Immigration Reform, FAIR, for short—that's ironic—argues on its Web site *fairus.org*, updated daily, that undocumented immigrants would displace American students and siphon away critically needed financial aid. The *Denver Post* of March 8, 2007, delineates that this argument assumes that these students are somehow less American. They grew up in our culture, succeeded in the same institutions, and abided by the same standards as everyone else. Their identity and therefore their right to a better life shouldn't be contingent on a label.

Finally, former U.S. congressman J. D. Hayworth argues in his 2006 book *Whatever It Takes* that these students shouldn't be granted a higher education because they are in violation of our rules. As one person put it, "It's hard to feel sympathy for someone that broke the law." The 2006 book *Targeting Immigrants* interjects that this argument not only stifles critical analysis but also puts the issue to rest without any consideration for context or extenuating circumstances. Obviously, we shouldn't disregard legality, but at the same time it shouldn't be our only argument. History has repeatedly shown us that legality in no way assumes morality. The 13th Amendment, women's suffrage, and the civil rights movement each fought against things that were codified into law and we're a better nation for it.

What might the speaker do to further illustrate the problem?

Undocumented students have been completely criminalized. They can't vote, work, or even legally drive a car—the least we can do is let them learn. So let's take a look at solutions on both the institutional and personal level. Institutionally, our government needs to stop criminalizing children who are brought here at a very early age, because as dangerous as they might be, two-year-olds probably shouldn't be classified as federal criminals. Next, Congress needs to take a stand in favor of immigration reform by reintroducing and passing the National Dream Act. As quoted in the *Herald News* on May 13, 2011, Senator

In your opinion, does the speaker do a competent job of personalizing problems? What do you think of the suggestions the speaker offers for action? Are they sufficient?

Barbara Boxer said: "It is long past time to provide a path to success for these bright and hard-working young people, who grew up here and call America home." With bipartisan support, such legislation would grant residency to undocumented students seeking to attend college. It would also allow undocumented students to legally obtain employment after graduation. As a side note, the act would also help the United States maintain a mission-ready and fully volunteer military, populated by immigrants who chose not to pursue at least two years of higher education, but to serve two years in the armed forces instead.

On the personal level, to help these students I've started a blog focused on immigration at *breakingdownborders.org* that keeps track of pending legislation, tuition developments, and has links to immigrant-friendly colleges and scholarships. We've also partnered with other on-campus organizations to collect over 3,000 letters addressed to Arizona representatives. What I need from you is information. Ask your admissions department if it requires a Social Security number and shoot me an e-mail at jose@breakingdownborders.org, and I'll post whatever you find. Finally, don't use legality as an excuse for dismissing this issue. Instead, go beyond labels and critically analyze the context in order to form your own opinion. You may have noticed that I have not once used the word "illegal" to describe these students—this is why. And this is something that all of us can do because dialogue and discourse are essential to understanding any plight. You can even help do the same. For example, I asked my school newspaper to do a story on these students. When published, it triggered a two-week wave of response letters—some for, many against—but this is just the sort of critical discussion that needs to take place, and it all got started because of a single phone call. Surely, the educational advancement of over a million students is worth a single phone call.

It's time to move beyond the shallow reasoning the law provides for us on this issue. Should we call Susan B. Anthony "wrong" for illegally voting in the 1872 election? Rosa Parks "disorderly" for refusing to give up her seat? Gay couples "immoral" for coming together in marriage? All of these actions were "illegal." Yet, let's not forget that oftentimes today's law is tomorrow's injustice. By looking at the problem and overcoming the objections, we've seen that, in the case of these immigrants, less than a century removed from our ancestors stepping through the open doors of Ellis Island, it is essential to realize that, sometimes, the most driven, dedicated, and patriotic Americans simply lack the label and the title.

In closing, does the speaker provide receivers with a summary?

Do the examples offered in the conclusion advance the speaker's purpose?

Does the conclusion provide a sense of closure?

Were you the speaker, what would you have done differently in the speech?

WORKS CONSULTED

Plyler v. Doe, 1982

Report by the U.S. Census, 2006

Interview with admissions counselor Carolyn Tweedie, March 4, 2007

Pioneer Press, February 9, 2007

continued

How would you organize the *Works Consulted* page?

San Jose Mercury News, March 3, 2007

Salt Lake Tribune, February 8, 2007

Los Angeles Times, April 17, 2006

Denver Post, March 8, 2007

Alejandro Cano, "Proposals to Pass DREAM Act Are Revived, but Groups Opposing Illegal Immigration Are Standing Firm," *Herald News,* May 13, 2011.

"Dream Act Dies in U.S. Congress," as reported in *The People's Daily Online,* http://english.peopledaily.com.cn/90001/90777/90852/7372867.html, accessed on 5/9/2011.

"DREAM Act: Summary," National Immigration Law Center, updated December 2010.

J. D. Hayworth, *Whatever It Takes: Illegal Immigration, Border Security, and The War on Terror.* Regnery Publishing, 2006

Jonathan Xavier Inda, *Targeting Immigrants: Government, Technology, and Ethics.* Wiley-Blackwell, 2006.

Fairus.org

Sample Speaker's Notes

Topic:	Undocumented students[27]
Purpose:	To persuade the audience that undocumented students should be allowed to attend college.
Thesis:	Undocumented students should be permitted to attend college.

    I. The scene is the third annual underwater robotics competition hosted by NASA.

       A. Competing against schools like MIT, an unlikely team of four students from an inner-city high school was able to build a robot and do what was thought to be impossible—win.

       B. The four students were undocumented immigrants.

    II. Undocumented students don't have citizenship, residency, or any legal status and as a result are regularly denied the opportunity to attend college.

       A. 1982 Supreme Court decision *Plyler v. Doe* established that, unlike grades K–12, colleges and universities have no obligation to admit undocumented students.

       B. The systematic exclusion affects over one million students, most who came to the United States as children, not intending to break the law.

Body

    I. Reasons undocumented students can't attend college

    SS #

    Financial issues

       Out-of-state tuition rate

       Lack of financial aid

       Experiencing legalized poverty (2006 Census report earnings figures)

II. Issues of taxes, displacement, and legality

    Salt Lake Tribune of February 8, 2007—regarding no work & taxes

    Los Angeles Times of April 17, 2006—received phony SS cards

    March 8, 2007 *Denver Post* report on FAIR

    Congressman J. D. Haworth, *Whatever It Takes* (2006)— criminalize undocumented students

    Targeting Immigrants (2006)—legality is not morality

III. Solutions

    Institutionally. Pass DREAM Act, Sen. Boxer Quote

    Personally

        Blog

        3,000 letters

        You can help

        Not illegal

Conclusion

I. Move beyond law.

II. Today's law = tomorrow's justice.

III. Get over label and title.

Communication Skills

PRACTICE TIPS FOR EVALUATING THE PERSUASIVE SPEECH

Although the evaluation form featured in Chapter 13 can be used to evaluate persuasive speeches, there are a number of criteria to keep in mind when evaluating persuasive discourse. Use the following checklist as a guide.

Rate the following criteria from 1 to 5; 1 represents "not at all" or "barely accomplished" and 5 represents "fully accomplished."

_____ Did the speaker's introduction fulfill its purpose?

_____ Was the speaker's proposition clearly understood?

_____ Were the reasons the speaker offered in support of the proposition clear?

_____ Was the speaker's use of testimony effective?

_____ Was the organizational pattern used by the speaker appropriate and easy to follow?

_____ Was the speaker's use of language vivid, appropriate, and motivating?

_____ Was the speaker effective in establishing his or her own credibility?

_____ Did the speaker's conclusion accomplish its purpose?

_____ Did the speaker conduct himself or herself ethically?

_____ Was the speaker's delivery effective?

Check *one* of the following:

The speech was _____ superior _____ above average _____ average _____ below average _____ poor

The Wrap-Up

SUMMARY

LO1 **Define** *persuasive speaking.*

Persuasive speaking is the means a speaker uses to modify the thoughts, feelings, or actions of receivers so that they eliminate the attitudes or behaviors of which the speaker does not approve and, instead, adopt attitudes and behavior compatible with the speaker's interests and worldview.

LO2 **Explain** the purposes of persuasion.

The speaker's objective, sometimes referred to as the proposition of the speech, indicates the type of change the speaker desires in audience members. Most propositions reflect at least one of the following persuasive goals: adoption, discontinuance, deterrence, or continuance of a way of believing or behaving.

LO3 **Distinguish** between types of persuasive speeches.

Persuasive speeches focus on questions of fact, value or policy. Propositions of fact seek to convince others of what is or is not, propositions of value seek to convince them of how good or bad something is, and propositions of policy seek to convince them of what ought to be done.

LO4 **Discuss** what it means to persuade responsibly, strategically, and credibly.

Responsible speakers do not coerce or manipulate audience members. Strategic persuaders use logos (logical proof), pathos (emotional proof), and ethos (judgments of the speaker's character) to advance their goals. Another word for ethos is credibility. In order for audiences to judge a speaker to be credible, they need to believe the speaker is a person of good character, knowledgeable, and personable. Assessments of speaker credibility can change during the course of a speech.

LO5 **Identify** guidelines for persuading effectively.

To persuade effectively speakers need to identify a goal, know the receivers they are trying to reach, understand factors affecting receivers' attitudes and beliefs, use consistency and social proof, reason logically and ethically, know how to gain the audience's attention, make receivers feel as well as think, evoke relevant needs and issues, and promise a reward.

LO6 Describe Monroe's motivated sequence.

Monroe's motivated sequence is a framework for persuasive speaking composed of five phases: attention, need, satisfaction, visualization, and action.

LO7 Develop and present a persuasive speech.

The job of the persuader is to build an effective case that includes well-supported reasons and appeals for accepting a speaker's proposition. The audience members must be drawn into the speech, sense the speaker's conviction and belief in the position he or she is advocating, and be reminded at the conclusion of the speech of what they need to believe and/or do.

KEY TERMS

argumentum ad hominem 421
argumentum ad populum 422
argumentum ad verecudiam 422
attitudes 416
backing 418
balance 423
beliefs 417
causal reasoning 420
claim 418
consistency 417
credibility 413
deduction 419
derived credibility 414
ethos 413
false division 421
induction 419
initial credibility 414
logos 412

Maslow's hierarchy of needs 424
Monroe's motivated sequence 425
pathos 412
persuasion 408
persuasive speech 408
post hoc, ergo propter hoc 422
proposition 409
proposition of fact 410
proposition of policy 410
proposition of value 410
qualifier 418
reasoning from analogy 420
reasons 418
rebuttal 418
red herring 421
social proof 417
terminal credibility 414
warrant 418

Looking Back and Ahead

CONSIDER THIS CASE: THE TOWN MEETING BLUES

"I don't know why you need to go through with this speech if it's making you so nervous," Mihwah said to her friend Daniel one evening.

"Because I really believe in what I'm going to say," said Daniel. "I just can't help being nervous about it, but I'm not going to let that stop me. At least, I'm going to try not to."

Mihwah and Daniel were housemates in a building near campus. Daniel was determined to speak at the upcoming town meeting in their community about an issue that was sure to be divisive. Mihwah had agreed to help him prepare and rehearse his speech, but as the day of the meeting drew closer, he was growing more apprehensive about his plan.

Daniel had been living off-campus for a year, and he'd become aware of a building boom that was taking place around the town. Private developers and contractors were busier than ever with home renovations and new commercial construction, and there was a shortage of workers for them to hire. At the same time, immigrants looking for work had begun gathering in the early morning hours, waiting on street corners for the contractors' trucks and vans to drive by. Often the contractors would stop, pick out a few men, hire them for the day, and drive on. An informal labor market had sprung up, and although it wasn't a perfect solution to the labor problem, or to the problems faced by the immigrant workers, it solved an immediate need, and local government hadn't made any attempt to interfere in it.

But a group of citizens had called a town meeting to try to force an end to the practice. They were mostly local business owners who claimed the small groups of men waiting for work were loitering in front of their stores, begging or scaring their customers away, and creating a public nuisance.

Daniel disagreed. As he'd explained to Mihwah, he believed the workers were sincerely looking for work. He'd never seen one of them begging, and he'd often observed how they kept quietly to themselves each morning until the contractors arrived. Anyone not hired for the day usually disappeared within a few minutes, and no disruptions or disorderly behavior had ever occurred that he knew of.

Daniel believed that a solution to the shopkeepers' objections could be found. He planned to speak at the town meeting to propose his solution—designating a small park in the center of town as the accepted gathering place for the workers and contractors to meet each morning. It would mean the drivers would have to go a little out of their way to find the men, but it would keep the workers away from the storefronts and allow them to continue finding the work they needed. And the contractors would benefit too, by having continued access to the informal labor pool.

Daniel knew he would have to be very persuasive to convince the business owners to consider his proposal. He thought the contractors would agree to it because it would benefit them, too, but he wasn't sure. He was even less sure about what the local government would do if it were finally forced to make some kind of decision in the matter. And he wondered what any of the meeting participants would think about his speaking out. After all, he was only a student. He suddenly wondered whether anyone else would be speaking on behalf of the immigrant workers.

"Well," said Mihwah, breaking in on his thoughts. "Since you're determined to speak, let's go over your outline again. Ready?"

DISCUSSION QUESTIONS

1. How many diverse parties are involved in the situation Daniel has observed in town? Has he considered all their possible interests?
2. What should Daniel do to make himself a more credible speaker at the town meeting? What advantages and disadvantages does he have as an observer, not a participant, in the immigrant labor situation?
3. What does he need to find out about his audiences, and how can he research this?
4. What kind of supporting material do you think Daniel will need to make his speech a success?
5. What kinds of questions should Daniel anticipate being asked at the meeting, and how can he prepare himself to answer them?

Interviewing and Developing Professional Relationships

After completing this chapter, you should be able to demonstrate mastery of the following learning outcomes:

LO1 **Define** and explain the nature of the *employment interview,* including a description of common interviewee fears.

LO2 **Describe** tools to use and tasks to complete in order to secure an interview.

LO3 **Explore** the particulars of an employment interview, including the various stages, the kinds of questions asked, and the roles and responsibilities of the interviewee.

LO4 **Explain** the practice of impression management.

LO5 **Identify** how diversity and technology affect the job search and the interview.

LO6 **Explain** your rights as an interviewee under the law.

Dear_____:

We enjoyed having you visit us here (last week) (last month) (recently). Everyone who talked with you was most impressed, and I personally feel that you are one of the most promising young (men) (women) I've seen in a long time. We all wish we could make you an offer at this time. However, . . .

—From a corporation's form letter

Twenty years from now, the typical American worker will have changed jobs four times and careers twice and will be employed in an occupation that does not exist today.

—Jeffrey Hallet

What does a job interview have to do with communication? A lot. In fact, when it comes to the kinds of skills that job recruiters look for, interpersonal skills top the list.[1] An employment interview is like an interaction on Match.com. However, instead of two people seeking to determine if they have what it takes to make a love connection, during a job interview, the candidate and the employer usually meet face-to-face to figure out if the organization's corporate culture and needs are a good match with the applicant's values and abilities.

During the course of our lives we all take part in interviews. From our vantage point, an interview incorporates many of the topics and principles of communication we have already discussed. Culture, self-concept, perception, listening, feedback, language and meaning, nonverbal cues, and assertiveness, together with team building, leadership, and presentation skills, have parts to play in determining your interviewing success. Let us explore the interview process and what you can do to succeed as an interviewee.

The Employment Interview: More Than Casual Conversation

LO1

Define and explain the nature of the employment interview, including a description of common interviewee fears.

employment interview
the most common type of purposeful, planned, decision-making, person-to-person communication

In comparison to ordinary conversations, the conversations we enact during employment interviews are planned and designed to achieve specific objectives. Thus, an **employment interview** is the most common type of purposeful, planned, decision-making, person-to-person communication. The person(s) hiring and the candidate(s) seeking to be hired engage in a process of personal contact and behavior exchange, giving and receiving information, to make educated career-related decisions.

The employment interview offers a unique opportunity for the potential employer and employee to share meaningful information that will permit each to determine whether their association would be beneficial and productive. It gives both participants a chance to test each other by asking and answering relevant questions. Employers hope to gather information about you during the interview that your résumé, references, and any personality tests you may have been asked to take do not provide. They also believe the person-to-person approach is an effective way to sell their organization to you. As an applicant, you seek information about the employer and the job during the interview. You can deduce from your interaction with the interviewer what your long-term relationship might be and what life in that organization might be like if you are hired.

Some interviews are over before they begin. Why? Because the interviewer asks a question that he or she thinks is easy but that the interviewee cannot answer. For example, on being asked what she had to offer the company, all one interviewee could respond was, "Hmmmmm, that's a toughie." Then she added, "I was more wanting to hear what you could do for me." The candidate did not get the job. How would you have replied to that question?

It is as a result of a hiring or selection interview that we find ourselves accepted or rejected by a prospective employer—an individual, a small business, a large corporation, and so on. The better prepared you are for an employment interview, the better your chances will be of performing effectively and realizing your job objectives. Remember, an interview is not "just talk."[2]

COMMON FEARS

How do you feel about interviewing for a job? Listed here are some fears that interviewees express frequently. Do you share them? Circle the numbers that most accurately reflect your level of interview apprehension: 0 = completely unconcerned; 1 = very mild concern; 2 = mild concern; 3 = more apprehensive than not; 4 = very frightened; 5 = a nervous wreck.

1. I will be asked questions I cannot answer.

    0   1   2   3   4   5

Piquing Career Interest

Have you found that you or your friends are taking more of an interest in criminal justice and forensics? If so, you are not alone. Even a large number of universities report having increased the scope of courses they offer in criminal justice. To what is this surge in interest attributed? Many people believe it is due to television.

The public appears fascinated with investigation and the justice system, as evidenced by the popularity of television shows such as *The Mentalist, Law and Order,* and *CSI.* Their popularity has spilled over into the real world, sparking an increasing interest in criminology careers. Even the Nevada law enforcement agency Field Services

Division has responded to popular interest in forensic science, changing its name to Crime Scene Investigations.[3]

In your opinion, to what extent, if any, is the portrayal of criminology careers on television and film contributing to unrealistic career expectations in those who now seek to become criminologists? For example, most of the crimes featured on *CSI*-type shows are solved in an hour, while they might take months or even years to solve in the real world. In addition, the programs on television rarely show the boring days, they reveal the staff working with state-of-the-art equipment that many cities cannot afford, and they have a crimes-solved rate that actual criminologists could never attain.

2. I will not dress properly for the interview.

   0   1   2   3   4   5

3. I will appear very nervous.

   0   1   2   3   4   5

4. I will not appear competent.

   0   1   2   3   4   5

5. The interviewer will cross-examine me.

   0   1   2   3   4   5

6. I will be caught in a lie.

   0   1   2   3   4   5

7. I will talk too much or too little.

   0   1   2   3   4   5

8. I will have poor rapport with the interviewer.

   0   1   2   3   4   5

9. I will undersell or oversell myself.

   0   1   2   3   4   5

10. I won't be hired.

    0   1   2   3   4   5

Total the numbers you circled to arrive at your "interviewee's anxiety" score.

Your scores indicate how frightened you are of assuming the role of interviewee. If you accumulated 45 to 50 points, you are a nervous wreck; if you scored 35 to 44 points, you are too frightened; if you scored 20 to 34 points, you are somewhat apprehensive; if you scored 11 to 20 points, you are too casual; if you scored 0 to 10 points, you are not at all concerned—that is, you simply do not care.

Review, Reflect, & Apply

Recall

Define employment interview.

Understand

Explain the goals of employer and applicant during an interview.

Apply

Describe your feelings about the job interview process and assess your level of interview anxiety.

Contrary to what you might assume, not being concerned at all about participating in an interview is just as much of a problem as being a nervous wreck, and being too casual can do as much damage as being too frightened. An interviewee should be apprehensive to a degree. If you are not concerned about what will happen during the interview, then you will not care about making a good impression and, as a result, will not perform as effectively as you could.

Securing the Interview: Tools and Tasks

LO2

Describe tools to use and tasks to complete in order to secure an interview.

There are a number of things you do to facilitate your job search, including networking, preparing an effective cover letter and résumé, and preliminary prepping.

NETWORKING AND THE JOB SEARCH

Networking may be responsible for 50 percent of the people looking for a job finding one, which means it makes sense for you to follow the ABC's of networking—Always Be Connecting. While being on social networking sites such as LinkedIn can be helpful, they are not the only answer. How should you be making those connections?

The following are among the networking options you should consider using: (1) Join a professional networking group. This would require you to attend regular meetings, reach out to others, and follow up on leads. (2) Seek membership in an industry and professional associations in or related to your field. Joining such groups will enable you to make industry connections and stay up with developments in your area of interest. (3) Become a member and stay active in your alumni association. This group can further your career and business life as well as your social life. (4) Keep databases containing names of family, friends, and friends of family members. Using friend and family ties—even if weak—can aid your job search. (5) Join civic organizations and clubs. You can be active in and make contacts through organizations such as Rotary, the Chamber of Commerce, and the PTA, or sports teams and clubs. (6) Supplement your education by obtaining an internship—even if unpaid. Interning or even volunteering gives you on-the-job experience that can set you apart from your competition. In fact, a survey by the National Association of Colleges and Employers (NACE) reveals that 42.3 percent of graduates with internship experience receive at least one job offer compared to only 30.7 percent of graduates without internship experience.[4] (7) Use social networks. If not misused or relied on exclusively, social networks can enhance your job search. Social networks such as Facebook, Twitter, and LinkedIn are an effective way to build your contact network by making it easy for you to reach out to former associates and classmates, as well as industry professionals and alumni. A Jobvite survey revealed that 80 percent of companies either now use or are planning to use social networking sites to fill openings.[5] Keep in mind, however, that you are more likely to be eliminated from consideration than to be hired because of what you reveal on your social networking sites. According to Careerbuilder.com, companies cease considering applicants because of their committing social networking mistakes such as posting provocative/inappropriate photographs and information or revealing a lack of interpersonal or communication skills.[6] Here's a rule to follow: If you wouldn't want your grandparent to see it, keep it offline.

PREPARING THE COVER LETTER AND RÉSUMÉ

The job of the applicant is to prepare fully for the interview. By completing two documents—a cover letter and a résumé—that are well written and register a positive impression, you provide the interviewer with a preview of who you are and why you are qualified for the position.

The Cover Letter

The cover letter introduces you to the interviewer. One career coach advices that it even be as short as 120 words because your average reader reads approximately six words per second and will give your letter about 20 seconds, providing it looks good to begin with.[7] The well-written cover letter reveals your purpose, whether you are replying to a posting, following up a referral, or writing an unsolicited introduction. Whatever type of cover letter you write, it should fulfill the following six criteria: (1) It expresses your interest in a position; (2) it tells how you learned of the position; (3) it reviews your primary skills and accomplishments; (4) it explains why these qualify you for the job; (5) it highlights any items of special interest about you that are relevant to your ability to perform the job; and (6) it contains a request for an interview. While a resume is always included with a cover letter, your cover letter needs to make a compelling statement about the value you will bring to the firm. This means putting in two or three important, high-impact accomplishments from your resume that you think will interest the reader.

Remember, your cover letter is the best—and may be the only—chance you have to convince the employer to read your resume. To help ensure this happens, when it comes to your cover letter, (1) Keep it short. (2) Make it easy to read. (3) Find out the name of the person you should address it to. (4) Customize it for every specific job opening. (5) Tell what you can do for the employer and employing company. (6) End it with a call for action—ask for the interview.

The Résumé

The résumé summarizes your abilities and accomplishments. It details what you have to contribute that will meet the company's needs and help solve the employer's problems. Although formats differ, the résumé typically includes the following:

1. contact information—your name, address, telephone number, and e-mail address
2. job objective—a phrase or sentence that focuses on your area of expertise

SIX CHIX © 2009 Anne Gibbons. King Features Syndicate.

www.thesixchix.com

Review, Reflect, & Apply

Recall

Identify the components in a cover letter and résumé, and the preparation required for a Web-based interview.

Understand

Explain why a cover letter should be brief.

Apply

Explain how you would prepare for a screening interview held via Webcam.

Evaluate

Assess the effectiveness of your current cover letter, résumé, and readiness for a Webcam-based screening interview.

Create

Create a new cover letter and résumé for a position of your choice.

3. employment history—your job experience, both paid and unpaid, beginning with the most recent

4. education—schools attended, degree(s) completed or expected, dates of completion, and a review of courses that relate directly to your ability to perform the job

5. relevant professional certifications and affiliations

6. community service

7. special skills and interests you possess that are relevant to the job

8. references—people who agree to elaborate on your work history, capabilities, and character; reveal only that references are available on request unless you are asked to provide specific references at the time you submit your résumé

Since the average resume gets about 15 seconds of the reader's time, creating an effective one is essential.[8] Also, although sending a video resume may intrigue you, many companies still do not accept them.

Preliminary Prepping

More and more companies are saving time and money by using video-chat software such as Skype as their tool of choice when conducting a preliminary screening of job candidates in the effort to narrow the field. While such long-distance interviews may not be as good as meetings, they tend to be better than phone calls.

When preparing for such a screening, be sure to: (1) Set the stage. Clean up the area so the interviewer isn't looking at your messy room. Be sure the space where you will be is quiet—no barking dogs or loud music allowed. Make sure there's no bright light behind you, as this will darken your face. Be sure to adjust the microphone settings. (2) Dress appropriately. Even though you are not meeting the interviewer in person, you are meeting face-to-face so dress as if you were in the same room as the person interviewing you. Don't wear white or bold patterns, as these could be distracting and white is noticed on a screen first. (3) Be video-genic. The interviewer will also be able to see your facial expressions and read your body language, Remember to sit tall, but don't lean too close to the Webcam as this offers the interviewer a close-up of your nose. Decide on a flattering angle. Try swiveling your chair toward the corner of your screen. Look at the interviewer's image when she or he talks, but when you answer, look at the camera so you make eye contact virtually with the interviewer. To look good on video, you need to look at the video lens. To sound good, you need to use your voice to communicate your enthusiasm.[9]

Explore the particulars of an employment interview, including the various stages, the kinds of questions, and the roles and responsibilities of the interviewee.

STRUCTURE: STAGES OF THE INTERVIEW

Most effective interviews have a clear structure. The beginning, or opening, is the segment of the process that provides an orientation to what will come. The middle, or body, is the longest segment and the one during which both parties really

Résumé Padding and Résumé Poaching

1. Résumé padding has been around for a long time. Would you lie on your résumé to get your foot in the door? Would you "fix up" your résumé to help you look better on paper than you really are?

   Not too long ago, Notre Dame's football coach, George O'Leary, had to step down from his head coach position after admitting that he had falsified the academic and athletic credentials listed on his résumé. In your opinion, should O'Leary have been fired for his résumé misrepresentations? Why or why not?

2. It is not merely some résumé writers who are ethically challenged. So are some recruiters. In fact, résumés posted on Internet job boards are not necessarily private or restricted to recruiters and other employers who pay a fee for access. While some sites may sell their résumés, résumé poaching also threatens the privacy of job seekers. The employees of competitive sites have been known to pose as recruiters in order to download thousands of résumés without permission. Persons who post their résumés on supposedly secure sites find themselves harassed by readers who object to their professions. For example, one job seeker in chemistry found herself harassed by activists against animal research.[10] In your opinion, should Internet job search sites be billboards for all to see, or should they be kept private, with recruiters and employers being screened adequately before being given access?

get down to business. The end, or close, is the segment during which the participants prepare to take leave of one another.

Just as the right kind of greeting at the start of a conversation can help create a feeling of friendliness, so the opening of an interview can help establish rapport between interviewer and interviewee.[11] The primary purpose of the opening is to make it possible for both parties to participate freely and honestly by creating an atmosphere of trust and goodwill and by explaining the purpose and scope of the meeting. Conversational icebreakers and orientation statements perform important functions at this stage. Typical icebreakers include comments about the weather, the surroundings, and current events—or a compliment. The idea is to use small talk to help make the interview a human encounter rather than a mechanical one. Typical orientation remarks include an identification of the interview's purpose, a preview of the topics to be discussed, and statements that motivate the respondent and act as a conduit, or transition, to the body of the interview.

In the body of the interview, the parties really get down to business. At this point, the interviewer and interviewee might discuss work experiences, including the applicant's strengths, weaknesses, major accomplishments, difficult problems tackled in the past, and career goals. Educational background and activities or interests are relevant areas to probe during this phase of the interview. Breadth of knowledge and the ability to manage time are also common areas of concern.

During the close of the interview, the main points covered are reviewed and summarized. Since an interview can affect any future meetings the parties may have, care must be taken to make the leave-taking comfortable.[12] Expressing appreciation for the time and effort given is important; neither interviewee nor interviewer should feel discarded. In other words, the door should be left open for future contacts.

Skill Builder

1. According to one résumé expert, "The biggest mistake that people are making is that their résumés have no real impact. . . . A good résumé won't get you a job, but it will get you in the door."[13]

   What steps can you take to ensure that your résumé doesn't end up as origami? Describe how you would market yourself so that the person who receives your résumé actually opens it and spends some time reading it. For example, one applicant for a marketing position included her résumé in a package of gourmet coffees that she sent to the potential interviewer with the slogan "Lindsay will wake up your marketing" affixed to the package. Do you think the interviewer read her résumé?

2. Once your résumé gets you in the door, give yourself an interview wake-up call. By exhibiting the following behaviors during your interview, you can help ensure you make the final cut: (1) Refer to the company you are interviewing with by name; (2) make it clear that you have researched the company; (3) respond enthusiastically to information the interviewer shares; (4) back up your answers to questions you are asked with specific examples; (5) use questions to demonstrate your knowledge of the industry and the company.

QUESTIONS: THE HEART OF THE INTERVIEW

> The only way to get the accurate answers is to ask the right questions.
>
> —Kevin J. Murphy,
> *Effective Listening:*
> *Your Key to Career Success*

> Each party has questions in the interview—both you and the employer. The essence of the interview is to find out the answers to those questions.
>
> —Richard N. Bolles

closed questions
highly structured questions answerable with a simple yes or no or in a few words

open questions
questions that offer the interviewee freedom with regard to the choice and scope of an answer

Questions are the primary means of collecting data in an interview. Not only do questions set the tone for an interview, but they also determine whether the interview will yield valuable information. Using the interrogatives *what*, *where*, *when*, *who*, *how*, and *why* throughout an interview lays a foundation of knowledge on which to base decisions or conclusions.

During the course of an interview, closed, open, primary, and secondary questions may all be used, in any combination.[14] **Closed questions** are highly structured and answerable with a simple yes or no or in a few words. Following are examples of closed questions:

Where do you live?

Did you graduate in the top quarter of your class?

What starting salary do you expect?

Open questions are broader than closed questions and are less restricting or structured; hence, they offer more freedom with regard to the choice and scope of an answer. Following are examples of open questions:

Tell me about yourself.

How do you judge success?

Why did you choose to interview for this job?

Describe a time you failed.

Describe a time when you failed to solve a conflict.

Open questions give you a chance to express your feelings, attitudes, and values. For example, let's consider the first question above. "Tell me about yourself" is not a request for your life story. The interviewer is really asking, "Why should I hire you?" Thus, your task when answering a question like this is to showcase your communication skills by crafting a statement shorter than two minutes, or about the length of an elevator ride, that lets the interviewer know more about you and what you can do for the company, that is, the benefits you will bring to your employer.[15]

Open and closed questions may be either primary or secondary. **Primary questions** introduce topics or begin the exploration of a new area. "What is your favorite hobby?" and "Tell me about your last job" are examples of primary questions—the first is closed; the second is open.

Interviewers use **secondary questions**—sometimes called probing questions—to follow up primary questions. They ask for an explanation of the ideas and feelings behind answers to other questions, and they are frequently used when answers to primary questions are vague or incomplete. Following are examples of secondary questions:

Go on. What do you mean?

Can you give me an example?

primary questions
questions used to introduce topics or explore a new area

secondary questions
probing questions that follow up primary questions

INTERVIEWEE ROLES AND RESPONSIBILITIES

An interviewer uses your interview in three ways: (1) to assess your probable performance if hired, (2) to determine if you and the organization's team can work well together, and assuming the first two goals result in a yes, then (3) to persuade you that the organization is a good one to work for.

What are your roles and responsibilities during this process? You need to speak and listen, and to provide information to help convince the interviewer that you are the right person for the job. At the same time, you need to collect information that will help you decide whether to accept the job if offered it. To accomplish these goals you need to research the organization to which you are applying and try to anticipate the questions the interviewer will ask. In addition, to help control the interview's direction and content, you also need to plan to ask questions. As your questions are answered, you will learn about work conditions and prospects for advancement.

Effective interviewees work hard at self-assessment. In effect, they take stock of themselves to determine who they are, what their career needs and their goals are, and how they can best sell themselves to an employer.

As a prospective interviewee, you will find it useful to prepare by thinking about and answering the following questions:

1. For what types of positions has my training prepared me?
2. What has been my most rewarding experience?
3. What type of job do I want?
4. Would I be happier working alone or with others?
5. What qualifications do I have that make me feel I would be successful in the job of my choice?
6. What type or types of people do I want to work for?
7. What type or types of people do I not want to work for?
8. How do I feel about receiving criticism?
9. What salary will enable me to meet my financial needs?
10. What salary will enable me to live comfortably?
11. What will interviewers want to know about me, my interests, my background, and my experiences?

In addition to conducting a self-survey, the interviewee needs to work to withstand the pressure of the interview situation. Are you prepared to maintain your composure while being stared at, interrupted, spoken to abruptly, or asked difficult questions? Have you practiced enough to keep cool when on the interview hot seat? How do you think you would react if you were asked tough questions? The following questions are favorites among interviewers. How would you answer them?

1. Tell me about yourself.
2. What do you think you're worth?
3. What are you good at?
4. If we hired you, what about this organization would concern you most?
5. What attributes do you think an effective manager should possess?
6. What are your short-term goals? How are they different from your long-term goals?
7. How has your background prepared you for this position?
8. What are your major strengths and weaknesses?
9. How would a former employer or instructor describe you?
10. Why did you leave your last job?
11. What do you consider your greatest accomplishment?
12. What's wrong with you?
13. What would you do if I told you that I thought you were giving a very poor interview today?
14. How long do you plan to remain with us if you get this job?
15. What would you like to know about us?

Some interviewers prefer to ask even more searching questions, such as the following:

Tell me about how you handled the last mistake you made.

Are there things at which you aren't very good?

At your weekly team meetings, your boss unexpectedly begins aggressively critiquing your performance on a current project. What would you do?

You're in a situation in which you have two very important responsibilities that both have deadlines that are impossible to meet. You cannot accomplish both. How do you handle that situation?[16]

Practice in answering questions like these—under both favorable and unfavorable conditions—is essential.[17] It is important that you know what you want to say during the interview and that you use the questions you are asked as an opportunity to say it. Along the way, you can flatter the interviewer by offering comments such as "I think you've touched on something really important."

The interviewer can, of course, consult a résumé to ascertain information about the applicant—about educational background and previous positions held, for example. However, gathering enough information to evaluate the personal qualities of an applicant is more difficult. Following is a list of personal qualifications, with the questions interviewers typically ask to evaluate them:

1. *Quality:* Skill in managing one's own career

   Question: What specific things have you done deliberately to get where you are today?

2. *Quality:* Skill in managing others

   Question: What are some examples of things you do and do not like to delegate?

3. *Quality:* Sense of responsibility

   Question: What steps do you take to see that things do not fall through the cracks when you are supervising a project?

4. *Quality:* Skill in working with people

   Question: If we assembled in one room a group of people you have worked with and asked them to describe what it was like to work with you, what would they be likely to say? What would your greatest supporter say? What would your severest critic say?

When it comes to answering questions about items listed on your résumé, one career coach suggests using the acronym S.T.A.R. (*s*ituation, *t*ask, *a*ction, *r*esult) as a guide. For example, let's say your résumé notes that you turned around a sales territory in decline, ultimately increasing sales by 10 percent in your first year. The interviewer asks: "How did you do that?" Your job is to walk the interviewer through the process by revealing the situation you faced, how you assessed your task, the action you took, and the result you achieved.[18]

Most employment interviews can be grouped into one of three categories: the behavioral, the case, and the stress interview. In the **behavioral interview,** an employer is looking for specific examples from the prospective employee of times when he or she has exhibited specific skills. When asked a question such as "Tell me about a time you acted in a leadership role," the interviewee might respond, "I was the director of a fund-raising group," or "I was an officer in Women in Communication." In the **case interview,** a company presents the interviewee with a business case and asks for him or her to work through it. To help prepare yourself for such an interview, check out the company Web site beforehand. Some companies post sample cases on their sites. The third type of interview, the **stress interview,** typically includes more than one interviewer firing questions at the interviewee to see how that person handles himself or herself during a stressful situation.

Because the interview is a conversation and not an interrogation, during the course of the interview, the interviewee should ask questions of the interviewer as a means of demonstrating interest in the job and the company.[19] When the interviewee asks questions, the interview becomes more balanced. What kinds of questions should you ask when in the interviewee role? You should not ask questions that you can answer easily by visiting the company's Web site. You should, however, ask questions that seek clarification; for example: "I read on your site that you will be introducing new products. Could you tell me more about how you plan to roll them out?"

behavioral interview
an employment interview in which an employer looks for the employee to provide specific examples of specific skills

case interview
an employment interview in which the interviewee is presented with a business case by the employer and asked to work through it

stress interview
an employment interview in which more than one person fires questions at an interviewee

Review, Reflect, & Apply

Recall

Name the stages in and kinds of questions asked in employment interviews.

Understand

Explain what occurs in each interview stage and discuss the nature of closed, open, primary, and secondary interview questions.

Apply

Describe how you would use conversational ice-breakers during an interview.

Analyze

Compare and contrast possible closed, open, primary, and secondary interview questions.

Evaluate

Assess the S.T.A.R. system's effectiveness in guiding your responses to questions based on your résumé.

Create

Compose a "position-wanted" advertisement for yourself, draft a two-minute response to the question: Why should I hire you?, and identify a list of questions you need to better prepare yourself to answer.

Let's Get Tough

Human relations consultant and interviewer trainer Justin Menkes helps employment recruiters learn how to gather a lot of information in a brief period of time. To accomplish this, he suggests they ask questions like those identified in the text. Try your hand at answering one of those questions: You have two very important responsibilities that both have deadlines that are impossible to meet. You cannot accomplish both. How do you handle that situation?

Which of the following possible responses does your answer most resemble?

1. I'd focus on the project I'm most comfortable with and give it my all.

2. I'd plan carefully, assign segments of the project to others, and multitask so that I could complete both.

3. I'd ask my supervisor which project is most important to the company.

According to Menkes, the first response suggests that the interviewee's focus is on himself or herself, the second response does not answer the question asked, and the third response reveals an interest in the needs of the company and an interest in developing a collaborative relationship.[20]

In general, interviewees ask questions about the company and corporate culture (rather than about salary or benefits), the industry, the position, and the people in the company. Following are some examples:

Why is this position open?

What would you say are the main challenges of this job?

What will be the priorities in the first 90 days?

With whom will I be working?

How is the department organized, and what will my role be?

How will performance be measured and evaluated?

How are conflicts resolved?

How are decisions made?

Why do you like working here?[21]

To be effective, both interview participants need to work hard. Questioner and respondent constantly exchange information. While one speaks, the other conveys nonverbal information through posture, facial expression, gestures, and so on. You may stop talking during an interview, but that does not mean that you stop communicating. Know what you want to accomplish with your verbal and nonverbal messages.

IMPRESSION MANAGEMENT: EFFECTIVE INTERVIEWING

LO4

Explain the practice of impression management.

How well do we need to know someone before we believe we understand him or her? Experience says not very long. According to psychologists Nalini Ambady and Frank Bernieri, the power of first impressions arms us with a kind of pre-rational ability or intuition for making judgments about others that colors the other impressions we gather over time.[22] It becomes a self-fulfilling prophecy. We assume that the way someone behaves in an interview is indicative of the way that person always behaves. Thus, in the context of interviewing, in an effort to manage the impression the interviewer forms of him or her, the interviewee makes a concerted

Voices and Impression Management

People from different cultures use their voices differently, a fact that could lead to misunderstandings between interviewers and interviewees. People from the Middle East, for example, tend to speak louder than Westerners, causing Westerners to perceive them as overly emotional. In contrast, the Japanese tend to be much more soft-spoken, leading Westerners to believe that they are extremely polite and humble.

How could such habitual ways of speaking affect the interview process? What can interviewers and interviewees do to diminish such perceptual barriers?

effort to influence the interviewer's perceptions of his or her image by engaging in behavior that causes the interviewer to view the interviewee favorably.

The adage that first impressions count apparently holds true for job interviews.[23] In fact, the word *interview* is derived from the French word *entrevoir*, meaning "to see one another" or "to meet." What happens when an interviewer and an interviewee meet for the first time? What variables influence the impressions the interviewer forms of the interviewee? Most interviewers make their decisions about an applicant during the course of the interview. In fact, although most decide in the last quarter of the interview whether or not to invite the applicant back, a bias for or against the candidate is established earlier in the interview, often during the first four to six minutes.

What can you do to help the interviewer judge you positively from the outset? Among the steps you should take are the following: (1) Look like the professional the interviewer wants to hire. (See Figure A.1.) Keep in mind that you're going on an interview, not a date. (2) Be smart going in. Know about the company, the competition, and industry trends. (3) Be enthusiastic and show that you are happy to be there. Smile, sit up, lean slightly forward, and maintain eye contact. Communicating a high level of energy works in your favor. (4) Vary your pitch and volume. The interviewer will view you more positively if you do not speak in a monotone, whisper, or shout, or if you speak without exhibiting vocal hesitations or signs of physical tension.[24]

According to researcher Lois Einhorn, the amount of time allotted for an interview also sends an important message.[25] She found that interviewees who were not hired had participated in interviews shorter than those of successful applicants. She also found that successful interviewees spoke a greater percentage of the time than their unsuccessful counterparts. In fact, the successful applicants spoke for some 55 percent of the total interview time, whereas the unsuccessful applicants spoke only 37 percent of the time. Seeming to control the interview also leaves an impression. In Einhorn's research, successful applicants initiated 56 percent of the comments made during their interviews, whereas unsuccessful applicants were viewed as followers—they initiated only 37 percent of the comments. It is important for you to send messages that you are active, not passive.

Companies are toughening their interviews, using more challenging techniques to sort through job candidates. Thus, you need to be prepared so that you make as good an impressible as possible. Here's where your team-building and presentation

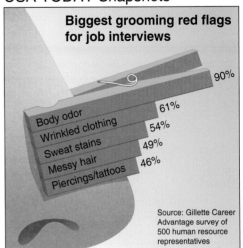

USA TODAY Snapshots®

Biggest grooming red flags for job interviews

- 90%
- Body odor 61%
- Wrinkled clothing 54%
- Sweat stains 49%
- Messy hair 46%
- Piercings/tattoos

Source: Gillette Career Advantage survey of 500 human resource representatives

By Jae Yang and Karl Gelles, USA TODAY

FIGURE A.1

skills come in handy. You need to be prepared to propose solutions to hypothetical or real problems. Employers want to know if you can think on your feet and stay composed. You need to be prepared to deliver an on-the-spot oral presentation about yourself—sometimes in front of your competition—so pay attention to their presentations as well, because employers also want to see how you treat others. Since employers may also conduct group interviews, try to pay attention to each person, addressing them by name, if possible.

The interviewer's assessment of you will determine whether or not you get the job. The following are some of the negative factors that turn off the interviewer and lead to applicant rejection:

Believe in yourself.

—The Wizard of Oz, to Dorothy

arrogance

lack of motivation or enthusiasm

immaturity

poor communication skills

unclear goals

unwillingness to relocate or travel

deficient preparation for the interview

lack of experience

too sloppy or too slick an appearance[26]

Among the factors leading to your receiving job offers are the following:

a pleasant personality (likableness)

enthusiasm

interpersonal skills

ability to function as part of a team

knowledge of the field

computer literacy

creativity

clear purpose and goals

flexibility and the ability to handle change

confidence in what you are doing and who you are

integrity and moral standards

global perspective

sense of humor[27]

Review, Reflect, & Apply

Recall

Define impression management.

Understand

Describe steps the interviewee should follow to ensure the interviewer will view him or her positively.

Apply

Discuss what you can do to convey to an interviewer that you possess the qualities sought.

Analyze

Identify variables influencing first impressions.

Evaluate

Assess your readiness to communicate a positive impression when interviewing.

Create

Compile a list of interview do's and don'ts.

You can cement a positive image in three ways. (1) Never ask about vacation, company benefits, and personal days during your first interview. Work, instead, to display your knowledge of the company, understand its goals, and identify how you fit in by asking questions that touch on strategic and tactical issues. (2) End an interview by reaffirming your interest in the position and restating why you believe you will be an asset to the company.[28] View this as your sales opportunity; that is, ask for the order. Saying something like, "I am very interested in the position. I would welcome the opportunity to work with you and your team," helps communicate that you really want the job. (3) Remember to send a thank you note to the person or persons who interviewed you. An essential step in the job-seeking process, this is also the one job seekers most often forget.[29] One successful job candidate sent her thank you via overnight carrier. Another who had interviewed for a job with Google delivered a handwritten thank you along with cupcakes for the recruiter and five other officials who interviewed him. One letter of the Google name appeared atop each cupcake.[30] Do you think he was hired?

Diversity and the Interview

Culture influences how we conduct ourselves during interviews. For example, in collectivistic cultures such as those in China, Japan, and Korea, interviewees habitually display modesty. If Americans, who are used to stressing their positive qualities, were interviewing in any of those countries, they could be perceived as arrogant and self-centered. On the other hand, if persons from a collectivistic culture were to interview in the United States, they could be perceived as unassertive, lacking in confidence, and unprepared to assume leadership. While Western culture encourages people to be assertive and showcase strengths, Eastern culture traditionally teaches members to be more modest and humble about their personal achievements, qualifications, and experience. Similarly, Native American culture teaches that cooperation is a benefit and that one leads through deeds, not words. Thus, not wanting to appear boastful, Native Americans could also be hesitant to discuss their personal strengths.[31]

LO5

Identify how diversity and technology affect the job search and the interview.

There are gender differences in what employees seek in a job. Survey results reveal that most men value compensation above all else, while most women put employee benefits first. Compensation is ranked third on most women's lists, after opportunities for skill development.[32]

Age also correlates with what employees want most in a job. In contrast with all other groups, the under-thirties do not even rank benefits among their top five concerns. What is important to most persons in this age bracket are opportunities to develop skills, chances for promotion, compensation, vacations, and an appealing culture and colleagues.[33]

Interviewers need to be sensitive to and demonstrate their respect for all cultures. Not hiring someone on the basis of age, sexual preference, national origin, or religion is illegal. Despite this, many Muslim workers report having thought about changing their last names to avoid alienating potential employers.[34] Would you ever change your name if you thought doing so would help you get the job you want? Why or why not?

Technology and the Job Search

The Web has changed the way we search for and find jobs. Regularly search online classified ads for job opportunities. In addition to Monster.com, aggregate sites such as Indeed.com and SimplyHired.com link you to job ads all over the Internet, including companies' career pages. Additionally, networking Web sites such as LinkedIn.com and Ryze.com can help you connect with business professionals in your field without your knowing them well or at all.[35]

Applicants should use a company's home page to get background information on the organization and its culture or to e-mail a résumé and cover letter. Following are some Web sites you can consult for information on companies and jobs:

Company Information

www.wsj.com

www.nytimes.com

www.bizweb.com

Job Information

http://stats.bls.gov The Bureau of Labor Statistics Web site, which offers information on positions by state, listing the average salary being paid per position

www.careerbuilder.com

www.NowHiring.com

www.monster.com

Usenet newsgroups, listserv mailing lists, and blogs are three other Internet resources you can use to learn about employment possibilities and company cultures. Of the three, blogs are becoming increasingly popular in electronic recruiting, functioning as a prime means that applicants use to find out about companies. Often they contain information such as what it is like to work at a company as well as what is going on in an industry.[36]

Job seekers also create their own home pages, featuring both their online résumé and business card.[37] A variety of online resources and computer programs exist to help you prepare your résumé. Many provide you with templates that you can complete as is or customize. You can also post your résumé on the Net by e-mailing it to a server.

In fact, more and more companies now request that potential employees submit an electronic résumé (a résumé that is obtained and analyzed electronically by the employer).[38] An electronic résumé includes keywords that describe the person's competencies and skills. Once the employer scans the résumé into the company's computer tracking system, when a job becomes available, the employer can efficiently search the résumés contained in the database by the keywords that describe the characteristics a person qualified for the position should have. Electronic résumés require standard formats and block letters that are plain and simple. A résumé that is going to be scanned should not use boldface type, underlining, or bullets, because these special effects interfere with the scanning process. To facilitate the initial résumé screening, which will be done by a bias-free computer, an electronic résumé typically contains a block paragraph of keywords, which immediately follows the identification information centered above it. Unlike your traditional résumé, which probably contains action verbs such as *communicates well*, your electronic résumé should contain nouns, such as *organizational skills*. A number of Internet sites can help you prepare an electronic résumé. By posting your résumé on a home page, you increase the likelihood that an employer looking for someone with your background and qualifications will access your résumé and contact you directly. It is possible to create a multipage, online portfolio that contains samples of your work, a page of references, and testimonials. It is advisable to provide your résumé in different formats, such as Microsoft Word, ASCII text, and a PDF file. This gives the employer a choice regarding how to download it. When posting your résumé online, you also may want to be more private. You might, for example, not include your home address but feature an e-mail address. You might also use a Google Voice phone number that keeps your actual phone number private.

As we noted, employers also use Webcams to add flexibility to currently available interviewing channels. By conducting a Webcam-based interview, for example, employers are able to conduct preliminary conversations with people geographically dispersed from them. In increasing numbers, in addition to telephones and videoconferences, employers are also conducting interviews via e-mail and chat groups. Although these channels do not enable interviewer and interviewee to shake hands with each other, and despite the fact that such interviews will probably not replace face-to-face interviews, they do expand the information resources used by organizations and can be used to supplement face-to-face interviews.[39]

You will want to avoid the following five blunders commonly made by people who use the Internet to search for a job.[40]

1. *Mismerged cover letters.* The interviewee sends a letter that expresses the desire to put skills to work for one company when applying for a job with another company.

2. *Goofy personal e-mail addresses.* Using a name like Snickerdoodle@pastrylover.com or egotisticalking @sold.com can make you look like a less than serious candidate. Use a business-sounding e-mail address instead.

3. *Fun with fonts.* It is a mistake to use bright colors and exotic fonts in résumés or e-mails. Use a plain-text format instead.

4. *Playing out of your league.* Because the Internet makes applying for a job so easy, many applicants apply for jobs for which they are not qualified.

5. *Thinking Send is the end.* Your work is not done when you click Send. Networking and follow-up remain essential components of any job search. Indeed, 61 percent of people surveyed report that networking and referrals remain the best sources for new jobs.[41]

Finally, here are some other warnings.

1. Do not post anything online, including in blogs and discussion boards, that you would not want an employer to see.

2. Do not request an interview or follow up using the too-casual tone of text-speak. Managers who were interviewed believe that text-speak, including the use of emoticons, has no place in interview communications.[42]

Review, Reflect, & **Apply**

Recall
Identify cultural and gender factors affecting interviewing.

Understand
Explain how Asians might view an American during an interview.

Apply
Explain how culture and gender factors, and the Web affect how you approach the job search and interview.

Analyze
Compare and contrast the following: (1) how a person from an individualistic culture and collective culture might perform during an interview; (2) an electronic and paper résumé.

Evaluate
Assess your ability to (1) adjust to the culture of the interviewer, and (2) use the Web to find a job.

Create
Develop a list of outcomes you seek in a job.

Getting a job today has much in common with reality-show contests. Hundreds of job candidates compete, but there will be only one winner.

Looking at the Law: Illegal Questions in Interviews

LO6

Explain your rights as an interviewee under the law.

We have seen that some interview questions are tough and probing. Others concerning age, race, marital status, and other personal characteristics are protected under antidiscrimination statutes and are illegal to ask. The Equal Employment Opportunity Commission (EEOC) is the arm of the federal government responsible for monitoring discriminatory practices in hiring decisions. The guidelines are updated periodically and the laws of the EEOC apply in all 50 states.

According to the EEOC, criteria that are legally irrelevant to job qualifications are discriminatory. Interviewees in all states are protected from answering questions about race, ethnicity, marital status, age, sex, disability, and arrest records. It is important for both interviewers and interviewees to realize which questions are legally impermissible in employment interviews. Both parties to the interview have to be well versed in their rights to be able to protect them. The determining factor in whether a question is lawful is simple: Is the information sought relevant to your ability to perform the job? The following are among the most commonly asked illegal questions:

1. Are you physically disabled?
2. How old are you?
3. Are you married?
4. Do you have or are you planning to have a family?
5. What political party do you belong to?
6. Have you ever served time in prison?
7. Is English your native language?
8. What is your religion?
9. Will you need to live near a mosque?
10. Is it hard for you to find child care?
11. Are you a United States citizen?
12. Where were your parents born?
13. Who lives with you?
14. When did you graduate from college?
15. What was the date of your last physical exam?
16. To what clubs or social organizations do you belong?
17. Have you had any recent or past illnesses or operations?
18. How is your family's health?
19. Have you ever been arrested?
20. If you have been in the military, were you honorably discharged?

Review, Reflect, & Apply

Recall

Identify illegal interview questions.

Understand

Explain the difference between legally relevant and illegal interview questions.

Apply

Illustrate the connection between illegal interview questions and discrimination.

Analyze

Distinguish between legally relevant and illegal interview questions.

Evaluate

Assess your ability to respond to an illegal question during an interview.

Create

Develop a list of answers to illegal interview questions.

On the other hand, it is legal to ask the following questions:

1. Are you authorized to work in the United States?
2. What languages do you read or speak fluently (if relevant to the job)?
3. Are you over 18?
4. Would you relocate?
5. Would you be willing to travel as needed?
6. Would you be able and willing to work overtime as necessary?
7. Do you belong to any groups that are relevant to your ability to perform this job?
8. What education do you have?
9. Have you ever been convicted of [fill in the blank]? (The crime must be reasonably related to the performance of the job.)
10. In what branch of the armed forces did you serve?[43]

What if an interviewer asks you an illegal question? You can object diplomatically and remind the interviewer that the question is inappropriate. Doing so, however, can make that interviewer defensive and less willing to select you for the job. Another option is to respond to the illegal question with only information that the interviewer could have legally sought from you. That is, you handle the question by answering the part you do not object to without providing any information you do not wish to provide. For example, if the interviewer asks whether English is your native language, you can respond, "I am fluent in English." If he or she asks whether you belong to a political group, you can respond, "The only groups with which I affiliate that are relevant to this job are the Public Relations Society of America and the American Society for Training and Development."

Communication Skills

PRACTICE TIPS FOR EFFECTIVE INTERVIEWING

As you can see, an interview, like any other interpersonal relationship, requires the cooperation, skill, and commitment of both participants to be effective. Interviewees can benefit from the following guidelines:

✔ Be Prepared

Understand the purpose of the interview; plan or anticipate the questions you will ask and be asked; understand your goals; and be able to communicate those goals clearly.

✔ Practice Sending and Receiving Messages

By its very nature, an interview demands skill at sending and receiving verbal and nonverbal messages. Not only must the parties clearly encode their messages, but they must also be skilled at reading the reactions and checking the perceptions of the other.

✔ Demonstrate Effective Listening Skills

Problems occur in interviews when either the interviewer or the interviewee fails to listen closely to what the other is saying. If participants listen carefully—rather than thinking about what they plan to say next—the interview has a better chance of being productive.

✔ Have Conviction

Ask and answer questions and express your opinions with enthusiasm. If you are not excited by your ideas, skills, and abilities, why should anyone else be?

✔ Be Flexible

Do not overprepare or memorize statements. Think things through thoroughly, and be prepared to handle questions or answers you did not anticipate. Be able to adjust to the other person's style and pace.

✔ Be Observant

Pay attention to the nonverbal signals sent to you and by you. Be sure that the signals you send are positive, not negative. Give the other person your total attention.

✔ Consider the Offer

Both interviewer and interviewee need to consider the ramifications of a job offer. A typical 40-hour-a-week job done for approximately 50 weeks a year adds up to 6,000 hours in only three years. Be sure that your choice is one both you and the organization can live with.

✔ Chart Your Progress

Each time you participate in an interview, fill out a copy of the following evaluation. Circle the number that best describes your response to each question.

a. How prepared were you for the interview?
    Not at all prepared   1   2   3   4   5   Fully prepared

b. What kind of climate did you help create?
    Hostile climate   1   2   3   4   5   Friendly climate

c. Were the questions you asked clear?
    Not clear   1   2   3   4   5   Clear

d. Were the responses you offered complete?
    Incomplete   1   2   3   4   5   Complete

e. How carefully did you listen to the other person?
    Not at all   1   2   3   4   5   Very carefully

f. How carefully did you pay attention to nonverbal cues?
    Not at all   1   2   3   4   5   Very carefully

g. To what extent were you distracted by external stimuli?

Very much   1   2   3   4   5   Not at all

h. How self-confident were you during the interview?

Not at all   1   2   3   4   5   Very confident

i. How flexible were you during the interview?

Not flexible   1   2   3   4   5   Very flexible

j. Would you like to change or improve your behavior for your next interview?

Very much   1   2   3   4   5   Little, or not at all

If your answer to the last question is 1, 2, 3, or 4, consider how you would like to change.

The Wrap-Up

SUMMARY

LO1   **Define** and explain the nature of the *employment interview,* including a description of common interviewee fears.

The employment interview is the most common type of purposeful, planned, decision-making, person-to-person communication. Among the fears interviewees have when it comes to interviewing for a job are not being able to asking questions, not dressing properly, appearing nervous, and not being hired.

LO2   **Describe** tools to use and tasks to complete in order to secure an interview.

In order to secure an interview, interviewees need to prepare an effective cover letter and résumé, and prepare themselves for a Webcam-based screening interview.

LO3   **Explain** the stages of, kinds of questions asked, and interviewee roles and responsibilities during employment interviews.

Effective interviews are well-structured interactions. They have a beginning, which provides an orientation to what is to come; a middle, when the participants get down to business; and an end, when the main points are reviewed and the participants take leave of one another. Good interviewees work hard during an interview, functioning simultaneously as information seekers, information givers, and decision makers.

LO4   **Explain** the practice of impression management.

Impression management, in the context of interviewing, has the interviewee making a concerted effort to influence the interviewer's perceptions of his or her image by engaging in behavior that causes the interviewer to view the interviewee favorably. To accomplish this, the interviewee dresses professionally, is knowledgeable about the company, uses verbal and nonverbal cues to convey his or her enthusiasm for the job, never asks about benefits during the first interview, ends the interview by affirming interest in the position, and remembers to send a thank you note following the interview.

LO5 **Identify** how diversity and technology affect the job search and the interview.

In order to avoid misunderstandings, interviewees need to be aware of how cultural differences can affect the interview. They also need to be adept at using the Web to research job openings and promote themselves.

LO6 **Explain** your rights as an interviewee under the law.

According to the Equal Employment Opportunity Commission criteria that are legally irrelevant to job qualifications are discriminatory. Interviewees in all states are protected from answering questions about race, ethnicity, marital status, age, sex, disability, and arrest records.

KEY TERMS

behavioral interview 449

case interview 449

closed questions 446

employment interview 440

open questions 446

primary questions 447

secondary questions 447

stress interview 449

Blindering Problem (page 64)

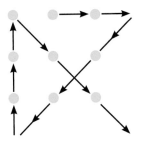

The Detective (page 66)

1. ?
2. ?
3. F
4. ?
5. ?
6. T
7. ?
8. ?
9. ?
10. ?
11. ?

A

accommodation the means by which co-culture members maintain their cultural identity while striving to establish relationships with members of the dominant culture

accommodator a person who, when faced with a conflict, overvalues the maintenance of relationships and undervalues the achievement of his or her own goals

achieved leader a person who exhibits leadership without being appointed

acquaintanceships relationships with persons we know by name and with whom we converse when the chance arises

affection the need to experience emotionally close relationships

aggressive stimulation theory the contention that the watching of violence stimulates aggression in the viewer

aggressiveness the expressing of one's own thoughts and feelings at another's expense

allness the erroneous belief that any one person can know all there is to know about anything

allocentric exhibiting a collectivistic orientation

appreciative listening listening for enjoyment or relaxation

argumentum ad hominem the use of name-calling in an argument

argumentum ad populum a bandwagon appeal; an appeal to popular opinion

argumentum ad verecudiam an appeal to authority

artifactual communication the use of personal adornments

assertiveness the expressing of one's thoughts and feelings while displaying respect for the thoughts and feelings of others

assimilation the means by which co-culture members attempt to fit in with members of the dominant culture

attitudes predispositions to respond favorably or unfavorably toward a person or subject

autistic society a society at home with computers but disadvantaged when it comes to establishing human intimacy

autocratic, or authoritarian, leaders directive leaders

avoider a person who, when faced with a conflict, uses the unproductive strategy of mentally or physically fleeing the situation

avoiding the relationship stage during which the participants intentionally avoid contact

B

backing support that answers concerns of others

balance a state of psychological comfort in which one's actions, feelings, and beliefs are related to one another as one would like them to be

bar graph a graph used to show the performance of one variable over time or to contrast various measures at a point in time

behavioral interview an employment interview in which an employer looks for the employee to provide specific examples of specific skills

beliefs confidence in the truth of something

blind area the part of the self known to others but not known to oneself

blindering the process by which one unconsciously adds restrictions that limit one's perceptual capabilities

blogs Web logs

bonding the relationship stage in which two people make a formal commitment to each other

Boolean search a keyword search

brainstorming a technique designed to generate ideas

breadth the number of topics one discusses with another person

bullying persistent teasing, name-calling, or social exclusion

bypassing miscommunication that occurs when individuals think they understand each other but actually miss each other's meaning

C

case interview an employment interview in which the interviewee is presented with a business case by the employer and asked to work through it

catalytic theory the contention that, while the media may play a role in real-life violence, they will trigger it only if a viewer is predisposed to violence or is particularly vulnerable

catharsis theory the contention that the viewing of violence makes one less apt to exhibit violence

causal reasoning speculation about the reasons for and effects of occurrences

cause-and-effect order an organizational format that categorizes a topic according to its causes and effects

channels media through which messages are sent

chronemics the study of the use of time

chronological, or time, order an organizational format that develops an idea using a time order

circumscribing the relationship stage in which both the quality and the quantity of communication between two people decrease

civil inattention the polite ignoring of others so as not to infringe on their privacy

claim debatable conclusion or assertion

closed question highly structured questions answerable with a simple yes or no or in a few words

closure the tendency to fill in missing perceptual pieces in order to perceive a complete world

co-cultures groups of persons who differ in some ethnic or sociological way from the parent culture

collectivistic cultures cultures in which group goals are stressed

communication the deliberate or accidental transfer of meaning

communication apprehension fear of communication, no matter what the context

communication privacy management theory theory that describes the establishment of the boundaries and borders that we decide others may or may not cross

comparison level an expectation of the kinds of rewards and profits we believe we ought to derive from a relationship

comparison level for alternatives the comparing of rewards derived from a current relationship with ones we expect to get from an alternative relationship

competitive forcer a person who, when faced with a conflict, adopts a win–lose orientation in which the attaining of personal goals is paramount

competitive goal structure a goal structure in which members hinder one another's efforts to obtain a goal

competitive set a readiness to perceive a conflict in all-or-nothing terms

complementarity the attraction principle that states that opposites attract

comprehensive listening listening to gain knowledge

compromiser a person who, when faced with a conflict, tries to find a middle ground

configural formats organizational patterns that are indirect and inexplicit

conflict perceived disagreement

conflict grid a model portraying the styles individuals use to resolve conflicts

connotative meaning subjective meaning; one's personal meaning for a word

consistency the desire to maintain balance in our lives by behaving according to commitments already formed

contact cultures cultures that promote interaction and encourage displays of warmth, closeness, and availability

content conflict a disagreement over matters of fact

context the setting

control the need to feel we are capable and responsible and are able to exert power and influence in our relationships

cooperative goal structure a goal structure in which the members of a group work together to achieve their objectives

cooperative set a readiness to share rewards to resolve conflicts

cost–benefit/social exchange theory the theory that we work to maintain a relationship as long as the benefits we receive outweigh the costs

credibility the receiver's assessment of the competence, trustworthiness, and dynamism of a speaker

critical listening listening to evaluate the worth of a message

critical thinking the careful and deliberate process of message evaluation

cultivation theory a theory propounded by George Gerbner and colleagues focusing on the mass media's ability to influence users' attitudes and perceptions of reality

cultural imperialism the expansion of dominion of one culture over another culture

cultural nearsightedness the failure to understand that we do not all attribute the same meanings to similar behavioral clues

cultural pluralism adherence to the principle of cultural relativism

cultural relativism the acceptance of other cultural groups as equal in value to one's own

culturally confused lacking an understanding of cultural difference

culture a system of knowledge, beliefs, values, customs, behaviors, and artifacts that are acquired, shared, and used by members during daily living

cyberbole exaggerated claims about the effects new technologies have on society

D

decision by consensus a decision that all members understand and will support, reached as a result of members' voicing feelings and airing differences

deduction reasoning that moves from the general to the specific

defensive behavior behavior that occurs when one perceives a threat

definitions explanations of what a stimulus is or what a word or concept means

democratic leaders leaders who represent a reasonable compromise between authoritarian and laissez-faire leaders

denotative meaning dictionary meaning; the objective or descriptive meaning of a word

depth a measure of how central the topics you discuss with another person are to your self-concept

derived credibility a measure of a speaker's credibility during a speech-making event

designated leader a person given the authority to exert influence within a group

dialectical tensions tensions that occur when opposing goals meet

dialogic listening listening that focuses on what happens to people as they respond to each other

differentiating the relationship stage in which two people identified as a couple seek to regain unique identities

digital divide information gap

disclaimers remarks that diminish a statement's importance

distance relating relating with persons via e-mail, chat rooms, and instant messages

distinctiveness theory the theory that states that a person's own distinctive traits are more salient to him or her than are the more prevalent traits possessed by others in the immediate environment

diversity the recognition and valuing of difference

dominant culture the culture in power; the mainstream culture

E

effect the communication outcome

ego conflict a disagreement in which persons believe that winning or losing is tied to their self-worth, prestige, or competence

emoticons symbols that replace nonverbal cues during machine-assisted communication

emotional contagion the catching of another person's mood

emotional intelligence the ability to motivate oneself, to control impulses, to recognize and regulate one's moods, to empathize, and to hope

emotional isolationists persons who seek to avoid situations that may require the exchange of feelings

empathic listening listening to help others

empathy experiencing the world from a perspective other than our own

employment interview the most common type of purposeful, planned, decision-making, person-to-person communication

equivocate use purposefully vague language to finesse a response

essentials of communication those components present during every communication event

ethnocentrism the tendency to see one's own culture as superior to all others

ethos audience's judgment of speaker's character or credibility

euphemism a pleasant word that is substituted for a less pleasant one

evaluative feedback a positive or negative judgment

examples representative cases

experimenting the relationship stage during which we begin to probe the unknown, often through the exchange of small talk

extemporaneous speech a speech that is researched, outlined, and delivered after careful rehearsal

external feedback a response from another

F

facework the means used to present a public image

facial management techniques the means we use to control the expressions we reveal to others

fact that which is known to be true based on observation

false division the polarization of options, when, in fact, many options exist

feedback information returned to a message source

feminine cultures cultures that value tenderness and relationships

figure-ground principle a strategy that facilitates the organization of stimuli by enabling us to focus on different stimuli alternately

first impressions initial judgments about people

fixed-feature space space that contains relatively permanent objects

flames online insults

formative feedback timed negative feedback

friendly relations the friendship stage in which we explore whether we have enough in common to continue building a relationship

friendships relationships characterized by enjoyment, acceptance, trust, respect, mutual assistance, confidences, understanding, and spontaneity

functional theory the leadership theory suggesting that several members of a group should be ready to lead because various actions are needed to achieve group goals

G

Galatea effect the principle that states that we fulfill our own expectations

gender-lects Deborah Tannen's term for language differences attributed to gender

globalization   the increasing economic, political, and cultural integration and interdependence of diverse cultures

gossip mill   the network through which unverified information is spread

grapevine   a type of informal, conversational network existing in organizations

grief process   a mourning process composed of five stages: denial, anger, guilt, depression, and acceptance

group   a collection of individuals who interact verbally and nonverbally, occupy certain roles with respect to one another, and cooperate to accomplish a goal

group climate   the emotional atmosphere of a group

group communication   interaction with a limited number of persons

group goals   a group's motivation for existing

group norms   informal rules for interaction in a group

group patterns of communication   patterns of message flow in a group

group role-classification model   a model that describes functions participants should seek to assume and to avoid in groups

group structure   group member positions and roles performed

groupthink   an extreme means of avoiding conflict that occurs when groups let the desire for consensus override careful analysis and reasoned decision making

H

habitual pitch   the characteristic pitch one uses

halo effect   the perceiving of qualities that are primarily positive

haptics   the study of the use of touch

hearing   the involuntary, physiological process by which we perceive sound

hidden area   the part of the self that contains information about the self known to oneself but that is hidden from others

high self-monitors   people highly attuned to impression management efforts

high-context communication   a tradition-bound communication system that depends on indirectness

high-intensity conflict   a conflict in which one person intends to destroy or seriously hurt the other

high-power-distance cultures   cultures based on power differences in which subordinates defer to superiors

high-tech–high-touch society   a technologically advanced society that values interpersonal relationships

horn effect   the perceiving of qualities that are primarily negative

HURIER model   a model of listening focusing on six skill areas or stages

hurtful messages   messages designed to upset or to cause emotional pain that further hampers trust

hyper-competitive culture   the contention that one needs to defeat another to achieve one's goals

I

"I" messages   nonevaluative responses that convey our feelings about the nature of a situation

idiocentric   exhibiting an individualistic orientation

illustrations   stories; narrative pictures

impression management   the creation of a positive image designed to influence others

impromptu speech   a speech delivered spontaneously or on the spur of the moment

inclusion   the need for social contact

individualistic cultures   cultures in which individual goals are stressed

induction   reasoning that moves from specific evidence to a general conclusion

inference   an assumption with varying degrees of accuracy

informal space   space that is highly mobile and can be quickly changed

information overload   the situation that occurs when the amount of information provided by a speech maker is too great to be handled effectively by receivers

information underload   the situation that occurs when the information provided by a speech maker is already known to receivers

informative speech   a speech that updates and adds to the knowledge of receivers

initial credibility   a measure of how an audience perceives a speaker prior to the speech-making event

initiating   the relationship stage during which contact is first made

integrating   the relationship stage in which two people are identified as a couple

intensifying   the relationship stage during which two people become good friends

intercultural communication   interaction with individuals from different cultures

interethnic communication   interaction with individuals of different ethnic origins

internal feedback   a response one gives oneself

internal summaries   rhetorical devices designed to help listeners remember content

international communication   communication between persons representing different nations

interpersonal communication   the relationship level of communication

interpersonal conflict   conflict between two or more people

interpersonal relationship a meaningful connection, such as friendship, between two persons

interracial communication the interpreting and sharing of meanings with individuals from different races

intimate distance a distance ranging from the point of touch to 18 inches from a person

intracultural communication interaction with members of the same racial or ethnic group or co-culture as one's own

intrapersonal communication communication with the self

intrapersonal conflict internal conflict

J

jargon a specialized vocabulary of technical terms that is shared by a community of users

Johari window a model containing four panes that is used to explain the roles that self-awareness and self-disclosure play in relationships

K

kaleidoscope thinking the taking of existing data and twisting it or looking at it from another angle

killer looks looks that discourage or inhibit the generation of ideas

killer phrases comments that stop the flow of ideas

kinesics the study of the relationship between human body motion, or body language, and communication

L

laissez-faire leader a nondirective leader

language a unified system of symbols that permits the sharing of meaning

leadership the ability to influence others

line graphs graphs used to illustrate trends, relationships, or comparisons over time

linear logic the step-by-step development of ideas; the reliance on facts and data to support main points

linguistic determinism the belief that language influences how we interpret the world

linguistic prejudice the use of prejudiced language

linguistic relativity the belief that persons who speak different languages perceive the world differently

listening the deliberate, psychological process by which we receive, understand, and retain aural stimuli

listserv an e-mail list of people who have interest in and knowledge of a particular topic

logos logical proof

loneliness the perceived discrepancy between desired and achieved social relationships

low self-monitors people who pay little attention to responses others have to them

low-contact cultures cultures that maintain more distance when interacting

low-context communication a system that encourages directness in communication

low-intensity conflict a conflict in which the persons involved work to discover a solution beneficial to all parties

low-power-distance cultures cultures that believe that power should be used only when legitimate

M

main ideas the main points of a speech; the subtopics of a speech

maintenance roles group roles designed to ensure the smooth running of a group

manuscript speech a speech read from a script

markers items that reserve one's space

masculine cultures cultures that value aggressiveness, strength, and material symbols of success

Maslow's hierarchy of needs a model that depicts motivation as a pyramid with the most basic needs at the base and the most sophisticated at the apex

mass communication the transmission of messages that may be processed by gatekeepers prior to being sent to large audiences via a channel of broad diffusion

media literacy the ability to mindfully interpret the meanings and effects of media messages

medium-intensity conflict a conflict in which each person feels committed to winning, but winning is seen as sufficient

melting-pot philosophy the view that different cultures should be assimilated into the dominant culture

memorized speech a manuscript speech committed to memory

message the content of a communicative act

mindfulness emptying one's mind of personal concerns and interfering emotions, and choosing to focus on the person and the here and now

mixed message message that occurs when words and actions contradict each other

Monroe's motivated sequence a speech framework composed of five phases—attention, need, satisfaction, visualization, and action

moving toward friendship the friendship stage in which we make small personal disclosures demonstrating the desire to expand our relationship

MUDs multiuser domains

multiculturalism engagement with and respect toward people from distinctly different cultures

MYGLO an acronym for "my eyes glaze over"

N

nascent friendship   the friendship stage that finds us considering each other friends

need for affection   the need to express and receive love

need for control   the need to feel we are capable and responsible

need for inclusion   the need for social contact

negative feedback   a response that extinguishes behavior in progress

noise   anything that interferes with or distorts the ability to send and receive messages

nonassertiveness   the hesitation to display one's feelings and thoughts

nonevaluative feedback   nondirective feedback

nonfluencies   meaningless sounds or phrases that disrupt the flow of speech

nonverbal communication   the kinds of human messages and responses not expressed in words

O

olfactics   the study of the sense of smell

online, or machine-assisted, communication   the building of relationships using computers and the Internet

onlinespeak   the informal communication style that marks electronic communication

open area   the part of the self containing information known to both the self and others

open questions   question that offer the interviewee freedom with regard to the choice and scope of an answer

P

paralanguage   vocal cues that accompany spoken language

paraphrasing   restating in one's own words what another person has said

pathos   emotional proof

perceived self   the self we believe ourselves to be

perception   the process by which we make sense out of experience

perceptual constancy   the desire to perceive experience exactly as we have perceived it in the past

perceptual sets   expectations that produce a readiness to process experience in a predetermined way

personal distance   a distance ranging from 18 inches to 4 feet from a person

persuasion   the attempt to change or reinforce attitudes, beliefs, values, or behaviors

persuasive speech   a speech whose primary purpose is to change or reinforce the attitudes, beliefs, values, and/or behaviors of receivers

phatic communication   communication designed to open the channels of communication

pictographs   graphs that use sketches to represent concepts

pie, or circle, graph   a circle with the various percentages of the whole indicated by wedges; a means of showing percentage relationships

pitch   the highness or lowness of the voice

polarization   the use of either/or language that causes us to perceive and speak about the world in extremes

pop language   words and phrases used to sell oneself as hip or cool

positive feedback   a behavior-enhancing response

post hoc, ergo propter hoc   the identification of a false cause

prejudice   a biased, negative attitude toward a particular group of people; a negative prejudgment based on membership in a social category

prejudiced language   sexist, ageist, or racist language; language disparaging to the members of a co-culture

primacy effect   the ability of one's first impression to color subsequent impressions

primary questions   questions used to introduce topics or explore a new area

primary research   the collection of information that does not already exist

probing   a nonevaluative technique in which we ask for additional information

problem-and-solution order   an organizational format that identifies the problems inherent in a situation and presents a solution to remedy them

problem-solving collaborator   a person who, when faced with a conflict, adopts a win-win orientation, seeking to satisfy his or her own goals as well as those of others

proposition   a statement that summarizes the purpose of a persuasive speech

proposition of fact   a persuasive speech with the goal of settling what is or is not so

proposition of policy   a persuasive speech on what ought to be

proposition of value   a persuasive speech that espouses the worth of an idea, a person, or an object

prosumers   consumers who produce the material of consumption themselves

proxemics   the study of the use of space

pseudoconflict   the situation that results when persons mistakenly believe that two or more goals cannot be achieved simultaneously

public communication   communication designed to inform, persuade, or entertain audience members

public distance   a distance of 12 feet and farther from a person

public speaking   the act of preparing, staging, and delivering a presentation to an audience

public speaking anxiety   fear of speaking to an audience

Pygmalion effect   the principle that states that we fulfill the expectations of others

Q

qualifier   indication of the strength of the connection

qualifiers   tentative phrases

quality circles   small groups of employees who meet regularly to discuss organizational life and the quality of their work environment

questions of fact   questions involving the truth or falsity of a statement

questions of policy   questions designed to help determine future actions

questions of value   questions involving subjective judgments

R

racial code words   words that are discriminatory but not literally racist

rate   speaking speed

reasoning from analogy   reasoning by comparison

reasons   facts or evidence for making the claim

rebuttal   potential counterarguments

receivers   persons who receive, decode, and interpret a message

red herring   a distraction used to lead the receiver to focus on an irrelevant issue

red-flag words   words that trigger emotional deafness, dropping listening efficiency to zero

reflective-thinking framework   a system for decision making and problem solving that is designed to encourage critical inquiry

role reversal   a strategy in which persons in conflict each act as the other in order to understand the other's position

role-limited interaction   the beginning stage of friendship

S

Sapir–Whorf hypothesis   the belief that the labels we use help shape the way we think, our worldview, and our behavior

secondary questions   questions that follow up primary questions

selective attention   the tendency to focus on certain cues and ignore others

selective exposure   the tendency to expose oneself to information that reaffirms existing attitudes, beliefs, and values

selective perception   the means of interpreting experience in a way that conforms to one's beliefs, expectations, and convictions

selective retention   the tendency to remember those things that reinforce one's way of thinking and forget those that oppose one's way of thinking

self-awareness   the ability to reflect on and monitor one's own behavior

self-concept   everything one thinks and feels about oneself

self-conflict   the type of conflict that occurs when a person has to choose between two or more mutually exclusive options

self-directed teams   autonomous groups of employees empowered to make decisions and supervise themselves

self-disclosure   the process of revealing to another person information about the self that he or she would not otherwise know

self-efficacy   an optimistic belief in one's own competence

self-esteem   how well one likes and values oneself

self-fulfilling prophecy   a prediction or an expectation that comes true simply because one acts as if it were true

self-image   the sort of person one perceives oneself to be

self-serving roles   group roles that impede the functioning of a group by preventing members from working together effectively

semi-fixed-feature space   space in which objects are used to create distance

senders   persons who formulate, encode, and transmit a message

separation   the means co-culture members use to resist interacting with members of the dominant culture

serial communication   a chain-of-command transmission

silence   the absence of both paralinguistic and verbal cues

situational theory   the theory of leadership that asserts that leadership depends on the situation

slang   informal vocabulary that bonds its users together while excluding others

social capital   social connections or networks

social distance   a distance ranging from 4 feet to 12 feet from a person

social penetration theory   the theory that states that our relationships begin with relatively narrow breadth and shallow depth and develop over time

social proof   the determination of what is right by finding out what other people think is right

spatial order   an organizational format that describes an object, a person, or a phenomenon as it exists in space

speech framework   a skeleton for speech development

speech–thought differential   the difference between speaking and thinking rates

stabilized friendship   the friendship stage in which we decide that our friendship is secure and will continue

stagnating   the relationship stage during which communication is at a standstill

statistics   facts expressed in numerical form

stereotype   a generalization about people, places, or events held by many members of a society

stereotypes   mental images or pictures that guide our re-actions to others

stress interview   an employment interview in which more than one person fires questions at an interviewee

subordinate ideas   ideas that amplify the main ideas or subtopics of a speech

supportive feedback   a nonevaluative response indicat-ing that the receiver perceives a problem as important

symbol   that which represents something else

T

tag questions   questions that are midway between out-right statements and yes–no questions

task roles   group roles designed to help the group achieve its goals

technopoly   a culture in which technology monopolizes the thought-world

terminal credibility   a measure of a speaker's credibility at the end of a speech-making event

termination   the relationship stage during which the rela-tionship ends

territoriality   the need to demonstrate a possessive or own-ership relationship to space

testimony   someone else's opinions or conclusions

time shifting   the ability to watch media offerings at a time convenient to you

tolerance of vulnerability   the degree of trust we place in another person to accept information we disclose without hurting us or the relationship

topical order   an organizational format that clusters mate-rial by dividing it into a series of appropriate topics

toxic communication   the consistent use of verbal abuse and/or physical or sexual aggression or violence

trait theory   the theory of leadership that asserts that cer-tain people are born to lead

transformational leader   a leader who gives a group a new vision, strengthening its culture or structure

transitions   connective words and phrases

triangle of meaning   a model that explains the relation-ship that exists among words, things, and thoughts

type X leader   a leader who does not trust group members to work and is unconcerned with the personal achievements of group members

type Y leader   a leader who displays trust in group members and is concerned with their sense of personal achievement

U

understanding   a nonevaluative response that uses re-statement to check comprehension

unknown area   the part of the self that is unknown to one-self and others

V

value conflict   a disagreement that arises when persons hold different views on an issue

virtual neighborhoods and communities   online, sur-rogate communities

virtual reality   an environment that exists as data in a computer system

visual dominance   a measure calculated by comparing the percentage of looking while speaking with the percentage of looking while listening

volume   the degree of loudness of the voice

W

waning friendship   the friendship stage during which friends begin to drift apart

warrant   explanation of the relationship between the claim and the data

Y

"you" messages   responses that place blame on another person

Chapter 1

1. Robert D. Putnam, *Bowling Alone: The Collapse and Revival of American Community*. New York: Simon & Schuster, 2000.

2. Alan Murray, *The Wealth of Choices*. New York: Crown Business, 2000.

3. An idea attributed to Leonard Lauder, as described in Della Bradshaw, "Old-World Leader, New World Vision," *Financial Times*, February 4, 2008, p. 8.

4. See, for example, Stephen R. Covey, *The 7 Habits of Highly Effective People*. New York: Simon & Schuster, 1989, pp. 236–260.

5. See Deborah Tannen, *That's Not What I Meant!* New York: Morrow, 1986.

6. Frank E. X. Dance, "Toward a Theory of Human Communication," in Frank E. X. Dance, ed., *Human Communication Theory: Original Essays*. New York: Holt, Rinehart & Winston, 1967.

7. See, for example, Alan E. Ivey and James C. Hurse, "Communication as Adaptation," *Journal of Communication*, 21 (1971), pp. 199–207. Ivey and Hurse reaffirm that communication is adaptive, like biological evolution—not an end in itself, but a process. Also see J. F. Nussbaum, ed., *Life-Span Communication: Normative Processes*. Hillsdale, NJ: Lawrence Erlbaum Associates, 1989.

8. O. Wiio, *Wiio's Laws and Some Others*. Espoo, Finland: Welin Goos, 1978.

9. C. Wade and C. Tarvis, *Learning to Think Critically: The Case of Close Relationships*. New York: HarperCollins, 1990.

10. Marshall McLuhan, *Understanding Media*. Cambridge: MIT Press, 1994.

11. Neil Postman, *Technopoly: The Surrender of Culture to Technology*. New York: Vintage, 1992.

12. See, for example, "The Information: How the Internet Gets Inside Us," *The New Yorker*, February 14 and 21, 2011, pp. 124–130.

13. Norman H. Nie and D. Sunshine Hillygus, "The Impact of Internet Use on Sociability: Time Diary Findings," *IT & Society*, 1:1 (Summer 2002), pp. 11–20.

14. Norman H. Nie, D. Sunshine Hillygus, and Lutz Erbring, "Internet Use, Interpersonal Relations, and Sociability: Findings from a Detailed Time Diary Study," in Wellman and Haythornthwaite, 2002.

15. BurstMedia, "Online Insights," July 2007, p. 1.

16. Ibid., p. 2.

17. "Exactly How Much Are the Times A-Changin'?" *Newsweek*, July 26, 2010, p. 56.

18. Sophie Terbush, "Glow of Electronic Devices Is Affecting Americans' Sleep," *USA Today*, March 7, 2011, p. 5D.

19. See, for example, Hector Jose Huyke, "Technologies and the Devaluation of What Is Near," *Technq* 6:3 (2003), pp. 57–70.

20. J. E. Katz and M. Aakhus, *Perpetual Contact: Mobile Communication, Private Talk, Public Performance*. Cambridge, U.K.: Cambridge University Press, 2002.

21. See, for example, K. Y. A. McKenna, A. S. Green, and M. E. J. Gleason, "Relation Formation on the Internet: What's the Big Attraction?" *Journal of Social Issues*, 58 (2002), pp. 9–31.

22. See, for example, www.theworldjournal.com/2003/realitycheck.htm.

23. William Schutz, *The Interpersonal Underworld*. Palo Alto, CA: Science & Behavior Books, 1966.

24. Diana Middleton, "Students Struggle for Words," *The Wall Street Journal*, March 2, 2011, p. B8.

25. National Association of Colleges and Employers. *Job Outlook*. 2008; and Sherwyn P. Morreale and Judy C. Pearson, "Why Communication Education Is Important: The Centrality of the Discipline in the 21st Century," *Communication Education*, 57:2 (April 2008), pp. 224–240.

26. See, for example, the National Association of Colleges and Employers (NACE) Job Outlook Survey (2010).

Chapter 2

1. See Walter Lippman, *Public Opinion*. New York: Macmillan, 1957, pp. 79–103; and C.S. Abbate, S. Boca, and P. Bocchiaro, "Stereotyping in Persuasive Communication: Influence Exerted by Disapproved Source," *Journal of Applied Social Psychology*, 34 (2004), p. 1192.

2. See Herb Jackson, "Muslim Leaders Angry over Inquiry," *The Record*, March 10, 2011, p. A1. Also see Neil MacFarquhar, "Abandon Stereotypes, Muslims in America Say," *New York Times* November 4, 2007, p. A12.

3. Devlin Barrett, "Emotions Run High at Hearing," *The Wall Street Journal*, March 11, 2011, p. A5.

4. Pamela Constable, "Racial Survey Unearths Tensions," *The Record*, December 11, 2007, p. A6.

5. Marshall McLuhan, *The Medium Is the Message*. New York: Bantam Books, 1967; Marshall McLuhan, *Understanding Media*. New York: Mentor, 1964.

6. Pew Research Center, "American Mobility," December 29, 2008, http://pewsocialtrends.org.

7. Robert D. Putnam, *Bowling Alone: The Collapse and Revival of American Community*. New York: Simon & Schuster, 2001.

8. See, for example, Christopher Caldwell, "Diversity Is Not Black and White," *Financial Times*, August 12, 2007, p. 7; and Michael Skapinker, "Why the Workplace Is Diversity's Best Bet," *Financial Times*, September 18, 2007, p. 11.

9. See William B. Gudykunst and Young Yun Kim, eds., *Readings on Communicating with Strangers*. New York: McGraw-Hill, 1991.

10. Haya El Nasser, "Multiracial No Longer Boxed In by the Census," *USA Today*, March 3, 2010, pp. 1A, 2A.

11. Edward T. Hall, *The Silent Language*. New York: Fawcett, 1959.

12. Griswold, pp. 22–24. Wendy Griswold, *Cultures and Society in a Changing World*. Thousand Oaks, CA: Pine Forge, 1994, pp. 22–24.

13. Carley H. Dodd, *Dynamics of Intercultural Communication*, 3rd ed. Dubuque, IA: Brown, 1991, p. 3.

14. See G. Hofstede, *Masculinity and Femininity: The Taboo Dimension of National Cultures*. Thousand Oaks, CA: Sage, 1998.

15. Gudykunst, *Bridging Differences*, 4th ed., pp. 12–13.

16. "Unhappy Meal for Muslims," *The Record*, June 8, 1993, p. C-3.

17. Griswold, p. 1.

18. Margaret H. DeFleur and Melvin L. DeFleur, "The Next Generation's Image of Americans: Attitudes and Beliefs Held by Teen-Agers in Twelve Countries," October 3, 2002. www.bu.edu/news/releases/2002/defleur/report.pdf.

19. William B. Gudykunst, *Bridging Differences: Effective Intergroup Communication*, 3rd ed. Thousand Oaks, CA: Sage, 1998, pp. 106–110; see also 4th ed., 2003.

20. W. Lippman, *Public Opinion*. New York: Macmillan, 1922.

21. For more on prejudice, see M. L. Hecht, ed., *Communicating Prejudice*. Thousand Oaks, CA: Sage, 1998.

22. Deborah Tannen, *You Just Don't Understand: Women and Men in Conversation*. New York: Morrow, 1990.

23. Judith Cornelia Person and Edward Nelson. *Understanding and Sharing: An Introduction to Speech Communication*, 6th ed. Dubuque, IA: Brown & Benchmark, 1994, p. 193.

24. Wendy Griswold. *Cultures and Societies in a Changing World*. Thousand Oaks, CA: Pine Forge, 1994, p. 57.

25. M. P. Orbe, "Laying the Foundation for Co-Cultural Communication Theory: An Inductive Approach to Studying 'Nondominant' Communication Strategies and the Factors That Influence Them." *Communication Studies*, 47 (1996), pp. 157–176.

26. See Judith N. Martin and Thomas K. Nakayama, *Intercultural Communication in Contexts*, 2nd ed. Mountain View, CA: Mayfield, 2000, pp. 265–266. Also see 3rd ed., 2003.

27. G. Hofstede, *Cultures and Organizations*. London: McGraw-Hill, 1991.

28. Hall, *The Silent Language*.

29. Edward T. Hall, *The Dance of Life: Other Dimensions of Time*. New York: Anchor/Doubleday, 1983, p. 42.

30. See G. Hofstede, *Masculinity and Femininity: The Taboo Dimension of National Cultures*. Thousand Oaks, CA: Sage, 1998.

31. Robert R. Harris and Robert T. Moran, *Managing Cultural Differences*, 3rd ed. Houston, TX: Gulf, 1991.

32. See Felicia Wu Song, *Virtual Communities: Bowling Alone, Online Together*. New York: Peter Lang Publishing, 2009; and Josh Meyrowitz, "Media Theory," in Erik P. Bucy, ed., *Living in the Information Age*. Belmont, CA: Wadsworth, 2002, p. 32.

33. See, for example, Bill Bishop with Robert G. Cushing, *The Big Sort: Why the Clustering of Like-Minded America Is Tearing Us Apart*. New York: Houghton Mifflin, 2009.

34. Christopher Chabris and Daniel Simons, "The Internet: Is It Reshaping Our Brains?" *The Record*, July 30, 2010, p. A21.

35. Clifford Stoll, "Further Explorations into the Culture of Computing," in Erick P. Bucy, ed., *Living in the Information Age*. Belmont, CA: Wadsworth, 2002, p. 32.

36. Anjali Mullany, "Egyptian Uprising Plays Out on Social Media Sites Despite Government's Internet Restrictions," *Daily News*, January 29, 2011.

37. Larry A. Samovar and Richard E. Porter, *Intercultural Communication: A Reader*, 11th ed. Belmont, CA: Wadsworth, 2006, p. 5.

Chapter 3

1. Ron Alsop, "The 'Trophy Kids' Go to Work," *Wall Street Journal*, October 21, 2008, pp. D1, D4.

2. See Steven R. Covey, *7 Habits of Highly Effective People*. New York: Simon & Schuster, 1990, p. 281. Also see Mark P. Orbe and Etusuko Kinefuchi, "Crash under Investigation: Engaging Complications of Complicity, Coherence, and Implication Through Critical Analyses," *Critical Studies in Media Communication* 25:2 (June 2008), pp. 135–156.

3. Natalie Angier, "Blind to Change, Even as IT Stares Us in the Face," *New York Times*, May 20, 2008, p. F5.

4. See Christopher Chabris and Daniel Simons, *The Invisible Gorilla and Other Ways Our Intuitions Deceive Us*. New York: Crown, 2010.

5. William V. Haney, *Communication and Organizational Behavior*. Homewood, IL: Irwin, 1973, p. 55.

6. Sara Reistad-Long, "Older Brain Really May Be a Wiser Brain," *New York Times*, May 20, 2008, p. F5.

7. See Jonathan Foer, *The Art and Science of Remembering Everything*. New York: The Penguin Press, 2011.

8. Chabris and Simons.

9. David A. Shaywitz, "The Future of Our Illusions," *Wall Street Journal*, June 11, 2010, p. W4.

10. Sharon Begley, "People Believe a 'Fact' That Fits Their Views Even If It's Clearly False," *Wall Street Journal*, February 4, 2005, p. B1.

11. See, for example, Steve Freiss, "Memory Does Not Always Serve, and That's No Lie," *USA Today*, September 14, 2004, p. 9D; and Daniel L. Schacter, "The Fog of War," *New York Times*, April 5, 2004, p. A21.

12. E. Rubin, "Figure and Ground," in D. Beardslee and M. Werthimer, eds., *Readings in Perception*. Princeton, NJ: Van Nostrand, pp. 194–203.

13. See, for example, C. N. Macrae and G. V. Bodenhausen, "Social Cognition: Categorical Person Perception," *British Journal of Psychology* 92 (2001), pp. 853–864.

14. K. G. Wilson and S. C. Hayes, "Why It Is Crucial to Understand Thinking and Feeling: An Analysis and Application to Drug Abuse," *Behavior Analyst*, 23 (Spring 2000), pp. 25–43.

15. C. Mruk, *Self-Esteem: Research, Theory, and Practice*. New York: Springer, 2005.

16. See Maureen Stout, *The Feel-Good Curriculum: The Dumbing Down of America's Kids in the Name of Self-Esteem*. New York: Perseus Books, 2000; and Mary Amorose, "Is Self-Esteem Overrated?" *The Record*, April 27, 2000, pp. HF-1, HF-3.

17. Roy E. Baumeister, Jennifer D. Campbell, Joachim I. Krueger, and Kathleen D. Vohs, "Exploding the Self-Esteem Myth," *Scientific American*, January 2005, pp. 84–91.

18. See Michele Orecklin, "Beware of the Crowd," *Time*, August 21, 2000, p. 69, and Valerie Strauss, "Most, Least Popular Kids Less Likely to Bully, Study Says," http://voices.washingtonpost.com/answer-sheet/bullying/most-least-popular-kids-less-1.html.

19. R. Baumeister, L. Smart, and J. Boden, "Relation of the Threatened Egotism to Violence and Aggression: The Dark Side of High Self-Esteem," *Psychological Review*, 103 (1996), pp. 5–33.

20. B. Bushman and R. T. Baumeister, "Threatened Egotism, Narcissism, Self-Esteem, and Direct and Displaced Aggression: Does Self-Love or Self-Hate Lead to Violence?" *Journal of Personality and Social Psychology*, 75 (1998), pp. 219–229.

21. Roy F. Baumeister, Jennifer D. Campbell, Joachim I. Krueger, and Kathleen D. Vohs, "Does High Self-Esteem Cause Better Performance, Interpersonal Success, Happiness, or Healthier Lifestyles?" *Psychological Science in the Public Interest*, 4:1 (May 2003), pp. 1–44.

22. Sharon Jayson, "Yep, Life'll Burst That Self-Esteem Bubble," *USA Today*, February 16, 2005, p. L7.

23. Marlene Zuk, "A Case of Unwarranted Self-Regard," *The Record*, May 30, 2005, p. L-7.

24. See Rosabeth Moss Kanter, *Confidence: How Winning Streaks and Losing Streaks Begin and End*. New York: Crown, 2004.

25. Sharon Begley, "Real Self-Esteem Builds on Achievement, Not Praise for Slackers," *The Wall Street Journal*, April 18, 2003, p. B1.

26. See D. Hamacheck, *Encounters with the Self*, 3rd ed. Fort Worth, TX: Holt, Rinehart & Winston, 1992, pp. 5–8.

27. Judith Martin and Thomas Nakayama, *Experiencing Intercultural Communication: An Introduction*, 3rd ed. New York: McGraw-Hill, 2008, p. 95.

28. Justine Coupland, John F. Nussbaum, and Nikolas Coupland, "The Reproduction of Aging and Ageism in Intergenerational Talk," in Nikolas Coupland, Howard Giles, and John Wiemann, eds., *Miscommunication and Problematic Talk*. Newbury Park, CA: Sage, 1991, p. 85.

29. See A. Bandura, *Self Efficacy: The Exercise of Control*. New York: Freeman, 1997.

30. Martin E. P. Seligman, interview in *Success*, July–August 1994, p. 41. Used by permission of *Success* magazine.

31. Carl Sandburg, *The People, Yes*. New York: Harcourt Brace Jovanovich, 1936.

32. Robert Rosenthal and Lenore Jacobson, *Pygmalion in the Classroom*. New York: Holt, Rinehart & Winston, 1968.

33. R. Rosenthal, "The Pygmalion Effect and Its Mechanisms," in J. Aronson, ed., *Improving Academic Achievement: Impact of Psychological Factors on Education*. San Diego: Academic, 2002, pp. 25–36.

34. See, for example, P. Watzlawick, "Self-Fulfilling Prophecies," in J. O'Brien and P. Kollock, eds., *The Production of Reality*, 3rd ed. Thousand Oaks, CA: Pine Force, 2001, pp. 411–423.

35. See Eric Berne, *Games People Play*. New York: Grove, 1964.

36. Joseph Luft, *Group Processes: An Introduction to Group Dynamics*, 2nd ed. Palo Alto, CA: Mayfield, 1970.

37. Liz Funk, "Women on Facebook Think Provocative Is Empowering," *USA Today*, September 19, 2007, p. 11A.

38. See E. Goffman, *The Presentation of Self in Everyday Life*. Garden City, NY: Doubleday, 1959; and *Relations in Public*. New York: Basic Books, 1971.

39. Peggy Orenstein, "I Tweet, Therefore I Am," *The New York Times Magazine*, August 1, 2010, pp. 11–12.

40. Shankar Verdantam, "Shades of Prejudice," *The New York Times*, January 19, 2010, p. A31.

41. Paul Chance, "Seeing Is Believing," *Psychology Today*, January–February 1989, p. 26.

42. See Charles G. Russel, "Culture, Language and Behavior: Perception," *ETC*, 57:2 (Summer 2000), pp. 189–218.

43. M. Sunnafrank, A. Ramirez, and S. Metts, "At First Sight: Persistent Relational Effects of Get Acquainted Conversations," *Journal of Social and Personal Relationships*, 21:3 (February 2005), pp. 361–379.

44. Marina Krakovsky, "Mixed Impressions," *Scientific American Mind*, January/February, 2010, p. 12.

45. Jerry Bembry, "The Pain That Whites Don't See," *The Record*, January 23, 1994, p. E-3. From Jerry Bembry, "Black's Anguish Gives 'Rage' Its Strength," *Baltimore Sun*, December 30, 1993, p. 8D. Reprinted by permission of the *Baltimore Sun*.

46. Marie T. Padilla, "Studying Stereotypes Among Minority Groups," *The Record*, July 19, 1998, p. L1, L3.

47. Sharon Begley, "Racism Studies Find Rational Part of Brain Can Override Prejudice," *Wall Street Journal*, November 19, 2004, p. B1.

48. Padilla, p. L1.

49. "Justice Stevens on 'Invidious Prejudice,'" *The New York Times*, November 10, 2010, p. A34.

50. Irving J. Lee, *How to Talk with People*. San Francisco: International Society for General Semantics, 1980.

51. Alfred Korzybski, *Science and Sanity*, 4th ed. San Francisco: International Society for General Semantics, 1980.

52. As told on *20/20*, ABC Television, June 30, 2000.

53. Peggy Orenstein, "I Tweet, Therefore I Am," *The New York Times Magazine*, August 1, 2010, pp. 11–12.

54. "The Boss's Daughter," *Wall Street Journal*, March 5–6, 2011, p. C4.

55. Julia T. Wood, *Gendered Lives: Communication, Gender, and Culture*, 9th ed. Belmont, CA: Wadsworth, 2011.

56. Diane Hales, *Just Like a Woman*. New York: Bantam, 1999, p. 136.

57. See, for example, Susan Faludi, *Fear and Fantasy in Post-9/11 America*. New York: Metropolitan Books, 2008; and Wood.

58. David Firestone. "While Barbie Talks Tough, G. I. Joe Goes Shopping," *New York Times*, December 31, 1993, p. A-12.

59. Peggy Orenstein, "Girls Will Be Girls," *New York Times Magazine*, February 10, 2008, pp. 17–18.

60. Kristen Homstedt, *Band of Sisters: American Women at War in Iraq*. New York: Stackpole Books, 2007.

61. J. S. Bagby, "A Cross-Cultural Study of Perceptual Predominance in Binocular Rivalry," *Journal of Abnormal and Social Psychology*, 54 (1957), pp. 331–334.

62. H. A. Elfenbein and N. Ambady, "Is There an Ingroup Advantage in Emotion Recognition?" *Psychological Bulletin*, 128, pp. 243–249.

63. "Textbooks Show Students' Conflicting Views of Past," *Wall Street Journal*, August 6, 2007.

64. Richard Breslin, *Understanding Culture's Influence on Behavior*. Orlando, FL: Harcourt Brace Jovanovitch, 1993, p. 47.

65. "Hey, I'm Terrific," *Newsweek*, February 17, 1992, p. 48.

66. Steven J. Heine, "Self as Cultural Product: An Examination of East Asian and North American Selves," *Journal of Personality*, 69:6 (December 2001), pp. 881–906.

67. Larry Samovar and Richard Porter, *Communication Between Cultures*. Belmont, CA: Wadsworth, 1991, p. 91.

68. Osei Appiah, "Americans Online: Differences in Surfing and Evaluating Race-Targeted Web Sites by Black and White Users," paper presented at the annual meeting of the Association for Education in Journalism and Mass Communication, Miami, FL, August 2002.

69. Steven D. Strak, *Glued to the Set: The 60 Television Shows and Events That Made Us Who We Are Today*. New York: Free Press, 1997.

70. Erin Texeira, "Multicultural Socializing in Ads Doesn't Reflect Reality in U.S.," *The Record*, February 18, 2005, p. A24.

71. V. Rohan, "Defining the Face of Evil," *The Record*, January 23, 2005, p. E1.

72. G. Gerbner, L. P. Gross, M. Morgan, and N. Signorielli, "The 'Mainstreaming' of America: Violence Profile No. 11," *Journal of Communication*, 30, pp. 10–29; J. Shanahan and M. Morgan, *Television and Its Viewers: Cultivation Theory and Research*. New York: Cambridge University Press, 1999.

73. See "Mirror, Mirror on My Facebook Wall: Effects of Exposure to Facebook on Self-Esteem," *Cyberpsychology, Behavior and Social Networking*, February 24, 2011, www.lieberpub.com/products/product.aspx?pid=10 and www.pressoffice.cornell.edu/releases/release.cfm?r=55003.

74. "Internet Use Tied to Depression in Youths," *The New York Times*, August 2, 2010, p. D6.

75. See Nicholas Carr, *The Shallows: What the Internet Is Doing to Our Brains*. New York: W. W. Norton, 2010.

76. Sherry Turkle, *Alone Together. Why We Expect More from Technology and Less from Each Other*. New York: Basic Books, 2011.

77. Susan B. Barnes, *Online Connections: Internet Interpersonal Relationships*. Creskill, NJ: Hamptoin, 2001, p. 102.

78. Alan Fram and Trevor Tompson, "Many Teens Take IM Route to Dating, Breaking Up," *The Record*, November 21, 2007, p. A19.

79. For an early work discussing this possibility, see Sherry Turkle, *Life on the Screen*. New York: Simon & Schuster, 1995.

80. A. Lenhart, L. Rainie, and O. Lewis, *Teenage Life Online*. Washington, D.C.: Pew Internet and American Life Project, 2001.

81. Turkle, *Life on the Screen*, p. 12.

82. John A. Bargh, Y. A. Katelyn McKenna, and Grainne M. Fitzsimons, "Can You See the Real Me? Activation and Expression of the 'True Self' on the Internet," *Journal of Social Issues*, 58:1 (January 2002), pp. 33–49.

83. Turkle, *Life on the Screen*, p. 179.

84. Marco R. Della Cava, "Attention Spans Get Rewired," *USA Today*, August 4, 2010, pp. 1D, 2D.

85. Turkle, *Life on the Screen*, p. 267.

86. "The Camera Lies," *Financial Times*, August 25/26, 2007, p. 6.

Chapter 4

1. Barry Gottlieb, "My Word," *The Record*, February 18, 2009, p. A11.

2. C. K. Ogden and I. A. Richards, *The Meaning of Meaning*. Orlando, FL: Harcourt Brace Jovanovich, 1993.

3. Charles F. Vich and Ray V. Wood, "Similarity of Past Experience and the Communication of Meaning," *Speech Monographs*, 36, pp. 159–162.

4. For a discussion of how the mindless use of language affects behavior, see Ellen Langer, "Interpersonal Mindlessness and Language," *Communication Monographs*, 59:3 (September 1992), pp. 324–327.

5. Michael Agar, *Language Shock: Understanding the Culture of Conversation*. New York: Morrow, 1994.

6. Steven Pinker, *The Stuff of Thought: Language as a Window into Human Nature*. New York: Viking, 2007.

7. Jill Lawless, "Texting Terms Make Oxford," *The Record*, March 26, 2011, p. A8.

8. Michiko Kakutani, "When the Geeks Get Snide," *New York Times*, June 27, 2000, p. E1.

9. See "Words to Live By, Depending on Where You're From," *The Record*, March 24, 2009, p. A3.

10. Laura Landro, "Taking Medical Jargon out of Doctors' Visits," *Wall Street Journal*, July 6, 2010, pp. D1, D2.

11. See, for example, S. I. Hayakawa and Alan R. Hayakawa, *Language in Thought and Action*, 5th ed. Orlando, FL: Harcourt Brace Jovanovich, 1990.

12. "'Hi, Jack' Greeting to Co-Pilot Causes Stir," *The Record*, June 8, 2000, p. A-13. Used by permission of the Associated Press. Copyright © 2000. All rights reserved.

13. See William V. Haney, *Communication and Organizational Behavior*, 3rd ed. Homewood, IL: Irwin, 1973, pp. 247–248.

14. For a discussion of names and how they affect us, see Mary Marcus, "The Power of a Name," *Psychology Today*, October 1976, pp. 75–76, 108.

15. Thomas N. Robinson, Dina L. G. Borzekowski, Donna M. Matheson, and Helena C. Kraemer, "Effects of Fast Food Branding on Young Children's Taste Preferences," *Archives of Pediatrics and Adolescent Medicine*, 161 (2007), pp. 792–797.

16. "Washington Wire," *Wall Street Journal*, October 14, 1994.

17. William Lutz, *The New Doublespeak: Why No One Knows What Anyone's Saying Anymore*. New York: Harper Collins, 1996.

18. Jennifer Lee, "A Call for Softer, Greener Language," *New York Times*, March 2, 2003, p. 24.

19. See William Lutz, *Doublespeak Defined*. New York: Harper Resource, 1999; and National Council of Teachers of English, "The 1999 Doublespeak Awards," *ETC*, 56:4 (Winter 1999–2000), p. 484.

20. Henry Beard and Christopher Cerf, *The Official Politically Correct Dictionary and Handbook*. New York: Villard Books, 1992.

21. Diane Ravitch, "You Can't Say That," *Wall Street Journal*, February 13, 2004, p. W15.

22. Donald G. McNeil, Jr., "Like Politics, All Political Correctness Is Local," *New York Times*, October 11, 1998, p. WK-5.

23. John Zeaman, "There's Way Too Much Katakarktanq," *The Record*, February 15, 2004, pp. F1, F4.

24. Nicholas D. Kristof, "Chinese Relations," *New York Times Magazine*, August 18, 1991, pp. 8–10.

25. Guy Deutscher, "You Are What You Speak," *New York Times Magazine*, August 29, 2010, pp. 42–47; and Guy Deutscher, *Through the Language Glass: Why the World Looks Different in Other Languages*. New York: Metropolitan Books/Henry Holt & Company, 2010.

26. Liz Sly, "In China, the Right Name Is Crucial," *The Record*, October 6, 1996, p. A-31.

27. Elizabeth Llorente and Ovetta Wiggins, "Human Services Agency to Correct Letter," *The Record*, February 7, 1997, p. A-3.

28. See, for example, Deborah Tannen, *Talking from 9 to 5: How Women's and Men's Conversational Styles Affect Who Gets Heard, Who Gets Credit, and What Gets Done at Work*. New York: Morrow, 1994.

29. Tannen.

30. Sharon Begley, "West Brain, East Brain: What a Difference Culture Makes," *Newsweek*, March 1, 2010, p. 22.

31. Lera Boroditsky, "Lost in Translation," *The Wall Street Journal*, July 24–25, 2010, p. W3.

32. Michael Slackman, "The Fine Art of Hiding What You Mean to Say," *New York Times*, August 6, 2006, p. WK-5.

33. See, for example, Carolyn Calloway-Thomas, Pamela J. Cooper, and Cecil Blake, *Intercultural Communication: Roots and Routes*. Boston: Allyn & Bacon, 1999, pp. 154–155; and William B. Gudykunst, *Bridging Differences: Effective Intergroup Communication*, 2nd ed. Thousand Oaks, CA: Sage, 1994, p. 83.

34. "Work Week," *Wall Street Journal*, p. A1.

35. J. J. Hemmer, Jr., "Exploitation of Native American Symbols: A First Amendment Analysis," paper presented at the National Communication Association annual convention, New Orleans, LA, November 22, 2002.

36. Suzanne Daily, "In Europe, Some Fear National Languages Are Endangered," *New York Times*, April 16, 2001, pp. A1, A10.

37. Steven Komarow, "Some Germans Fear Language Is Being Infected by English," *USA Today*, May 16, 2001, p. 6A.

38. Andrew Jacobs, "Shanghai Is Trying to Untangle the Mangled English of Chinglish," *The New York Times*, May 3, 2010, p. A12.

39. B. Kitwana, *The Hip Hop Generation: Young Blacks and the Crisis in African American Culture*. New York: Basic Books, 2002.

40. See Adam Bradley and Andrew DuBois, ed., *The Anthology of Rap*. New Haven: Yale University Press, 2011, and William Buckhoz, *Understanding Rap: Explanations of Confusing Rap Lyrics You & Your Grandma Can Understand*. New York: Abrams, 2011

41. Associated Press, "Congress Looks at Hip-Hop Language," *New York Times*, September 25, 2007.

42. Jeff Leeds, "Hearing Focuses on Language and Violence in Rap Music," *New York Times*, September 26, 2007, p. A24.

43. Monica Davey, "Fighting Words," *New York Times*, February 20, 2005, pp. ARI, 34.

44. Judy Rosen, "Rap: A Celebration of Language," *The Record*, December 2, 2002, p. L15.

45. A. Nilsen, "Sexism as Shown through the English Vocabulary," in A. Nilsen, H. Bosmajian, H. Gershuny, and J. Stanley, eds., *Sexism and Language*. Urbana, IL: National Council of Teachers of English, 1977.

46. Ibid.

47. Sam Kean, "What's in a Name?" *New York Times Magazine*, October 28, 2007, p. 25.

48. Simon Romero, "A Culture of Naming That Even a Law May Not Tame," *New York Times*, September 5, 2007, p. A4.

49. Thomas Fuller, "In Thai Cultural Battle, Name-Calling Is Encouraged," *New York Times*, August 29, 2007, p. A4.

50. Michael Wines, "In a Land of Homemade Names, Tiffany Doesn't Cut It," *New York Times*, October 1, 2007, p. A4.

51. Alexander Alter, "The Baby-Name Business," *Wall Street Journal*, June 22, 2007, pp. W1, W12.

52. Frank Luntz, *Words That Work: It's Not What You Say, It's What People Hear*. New York: Hyperion, 2007, p. 108.

53. A. Mulac, J. Bradac, and S. Mann. "Male/Female Language Differences and Attributional Consequences in Children's Television," *Human Communication Research*, 11 (1985), pp. 481–506.

54. C. Kramer, "Stereotypes of Women's Speech: The Word from Cartoons," *Journal of Popular Culture*, 8 (1974), pp. 624–630.

55. C. Kramer, "Male and Female Perceptions of Male and Female Speech," *Language and Speech*, 20 (1978), pp. 151–161.

56. Patricia Hayes Bradley, "The Folk-Linguistics of Women's Speech: An Empirical Examination," *Communication Monographs*, 48, pp. 73–90.

57. Nancy M. Henley and Cheris Kramarae, "Gender, Power and Miscommunication," in Nickolas Coupland, Howard Giles, and John Weimann, eds., *Miscommunication and Problematic Talk*. Newbury Park, CA: Sage, 1991, p. 42.

58. Deborah Tannen, *You Just Don't Understand*. New York: Ballantine, 1991, p. 42.

59. M. Hiller and F. L. Johnson, "Gender and Generation in Conversational Topics: A Case Study of Two Coffee Shops," paper presented at the annual meeting of the Speech Communication Association, San Diego, CA, November 1996.

60. Cited in Craig Johnson and Larry Vinson, "Placement and Frequency of Powerless Talk and Impression Formation," *Communication Quarterly*, 38:4 (Fall 1990), p. 325.

61. Cheris Kramarae, *Women and Men Speaking*. Rowley, MA: Newbury House Publishers, 1981, p. 1.

62. Deborah Tannen, *You Just Don't Understand*. New York: Ballantine, 1991.

63. "When Cheers Turn to Abuse, Colleges Need to Take Action," *USA Today*, March 7, 2008, p. 12A.

64. Melanie B. Glover, "Experts See Epidemic of Foul-Mouthed Kids," *The Record*, February 28, 2008, p. A6.

65. Rachel Emma Silverman, "On the Job Cursing: Obscene Talk Is the Latest Target of Workplace Ban," *Wall Street Journal*, May 8, 2001, p. B12.

66. See, for example, James O'Connor, *Cuss Control: The Complete Book on How to Curb Your Cursing*. New York: Three Rivers, 2000.

67. "The Informed Reader; Swearing Is the Best Way to Capture Connotations," *Wall Street Journal*, October 9, 2007, p. B14.

68. Randall Kennedy, *Nigger: The Strange Career of a Troublesome Word*. New York: Pantheon, 2002.

69. Anahad O'Connor, "In Bid to Ban Racial Slur, Blacks Occupy Both Sides," *New York Times*, February 25, 2007, pp. 23, 26.

70. Joseph Plambeck, "'Dr. Laura' Retreats after Use of Epithet," *The New York Times*, August 19, 2010, p. C3.

71. DeWayne Wickman, "'N-Word' Has Become an Indelible Part of the American Lexicon," *USA Today*, January 11, 2011, p. 9A.

72. Stephanie Raposo, "Quick! Tell Us What KUTGW Means," *Wall Street Journal*, August 5, 2009, pp. D1, D3.

73. Amy Harmon, "Internet Changes Language for :-) & :-(." *New York Times*, February 20, 1999, p. B-7.

74. See Katie Roiphe, "The Language of Fakebook," *The New York Times*, August 15, 2010, p. 2. (JK)," *New York Times*, March 19, 2008, pp. BU1, BU9.

75. Hayakawa and Hayakawa.

76. For more information, see Richard Lacayo, "Mixed Signals on Sanctions," *Time*, December 17, 1990, p. 114.

Chapter 5

1. Ann Davis, Joseph Pereira, and William M. Bulkeley, "Security Concerns Bring New Focus on Body Language," *Wall Street Language*, August 15, 2002, pp. A1, A6.

2. See, for example, H. A. Elfenbein and N. Ambady, "Predicting Workplace Outcomes from the Ability to Eavesdrop on Feelings," *Journal of Applied Psychology* (October 2002), pp. 963–972.

3. Ray Birdwhistell, *Kinesics and Context*. Philadelphia: University of Pennsylvania Press, 1970; Mark L. Knapp and Judith A. Hall, *Nonverbal Communication in Human Interaction*, 6th ed. Belmont, CA: Wadsworth, 2005; and Albert Mehrabian, *Silent Messages*, 2nd ed. Belmont, CA: Wadsworth, 1981.

4. From the opening scene in the film *Primary Colors*.

5. For some practical advice, see Dale G. Leathers. *Successful Nonverbal Communication: Principles and Applications*. New York: Macmillan, 1992.

6. Knapp and Hall.

7. Kathleen Fackelmann, "Look Who's Talking with Gestures," *USA Today*, July 5, 2000, p. 7D.

8. Quoted in Daniel Goleman, "Sensing Silent Cues Emerges as Key Skills," *New York Times*, October 10, 1989.

9. M. D. Licke, R. H. Smith, and M. L. Klotz, "Judgements of Physical Attractiveness: The Role of Faces and Bodies," *Personality and Social Psychology Bulletin*, 12 (1986), pp. 381–389.

10. T. R. Levine et al., "The Lying Chicken and the Avoidant Egg: Eye Contact, Deception, and Causal Order," *Southern Communication Journal*, 71:4 (December 2006), pp. 401–411; and D. S. Berry, "What Can a Moving Face Tell Us?" *Journal of Personality and Social Psychology*, 58 (1990), pp. 1004–1014.

11. Helmut Morsbach, "Aspects of Nonverbal Communication in Japan," in Larry Samovar and Richard Porter, eds., *Intercultural Communication: A Reader*, 3rd ed. Belmont, CA: Wadsworth, 1982, p. 308.

12. V. Richmond, "Teacher Nonverbal Immediacy: Use and Outcomes," in J. L. Chesebro and J. C. McCroskey, eds., *Communication for Teachers*. Boston: Allyn & Bacon, 2002, pp. 65–82.

13. See Julie Woodzicka, "Sex Differences in Self-Awareness of Smiling during a Mock Job Interview," *Journal of Nonverbal Behavior*, 32:2 (June 2008), pp. 109–121.

14. Warren St. John, "They're Not Just Saying Ah," *New York Times*, October 2, 2005, p. 13.

15. Nancy Henley, *Body Politics: Power, Sex and Nonverbal Communication* New York: Simon & Schuster, 1986.

16. For a summary of Mehrabian's work in this area, see his article "Significance of Posture and Position in the Communication of Attitude and Status Relationship," *Psychological Bulletin*, 71(1969), pp. 359–372.

17. Natalie Angier, "Abstract Thoughts? The Body Takes Them Literally," *The New York Times*, February 2, 2010, p. D2.

18. Lauren Neergaard, "Experts Find Gesturing Helps Tots Learn Words," *The Record*, February 15, 2009, p. A-13.

19. Christina Binkley, "Heelpolitik: The Power of a Pair of Stilettos," *Wall Street Journal*, August 2, 2007, p. D8.

20. Del Jones, "The Bald Truth about CEOs," *USA Today*, March 14, 2008, pp. 1B, 2B.

21. Malcolm Gladwell, *Blink*. New York: Little, Brown, 2005.

22. Del Jones, "Does Height Equal Power?" *USA Today*, July 18, 2007, pp. 1B, 2B.

23. Paul Ekman, W. V. Friesen, and J. Baer, "The International Language of Gestures," *Psychology Today*, May 1984, pp. 64–69.

24. L. Samovar, R. Porter, and E. McDaniel, *Communication between Cultures*. Belmont, CA: Wadsworth, 2006.

25. See, for example, Scott Shane, "Language Help from, Um, Almost-Words," *Sunday Record*, September 12, 1999, pp. L3, L7.

26. Cited in Peter Jaret, "My Voice Has Got to Go." *New York Times*, July 21, 2003, p. G1.

27. Mehrabian.

28. For background on how culture affects rate, see Hyun O. Lee and Franklin J. Boster," Collectivism-Individualism in Perceptions of Speech Rate: A Cross-Cultural Comparison," *Journal of Cross Cultural Psychology*, 23:3 (September 1992), pp. 377–388.

29. F. Goldman-Eisler, "Continuity of Speech Utterance, Its Determinance and Its Significance," *Language and Speech*, 4 (1961), pp. 220–231.

30. Adam Jaworski, *The Power of Silence: Social and Pragmatic Perspective*. Thousand Oaks, CA: Sage, 1993.

31. Pamela Paul, "A Failure to Communicate," *The New York Times*, August 29, 2010, p. 6.

32. Sarah E. Needleman, "Office Personal Space Is Crowded Out," *The Wall Street Journal*, December 7, 2009, p. B7.

33. Edward Hall, *The Hidden Dimension*. New York: Doubleday, 1969.

34. Lizette Alvarez, "Where the Healing Touch Starts with the Hospital Design," *New York Times*, pp. F5, F10.

35. See J. K. Burgoon, "Privacy and Communication," in M. Burgoon, ed., *Communication Yearbook 6*. Beverly Hills, CA: Sage, 1982, pp. 206–249; J. K. Burgoon and L. Aho, "Three Field Experiments on the Effects of Violations of Conversational Distance," *Communication Monographs*, 49 (1982), pp. 71–88; and J. K. Burgoon and J. B. Walther, "Nonverbal Expectations and the Evaluative Consequence of Violations," *Human Communication Research* 17:2 (1990), pp. 232–265.

36. See, for example, A. G. White, "The Patient Sits Down: A Clinical Note," *Psychosomatic Medicine*, 15 (1953), pp. 256–257.

37. D. Diamond, "Behind Closed Gates," *USA Today*, January 31, 1997, pp. 4–5.

38. Dahlia Lithwick, "Our Beauty Bias Is Unfair," *Newsweek*, June 14, 2010, p. 20; and Jessica Bennett, "The Beauty Advantage, *Newsweek*, July 26, 2010, pp. 46–48.

39. Valerie Ross, "Color TV," *Scientific American Mind*, July/August 2010, p. 13.

40. See L. K. Guerrero, J. A. DeVito, and M. L. Hecht, eds., *The Nonverbal Communication Reader: Classic and Contemporary Readings*, 2nd ed. Prospect Heights, IL: Waveland, 1999; and Joseph Kahn, "Chinese People's Republic is Unfair to Its Short People," *New York Times*, May 21, 2004, p. A13.

41. "Cold Shoulder for Fat Customers," *New York Times*, April 5, 2005, p. F6.

42. Maureen Dowd, "Dressed to Distract," *New York Times*, June 6, 2010, p. WK11.

43. Harriet Brown, "For Obese People, Prejudice in Plain Sight," *The New York Times*, March 16, 2010, p. D6.

44. Ibid.

45. V. Ritts, M. L. Patterson, and M. E. Tubbs, "Expectations, Impressions, and Judgments of Physically Attractive Students: A Review," *Review of Educational Research*, 62 (1992), pp. 413–426.

46. See, for example, J. Kilbourne, "The More You Subtract, the More You Add: Cutting Girls Down to Size," in J. Spade and C. Valentine, eds., *The Kaleidoscope of Gender*, Belmont, CA: Wadsworth, 2004, pp. 234–244.

47. Choe Sang-Hun, "South Korea Stretches Standards for Success," *The New York Times*, December 24, 2009, pp. A6, A10.

48. Ruth La Ferla, "Generation E. A.: Ethnically Ambiguous," *New York Times*, December 28, 2003, pp. ST1, ST9.

49. Karin Nelson, "What's Vision Got to Do With It?" *New York Times*, September 27, 2007, p. G9.

50. John T. Molloy, *New Dress for Success*. New York: Warner, 1990.

51. See, for example, M. S. Singer and A. E. Singer, "The Effect of Police Uniforms on Interpersonal Perception," *Journal of Psychology*, 119 (1985), pp. 157–161.

52. Cathy Horyn, "A New Year, A New Color. But Are We Blue?" *New York Times*, December 20, 2007, pp. C1, C11.

53. Horyn, p. C11.

54. Horyn, p. C11.

55. Roy A. Smith, "The Color of Confidence," *The Wall Street Journal*, September 25–26, 2010, p. D3.

56. Pam Belluck, "Reinvent Wheel? Blue Room. Defusing a Bomb? Red Room," *The New York Times*, February 6, 2009, pp. A1, A15.

57. Susan Carey, "More U. S. Companies Are Blue, and It's Not Just the Stock Market," *Wall Street Journal*, August 30, 2001, pp. A1, A2.

58. Robert Levine, *A Geography of Time, or How Every Culture Keeps Time Just a Little Differently*. New York: Basic Books, 1997.

59. Del Jones, "I'm Late, I'm Late, I'm Late," *USA Today*. November 26, 2003, p. B1.

60. Hall.

61. Alex MacKenzie, *The Time Trap*. New York: McGraw-Hill, 1975.

62. See Robert J. Samuelson, "The Sad Fate of the Comma," *Newsweek*, July 23, 2007, p. 41.

63. J. Burgoon, J. Walther, and J. Baesler, "Interpretations, Evaluations, and Consequences of Interpersonal Touch," *Human Communication Research*, 19 (1992), pp. 237–263.

64. Marilyn Elias, "Study: Hugging Warms the Heart, and Also May Protect It," *USA Today*, March 10, 2003, p. 7D.

65. An especially persuasive argument is made by Ashleu Montagu in *Touching: The Human Significance of the Skin*. New York: Harper & Row, 1971.

66. Marilyn Elias, "Hugs Can Do a Heart Good," *USA Today*, March 8, 2004, p. 7D.

67. Nicholas Bakalar, "Five-Second Touch Can Convey Specific Emotion, Study Finds," *The New York Times*, August 11, 2009, p. D3.

68. Benedict Carey, "Evidence That Little Touches Do Mean So Much," *The New York Times*, February 23, 2010, p. D5.

69. See D. F. Fromme, W. E. Jaynes, D. K. Taylor, E. G. Harold, J. Daniell, J. R. Roundtree, and M. Fromme, "Nonverbal Behaviors and Attitudes toward Touch," *Journal of Nonverbal Behavior*, 13 (1989), pp. 3–14.

70. Barbara Bales, *Communication and the Sexes*. New York: Harper & Row, 1988, p. 60.

71. See, for example, R. Heslin and T. Alper, "Touch: A Bonding Gesture," in J. M. Wiemann and R. P. Harrison, eds., *Nonverbal Interaction*. Beverly Hills, CA: Sage, 1983, pp. 47–75.

72. See, for example, J. T. Wood, *Interpersonal Communication in Everyday Encounters*, 5th ed. Belmont, CA: Wadsworth, 2009.

73. Henley.

74. James L. Lynch, *The Broken Heart*. New York: Basic Books, 1979. See also James L. Lynch, *The Language of the Heart*. New York: Basic Books, 1986.

75. Jim Beckerman, "A Whiff of Vanilla Seems to Please Us All," *The Record*, September 16, 2003, pp. F1, F2.

76. N. Wade, "Scent of a Man Is Linked to a Woman's Selection," *New York Times*, January 22, 2002, p. F2.

77. N. Wade, "For Gay Men, Different Scent of Attraction," *New York Times*, May 10, 2005, pp. A1, A14.

78. Lauran Neergaard, "Researchers Find Bad Times Really Do Stink," *The Record*, March 28, 2008, p. A6.

79. M. G. Millar and K. U. Millar, "The Effects of Suspicion on the Recall of Cues to Make Veracity Judgments," *Communication Reports*, 11 (1998), pp. 57–64.

80. R. G. Riggio and H. S. Freeman, "Individual Differences and Cues to Deception," *Journal of Personality and Social Psychology*, 45 (1983), pp. 899–915.

81. D. B. Buller and J. K. Burgoon, "Deception: Strategic and Nonstrategic Communication," in J. Daly and J. M. Wiemann, eds., *Interpersonal Communication*. Hillsdale, NJ: Erlbaum, 1994.

82. Paul Ekman and Mark G. Frank, "Lies That Fail," in Michael Lewis and Carolyn Saarni, eds., *Lying and Deception in Everyday Life*. New York: Guilford, 1993, pp. 184–200.

83. David J. Lieberman, *Never Be Lied to Again*. New York: St. Martin's, 1998.

84. See, for example, L. Case et al., "The Impact of Deception and Suspicion on Different Hand Movements," *Journal of Nonverbal Behavior*, 30:1 (Spring 2006), pp. 1–19.

85. B. Veland, "Tell Me More: On the Fine Art of Listening," *Utne Reader*, 1992, pp. 104–109; A. Mulac, "Men's and Women's Talk in Same Gender and Mixed Gender Dyads: Power or Polemic?" *Journal of Language and Social Psychology*, 8 (1989), pp. 249–270.

86. J. F. Dovidio, S. L. Ellyson, C. F. Keating, K. Heltman, and C. E. Brown, "The Relationship of Social Power to Visual Displays of Dominance between Men and Women," *Journal of Personality and Social Psychology*, 54 (1988), pp. 233–242.

87. Shelly Branch, "Forget Standing Tall, Female Models Make Slouching Look Good," *Wall Street Journal*, pp. A1, A9.

88. Julia T. Wood, *Gendered Lives*. Belmont, CA: Wadsworth, 1994, p. 154.

89. N. G. Rotter and G. S. Rotter, "Sex Differences in the Encoding and Decoding of Negative Facial Emotions," *Journal of Nonverbal Behavior*, 12:2 (1998), pp. 139–148.

90. P. Anderson, "Exploring Intercultural Differences in Nonverbal Communication," in L. Samovar and R. Porter, eds, *Intercultural Communication: A Reader*, 3rd ed. Belmont, CA: Wadsworth, 1982, pp. 272–282.

91. E. R. McDaniel, "Japanese Nonverbal Communication: A Review and Critique of Literature," paper presented at the annual meeting of the Speech Communication Association, Miami Beach, FL, November 18–21, 1993.

92. Rebecca Knight, "Interactions Speak Louder than Words," *Financial Times*, July 2, 2007, p. 12.

93. Neil MacFarquhar, "A Kiss Is Not Just a Kiss to an Angry Arab TV Audience," *New York Times*, March 5, 2004, p. A3.

94. Kaet Saks, "In Perfect Harmony," *The Record*, August 19, 1999, pp. HF1, HF3.

95. Steven G. Jones, *Cybersociety: Computer-Mediated Communication and Community*. Thousand Oaks, CA: Sage, 1995, p. 116.

96. Jina Yoo, "To Smile or Not to Smile:) : Defining the Effects of Emoticons on Relational Outcomes," paper presented at the annual meeting of the International Communication Association, 2007; and C. Constantin, S. Kalyanaraman, C. Stavrositu, and N. Wagoner, "To Be or Not to Be Emotional: Impression Formation Effects of Emoticons in Moderated Chatrooms," paper presented at the annual meeting of the Association for Education in Journalism and Mass Communication, Miami Beach, FL, August 7–10, 2002.

97. Jones, p. 172

98. Karen De Witt, "So, What Is That Leather Bustier Saying?" *New York Times*, January 1, 1995, p. 2E.

99. Bret Lortie, "Your Lying Eyes," *Bulletin of the Atomic Scientists*, 58:6 (November/December 2002).

100. Christopher De Vinck, "A Digital Hug," *The Record*, November 26, 2009, p. A23.

Chapter 6

1. Karen Arenson, "The Fine Art of Listening," *New York Times Education Life*, January 13, 2002, pp. 34–35.

2. Cesar G. Soriano, "News Flash: Teen Stops Speaking!" *USA Today*, August 9, 2000, p. 1D.

3. Brendan Schurr, "Teenager Vows Not to Speak for a Year," *The Record*, August 16, 2000, p. A-5.

4. See Jane Allan, "Talking Your Way to Success (Listening Skills)," *Accountancy*, February 1993, pp. 612–663; and John W. Haas and Christina L. Arnold, "An Examination of the Role of Listening in Co-Workers," *Journal of Business Communication*, April 1995, pp. 123–139.

5. The Office Team Survey, 2000, was cited in *Sssh! Listen Up!* HighGain, Inc. Newsletter, June 2000, p. 4.

6. K. W. Hawkins and B. P. Fullion, "Perceived Communication Skill Needs for Work Groups," *Communication Research Reports*, 16 (1999), pp. 167–174.

7. J. T. Wood, "Buddhist Influences on Scholarship and Teaching," *Journal of Communication and Religion*, 2004, pp. 32–39.

8. See, for example, M. Levine, "Tell the Doctor All Your Problems but Keep It to Less Than a Minute," *New York Times*, June 1, 2004, p. F6; and M. Nichols, "Listen Up for Better Sales," *Business Week Online*, September 15, 2006, p. 12.

9. Jared Sandberg, "Bad at Complying? You Might Just Be a Very Bad Listener," *Wall Street Journal*, September 25, 2007, p. B1.

10. Jim Adams et al. "How College Students Spend Their Time Communicating," *International Journal of Listening*, 22:1 (2008), pp. 13–28.

11. Brigitta R. Brunner, "Listening, Communication & Trust: Practitioners' Perspectives of Business/Organizational Relationships," *International Journal of Listening*, 22:1 (2008), pp. 73–82.

12. See A. D. Wolvin and C. G. Coakley, "A Survey of the Status of Listening Training in Some Fortune 500 Corporations," *Communication Education*, 40 (1991), pp. 152–164.

13. Denisa R. Superville, "Hours Spent Wired Changing How Kids Think and Interact," *The Record*, May 15, 2010, pp. A1, A8.

14. See "Generation M2: Media in the Lives of 8- to 18-Year-Olds," The Kaiser Family Foundation, January 2010.

15. For a detailed discussion, see Ralph G. Nichols and Leonard A. Stevens, *Are You Listening?* New York: McGraw-Hill, 1956. See also K. Watson and L. Barker, "Listening Behavior: Definition and Measurement," in R. Bostrom, ed., *Communication Yearbook 8*. Beverly Hills, CA: Sage, 1984, pp. 178–197; and Andrew Wolving and Carolyn Gwynn Coakly, *Listening*, 4th ed. Dubuque, IA: Brown, 1988.

16. John R. Freund and Arnold Nelson, "Distortion in Communication," in B. Peterson, G. Goldhaber, and R. Pace, eds., Chicago: Science Research Associates, 1974, pp. 122–124.

17. Gerald Goldhaber, *Organizational Communication*, 4th ed. Dubuque, IA: Brown, 1988.

18. See L. Wheeless, A. Frymier, and C. Thompson, "A Comparison of Verbal Output and Receptivity in Relation to Attraction and Communication Satisfaction in Interpersonal Relationships," *Communication Quarterly*, Spring 1992, pp. 102–115.

19. See, for example, Judi Brownell, *Listening: Attitudes, Principles, and Skills*. Boston: Allyn & Bacon, 1996.

20. Janel Beavin Bavelas, Linda Coates, and Trudy Johnson, "Listener Responses as a Collaborative Process: The Role of Gaze," *Journal of Communication*, 52:3 (September 2002), pp. 566–579.

21. Frank Luntz, *Win*. New York: Hyperion, 2011.

22. For insight into empathic listening, also see Judi Brownell, *Listening: Attitudes, Principles, and Skills*, 3rd ed. Boston: Allyn & Bacon, 2006.

23. B. L. Omdahl, *Cognitive Appraisal, Emotion, and Empathy*. Mahwah, NJ: Erlbaum, 1995.

24. T. Holtgraves, *Language as Social Action: Social Psychology and Language Use*. Mahwah, NJ: Erlbaum, 2002.

25. See, for example, J. B. Weaver III and M. B. Kirtley, "Listening Styles and Empathy," *Southern Communication Journal*, 60 (1995), pp. 131–140.

26. Karen S. Peterson, "Sharing Memorable Moments Can Calm the Soul, Heal the Body," *USA Today*, February 15, 1999, p. 4D.

27. Angela Delli Santi, "N.J. Doctors to Learn Cultural Sensitivity," *The Record*, April 11, 2005, p. A3.

28. Nissa Simon, "Can You Hear Me Now?" *Time*, August 18, 2003; and Kim Painter, "Getting Bad Reception?" *USA Today*, October 3, 2005, p. 6D.

29. C. Crosen, "Blah, Blah, Blah," *Wall Street Journal*, July 10, 1997, pp. 1A, 6A; and Betsy A. Lehman, "Getting an Earful Is Just What the Doctor Needs," *The Record*, March 21, 1994, p. B4.

30. See also Judi Brownell, *Listening: Attitudes, Principles, and Skills*, 2nd ed. Boston: Allyn & Bacon, 2004.

31. Ralph G. Nichols and Leonard A. Stevens. *Are You Listening?* New York: McGraw-Hill, 1956.

32. Harry Jackson, Jr., "Fear of Forgetting," *The Record*, April 5, 2005, pp. F1, F12.

33. See A. Vangelisti, M. Knapp, and J. Daly, "Conversational Narcissism," *Communication Monographs*, December 1990, pp. 251–271.

34. Alfie Kohn, "Girl Talk, Guy Talk," *Psychology Today*, February 1988, pp. 65–66.

35. Christine Kenneally, *The First Word: The Search for the Origins of Language*. New York: Viking, 2007.

36. Deborah Tannen, *The Argument Culture: Moving from Debate to Dialogue*. New York: Ballentine, 1998.

37. Don Tosti, "Operant Conditioning," speech presented at Operant Conditioning Seminar, New York, Fall 1983.

38. David W. Johnson, *Reaching Out: Interpersonal Effectiveness and Self-Actualization*. Englewood Cliffs, NJ: Prentice-Hall, 1972; and Thomas Gordon, *Leader Effectiveness Training*. New York: Wyden, 1977.

39. For a discussion of the benefit of questioning, see John F. Monoky, "Listen by Asking." *Industrial Distribution*, April 1995, p. 123.

40. Quoted in "Making TLC a Requirement," *Newsweek*, August 12, 1991, p. 56.

41. See Richard Paul and Linda Elder, *The Miniature Guide to Critical Thinking*, 6th ed. Tomales, CA: Foundation for Critical Thinking Press, 2009.

42. See R. Boostrom, *Developing Creative and Critical Thinking*, Lincolnwood, IL: National Textbook, 1992.

43. Teri Gamble and Michael Gamble, *Public Speaking in the Age of Diversity*. Boston: Allyn & Bacon, 1994, p. 18.

44. Deborah Tannen, *You Just Don't Understand: Women and Men in Conversation*. New York: Morrow, 1990.

45. See, for example, Deborah M. Saucier et al. "Are Sex Differences in Navigation Caused by Sexually Dimorphic Strategies or by Differences in the Ability to Use the Strategies?" *Behavioral Neuroscience*, 116:3 (2002), pp. 403–410; and Bia Kim, Sewon Lee, and Jaesik Lee, "Gender Differences in Spatial Navigation," *Proceedings of the World Academy of Science, Engineering and Technology*, 25 (November 2007), pp. 297–300.

46. S. Petronio, J. Martin, and R. Littlefield, "Prerequisite Conditions for Self-Disclosing: A Gender Issue," *Communication Monographs*, 51 (1984), pp. 282–292.

47. See also Michael Purdy and Deborah Borisoff, *Listening in Everyday Life: A Personal and Professional Approach*, 2nd ed. Lanham, MD: University Press of America, 1997.

48. Judi Brownell, *Listening*, 2nd ed.

49. B. R. Burleson, "Emotional Support Skills," in J. O. Green and B. R. Burleson, eds., *Handbook of Communication and Social Interaction Skills*. Mahwah, NJ: Erlbaum, 2003.

50. C. Y. Cheng, "Chinese Philosophy and Contemporary Communication Theory," in D. I. Kincaid, ed., *Communication Theory: Eastern and Western Perspectives*. New York: Academic Press, 1987.

51. Documented by T. S. Lebra in *Japanese Patterns of Behavior*. Honolulu: University Press of Hawaii, 1976.

52. C. Kiewitz, J. B. Weaver III, H. B. Brosius, and G. Wiemann, "Cultural Differences in Listening Style Preferences: A Comparison of Young Adults in Germany, Israel, and the United States," *International Journal of Public Opinion Research*, 9:3 (Fall 1997), p. 233.

53. John Stewart and M. Thomas, "Dialogic Listening: Sculpting Mutual Meanings," in J. Stewart, ed., *Bridges, Not Walls: A Book about Interpersonal Communication*, 6th ed. New York: McGraw-Hill, 1995, pp. 184–201.

54. Larry A. Samovar and Richard E. Porter, *Communication between Cultures*. Belmont, CA: Wadsworth, 1995, pp. 211–212.

55. For more information on this topic, also see Julia T. Wood, *Gendered Lives: Communication, Gender and Culture*, 7th ed. Belmont, CA: Wadsworth, 2007.

56. D. A. Christakis, F. J. Zimmerman, D. L. DiGuiseppe, and C. A. McCarty, "Early Television Exposure and Subsequent Attentional Problems in Children," *Pediatrics*, 113 (2004), pp. 707–713.

57. See, for example, "Personality Typing," *Wired*, July 1999, p. 71.

58. Jay Reeves, "Texting as Life-Changer," *The Record*, September 20, 2010, p. A4.

59. See, for example, Gui Qing Koh et al., "Presence and Podcasting: The Role of Contextual and Formal Attributes," paper presented at the annual meeting of the International Listening Association, 2007.

60. Patricia Alex, "Texting in Class Getting out of Hand," *The Record*, October 11, 2010, pp. A1, A8.

61. Sharon White Taylor, "Wireless and Witless," *New York Times*, July 5, 2000, p. A-17; and "Cell Phone Rage: Helpful Hints," *New York Times*, July 8, 2000, p. A-14.

62. Rita Rubin, "Merely Listening on Phone Shown to Distract Drivers," *USA Today*, March 10, 2008, p. 5D.

63. David Shenk, *Data Smog*. New York: Harper-Edge, 1997.

64. Todd Gitlin, "Supersaturation, or the Media Torrent and Disposable Feeling," in E. Bucy, ed., *Living in the Information Age: A New Media Reader*, 2nd ed. Belmont, CA: Thomson Wadsworth, 2005, pp. 139–146.

65. Sheila C. Bentley, "Listening in the 21st Century," paper presented at the annual convention of the National Communication Association, Chicago, November 1999.

66. Mickey Meece, "Who's the Boss, You or Your Gadget?" *The New York Times*, February 6, 2011, pp. BU 1, BU 8.

67. Jenna Wortham, "Everyone's Using Cellphones, But Not So Many Are Talking," *The New York Times*, May 14, 2010, pp. B1, B4.

68. Michael Fitzgerald, "The Coming Wave of Gadgets That Listen and Obey," *New York Times*, January 27, 2008, p. BU4.

69. Cynthia B. Leshin, *Internet Investigations in Business Communication*. Upper Saddle River, NJ: Prentice Hall, 1997, pp. 53–56.

Chapter 7

1. Virginia Satir, *The New Peoplemaking*. Palo Alto, CA: Science and Behavior Books, 1998, p. 51.

2. Sharon Jayson, "The Year We Stopped Talking," *USA Today*, December 30, 2010–January 2, 2011, pp. 1A, 2A.

3. Sherry Turkle, *Alone Together: Why We Expect More from Technology and Less from Each Other*. New York: Basic Books, 2011.

4. J. O'Neill, "Help Others for a Longer Life," *New York Times*, November 2, 2002, p. F6.

5. Lori Oliwenstein, "Marry Me," *Time*, January 28, 2008, pp. 73–76.

6. "Sick? Lonely? Genes Tell the Tale," September 15, 2007, accessed at www.theage.com.au/news/World/Sick-Lonely-Genes-tell-the-tale/2007/09/15/11892; and Kathleen Fackelmann, "For Lonely Hearts, 1 Can Be an Unhealthy Number," *USA Today*, August 27, 2007, p. 8D.

7. William C. Schutz, *The Interpersonal Underworld*. Palo Alto, CA: Science and Behavior Books, 1966, pp. 18–20.

8. See, for example, Robert A. Bell, "Conversational Involvement and Loneliness," *Communication Monographs*, 52 (1985) pp. 218–235.

9. Robert A. Bell and Michael Roloff, "Making a Love Connection: Loneliness and Communication Competence in the Dating Marketplace," *Communication Quarterly*, 39:1 (Winter 1991), pp. 58–74.

10. Steve Duck, *Human Relationships*, 3rd ed. Thousand Oaks, CA: Sage, 1999, p. 57.

11. *Time*, December 20, 1993, p. 15.

12. John T. Cacioppo and William Patrick, *Loneliness: Human Nature and the Need for Social Connection*. New York: W. W. Norton, 2008.

13. Schutz, p. 24.

14. J. A. Bryant, A. Sanders-Jackson, and A. M. K. Smallwood, "IMing, Text Messaging, and Adolescent Social Networks," *Journal of Computer Mediated Communication*, 11, 2006.

15. Andrea Heiman, "Flirting Still Has Its Attractions," *Sunday Record*, March 20, 1994.

16. Robert E. Nofsinger, *Everyday Conversation*. Newbury Park, CA: Sage, 1991, p. 1.

17. See Deborah Cameron, *Good Talk? Living and Working in a Communication Culture*. Thousand Oaks, CA: Sage, 2000.

18. Deborah Tannen, "Why Sisterly Chats Make People Happier," *The New York Times*, October 26, 2010, p. D6.

19. Anita L. Vangelisti and Mary A. Banski, "Couples' Debriefing Conversations: The Impact of Gender, Occupation, and Demographic Characteristics," *Family Relations*, 42:2 (April 1993) pp. 149–157.

20. See Steven W. Duck, *Human Relationships*, 4th ed. London: Sage, 2007; and Steven W. Duck, *Meaningful Relationships: Talking Sense, and Relating*. Thousand Oaks, CA: Sage, 1994.

21. Karen Shafer, "Talk in the Middle: Two Conversational Skills for Friendship," *English Journal*, 82:1 (January 1993) pp. 53–55.

22. See M. R. Parks and K. Floyd, "Making Friends in Cyberspace," *Journal of Communication* 46, 1996, p. 85.

23. See for example, A. Ramirez Jr. and Judee K. Burgoon, "The Effect of Interactivity on Initial Interactions: The Influence of Information Valence and Modality and Information Richness on Computer-Mediated Interaction," *Communication Monographs* 71, 2004, pp. 422–447.

24. Bob Smith, "Care and Feeding of the Office Grapevine," *Management Review*, 85 (February 1996), p. 6; and Lisette Hilton, "They Heard It through the Grapevine," *South Florida Business Journal*, 21 (August, 2000), p. 53.

25. See Joann Klimkiewicz, "Society Has Become Addicted to Gossip," *The Record*, April 29, 2007, p. F4; Graeme Turner. *Understanding Celebrity*. London: Sage, 2004; and F. T. McAndrew, E. K. Bell, and C. M. Garcia, "Who Do We Tell and Whom Do We Tell On? Gossip as a Strategy for Status Enhancement," *Journal of Applied Social Psychology*, 37:7 (July 2007), pp. 1562–1577.

26. M. M. Turner, M. A. Mazur, N. Wendel, and R. Winslow, "Relational Ruin or Social Glue? The Joint Effect of Relationship Type and Gossip Valence on Liking, Trust, and Expertise," *Communication Monographs*, 70 (June 2003), pp. 129–141.

27. I. Altman and D. A. Taylor, *Social Penetration: The Development of Interpersonal Relationships*. New York: Holt, Rinehart & Winston, 1973.

28. Sandra Petronio, *Boundaries of Privacy: Dialectics of Disclosure*. Albany: State University of New York Press, 2003. See also Sandra Petronia, "Translational Research Endeavors and the Practices of Communication Privacy Management," *Journal of Applied Communication Research*, 35:3 (August 2007), pp. 218–222.

29. Mark L. Knapp and Anita L. Vangelisti, *Interpersonal Communication and Human Relationships*, 2nd ed. Boston: Allyn & Bacon, 1992, p. 33.

30. Alan Garner, *Conversationally Speaking*. New York: McGraw-Hill, 1981, p. 69.

31. Knapp and Vagelisti.

32. Michael Korda, "Small Talk," *Signature*, 1986, p. 78.

33. See Lawrence B. Rosenfield and Daniella Bordaray-Sciolino, "Self-Disclosure as a Communication Strategy during Relationship Termination," paper presented at the national meeting of the Speech Communication Association, Denver, CO, November 1985.

34. Rosenfield and Bordaray-Sciolino.

35. Steve Duck, "A Topography of Relationship Disagreement and Dissolution," in *Personal Relationships 4: Dissolving Personal Relationships*. New York: Academic Press, 1982.

36. Leslie Kaufman, "When the Ex Writes a Blog, the Dirtiest Laundry Is Aired," *New York Times*, April 18, 2008, pp. A1, A23; and Emily Gould, "Exposed," *New York Times Magazine*, May 25, 2008, pp. 32–40, 52, 56.

37. See S. W. Duck and J. T. Wood, "What Goes Up May Come Down: Sex and Gendered Patterns in Relational Dissolution," in M. A. Fine and J. H. Harvey, eds., *The Handbook of Divorce and Relationship Dissolution*. Mahwah, NJ: Erlbaum, pp. 169–187; and J. T. Wood, *Gendered Lives: Communication, Gender and Culture*, 9th ed., Belmont, CA: Wadsworth, 2011.

38. Lee Siegel, *Against the Machine: Being Human in the Age of the Electronic Mob*. New York: Random House, 2008.

39. Laura M. Holson, "Breaking Up in a Digital Fishbowl," *The New York Times*, January 7, 2010, pp. E1, E6.

40. See, for example, Harold S. Kushner, *When Bad Things Happen to Good People*. New York: Schocken Books, 1981.

41. Erica Goode, "Experts Offer Fresh Insights into the Mind of the Grieving Child," *New York Times*, March 28, 2000, pp. F7, F12.

42. N. Stevens, "Re-engaging: New Partnerships in Late-Life Widowhood," *Aging International*, 27:4 (Spring 2003), pp. 27–43.

43. J. W. Thibaut and H. H. Kelly, *The Social Psychology of Groups*. New York: Wiley, 1959.

44. See Richard West and Lynn H. Turner, *Introducing Communication Theory: Analysis and Application*. Mountain View, CA: Mayfield, 2000, pp. 180–190.

45. L. A. Baxter and B. M. Montgomery, *Relating Dialogues and Dialectics*. New York: Guilford, 1996; and L. A. Baxter, "Dialectical Contradictions in Relationship Development," *Journal of Social and Personal Relationships*, 7 (1990), pp. 69–88.

46. See also Sandra Petronio, ed., *Balancing the Secrets of Private Disclosures*. Mahwah, NJ: Erlbaum, 1999.

47. C. A. VanLear, "Testing a Cyclical Model of Communicative Openness in Relationship Development," *Communication Monographs*, 58 (1991), pp. 337–361.

48. J. T. Wood, L. Dendy, E. Dordek, M. Germany, and S. Varallo, "Dialectic of Difference: A Thematic Analysis of Intimates' Meanings for Differences," in K. Carter and M. Presnell, eds., *Interpretive Approaches to Interpersonal Communication*. New York: State University of New York Press, 1994, pp. 115–136.

49. See, for example, L. Anolli, M. Balconi, and Rita Ciceri, "Deceptive Miscommunication Theory (DeMiT): A New Model for the Analysis of Deceptive Communication," in A. Luigi, R. Ciceri et al., eds., *Say Not to Say: New Perspectives on Miscommunication. Studies in New Technologies and Practices in Communication*. Amsterdam, Netherlands Antilles: IOS Press, pp. 73–100.

50. See Mark L. Knapp, *Lying and Deception in Human Interaction*, Boston: Penguin Academics, 2008.

51. Cal Thomas and Bob Beckel, "Lies, Lies, Lies," *USA Today*, June 3, 2010, p. 11A.

52. Maureen Dowd, "Lies as Wishes," *The New York Times*, May 23, 2010, p. WK 9.

53. C. Camden, M. T. Motley, and A. Wilson, "White Lies in Interpersonal Communication: A Taxonomy and Preliminary Investigation of Social Motivations," *Western Journal of Speech Communication*, 48 (1984), pp. 309–325.

54. See, for example, J. B. Bavelas, A. Black, N. Chovil, and J. Mullett, *Equivocal Communication*. Newbury Park, CA: Sage, 1990, p. 171.

55. Benedict Carey, "I'm Not Lying, I'm Telling a Future Truth. Really," *New York Times*, May 6, 2008, p. F5.

56. Sissela Bok, *Lying*. New York: Pantheon, 1978. See also Sissela Bok, *Secrets*. New York: Random House, 1989.

57. J. K. Rempel and J. G. Holmes, "How Do I Trust Thee?" *Psychology Today*, February 1986.

58. A. L. Vangelisti and L. P. Crumley, "Reactions to Messages That Hurt: The Influence of Relational Contexts," *Communication Monographs*, 65 (1998), pp. 173–196.

59. Natalie Angier, "Laughs: Rhythmic Bursts of Social Glue," *New York Times*, February 27, 1996, pp. C-1, C-5.

60. Angier. See also Regina Barreca, *They Used to Call Me Snow White . . . but I Drifted: Women's Strategic Use of Humor*. New York: Penguin Books, 1991.

61. Seth Borenstein, "Why Have Sex?" *The Record*, August 1, 2007, p. A8.

62. L. A. Rudman and J. E. Phelan, "The Interpersonal Power of Feminism: Is Feminism Good for Romantic Relationships?" *Sex Roles*, 2007.

63. Heiman.

64. Heiman.

65. Sharon Jayson, "Women Say Sorry More Because of a Sense of 'I'm Wrong,'" *USA Today*, September 29, 2010, p. 5D.

66. ScienceDaily.com, "Women More Perceptive Than Men in Describing Relationships," www.sciencedaily.com/releases/2008/02/080213111055.htm.

67. N. M. Punyanunt-Carter, "An Analysis of College Students' Self-Disclosure Behavior on the Internet," *College Student Journal*, 40 (2006), pp. 329–331.

68. Liz Funk, "Women on Facebook Think Provocative Is Empowering," *USA Today*, September 19, 2007, p. 11A.

69. Stephanie Rosenbloom, "Sorry, Boys, This Is Our Domain," *New York Times*, February 21, 2008, pp. G1, G8.

70. J. D. Ragsdale, "Gender, Satisfaction Level, and the Use of Relational Maintenance Strategies in Marriage," *Communication Monographs*, 63 (1996), pp. 354–369.

71. A. M. Sherman, H. E. Lansford, and B. L. Volling, "Sibling Relationships and Best Friendships in Young Adulthood: Warmth, Conflict, and Well-Being," *Personal Relationships*, 13 (2006), pp. 151–165.

72. Julia T. Wood and C. Inmam, "In a Different Mode: Recognizing Male Modes of Closeness," *Journal of Applied Communication Research*, August 1993.

73. Julia T. Wood, *Gendered Lives*, 3rd ed. Belmont, CA: Wadsworth, 1999, p. 201.

74. Deborah Tannen, *The Argument Culture: Moving from Debate to Dialogue*. New York: Random House, 1998, pp. 186–187.

75. See M. Hecht, S. Ribeau, and J. Alberts, "An Afro-American Perspective on Interethnic Communication," *Communication Monographs*, 56 (1989), pp. 385–410; and M. Hecht, S. Ribeau, and M. Sedano, "A Mexican-American Perspective on Interethnic Communication," *International Journal of Intercultural Relations*, 14 (1990), pp. 31–55.

76. H. C. Triandis, *Culture and Social Behavior*. New York: McGraw-Hill, 1994, p. 30.

77. M. J. Collier, "Communication Competence Problematics in Ethnic Friendships," *Communication Monographs*, 63 (1996), pp. 314–336.

78. See Ann S. Wildemuth, "Love on the Line: Participants' Descriptions of Computer Mediated Close Relationships," *Qualitative Research Reports in Communication*, 2 (2001), pp. 89–95.

79. Sharon Jayson, "Internet Changing the Game of Love," *USA Today*, February 11, 2010, pp. 8A, 8B.

80. J. McQuillen, "The Influence of Technology on the Initiation of Interpersonal Relationships," *Education*, 1123 (2003), pp. 616–624.

81. Sherry Turkle, *Life on the Screen: Identity in the Age of the Internet*. New York: Simon & Schuster, 1995; and Katie Hafner, "At Heart of a Cyberstudy, the Human Essence," *New York Times*, June 18, 1998, p. G-9.

82. Scott McCartney, "Society's Subcultures Meet by Modem," *Wall Street Journal*, December 8, 1994, p. B1.

83. "Living a Second Life Online," *Newsweek*, July 28, 2008, p. 10.

84. Marie Puente, "Blogger Gives Dark Secrets the First-Class Treatment," *USA Today*, March 15, 2006, pp. 1A, 6A.

85. Sharon Jayson, "Thanks for Oversharing?" *USA Today*, September 14, 2010, pp. 1D, 2D.

86. See John Locke, *Eavesdropping: An Intimate History*, Claude Fischer, *Made in America: A Social History of American Culture and Character*, and W. Keith Campbell, *The Narcissism Epidemic*.

87. Austin Considine, "Defriended, Not De-Emoted," *The New York Times*, September 5, 2010, p. ST6.

88. Alex Mindlin, "Girl Power Is in Full Force Online," *New York Times*, December 24, 2007, p. C3.

89. Charles McGrath, "The Pleasures of the Text," *New York Times Magazine*, January 22, 2006, pp. 15, 19.

90. Joanne Kaufman, "Romancing the Phone," *The Wall Street Journal*, June 11, 2010, p. W8.

91. For a discussion of how to enhance the teaching of relationships in a basic course, see Diane Tkinson Gorcyca, "Enhancing the Instruction of Relationship Development in the Basic Communication Course," paper presented at the annual meeting of the Speech Communication Association, Miami Beach, FL, November 18–21, 1993.

Chapter 8

1. For example, Ellen Bercheid and Elaine Hatfield Walster, *Interpersonal Attraction*, 2nd ed. Reading, MA: Addison-Wesley, 1978.

2. Emily Prager, "The Science of Beauty," *New York Times*, April 17, 1994.

3. Berscheid and Walster.

4. Eliot Aronson, *The Social Animal*, 3rd ed. San Francisco: Freeman, 1980, p. 239.

5. See Katherine C. Maguire, "Will It Ever End? A (Re) Examination of Uncertainty in College Student Long-Distance Dating Relationships," *Communication Quarterly*, November 2007, pp. 415–432; and Charles Berger, "Uncertainty and Information Exchange in Developing Relationships," in Steve Duck, ed., *Handbook of Personal Relationships*. New York: Wiley, 1988, p. 244.

6. C. R. Berger and R. J. Calabrese, "Some Explorations in Initial Interactions and Beyond: Toward a Developmental Theory of Interpersonal Communication," *Human Communication Research*, 1 (1975), pp. 98–112.

7. See, for example, W. Gudykunst, "Uncertainty and Anxiety," in Y. Y. Kim and W. Gudykunst, eds., *Theories in Intercultural Communication*. Newbury Park, CA: Sage, 1988, pp. 123–156.

8. M. Sunnafrank, "A Communication-Based Perspective on Attitude Similarity and Interpersonal Attraction in Early Acquaintance," *Communication Monographs*, 51 (1984), pp. 372–380.

9. Keith E. Davis, "Near and Dear: Friendship and Love Compared," *Psychology Today*, February 1985, pp. 22–30.

10. Keith J. Winstein, "Ability to Quit Smoking Is Affected by Friendships," *Wall Street Journal*, May 22, 2008, p. D6.

11. See W. Samter, "Friendship Interaction Skills across the Lifespan," in J. O. Freene and B. R. Burleson, eds., *Handbook of Communication and Social Interaction Skills*. Mahwah, NJ: Erlbaum, 2003; Daniel Goleman, "'Friends for Life': An Emerging Biology of Emotional Healing," *New York Times*, October 10, 2006; and Alan K. Goodby and Scott A. Myers, "Relational Maintenance Behaviors of Friends with Benefits: Investigating Equity and Relational Characteristics," *Human Communication*, 11:1 (Spring 2008), pp. 71–85.

12. W. K. Rawlins, "Friendship as a Communicative Achievement: A Theory and an Interpretive Analysis of Verbal Reports," doctoral dissertation, Temple University, Philadelphia, 1981.

13. Sharon Jayson, "Is Dating Dead?" *USA Today*, March 31, 2011, pp. 1A, 2A.

14. Robert J. Sternberg, "A Triangular Theory of Love," *Psychological Review*, 93 (1986), pp. 119–135; and Robert L. Sternberg, *The Triangle of Love: Intimacy, Passion, Commitment*. New York: Basic Books, 1988.

15. Alice Park, "Love Hurts," *Time*, April 11, 2011; Nanci Hellmich, "Heartbreak Hurts Physically, Too," *USA Today*, p. 1A; and www.cnn.com/s011/HEALTH/03/28/burn .heartbreak.same.to.brain/index.html?hpt=Sbin

16. See Sally A. Lloyd and Beth C. Emery, *The Dark Side of Courtship: Physical and Sexual Aggression*. Thousand Oaks, CA: Sage, 2000; and J. D. Cunningham and J. K. Antill,

"Current Trends in Nonmarital Cohabitation: The Great POSSLQ Hunt Continues," in Julia Wood and Steve W. Duck, eds., *Understanding Relationship Processes, 6: Off the Beaten Track: Understudied Relationships*. Thousand Oaks, CA: Sage, 1995, pp. 148–172.

17. D. Holmberg, "So Far So Good: Scripts for Romantic Relationship Development as Predictors of Relational Well-Being," *Journal of Social and Personal Relationships*, 19:6 (December 2002), pp. 777–796.

18. Julia T. Wood, *Gendered Lives*, 3rd ed. Belmont, CA: Wadsworth, 1999, p. 340.

19. Virginia Satir, *The New Peoplemaking*. Mountain View, CA: Science and Behavior Books, 1988, p. 79; and A. Vangelisti, K. C. Maguire, A. Alexander, and G. Clark, "Hurtful Family Environments: Links with Individual and Relationship and Perceptual Variables," *Communication Monographs*, 74:3 (September 2007), pp. 357–385.

20. See the 2000 U.S. Census Report.

21. Sharon Jayson and Anthony DeBarros, "Young Adults Delaying Marriage," *USA Today*, September 12, 2007, p. 6D.

22. Sharon Jayson, "Families Feel Effect of Financial Stress for Generations," *USA Today*, April 11, 2011, p. 6D.

23. D. Gibbons and P. M. Olk, "The Individual and Structural Origins of Friendship and Social Position among Professionals," *Journal of Personality and Social Psychology*, 84:2 (February 2003), pp. 340–352; and "The Power of Nice," *Workforce*, 82:1 (January 2003), pp. 22–24.

24. See, for example, Susan A. Wheelan, *Creating Effective Teams: A Guide for Members and Leaders*. Thousand Oaks, CA: Sage, 1999; and James R. Barker, *The Discipline of Teamwork: Participation and Concertive Control*. Thousand Oaks, CA: Sage, 1999.

25. Daniel Goleman, *Emotional Intelligence*. New York: Bantam, 1995, p. 34. See also *Social Intelligence: The New Science of Human Relationships*. New York: Bantam, 2006.

26. Alan V. Horwitz, Jerome C. Wakefield, and Robert L. Spitzer, *The Loss of Sadness: How Psychiatry Transformed Normal Sorrow into Depressive Disorder*. Boston: Oxford University Press, 2007.

27. Eric G. Wilson, *Against Happiness*. New York: Farrar, Straus & Giroux, 2008.

28. John Cloud, "When Sadness Is a Good Thing," *Time*, August 27, 2007, p. 56.

29. Carroll E. Izard, *Human Emotions*. New York: Plenum, 1977, p. 10.

30. Izard.

31. Earl Ubell, "The Deadly Emotions," *Parade*, February 11, 1990, pp. 3–5; and Jane E. Brody, "Controlling Anger Is Good Medicine for the Heart," *New York Times*, November 20, 1996, p. C15.

32. See *The Record*, June 20, 2004, p. B1; and Thomas Sancton, "Oedipus, Schmoedipus," *Time*, December 9, 1996, p. C15.

33. E. Nagourney, "Blow a Gasket, for Your Heart," *New York Times*, February 11, 2003, p. F6.

34. Ann Kreamer, "Go Ahead Cry at Work," *Time*, April 4, 2011, pp. 52–55.

35. See Daniel Goleman, "A Feel-Good Theory: A Smile Affects Mood," *New York Times*, July 18, 1989, pp. C1, C9.

36. Ellen O' Brien, "Moods Are as Contagious as the Office Cold," *The Record*, November 15, 1993, p. B3.

37. John Powell, *Why am I Afraid to Tell You Who I Am?* Niles, IL: Argus, 1969. For a more recent discussion, see Katherine J. Miller and Joy Koesten, "Financial Feeling: An Investigation of Emotion and Communication in the Workplace," *Journal of Applied Communication Research*, 36:1 (February 2008), pp. 8–32.

38. Sandra Petronio, ed., *Balancing the Secrets of Private Disclosures*. Mahwah, NJ: Erlbaum, 1999.

39. Theodore Isaac Rubin, *The Angry Book*. New York: Macmillan, 1970; and *Emotional Common Sense*. New York: Harper & Row, 1986.

40. Sharon Jayson, "Emotions Show Our True Colors," *USA Today*, April 4, 2011, p. 4D.

41. Rubin, *The Angry Book*.

42. Marilyn Elias, "The Traits of Wrath in Men and Women," *USA Today*, August 11, 1994, p. 1D.

43. Elias, p. 2D.

44. See Stephanie A. Shields, *Speaking from the Heart: Gender and the Social Meaning of Emotion*. New York: Cambridge University Press, 2002; and Stephanie Armour, "Tears at Work Not Recommended," *USA Today*, January 18, 2008, p. 9B.

45. See Anne Kreamer, *It's Always Personal*. New York: Random House, 2011.

46. Kay Deaux, *The Behavior of Women and Men*. Belmont, CA: Brooks/Cole, 1976.

47. See, for example, Michael Ryan, "Go Ahead—Cry!" *Parade*, January 5, 1997, p. 22.

48. Paul Ekman and Wallace Friesen, *Unmasking the Face*. Los Angeles: Consulting Psychology, 1984. For an intercultural perspective, see Stella Ting-Toomey, *The Challenge of Facework*. Albany: State University of New York Press, 1994.

49. Jerry Gillies, *Friendship: The Power and Potential of the Company You Keep*. New York: Coward-McCann, 1976.

50. Sidney Jourard, *The Transparent Self*. New York: Van Nostrand, 1971; and Sidney Jourard and Ted Landsman, *Health Personality*. New York: Macmillan, 1980.

51. Elizabeth Bernstein, "Friendly Fights: A Smarter Way to Say 'I'm Angry,'" *The Wall Street Journal*, April 19, 2011, pp. D1, D4.

52. Elizabeth Bernstein, "Fighting Happily Ever After," *The Wall Street Journal*, July 27, 2010, pp. D1, D4.

53. Alan C. Filley, *Interpersonal Conflict Resolution*. Glenview, IL: Scott, Foresman, 1975.

54. See, for example, Denise H. Cloven and Michael E. Roloff, "The Chilling Effect of Aggressive Potential on the Expression of Complaints in Intimate Relationships," *Communication Monographs*, 60:3 (September 1993), pp. 199–219.

55. David Johnson, *Reaching Out: Interpersonal Effectiveness and Self-Actualization*. Englewood Cliffs, NJ: Prentice-Hall, 1972.

56. Susan Chira, "Study Finds Benefits in Emotional Control," *New York Times*, May 26, 1994.

57. See Myra Warren Isenhart and Michael L. Spangle, *Collaborative Approaches to Resolving Conflict*. Thousand Oaks, CA: Sage, 2000.

58. J. M. Gottman, *The Marriage Clinic: A Scientifically Based Marital Therapy*. New York: Norton, 1999.

59. Cited in Mireya Navarro, "We're Friends, Right?" *New York Times*, February 10, 2008, pp. ST 1–2.

60. J. M. Gottman and R. W. Levinson, "Observing Gay and Lesbian Heterosexual Couples' Relationships: Mathematical Modeling of Conflict Interaction," *Journal of Homosexuality*, 45:1 (2003), pp. 711–720.

61. Ibid.

62. Lori Oliwenstein, "Marry Me," *Time*, January 28, 2008, pp. 73–76.

63. Also see J. W. Pennebaker, B. Rime, and V. E. Blankenship, "Stereotypes of Emotional Expressiveness of Northerners and Southerners: A Cross-Cultural Test of Montesquieu's Hypotheses," *Journal of Personality and Social Psychology*, 70 (1996), pp. 372–380.

64. See F. E. Jandt, *Intercultural Communication: An Introduction*, 3rd ed. Thousand Oaks, CA: Sage, 2001; and L. A. Samovar, R. E. Porter, and E. R. McDaniel, *Communication between Cultures*, 4th ed. Belmont, CA: Thomson Wadsworth, 2007.

65. For additional information, see J. D. Pearson, *Gender and Communication*, 2nd ed. Dubuque, IA: Brown, 1991, pp. 183–184; and Stella Ting-Toomey, "Managing Intercultural Conflict Effectively," in Larry A. Samovar and Richard E. Porter, eds., *Intercultural Communication: A Reader*, 7th ed. Belmont, CA: Wadsworth, 1994, pp. 360–372.

66. Philip G. Zimbardo and Shirley L. Radl, *The Shyness Workbook*. New York: A&W, Visual Library, 1979.

67. Ibid.

68. Lynn Z. Bloom, Karen Coburn, and Joan Pearlman, *The New Assertive Woman*. New York: Dell, 1975.

69. Arthur J. Lange and Patricia Jakubowski, *Responsible Assertive Behavior*. Champaign, IL: Research Press, 1976.

70. Sherwin B. Cotler and Julio J. Guerra, *Assertive Training*. Champaign, IL: Research Press, 1976, pp. 15–22.

71. For exercises related to the topics covered, see Danny Saunders, "Exercises in Communicating," *Simulation/Games for Learning*, 21:2 (June 1991), pp. 186–200.

72. Alan Wright, "Friending, Ancient or Otherwise," *New York Times*, December 2, 2007, p. WK 4.

73. Craig Wilson, "Suddenly, You've Got a Friend—Tons of Them," *USA Today*, February 6, 2008, p. 1D.

74. Steven Levy, "How Many Friends Is Too Many?" *Newsweek*, May 26, 2008, p. 15.

75. Robin Dunbar, *How Many Friends Does One Person Need? Dunbar's Number and Other Evolutionary Quirks*. Cambridge, MA: Harvard University Press, 2010.

76. Lee Siegel, *Against the Machine: Being Human in the Age of the Electronic Mob*. New York: Spiegel & Grau, 2008.

77. S. B. Barnes, *Computer-Mediated Communication: Human-to-Human Communication across the Internet*. Boston: Allyn & Bacon, 2003.

78. See Nicholas Negroponte, *Being Digital*. New York: Vintage Books, 1995.

79. Lisa Takeuchi Cullen and Coco Masters, "We Just Clicked," *Time*, January 28, 2008, pp. 84, 88–89.

80. Kimberly C. Moore, "Mother's Tweet as Son, 2, Died Stirs Debate," *USA Today*, p. 3A.

81. See Noam Cohen, "The Global Sympathetic Audience," *New York Times*, November 4, 2007, pp. 2ST, 8ST.

82. Stephanie Armour, "Boss: It's in the E-Mail," *Wall Street Journal*, April 10, 1999, p. B3.

Chapter 9

1. D. Johnson and F. Johnson, *Joining Together: Group Theory and Group Skills*, 9th ed. Boston: Allyn & Bacon, 2006.

2. See www.creativity-engineering.com/client.html for a list of current companies providing training in team building.

3. Henry Jenkins, "From YouTube to YouNiversity," *The Chronicle of Higher Education*, February 16, 2007, B10; and Association of American Colleges and Universities, *College Learning for the New Global Age*, Washington D.C.: Association of American Colleges and Universities, 2007.

4. See, for example, G. Lumsden and D. Lumsden, *Communicating in Groups and Teams*, 4th ed. Belmont, CA: Wadsworth, 2004; and T. E. Harris and John C. Sherblom, *Small Group and Team Communication*. New York: Addison Wesley, 2007.

5. Natalie Angier, "Why We're So Nice: We're Wired to Cooperate," *New York Times*, July 23, 2002, pp. F1, F8.

6. See, for example, H. Lancaster, "The Team Spirit Can Lead Your Career to New Victories," *Wall Street Journal*,

January 14, 1996, p. B1; and "Work Week," *Wall Street Journal*, November 28, 1995, p. A1.

7. See www.organizedchange.com/selfdir.htm (2008); Daniel S. Iacofano, *Meeting of the Minds*. New York: MIG Communication, 2001; M. A. Verspeij, "When You Put the Team in Charge," *Industry Week*, December 1990, pp. 30–32; A. Versteeg, "Self-Directed Work Teams Yield Long-Term Benefits," *Journal of Business Strategy*, November/December 1990, pp. 9–12; and R. S. Wellins, C. W. Byham, and J. M. Wilson, *Empowered Teams: Creating Self-Directed Workgroups That Improve Quality, Productivity, and Participation*. San Francisco: Jossey-Bass, 1991.

8. J. Hackman, "The Design of Work Teams," in J. Lorsch, ed. *Handbook of Organizational Behavior*. Englewood Cliffs, NJ: Prentice-Hall, 1987, pp. 315–342.

9. Charles Redding, *Communication within the Organization*. New York: Industrial Communication Council, 1972.

10. Douglas McGregor, *The Human Side of Enterprise*. New York: McGraw-Hill, 1960.

11. B. Tuchman, "Developmental Sequence in Small Groups," *Psychological Bulletin*, 63 (1965), pp. 384–399; and S. A. Wheelen and J. M. Hockberger, "Validation Studies of the Group Development Questionnaire," *Small Group Research*, 27:1 (1996), pp. 143–170.

12. See, for example, J. Keyton, "Group Termination: Completing the Study of Group Development," *Small Group Research*, 24 (1993), pp. 84–100.

13. See, for example, Marshall Scott Poole, "Do We Have Any Theories of Group Communication?" *Communication Studies*, 41:3 (1990), p. 237.

14. Dave Logan, John King, and Hale Fischer-Wright, *Tribal Leadership: Leveraging Natural Groups to Build a Thriving Organization*. New York: Collins, 2008.

15. Kenneth Benne and Paul Sheats, "Functional Roles of Group Members," *Journal of Social Issues*, 4 (1948), pp. 41–49.

16. Max H. Bazeerman and Ann E. Tenbrunsel, "Stumbling into Bad Behavior," *The New York Times*, April 21, 2011, p. A27.

17. For a discussion of supportive leadership, see Peter G. Northouse, *Leadership: Theory and Practice*, 2nd ed. Thousand Oaks, CA: Sage, 2001.

18. Linden L. Nelson and Spencer Kagen, "Competition: The Star Spangled Scramble," *Psychology Today*, September 1972, pp. 53–56, 90–91.

19. Morton Deutsch, "A Theory of Cooperation and Competition," *Human Relations*, 2 (1949), pp. 129–152.

20. Jack R. Gibb, "Defensive Communication," *Journal of Communication*, 2 (1961), pp. 141–148.

21. Gibb.

22. See Y. Otsubo, A. Masuchi, and D. Nakanishi, "Majority Influence Process in Group Judgment: Test of the Social Judgment Scheme Model in a Group Polarization Context," *Group Process and Intergroup Relations*, 5:3 (July 2002), pp. 249–262; and D. G. Meyers, *Social Psychology*, 7th ed. New York: McGraw-Hill, 2002, pp. 302–303.

23. John Dewey, *How We Think*. Boston: Heath, 1910.

24. Jay Cocks, "Let's Get Crazy!" *Time*, June 11, 1990, p. 40.

25. Betty Edwards, *Drawing on the Right Side of the Brain*. New York: St. Martin's, 1979.

26. See James Webb Young, *A Technique for Producing Ideas*. New York: McGraw-Hill, 2003; and Luke Johnson, "How to Find Ideas for Challenging Times," *Financial Times*, June 18, 2008, p. 10.

27. Alex Osborn, *Applied Imagination*. New York: Scribner's, 1957.

28. Kelly K. Spors, "Productive Brainstorms Take the Right Mix of Elements," *Wall Street Journal*, July 24, 2008, p. B5.

29. Sidney Parnes, *A Source Book for Creative Thinking*. New York: Scribner's, 1962.

30. Leslie Dorman and Peter Edidin, "Original Spin," *Psychology Today*, July 8, 1989, p. 46.

31. Rosabeth Moss Kanter, "How to Be an Entrepreneur without Leaving Your Company," *Working Woman*, November 1988, p. 44. See also Rosabeth Moss Kanter, *When Giants Learn to Dance*. New York: Touchstone, 1990.

32. G. Hofstede, *Culture and Organizations: Software of the Mind*. New York: McGraw-Hill, 1997.

33. Paul B. Brown, "A Defense of the Boss' Pay," April 12, 2008, p. C5.

34. Francesco Guerrera, "Women Crack Glass Ceiling from Above," *Financial Times*, July 23, 2008, p. 3.

35. See, for example, L. P. Stewart, P. J. Cooper, A. D. Stewart, and S. H. Friendley, *Communication and Gender*, 4th ed. Boston: Allyn & Bacon, 2003, p. 44–50.

36. S. Helgesen, *The Female Advantage: Women's Use of Leadership*. New York: Doubleday, 1990.

37. Julia T. Wood, *Gendered Lives*, 7th ed. Belmont, CA: Wadsworth, 2006; and Iris Aaltio and Pila Lapisto, "Discursive Practice in Ways Male and Female Managers Talk about Careers," www.mngtworkato/ac/nz.ejrot.conference2003/proceeding/gender/Aaltio.pdf.

38. Shirley S. Wang, "Why So Many People Can't Make Decisions," *The Wall Street Journal*, September 28, 2010, pp. D1, D2.

39. See, for example, S. B. Paletz, K. Peng, M. Erez, and C. Maslach, "Ethnic Composition and Its Differential Impact on Group Processes in Diverse Teams," *Small Group Research*, 35 (2004), pp. 128–157.

40. J. T. Materson, *Communication in Small Groups: Principles and Practices*, 8th ed., Boston: Allyn & Bacon, 2006.

41. Delores Cathcart and Robert Cathcart, "The Group: A Japanese Context," in Larry A. Samovar and Richard E. Porters, eds., *Intercultural Communication: A Reader*, 8th ed. Belmont CA: Wadsworth, 1997, pp. 329–339.

42. Harry C. Triandis, Richard Brislin, and C. Harry Hul, "Cross-Cultural Training across the Individualism-Collectivism Divide," *International Journal of Intercultural Relations*, 12 (1988), pp. 269–289.

43. Cathcart and Cathcart.

44. Michiyo Nakamoto, "Modernisers Span a Cultural Divide," *Financial Times*, May 22, 2008, p. 14.

45. Erin White, "Making the Generation Gap Work for You," *The Record*, July 27, 2008, pp. J1–J2.

46. Stefan Stern, "Y's and Wherefores of a Multi-Generational Workplace," *Financial Times*, April 15, 2008, p. 12.

47. Laurie J. Flynn, "MySpace Mind-Set Finally Shows Up at the Office," *New York Times*, April 9, 2008, p. 7.

48. Clive Thompson, "Close Encounters," *Wired*, August 2008.

49. Brad Stone, "At Social Site, Only the Businesslike Need Apply," *New York Times*, June 18, 2008, pp. C1, C2.

50. Adam Bryant, "Views from the Top," *The Wall Street Journal*, April 21, 2011, p. A11.

51. Mark Tutton, "Going to the Virtual Office in Second Life," CNN.com, accessed November 9, 2009.

52. Laura Rich, "Tapping the Wisdom of the Crowd," *The New York Times*, August 5, 2010, p. B8.

53. David Gelles, "The Personal at Work Can Be a Disruptive Mix," *The Financial Times*, April 20, 2011, p. 2.

54. Eileen Zimmerman, "Staying Professional in Virtual Meetings," *The New York Times*, September 26, 2010, p. BU9.

55. Caroline Winter, "Is the Vertical Pronoun Really Such a Capital Idea?" *New York Times Magazine*, August 3, 2008.

56. Joanne S. Lublin, "Video Comes to Board Meetings," *The Wall Street Journal*, April 25, 2011, p. B6.

57. Bobby R. Patton and Kim Griffin, *Decision Making: Group Interaction*. New York: Harper & Row, 1978.

Chapter 10

1. Jason Zweig, "How Group Decisions End Up Wrong-Footed," *The Wall Street Journal*, April 25, 2009, p. B1.

2. For creative ideas on how to use film to better understand leadership, see Roy V. Leeper, "Mutiny on the Bounty: A Case Study for Leadership Courses," paper presented at the joint meeting of the Southern States Communication Association, Lexington, KY, April 14–18, 1993; and Michael Z. Hackman and Craig E. Johnson, *Leadership: A Communication Perspective*, 4th ed., Long Grove, IL: 2004.

3. Paul B. Brown, "What Sets Leaders Apart from the Pack?" *New York Times*, February 5, 2006, p. BU8.

4. For a historical perspective and a summary and critique of 114 studies on small groups, focusing on leadership, discussion, and pedagogy, see John F. Cragan and David W. Wright, "Small Group Communication Research of the 1970s: A Synthesis and Critique," *Central States Speech Journal*, 31 (1980), pp. 197–213;

and Michael S. Frank, "The Essence of Leadership," *Public Personnel Management*, 22:3 (Fall 1993), pp. 381–389.

5. For a discussion on how to develop leadership skills, see Stephen S. Kaagan, *Leadership Games*. Thousand Oaks, CA: Sage, 1999; and Lois B. Harle and Charlotte S. Waisman, *The Leadership Training Activity Book*, New York: Amacom, 2004.

6. Craig L. Pearce, "Follow the Leaders," *Wall Street Journal*, July 7, 2008, pp. R8, R12.

7. Douglas McGregor, *The Human Side of Enterprise*. New York: McGraw-Hill, 1960.

8. Norman Augustine and Kenneth Adelman, *Shakespeare in Charge*. New York: Hyperion, 1999.

9. For a classic study on leadership style, see K. Lewin, R. Lippit, and R. K. White, "Patterns of Aggressive Behavior in Experimentally Created Social Climates," *Journal of Social Psychology*, 10 (1939), pp. 271–299.

10. For an early study on trait theory, see Frederick Thrasher, *The Gang: A Study of 1313 Gangs in Chicago*. Chicago: University of Chicago Press, 1927.

11. Marvin Shaw, *Group Dynamics: The Psychology of Small Group Behavior*, 3rd ed. New York: McGraw-Hill, 1981.

12. See Fred Fiedler, *A Theory of Leadership Effectiveness*. New York: McGraw-Hill, 1967.

13. Keith Davis, *Human Relations at Work*. New York: McGraw-Hill, 1967.

14. See, for example, F. E. Fiedler, "Personality and Situational Determinants of Leadership Effectiveness," in D. Cartwright and A. Zander, eds., *Group Dynamics: Research and Theory*, 3rd ed. New York: Harper & Row, 1968, pp. 389–398.

15. P. Hersey and K. Blanchard, *Management Organizational Behavior: Utilizing Human Resources*. Englewood Cliffs, NJ: Prentice Hall, 1988.

16. See Stephen R. Covey, *The 7 Habits of Highly Effective People*. New York: Simon & Schuster, 1989.

17. Phred Dvorak and Jaclyne Badal, "Neuroscientists Are Finding That Business Leaders Really May Think Differently," *The Wall Street Journal*, September 20, 2007, pp. B1, B6.

18. See, for example, M. Z. Hackman and C. E. Johnson, *Leadership: A Communication Perspective*, 4th ed. Long Grove, IL: Waveland, 2004.

19. For an interesting discussion of how conformity pressures can hamper decision making, see Russel F. Proctor, "Do the Ends Justify the Means? Thinking Critically about 'Twelve Angry Men'," paper presented at the annual meeting of the Central States Communication Association, Chicago, April 11–14, 1991.

20. M. T. Claes, "Women, Men, and Management Styles," in P. J. Dubeck and D. Cunn, eds., *Workplace/Women's Place: An Anthology*, 2nd ed. Los Angeles: Roxbury, 2002, pp. 121–125; and A. H. Eagly and S. J. Karau, "Role

Congruity Theory of Prejudice Toward Female Leaders," *Psychological Review*, 109:3 (2002), pp. 573–598.

21. J. K. Fletcher, "The Paradox of Post Heroic Leadership: Gender Matters" (Working Paper No. 17). Boston: Center for Gender in Organization, Simmons Graduate School of Management, 2003.

22. R. I. Kabacoff, "Gender Difference in Organizational Leadership: A Large Sample Study," paper presented at the meeting of the American Psychological Association, San Francisco, CA, 1998.

23. See, for example, T. D. Daniels, B. K. Spiker, and M. J. Papa, *Perspectives on Organizational Communication*, 4th ed. New York: McGraw-Hill, 1997.

24. Jennie Yabroff, "Betas Rule," *Newsweek*, June 4, 2007, pp. 64–65.

25. Deborah Tannen, *The Argument Culture: Moving from Debate to Dialogue*. New York: Random House, 1998, pp. 170, 194.

26. J. F. Benenson, S. A. Ford, and N. H. Apostoleris, "Girls' Assertiveness in the Presence of Boys," *Small Group Research*, 29 (1998), pp. 198–211.

27. See, for example, Daniel Canary, William R. Cupach, and Susan J. Messman, *Relational Conflict*. Thousand Oaks, CA: Sage, 1995.

28. Majaana Lindeman, Tuija Harakka, and Liisa Keltikangas-Jarvinen, "Age and Gender Differences in Adolescents' Reactions to Conflict Situations: Aggression, Prosociality, and Withdrawal," *Journal of Youth and Adolescence*, 26 (1997), pp. 339–351.

29. Canary, Cupach, and Messman.

30. Anthony De Palma, "It Takes More Than a Visa to Do Business in Mexico," *New York Times*, June 26, 1994.

31. Lea P. Stewart, "Japanese and American Management: Participative Decision Making," in Larry A. Samovar and Richard E. Porter, eds., *Intercultural Communication: A Reader*. Belmont, CA: Wadsworth, 1985, pp. 186–189.

32. Delores Cathcart and Robert Cathcart, "Japanese Social Experience and Concept of Groups," in Samovar and Porter, pp. 293–304.

33. John Gapper, "Corporate Culture Shock Is a Big Deal," *Financial Times*, July 31, 2008, p. 9; and Geoffrey A. Fowler, "In China's Offices, Foreign Colleagues Might Get an Earful," *Wall Street Journal*, February 13, 2007, p. B1.

34. Paul B. Brown, "Boardroom Types," *New York Times*, May 3, 2008, p. C5.

35. Phred Dvorak, "Firms Push New Methods to Promote Diversity," *Wall Street Journal*, December 18, 2006, p. B3.

36. Marie Brennan, "Mismanagement and Quality Circles: How Middle Managers Influence Direct Participation," *Employer Relations*, 13 (1991), pp. 22–32.

37. Pearce, 2008.

38. Pearce, 2008.

39. Rebecca Knight, "When Three Generations Can Work Better Than One," *The Financial Times*, September 15, 2009, p. 10.

40. Deborah Tannen, *Talking from 9 to 5*. New York: Morrow, 1994.

41. Adapted from Aesop's Fables.

42. See, for example, Larry K. Leslie, *Mass Communication Ethics: Decision Making in Post Modern Culture*. Boston: Houghton Mifflin, 2000, pp. 263–266; Barbara Ehrenreich, "In Defense of Talk Shows," *Time*, December 4, 1995, p. 92; and Howard Kurtz, *Hot Air*. New York: Basic Books, 1997.

43. For a description of how to promote a win-win approach to conflict, see Deborah Weider-Hatfield, "A Unit in Conflict Management Communication Skills," *Communication Education*, 30 (1981), pp. 265–273; Joyce L. Hocker and William W. Wilmot, *Interpersonal Conflict*, 3rd ed. Dubuque, IA: Brown, 1991; and Herb Cohen, *Negotiate This!* New York: Warner Business Books, 2003.

44. Robert Blake and Jane Mouton, "The Fifth Achievement," *Journal of Applied Behavioral Science*, 6 (1970), pp. 413–426.

45. Alan Filley, *Interpersonal Conflict Resolution*. Glenview, IL: Scott, Foresman, 1975.

46. John Schwartz and Matthew L. Wald, "NASA's Curse?" *New York Times*, March 9, 2003, p. WK5.

47. Morton Deutsch, "Conflicts: Productive and Destructive," *Journal of Social Issues*, 25 (1969), pp. 7–43; H. Whitteman, "Group Member Satisfaction: A Conflict-Related Account," *Small Group Research*, 22 (1992), pp. 24–58; and R. C. Pace, "Personalized and Depersonalized Conflict in Small Group Discussion: An Examination of Differentiation," *Small Group Research*, 21 (1991), pp. 79–96.

48. Jim Collins, *How the Mighty Fall*. New York: Random House, 2010.

49. Irving Janis, *Victims of Groupthink: A Psychological Study of Foreign Policy Decisions and Fiascos*. Boston: Houghton Mifflin, 1972.

50. Benedict Carey, "How to Turn a Herd on Wall St." *New York Times*, April 6, 2008, pp. WK1, WK4.

51. See Ori Brafman and Rom Brafman, *Sway: The Irresistible Pull of Irrational Behavior*. New York: Doubleday, 2008; and Robert Thaler and Cass Sunstein, *Nudge: Improving Decisions about Health, Wealth, and Happiness*. New Haven: Yale University Press, 2008.

52. Joseph Nye, "Good Leadership Is Deciding How to Decide," *Financial Times*, April 1, 2008, p. 13.

53. See Deborah L. Duarte and Nancy Tennant Snyder, *Mastering Virtual Teams*, 3rd ed. San Francisco: Jossey Bass, 2007.

54. T. Silverman, "Expanding Community: The Internet and Relational Theory," *Community, Work, and Family*, 4 (2001), pp. 231–237.

55. A. Lantz, "Meetings in a Distributed Group of Experts: Comparing Face-to-Face, Chat, and Collaborative Virtual Environments," *Behavior and Information Technology*, 20 (2001), pp. 111–117.

56. B. R. Patton and T. M. Downs, *Decision-Making Group Interaction*, 4th ed. Boston: Allyn & Bacon, 2003.

57. Eric Timmerman and Craig Scott, "Virtually Working: Communicative and Structural Predictors of Media Use and Key Outcomes in Virtual Work Teams," *Communication Monographs*, 73 (2006), pp. 108–136.

58. Simone S. Oliver, "Who Elected Me Mayor? I Did," *The New York Times*, August 19, 2010, pp. E1, E2.

59. David Gelles, "The Personal at Work Can Be a Disruptive Mix," *The Financial Times*, April 20, 2011, p. 2.

60. Teresa McAleavy, "Don't Let Bullies Do a Job on You," *The Record*, October 23, 2007, p. B3.

Chapter 11

1. David Wallechinsky, Irving Wallace, and Amy Wallace, *The Book of Lists*. New York: Morrow, 1977, p. 469.

2. Ellen Joan Pollock, "The Selling of a Golden Speech," *Wall Street Journal*, March 12, 1999, p. B1. The Wall Street Journal Eastern Edition by Robert L. Bartley. Copyright 1999 By Dow Jones & Co. Inc. Reproduced with permission of Dow Jones & Co. via the Copyright Clearance Center.

3. See, for example, Betty Horwitz, *Communication Apprehension: Origins and Management*. Florence, KY: Cengage Learning, 2001; Timothy L. Sellnow, "Controlling Speech Anxiety," paper presented at the annual meeting of the Speech Communication Association, Chicago, IL, October 29–November 1, 1992; Marianne Martin, "The Communication of Public Speaking Anxiety: Perception of Asian and American Speakers," *Communication Quarterly* 40 (Summer 1992), pp. 279–288; James McCroskey, Steven Booth Butterfield, and Steven K. Payne, "The Impact of Communication Apprehension on College Student Retention and Success," *Communication Quarterly* 37 (Spring 1989), pp. 100–107; and Judy C. Pearson and Jeffrey Child, "Preparation Meeting Opportunity: How Do College Students Prepare for Public Speakers," *Communication Quarterly* 54 (August 2006), pp. 351–366.

4. Eleanor Blau, "Taking Arms against Stage Fright," *New York Times*, September 20, 1998, p. AR-33; and Holina Ablamowicz, "Using a Speech Apprehension Questionnaire as a Tool to Reduce Students' Fear of Public Speaking," *Communication Teacher* 19 (July 2005), pp. 98–102.

5. J. D. Mladenka, C. R. Sawyer, and R. R. Behnke, "Anxiety Sensitivity and Speech Trait Anxiety as Predictors of State Anxiety during Public Speaking," *Communication Quarterly* 46 (1998), pp. 417–429; and Penny Addison, Elc Clay, Shuang Xie, Chris R. Sawyer, and Ralph R. Behnke, "Worry as a Function of Public Speaking State Anxiety Type," *Communication Reports* 16 (2003).

6. For a more detailed guide to fear-control training, see Joe Ayres and Tim Hopf, "Visualization: Reducing Speech Anxiety and Enhancing Performance," *Communication Reports* 1:1 (winter 1992), pp. 1–10.

7. Elie Wiesel, *Souls on Fire*. New York: Summit, 1982.

8. See Erica Orden, "This Book Brought to You by . . . ," *The Wall Street Journal*, April 26, 2011, p. A19.

9. See Charles Francis, "How to Stop Boring Your Audience to Death," *Vital Speeches of the Day*, February 15, 1996, p. 283.

10. Michael Skapinker, "Chief Execs Should Learn the Art of Oratory," *Financial Times*, January 29, 2008, p. 11.

11. Wynton C. Hall, "Do Effective Speakers Make Effective Presidents?" *USA Today*, February 28, 2008, p. 11A.

12. Roger Ailes, *You Are the Message*. New York: Doubleday, 1989.

13. Robert Orben, "Speech Writing for Presidents," presentation delivered to the Speech Communication Association in Washington, DC, April 1983.

14. Q. McGuire, "Attitudes and Attitude Change," in G. Lindsley and E. Aronson, eds., *The Handbook of Social Psychology*, vol. 2. New York: Random House, 1985, pp. 287–288.

15. Thomas M. Scheidel, "Sex and Persuasability," *Speech Monographs*, 30 (1963), pp. 353–368.

16. Larry A. Samovar, Richard E. Porter, and Edwin R. McDaniel, *Communication between Cultures*, 6th ed. Belmont, CA: Thomson, 2007; and Barbara Mueller, *Communicating with the Multicultural Consumer: Theoretical and Practical Perspectives*. New York: Peter Lang, 2008.

17. See Jill Givson and Trudy L. Hanson, "The Breakfast of Champions: Teaching Audience Analysis Using Cereal Boxes," *Texas Speech Communication Journal*, 31:1 (Winter 2007), pp. 49–50; and Lawrence R. Wheeless, "The Effects of Attitude Credibility and Homophily on Selective Exposure to Information," *Speech Monographs*, 41 (1974), pp. 329–338.

18. For a look at the topics treated recently in public speeches by the leaders of the largest corporations in the United States, see 2006–2009 issues of *Vital Speeches of the Day*.

19. Thomas Leech, *How to Prepare, Stage, and Deliver Winning Presentations*. New York: Amacom, 1982, p. 11.

Chapter 12

1. Randy Reddict and Elliot King, *The OnLine Student*. Fort Worth: TX: Harcourt Brace College, 1996, p. 3. Information on conducting research, pp. 161–179, is particularly valuable.

2. Danny Sullivan, "Nielsen Net Ratings Search Engine Ratings," August 27, 2006, accessed on August 11, 2008, at Searchenginewatch.com.

3. Russ Juskalian, "Video Search Engines Help Sort It All Out," *USA Today*, July 30, 2008, p. 3B.

4. For a more comprehensive treatment of supporting materials see Teri Gamble and Michael Gamble, *Public Speaking in the Age of Diversity*, 2nd ed. Boston: Allyn & Bacon, 1998, chaps. 7 and 8.

5. Paul Starbuck, "Exercise Anorexia: The Deadly Regimen," in *Winning Orations*. Mankato, MN: Interstate Oratorical Association, 2007, p. 5.

6. See, for example, "In Fighting Anorexia, Recovery Is Elusive," *The New York Times*, April 26, 2011, p. D5.

7. Megan Solan, "Serving Those Who Serve," in *Winning Orations 2004*. Mankato MN: Interstate Oratorical Association, 2005.

8. Solan.

9. Suan E. Rice, "Why America Needs the U.N.," *Vital Speeches of the Day*, April, 2011, pp. 147–150.

10. Amy Solomito, "Untitled," in *Winning Orations*. Mankato, MN: Interstate Oratorical Association, 2007, p. 73.

11. Lev Grossman, "The Off-Line American," *Time*, August 25, 2008, p. 52.

12. For a discussion of the power of examples in public speaking, see Gamble and Gamble; and Scott Consigny, "The Rhetorical Example," *Southern Speech Communication Journal* 41 (1976), pp. 121–134.

13. Solomon D. Trujillo, "Two Lives: The One We Make Defines Our Legacy," *Vital Speeches of the Day* 66:6 (January 1, 2000), p. 169. Reprinted with permission.

14. Risa Lavizzo-Mourey, M.D., "Changing the Norms of Medicine and Health," *Vital Speeches of the Day*, June 2010, pp. 276–282.

15. Harvey Mackay, "Postgraduate Life," *Vital Speeches of the Day* (August 2008), p. 359.

16. Theresa McGuiness, "Greeks in Crisis," in *Winning Orations*. Mankato, MN: Interstate Oratorical Association, 2000, p. 75. Reprinted by permission.

17. William L. Laurence, "Eyewitness Account: Atomic Bomb Mission over Nagasaki," *New York Times*, September 9, 1945.

18. Lady Gaga, "The Prime Rib of America," *Vital Speeches of the Day*, November 2010, pp. 521–522.

19. "I Have a Dream," by Martin Luther King, Jr. Reprinted by arrangement with the Estate of Martin Luther King, Jr., c/o Writers House as agent for the proprietor, New York, NY. Copyright 1963 Dr. Martin Luther King, Jr., copyright renewed 1991 Coretta Scott King.

20. For decades, studies revealed how organization affects reception. For example, see Christopher Spicer and Ronald E. Bassett, "The Effect of Organization on Learning from an Informative Message," *Southern States Communication Journal* 41 (1976), pp. 290–299; and Johen E. Baird, Jr., "The Effects of Speech Summaries upon Audience Comprehension of Expository Speeches of Varying Quality and Complexity," *Central States Speech Journal* 25 (1974), pp. 119–127.

21. Richard Nisbett, *The Geography of Thought: How Asians and Westerners Think Differently . . . and Why*. New York: Free Press, 2003.

22. National Public Radio, "Analysis: Geography of Thought," *Talk of the Nation* broadcast of interview of Richard Nisbett by Neal Conan, March 3, 2003. © 2003 National Public Radio, Inc. Used with permission.

23. Ibid.

24. D. L. Thislethwaite, H. DeHaan, and J. Kamenetsky suggest that a message is more easily understood and accepted if transitions are used: see "The Effect of 'Directive' and 'Non-Directive' Communication Procedures on Attitudes," *Journal of Abnormal and Social Psychology* 51 (1955), pp. 107–118. Also of value on this aspect of speech organization is E. Thompson, "Some Effects of Message Structure on Listeners' Comprehension," *Speech Monographs* 34 (1967), pp. 51–57.

25. See for example, Arran Gare, "Narratives and Culture: The Role of Stories in Self-Creation," *Telos* (Winter 2002); and Jessica Lee Shumake, "Reconceptualization Communication and Rhetoric from a Feminist Perspective," *Guidance & Counseling* (Summer 2002).

26. Myron W. Lustig and Jolene Koester, *Intercultural Competence: Interpersonal Communication across Cultures*, 3rd ed. New York: Longman, 1999.

27. See R. S. Zaharna, "Rhetorical Ethnocentrism," for example, http://nw08.american.edu/~zaharna/rhetoric.htm.

28. For a more comprehensive treatment of introductions and conclusions, see Gamble and Gamble, *Public Speaking in the Age of Diversity*, 2nd ed. Boston: Allyn & Bacon, 1998, chap. 10.

29. David H. Petraeus, "The Surge of Ideas," *Vital Speeches of the Day*, July 2010, pp. 314–320.

30. Brittany Young, "Prisoner Abuse: The Stain on American Democracy," in *Winning Orations*. Mankato, MN: Interstate Oratorical Association, 2007, p. 89.

31. Erin Gallaher, "Upholstered Furniture: Sitting in the Uneasy Chair." *Winning Orations*. Mankato, MN: Interstate Oratorical Association, 2000, p. 99. Reprinted with permission.

32. Adrienne Hallett, "Dying in Your Sleep," in *Winning Orations* Northfield, MN: Interstate Oratorical Association, 1995, p. 27. Reprinted with permission.

33. Richard L. Trumka, "Why Working People Are Angry, and Why Politicians Should Listen," *Vital Speeches of the Day*, June 2010, pp. 268–271.

34. Marie S. Bilik, "Public Schools Must Thrive—Not Just Survive—in Troubled Times," *Vital Speeches of the Day,* July 2010, pp. 324–325.

35. Jesse Ohl, "Rising Sun, Rising Cancer," *in Winning Orations.* Mankato, MN: Interstate Oratorical Association, 2007, p. 31.

36. Brian Swenson, "Gun Safety and Children," *in Winning Orations.* Mankato, MN: Interstate Oratorical Association, 1990, p. 101. Reprinted with permission.

37. This Kennedy quote has been attributed to G. B. Shaw, as well as the poet Robert Browning.

Chapter 13

1. Mary Panzer, "Photojournalism for the Web Generation," *Wall Street Journal,* July 8, 2008, p. D7.

2. Jae Yang and Kari Gelles, "USA Today Snapshots," *USA Today,* August 13, 2008, p. 1B.

3. "America Incarcerated," *Time,* March 17, 2008, p.14.

4. Anne R. Caarey and Julie Snider, "Where Nuclear Plants Are," *USA Today,* July 17, 2008, p. 1A.

5. Karen Sudo, "Deadly Riptides," *The Record,* August 1, 2008, p. A1.

6. *Discover,* June 2003, pp. 42–47.

7. See Richard B. Woodward, "Debatable 'Evidence,'" *The Wall Street Journal,* May 4, 2011, p. D 5, and David W. Dunlap, "Fake Bin Laden Death Photos Spread on Web and Fool Some Newspapers," *The New York Times,* May 5, 2011, p. A 17.

8. W. I. Ringle and W. D. Thompson, *TechEdge: Using Computers to Present and Persuade.* Needham Heights, MA: Allyn & Bacon, 1998.

9. Nancy Duarte, "Avoiding the Road to PowerPoint Hell," *The Wall Street Journal,* January 22–23, 2011, p. C 12.

10. L. Zuckerman, "Words Go Right to the Brain, But Can They Stir the Heart," *New York Times,* April 17, 1999, pp. A17–A19.

11. Greg Jaffe, "What's Your Point, Lieutenant? Just Cut to the Pie Charts," *Wall Street Journal,* April 26, 2000, pp. A1, A6.

12. Dean Dad, "PowerPoint Hates Freedom," http://www.insidehighered.com/layout/set/print/blogs/confessions, accessed 4/29/10.

13. June Kronholz, "PowerPoint Goes to School," *Wall Street Journal,* November 12, 2002, pp. B1, B6.

14. Elizabeth Bumiller, "We Have Met the Enemy and He Is PowerPoint," *The New York Times,* April 27, 2010, pp. A1, A8.

15. Jan Parker, "Absolute PowerPoint," *New Yorker,* May 28, 2001, pp. 76–87.

16. Frances Cole Jones, *How to WOW.* New York: Ballentine Books, 2008, p. 132; also see Dale Cyphert, "Presentation Technology in the Age of Electronic Eloquence: From Visual Aid to Visual Rhetoric," *Communication Education* 56:2 (April 2007), pp 168–192.

17. Parker; also see Mark R. Stoner, "PowerPoint in a New Key," *Communication Education* 56:3 (July 2007), pp. 354–381.

18. Lee Gomes, "PowerPoint Turns 20, as Its Creators Ponder a Dark Side to Success," *Wall Street Journal,* June 20, 2007, p. B1.

19. "College Faked Photo in Pitch for Diversity," *The Record,* September 21, 2000, p. A13; for more on this subject see David D. Perlmutter and Nicole Smith Dahman, "(In) Visible Evidence in the Apollo Moon Landings," *Visual Communication* 7:2 (May 2008), pp. 229–251.

Chapter 14

1. See Francis Cairncross, "The Roots of Revolution and the Trendspotter's Guide to New Communications," in Erik P. Bucy, *Living in the Information Age: A New Media Reader.* Stamford, CT: Wadsworth/Thomson Learning, 2002, pp. 3–10.

2. Daniel Pink, *A Whole New Mind: Moving from the Information Age to the Conceptual Age.* New York: Riverhead Books, 2005; and Garr Reynolds, *Presentation Zen.* New York: New Ridges Press, 2008.

3. Although compiled years ago, a valuable source to consult is Charles Petrie, "Informative Speaking: A Summary and Bibliography of Related Research," *Speech Monographs* 30 (1963), pp. 79–91.

4. See, for example, Katherine E. Rowan, "Informing and Explaining Skills: Theory and Research on Informative Communication," in John O. Greene and Brant R. Burleson, eds., *Handbook of Communication and Social Interaction Skills.* Mahwah, NJ: Lawrence Erlbaum Associates, 2003, pp. 403–438.

5. David Shenk, *Data Smog: Surviving the Information Glut.* San Francisco: Harper Edge, 1997, p. 93.

6. See, for example, Brendan Lemon, "Audiences Today Are Getting in on the Act," *New York Times,* October 8, 2000, pp. AR-5, AR-22.

Chapter 15

1. Robert B. Cialdini, *Influence: Science and Practice,* 4th ed. Boston: Allyn & Bacon, 2001, p. 239.

2. For an excellent explanation of why we study persuasion, see Deirdre D. Johnston, *The Art and Science of Persuasion.* Dubuque, IA: Brown & Benchmark, 1994. For an analysis of key theories of persuasion, see Dominick A. Infante, Andrew S. Rancer, and Deanna F. Womack, *Building Communication Theory,* 3rd ed. Prospect Heights, IL: Waveland, 1997. An interesting discussion also occurs in Jay A. Conger, "The Necessary

Art of Persuasion," *Harvard Business Review* 76:3 (May–June 1998), pp. 84–95.

3. See Wallace Folderingham, *Perspectives on Persuasion*. Boston: Allyn & Bacon, 1966, p. 33; and James Price Dillard, "Persuasion Past and Present: Attitudes Aren't What They Used to Be," *Communication Monographs* 60:1 (March 1993), pp. 90–97.

4. For an interesting definition and discussion of persuasion, see Anthony Pratkanis and Elliot Aronson, *The Age of Propaganda*, rev. ed. New York: Freeman, 2000; and Cialdini, 2000.

5. Patrick D. Healy, "Weld Aides Find a Way to Deal with Negative Press: Re-edit It," *New York Times*, February 4, 2006, pp. B1, B4.

6. Credibility has received much attention from researchers. See, for example, James M. Kouzes and Barry Z. Posner, *Credibility*. San Francisco: Jossey-Bass, 1993.

7. J. W. Anderson, "A Comparison of Arab and American Conceptions of 'Effective' Persuasion," *Howard Journal of Communications* 2:1 (Winter 1989–1990), pp. 81–114.

8. Speakers can establish credibility early in a speech. For example, see R. Brooks and T. Scheidel, "Speech as Process: A Case Study," *Speech Monographs* 35 (1968), pp. 1–7.

9. Nonverbal aspects of credibility are discussed in more detail in Chapter 16.

10. Bob Ivry, "From White Lies to the White House," *The Record*, June 8, 2003, pp. A-1, A-16.

11. Mark Bowden, "Sometimes Heroism Is a Moving Target," *New York Times*, pp. WK1, WK4.

12. Bowden.

13. For a discussion of now-classic studies, see M. Sherif and C. Hovland, *Social Judgment*. New Haven, CT: Yale University Press, 1961; and C. Sherif, M. Sherif, and R. Nebergall, *Attitude and Attitude Change*. Philadelphia: Saunders, 1965. For a very understandable explanation, see also E. Griffin, *A First Look at Communication Theory*, 4th ed. New York: McGraw-Hill, 2000.

14. Scott Cutlip and Alan Center, *Effective Public Relations*. Englewood Cliffs, NJ: Prentice-Hall, 1985, p. 122.

15. A framework for understanding the importance of beliefs is provided by Martin Fishbein and Icek Ajzaen, *Belief, Attitude, Intention and Behavior: An Introduction to Theory and Research*. Reading, MA: Addison-Wesley, 1975. See especially Chapters 1 and 8.

16. Milton Rokeach, *The Open and Closed Mind*. New York: Basic Books, 1960.

17. Prominent theorists such as Leon Festinger, Fritz Hieder, and Theodore Newcomb consider the desire for consistency a central motivator of behavior. For a more contemporary discussion of the topic, see Robert B. Cialdini, *Influence*, rev. ed. New York: Quill, 2000.

18. Cialdini, p. 116.

19. Cialdini; see also Mike Allen, "Determining the Persuasiveness of Message Sidedness: A Prudent Note about Utilizing Research Summaries," *Western Journal of Communication* 57:1 (Winter 1993), pp. 98–103.

20. John P. Walters, "Drugs: To Legalize or Not," *The Wall Street Journal*, April 25–26, 2009, pp. W1–W2.

21. Wayne Minnick, *The Art of Persuasion*. Boston: Houghton Mifflin, 1968.

22. For a discussion of the role of affect, see, for example, Mary John Smith, *Persuasion and Human Action*. Belmont, CA: Wadsworth, 1982.

23. Abraham Maslow, *Motivation and Personality*. New York: Harper & Row, 1954, pp. 80–92.

24. Bruce E. Gronbeck, Rayme E. McKerrow, Douglas Ehninger, and Alan H. Monroe, *Principles and Types of Speech Communication*, 15th ed. New York, Allyn & Bacon, 2002.

25. Based on a speech by Amanda Taylor, "Drowsy Driving: A Deadly Epidemic," in *Winning Orations*. Mankato, MN: Interstate Oratorical Association, 2000, pp. 12–15.

26. Developed as part of a class exercise by students in communication courses at the College of New Rochelle in New Rochelle, New York, and at the New York Institute of Technology in New York City, using a transcript made of the videotaped speech by Jose Magana, "Breaking Down Borders: Allowing Immigrants to Obtain a Higher Education," in *Winning Orations*. Mankato, MN: Interstate Oratorical Association, 2007, pp. 1–2.

27. Transcribed from a speech by Jose Magana of Arizona State University appearing in *Winning Orations*. Mankato, MN: Interstate Oratorical Association, 2007, pp. 1–2.

Appendix Notes

1. Eli Amdur, "How Workers Should Prepare for the World in 2050," *The Record*, May 23, 2008, pp. J1, J2.

2. Melinda Ligos, "Young Job Seekers Need New Clues," *New York Times*, August 8, 2001, p. G1; and Lois J. Einhorn report in "An Inner View of the Job Interview: An Investigation of Successful Communicative Behavior," *Communication Education* 30 (1981), pp. 217–228, that successful candidates were able to identify with the employer, support their arguments, organize their thoughts, clarify their ideas, and speak fluently.

3. Rick Bentley, "Interest in Forensic Science Has Surged during 'CSI'," (Rock Hill, SC) *Herald*, January 12, 2002, www.heraldonline.com.

4. John A. Challenger, "Internships Are Critical, But Difficult to Land," *The Record*, September 19, 2010, p. J 1.

5. John A. Challenger, "Social Networking Explodes as Job-Search Tool," *The Record*, February 27, 2011, p. J 1.

6. Ibid.

7. Eli Amdur, "The 'Great All-American Cover Letter Challenge'," *The Record*, September 12, 2010, pp. J1–J2.

8. Eli Amdur, "On a Resume, There's Nothing Like a Good Opening," *The Record*, January 27, 2008, pp. Jl, J2.

9. Barbara Kiviat, "Resume? Check. Nice Suit? Check. Webcam?" *Time*. November 9, 2009, pp. 89–90; Jonnelle Marte, "Nailing the Interview," *The Wall Street Journal*, March 14, 2010, p. B-4.

10. Leonard Zunin and Natalie Zunin, *Contact: The First Four Minutes*. Los Angeles: Nash, 1972, pp. 8–12.

11. Adam Geller, "Problem Postings," *The Record*, March 17, 2003; and Kris Maher, "Resume Rustling Threatens Online Job Sites," *Wall Street Journal*, February 25, 2003, pp. Bl, B10.

12. See Mark L. Knapp, Roderick P. Hart, Gustav W. Friedrich, and Gary M. Schulman, "The Rhetoric of Goodbye: Verbal and Nonverbal Correlates of Human Leave-Taking," *Speech Monographs* 40 (1973), pp. 182–198.

13. David Koeppel, "On a Resume, Don't Mention Moon Pies or Water Cannons," *New York Times*, November 24, 2001, Section 10, p. 1.

14. Charles J. Stewart and William B. Cash, Jr., *Interviewing: Principles and Practices*, 6th ed. Dubuque, IA: Brown, 1991.

15. Arlene Hirsch, "Tell Me about Yourself Doesn't Mean 'Tell It All'," *The Record*, November 28, 2004, pp. Jl, J2; and Anthony DePalma, "Preparing for 'Tell Us about Yourself'," *New York Times*, July 27, 2003, p. NJ1.

16. Malcolm Gladwell, "What Do Job Interviews Really Tell Us?" *New Yorker*, May 29, 2000, p. 84.

17. Ibid.

18. Eli Amdur, "Train Yourself to Be a S.T.A.R. during the Job Interview," *The Record*, September 4, 2005, p. Jl.

19. Eli Amdur, "An Interview Is a Two-Way Deal, So Ask Questions," *The Record*, April 17, 2005, pp. Jl, J2.

20. For a study confirming that employers use a candidate's speech characteristics to judge competence and likability, see Robert Hopper, "Language Attitudes in the Employment Interview," *Speech Monographs* 44 (1974), pp. 346–351.

21. Eli Amdur, "Be the Person Companies Will Want to Hire," *The Record*, October 24, 2004, pp. Jl, J2.

22. Gladwell, pp. 68–86.

23. "Initial Minutes of Job Interview Are Critical," *USA Today*, January 2000, p. 8.

24. Eli Amdur, "The 10 General Rules to Help You Be a Good Interviewee," *The Record*, August 5, 2007, pp. Jl, J2.

25. Einhorn.

26. Rachel Emma Silverman and Kemba J. Dunham, "Even in a Tight Market, Job Hunters Can Blunder," *Wall Street Journal*, June 20, 2000, p. B12.

27. Also see Gladwell, pp. 68–72, 84–86; and C. J. Stewart and W. B. Cash, Jr., *Interviewing Principles and Practices*, 7th ed. Dubuque, IA: Brown, 1994.

28. Marvin Walberg, "Interviewing: Expected the Unexpected," *The Record*, September 4, 2009, p. A9.

29. Joann S. Lublin, "Notes to Interviewers Should Go Beyond a Simple Thank You," *Wall Street Journal*, February 5, 2008, p. Bl.

30. Lublin.

31. See, for example, F. Mahoney, "Adjusting the Interview to Avoid Cultural Bias," *Journal of Career Planning and Employment* 52 (1992), pp. 41–43.

32. Mary Williams Walsh, "Money Isn't Everything," *New York Times*, January 30, 2001, p. 10.

33. Ibid.

34. Marjorie Valbrun, "More Muslims Claim They Suffer Job Bias," *Wall Street Journal*, April 15, 2003, pp. B1, B8.

35. Sarah E. Needleman, "Job Seekers: Put Your Web Savvy to Work," *Wall Street Journal*, September 9, 2007, p. B3.

36. Kris Maher, "Blogs Catch on as Online Tool for Job Seekers and Recruiters," *Wall Street Journal*, September 28, 2004, p. B10.

37. For a discussion of online search techniques, see Cynthia B. Leshin, *Internet Investigations in Business Communication*. Saddle River, NJ: Prentice Hall, 1997, pp. 95–134.

38. See Zane K. Quible, "Electronic Resumes: Their Time Is Coming," *Business Communicaiton Quarterly* 58 (September 1995), pp. 5–9.

39. Wallace V. Schmidt and Roger N. Conaway, *Results-Oriented Interviewing: Principles, Practices, and Procedures*. Boston: Allyn & Bacon, 1999, p. 11.

40. Mark Cendella, "Top 10 Blunders of Online Job Hunters," *The Record*, September 5, 2004, p. Jl.

41. David Koeppel, "Web Can Help, but a Job Hunt Still Takes Lots of Hard Work," *New York Times*, September 12, 2004, pp. MB1, 3.

42. Sarah E. Needleman, "Thx for the Iview! I Wud (Heart) to Work 4 U!!" *Wall Street Journal*, July 29, 2008, pp. Dl, D4.

43. From David Kirby, "Selling Yourself: There Are Questions You Shouldn't Answer." Adapted from *The New York Times*, January 30, 2001, p. 2. Copyright © 2001 by the New York Times Co. Reprinted with permission.

Online Chapter

1. Nick Wingfield, "Facebook, Microsoft Deepen Search Ties," *The Wall Street Journal*, May 17, 2011, p. B6

2. See W. James Potter, *Media Literacy*, 4th ed. Thousand Oaks, CA: Sage, 2008.

3. B. Haring, "Internet Vet Wary of Superhighway's Direction," *USA Today*, April 6, 1995, p. 7D.

4. J. Hancock and P. Dunham, "Impression Formation in Computer-Mediated Communication Revisited: An Analysis of the Breadth and Intensity of Impressions,"

Communication Research 28 (2001), pp. 325–332; and L. Pratt, R. Weisman, M. Cody, and P. Wendt, "Interrogative Strategies and Information Exchange in Computer-Mediated Communication," *Communication Quarterly* 47 (1999), pp. 36–66.

5. Roger Fidler, "New Media Theory," in Eric P. Bucy, ed., *Living in the Information Age.* Belmont, CA: Wadsworth, 2002, pp. 21–29.

6. Bill Maxwell, "Civility Can Prevail in an Age of Rage," *The Record*, May 18, 2011, p. A-11.

7. Neil Postman, *Amusing Ourselves to Death.* New York: Viking, 1985.

8. See, for example, "The Veronis Suhler Stevenson Communications Industry Forecast, 2007–2011."

9. Ibid.

10. See "Generation M: Media in the Lives of 8- to 18-Year-Olds," a Kaiser Family Foundation Study, p. 10, www.kff.org/entmedia/upload/8010.pdf. Accessed May 1, 2011; and Steven Reinberg, "U.S. Kids Using Media Almost 8 Hours a Day," *Bloomberg BusinessWeek*, January 20, 2010, www.businessweek.com/print/lifestyle/content/healthday/635134.html. Accessed 5/18/2011.

11. Alexandra Petri, "More Time Spent Consuming Media? Of Course—the Internet is Better Now," www.washingtonpost.com/blogs, posted 4/12/11. Accessed 5/18/2011.

12. "Who Tweets?" *The Wall Street Journal*, May 21–22, 2011, p. C4.

13. See "Television and Health" accessed at www.csun.edu/science/health/docs/tv&health.html.

14. Ellen Graham, "The New Living-Room Détente," *Wall Street Journal*, June 27, 1997, p. R4.

15. See Alex Williams, "Quality Time, Redefined," *The New York Times*, May 1, 2011, p. ST1, ST2.

16. Douglas Foster, "Burdened with Being Everywhere," *New York Times*, August 19, 2000, p. A15.

17. See Bill Keller, "The Twitter Trap," *The New York Times Magazine*, May 22, 2011, pp. 11–12.

18. James Alexander Thom, "The Perfect Picture," *Reader's Digest*, August 1976, p. 113. Reprinted with permission.

19. Richard Soklos, "I Cannot Tell a Lie (from an Amplification)," *New York Times*, February 5, 2006, p. BU3.

20. Andrew Keen, *The Cult of the Amateur: How Today's Internet Is Killing our Culture.* New York: Doubleday, 2007.

21. Clarence Page, "Someone's Watching Your Web Searches," *The Record*, January 26, 2006, p. L-9.

22. Ken Belson, "Lipstick on Your Caller," *New York Times*, February 5, 2006, p. WK4.

23. Janice Kaplan, "Are Talk Shows Out of Control?" *TV Guide*, April 1, 1995, pp. 10–15.

24. Thomas E. Weber, "Privacy Concerns Force Public to Confront Thorny Issues," *Wall Street Journal*, June 19, 1997, p. B6.

25. Joshua Quittner, "Invasion of Privacy," *Time*, August 25, 1997, pp. 28–35.

26. Albert Bandura, *Social Learning Theory.* Englewood Cliffs, NJ: Prentice Hall, 1977.

27. U.S. Department of Health and Human Services, *Youth Violence: A Report of the Surgeon General, 2001*, retrieved from www.surgeongeneral.gov.

28. American Academy of Pediatrics, "Children, Adolescents, and Television," *Pediatrics* 107 (2001), pp. 423–426.

29. Wilbur Schramm, Jack Lyle, and Edwin Parker, *Television in the Lives of Our Children.* Palo Alto, CA: Stanford University Press, 1961.

30. Ibid., p. 13.

31. Lee Siegel, *Against the Machine: Being Human in the Age of the Electronic Mob.* New York: Spiegel and Grau, 2008.

32. David Browne, "On the Internet, It's All about 'My'," *New York Times*, April 30, 2008, p. ST7.

33. Jean M. Twenge, *Generation Me: Why Today's Young Americans Are More Confident, Assertive, Entitled—and More Miserable Than Ever Before.* New York: Free Press, 2007.

Chapter 8

Chapter 9

Chapter 10

Chapter 11

Chapter 12

Chapter 13

Chapter 14

Chapter 15

on speech analysis, 319–320
See also Skill Builder exercises
Communication within the Organization
(Redding), 239
community and technology, 36–38
company information, 454
comparison level for alternatives, **186**
comparison level for relationships, **186**
comparisons and contrasts, 334–335
competent communication, 12
competitive forcer, **281**
competitive goal structure, **247**
competitive set, **279**
complementarity, **203**
completers, 151
comprehensive listening, **147**
compromiser, **280–281**
computer-assisted presentations, 370–374
PowerPoint used for, 370–371
sample slide presentation, 372–374
computer graphics, 366–368, 368f, 369f
computer-mediated communication
(CMC), 72
conclusion of speech, 352–354
functions of, 352–353
types of, 353–354
concrete language, 84
confidence, 380–381
configural formats, 347–348
conflict, 217–227
categorizing, 217–220
cooperative vs. competitive,
279–280
culture and, 223
definition of, **217, 275**
gender and, 221–223, 276
groupthink and, **282–284**
intensity of, 218–219
management of, 220–221, 222f
online interactions and, 228, 284
practice tips for resolving, 285–286
role reversal and, **280**
self-assessment about, 274–275
styles of handling, 223–227, 280–282
summary points on, 287
conflict grid, **280–282**, 281f
conformity, pressure for, 283
confrontational communication
approach, 32, 33t
confusion, cultural, **27–28**
connecting ideas, 346
connection vs. autonomy, 186
connotative meaning, **81,** 91
consensus
decision by, **250,** 252
groupthink and desire for, 282–284
seeking for, 253, 259
consequences, fear of, 296
consistency, **417**
contact cultures, **131**
content conflicts, 219

content of speeches
postpresentation evaluation of, 382
selection of, 300, 303, 314–315
See also topics
content-oriented listeners, **161**
context, **8**
contingency theory, 273
continuance, goal of, 410
contrasts and comparisons, 334–335
control
need for, **17, 174**
problem orientation vs., 249
conversation
connecting through, 175–177
gender differences in, 95–96
Conversationally Speaking (Garner), 180
cooperative goal structure, **247**
cooperative set, **279**
cost-benefit/social exchange theory,
185–186
cover letters, 443, 455
Crane, Frank, 204
creative speech, 394
credibility, **413**
lying related to, 415
persuasive speech and, 413–414
three types of, 414
criminology careers, 441
critical listening, **147**
critical thinking, **157–159**
questions to facilitate, 159
uncritical thinking vs., 158–159
Crump, Levell, 93
cultivation theory, **72**
cultural confusion, **27–28**
cultural differences
interpretation of, 36
language translations and, 90
speeches and, 340–341, 348, 381
cultural identity, 29–30, 70
cultural imperialism, 28
cultural nearsightedness, **70**
cultural pluralism, **26**
cultural relativism, **28–29,** 33
cultural storytelling, 31
culture
attitudes influenced by, 417
audience demographics and, 308
co-cultures and, **30,** 31–33, 31f
communication and, 12, 26–29, 90–91
conflict and, 223
contact level in, 131
definition of, **30,** 31
dimensions of, 33–36
diversity and, 24–25
dominant, **88**
emotional display and, 131, 215–216
employment interviews and, 453
gender related to, 30, 70
group interaction and, 258–260, 277
hyper-competitive, **17**

identity based on, 29–30
individualist vs. collectivist, 34, 36, 70
interaction etiquette and, 133
language and, 88–94
leadership and, 276–278
listening influenced by, 160–162
masculine vs. feminine, 35
melting-pot philosophy of, **25**–26
monochromatic vs. polychromatic, 35
nonverbal communication and,
131–133, 381
power distance and, 35, 36
relationships and, 193–194
speech delivery and, 381
technology and, 36–38
culture effect, 69
cyber-bullying, 285
cyberspace. *See* Internet

D

Dalai Lama, 413
Dance, Frank, 10
database research, 326
Data Smog: Surviving the Information Glut
(Shenk), 163, 390
date/time of speeches, 311–312
dating sites, 194, 194f, 229
Davis, Keith, 272
deaf people, 163
death of relations, 184–185
Deaux, Kay, 215
decentering process, 147
deception
nonverbal communication and, 129–130
relationship development and, 187–188
decision by consensus, **250,** 252
decision making, 250–257
avoiding groupthink in, 282–284
brainstorming and, **254**–257
golden rules of, 243
groups used for, 242–244, 250–257
questions related to, 253
reflective-thinking framework for,
253–254
strategies and methods of, 250–253
deduction, **419**
deep-muscle relaxation, 297
defensive behavior, 247–250
defensive listeners, 151–152
deferred-thesis pattern, 347
definitions
as informative speech, 390
as supportive material, **332**
defriending practice, 196
delivery of speeches, 300, 382
cultural norms and, 381
persuasive speeches, 427–428
postpresentation evaluation of, 383
styles of delivery, 375–376
summary tips on, 382

Ramirez, Artemio, 62
rapport talk, 296
rap talk, 93–94
rate of speech, **117,** 380
rationalization, 283
Ravitch, Diane, 87
Rawlins, William, 189, 205
    Six-Stage Model of Friendship, 205, 205f
    Trust Matrix, 189–190, 189f
readiness theory, 273
reality TV shows, 17, 171
reasoning
    from analogy, **420**
    causal, **420**
    deductive, 419
    ethical, 420–422
    inductive, 419
    logical, 417–420
reasons, **418**
rebuttals, **418**
receivers, **6**
receptive listening, 146
recording research information, 329–331
Redding, Charles, 239
red-flag words, **149**
red herring, **421**
redundancy, principle of, 336
Reference Desk Web site, 325
reference works, 325–326
reflective-thinking framework, 253–254
rehearsing speeches, 300, 376–381
    confidence connected to, 380–381
    eye contact, 379
    facial expressions, 379
    gestures, 378–379
    movements, 379
    posture, 378
    tryouts in, 377–378
    verbal tune-up, 380
    visual tune-up, 378
    vocal tune-up, 379–380
Reik, Theodore, 203
reinforcement, 108–109, 202
relationships, 171–233
    acquaintanceships, **204**
    attraction in, 202–203
    breadth of, **177**–179, 177f
    casual and intimate, 177f
    conflict in, 217–227
    conversation in, 175–177
    costs and benefits of, 185–186
    culture and, 193–194
    depth of, **177**–179, 177f
    dialectical tensions in, **186**–187
    emotions in, 209–217, 230–231
    family, 207–208
    forming meaningful, 16–17
    friendships, **204**–206
    gender and, 191–193
    guidelines for, 197, 230–231
    interpersonal, **172**

laughter in, 190–191
lying in, 187–188
model of communication in, 10, 10f
needs fulfilled through, 173–175
predicting outcomes of, 204
privacy needs in, 179
role of, 172–177
romantic, 206–207
self-disclosure in, **178**–179
stages of, 179f, 180–184
summary points on, 198–199, 231–232
technology and, 194–197, 227–229
termination of, **182**–185, 184f
trust in, 189–190, 189f
types of, 204–209
uncertainty reduction in, 203–204
work, 208–209
relationship window, 226, 226f
relaxation, deep-muscle, 297
religion
    audience demographics and, 307–308
    listener attitudes and, 416
    religious identity and, 30
remembering stage of listening, 149–150
Rempel, John K., 189
repetition, 150, 335, 336, 393–394
report talk, 296
research
    audience, 304–306
    citing sources of, 331
    Internet resources for, 327–328
    listservs and newsgroups for, 327
    observational or experiential, 329
    online and offline, 325–328
    primary, **328**–329
    recording information from, 329–331
    surveys and interviews for, 329
    topic selection and, 315, 324–331
responding stage of listening, 150
restatement, 335
résumés
    electronic, 454–455
    format for, 443–444
    padding/poaching, 445
resurrection processes, 183
retention, selective, **45**
rewards, promising, 425
rhetorical questions, 351, 354
Rice, Susan E., 332
Richards, I. A., 80
Rihanna, 124
risky shift, 243
Robert, Cavett, 417
Rogers, Will, 242, 416
role constructs, 48
role-limited interaction, **204,** 205
role reversal, **280**
roles
    gender, 30
    group, 244–246
    interviewee, 447–450

romantic relationships, 206–207
Romeo and Juliet (Shakespeare), 86
Rosenthal, Robert, 55
Rubin, Theodore Isaac, 202, 214
Ryze.com Web site, 453

S

same-sex relationships, 194
Samovar, Larry A., 38
sample speeches
    informative, 398–403
    persuasive, 430–434
sample speech outlines, 355–357
    informative speech, 395–397
    persuasive speech, 428–430
Sandburg, Carl, 54, 75
Sapir-Whorf hypothesis, **89**–90
Sarkozy, Nicolas, 74
Satir, Virginia, 172
satisfaction, 426
Savan, Leslie, 95
scaled questions, 305
Scary Guy, 64
Schlessinger, Laura, 99
Schulberg, Budd, 268
Schutz, William, 17, 172, 173, 174
Science and Sanity (Korzybski), 64
scripts
    DESC, **227**
    life, 56–57
search engines, 327
searches
    Boolean, **325**
    Google, 326, 327
secondary questions, **447**
secondary tension, 241
Second Life Web site, 227, 261
Seeing a Color-Blind Future (Williams), 61
selective attention, **45**
selective exposure, **45**
selective listeners, 151
selective perception, **45**–46
selective retention, **45**
self
    awareness of, 49, 56–60
    perception of, 49–56
    symbolization of, 59
self-actualization, 424
self-analysis for speech making,
        301–303
    considering the moment, 302
    reviewing your life, 301–302
    searching the news, 302
    using online resources, 303
self-awareness, **49,** 56–60
    impression management and, **59**–60
    Johari window and, **56,** 57–59,
        57f, 58f
    life script identification and, 56–57
self-censorship, 283